49 AT LAST!

The Battle for
Alaska Statehood

Claus-M. Naske

Epicenter Press is a regional press publishing nonfiction books about the arts, history, environment, and diverse cultures and lifestyles of Alaska and the Pacific Northwest.

Publisher: Kent Sturgis
Photo research: Jill Shepherd
Indexer and Proofreader: Carolyn Acheson
Text design: Stephanie Martindale

Acquisitions Editor: Lael Morgan
Production: Book Publishers Network
Cover design: Laura Zugzda
Printer: Lighting Source

Front cover photos (clockwise, starting in upper-left corner): George Sundborg Jr., Dwight D. Eisenhower, Ernest Gruening, Evangeline Atwood, Anthony J. Dimond, Mildred Hermann, William A. Egan, James Wickersham, Vic Fisher (below), William C. Arnold (above), E.L. "Bob" Bartlett (below), Robert B. Atwood (above), Clinton P. Anderson, C.W. Snedden (lower left corner), Henry M. Jackson, Harry S. Truman.

Page i photo: Using four fountain pens, President Dwight D. Eisenhower signs the Alaska statehood proclamation on January 3, 1959. Looking on are, back row, from left, Alaska Rep.-elect Ralph Rivers; Sens.-elect Ernest Gruening and Bob Bartlett; Interior Secretary Fred Seaton; acting territorial Gov. Waino Hendrickson; unknown, possibly a presidential aide; former territorial Gov. Mike Stepovich, and Bob Atwood, president of the Alaska Statehood Commission. To the President's right is Vice President Richard Nixon; to his left, Sam Rayburn, speaker of the House of Representatives. *Photo courtesy of Fairbanks Daily News-Miner*

Library of Congress Control Number: 2009921843
ISBN 978-1-935347-02-6

Publishing history:
3rd Edition (revised) published February 2009 by Epicenter Press, Inc. under the title 49 AT LAST!
2nd Edition (revised) published 1985 by University of America Press under the title A HISTORY OF ALASKA STATEHOOD.
1st Edition published 1973 by Alaska Northwest Publishing Co. under the title AN IN-TERPRETATIVE HISTORY OF ALASKA STATEHOOD.

10 9 8 7 6 5 4 3 2 1
Printed in the United States of America

To order single copies mail $17.95 plus $5 for shipping (WA residents add $2.02 state sales tax) to Epicenter Press, PO Box 82368, Kenmore, WA 98028; call us at 800-950-6663, or visit www.EpicenterPress.com.

For Professor David H. Stratton:
teacher, mentor, and friend

Contents

Other books by Claus-M. Naske

Ernest Gruening: Alaska's Greatest Governor (2004)

Alaska's Builders: 50 Years of Construction in the 49th State (1999) with Gail West

Fairbanks: A Pictorial History, 2nd revised edition (1995) with L.J. Rowinski

Alaska: A History of the 49th State, 2nd revised edition (1987) with Herman Slotnick

Paving Alaska's Trails: The work of the Alaska Road Commission (1986)

A History of Alaska Statehood (1985)

Alaska, photographs by Hans Blohm, text by Claus-M. Naske (1984)

Alaska: A Pictorial History (1983) with L.J. Rowinski

Fairbanks: A Pictorial History (1981) with L.J. Rowinski

Anchorage: A Pictorial History (1981) with L.J. Rowinski

Edward Lewis "Bob" Bartlett of Alaska: A Life in Politics (1979)

Alaska: A History of the 49th State (1979) with Herman Slotnick

An Interpretative History of Alaskan Statehood (1973)

Acknowledgments

Three events in 20ᵗʰ century Alaska history are destined to stand out among all others. World War II brought rapid change to the territory, the struggle for statehood completed Alaska's process of modernization, and the discovery at Prudhoe Bay of the largest oilfield ever found in North America brought a measure of prosperity to the state.

Alaska's modest population together with relatively large revenues gave the state the possibility, if it so desired, to pioneer in building a unique model community with all the comforts and convenience of 21st century life in proximity to and in harmony with the natural environment. The reader must judge whether Alaskans fulfilled that potential.

This book first was published in 1973 as *An Interpretative History of Alaska Statehood*. It was republished in 1985, substantially revised, as *A History of Alaska Statehood* when Alaska celebrated twenty-five years of statehood. Initially prepared as a doctorial dissertation, this work remains a fitting reflection of the long fight for Alaska statehood as Alaskans celebrate the 50th anniversary of

Alaska coming into the Union. Many monumental changes have taken place in this half-century.

The main sources for this work include various Alaska newspapers, files of the Department of the Interior and the Office of Territories and Island Possessions, and the papers accompanying Senate and House bills, all located in the nation's capital. The papers in the Dwight D. Eisenhower and Harry S. Truman presidential libraries located, respectively, in Abilene, Kansas and Independence, Missouri yielded much valuable information. The Records of the Office of the Governor of Alaska, 1884-1958, then residing in the Federal Records Center in Seattle, Washington, furnished important materials, as did the James Wickersham diary and the Anthony J. Dimond Papers in the University of Alaska Fairbanks Archives. The E.L. Bartlett Papers in the same depository were invaluable. The Congressional Record was an important source.

I wish to thank the librarians and archivists at the various depositories who always extended unfailing help. I am particularly grateful to Professor Emeritus David H. Stratton of Washington State University who guided my dissertation and shaped many of my ideas. He was a superb editor. I thank my wife, Dinah A., who has given me help encouragement, understanding, and support over many years for this and other projects.

Thanks to my friend, James Johnsen, formerly vice president for administration at the University of Alaska, for his help on this project.

Special thanks, too, to Mark Hamilton, president of the University of Alaska System, who made possible the republication of this volume for the 50th anniversary of Alaska Statehood.

F O R E W O R D

"I believe that we will show the United States of America that we will be one of the greatest states in the union within the next fifty years," Alaska's last territorial governor, Mike Stepovich, said in Washington, D.C. a half-century ago.

As we look back on the last fifty years, it is evident that Alaska has made good on Governor Stepovich's prediction.

One reason for Alaska's greatness is that it is a land rich in natural resources, from North America's largest oilfield to abundant supplies of liquefied natural gas. Its past is known for its minerals, fur, and salmon. Today, Alaska is home to world-class sport fishing and boasts some of the richest mineral deposits and the largest zinc mine in the world.

Yet, Alaska's greatest resource is its people. The road to statehood was paved with the tireless efforts of so many pioneers. It was a road filled with obstacles, long debate, and hard lobbying right up until President Dwight D. Eisenhower signed the Alaska Statehood Proclamation on January 3, 1959. We owe a debt of gratitude to the great Alaskans who had the vision and tenacity to see statehood become a reality. Alaska is young enough that some of those early pioneers are still with us, still visionary, and still tenacious. We are also blessed with our First People, the Alaska Natives who have shaped our traditions and culture.

Our pioneers speak to us from the past. They speak to us through our constitution, carefully crafted and considered by many to be one of the finest of its kind. The Alaska Constitution is a model of simplicity and flexibility. For example, it outlined a policy of responsible resource development that has led to a vital economy and high quality of life for Alaskans.

Most important, perhaps unique among state constitutions, is the clear direction for self-determination. The Declaration of Rights in Article I, Section 2, states:

> *All political power is inherent in the people. All government originates with the people, is founded upon their will only, and is instituted solely for the good of the people as a whole.*

This simple declaration has become the cornerstone of how Alaskans govern themselves. It reflects a bold streak of independence and self-sufficiency that are hallmarks of the Alaska spirit is borne of centuries of human experience. It is the legacy of rugged individuals who made their way to this spectacular but often unforgiving land to carve out a new life.

As we move forward from this auspicious milestone of fifty years of statehood, we know that if we continue to be guided by the principles of our constitution, the future of this great land will be filled with promise. The history of Alaska is the story of a beautiful state and a fiercely spirited people who are determined to live in and off the land. We continue to write this story today.

I appreciate this faithful account of our state's journey. It's an important story. In this new edition of *A History of Alaska Statehood* (now titled *49 at Last!*), Claus-M. Naske continues his commitment to reporting Alaska history with excellence and authenticity. He examines the various stages of the fight for self-determination, including the first statehood campaign, the role of the federal government, some of the great crusaders for statehood over the years, the "Statehood Now" movement, and the final victory.

As Alaska's governor, it is my pleasure to lead Alaskans as we continue this journey of statehood together.

Governor Sarah Palin

INTRODUCTION

A Retrospective on
50 Years of Statehood

In 2008 Alaska marked 50 years of statehood. The U.S. House of Representatives passed an Alaska statehood measure on May 28, 1958 by a roll-call vote of 210 to 166, and the Senate passed the House version on June 30 by a roll-call vote of 64 to 20. Statehood had been achieved – almost. President Eisenhower signed the bill into law on July 7, 1958, and on January 3, 1959 the president signed the proclamation admitting Alaska and its 215,000 residents into the Union as the 49th state.

On May 28, 2008 celebrations kicked off in Fairbanks at the Pioneer Park with a barbecue for 2,000 and a bonfire. Despite the cool, rainy and windy weather, attendance was excellent. U.S. Senators Ted Stevens and Lisa Murkowski were in attendance and gave short addresses. U.S. Representative Don Young's Fairbanks staff person relayed his thoughts on this historic day. There is much to celebrate. Alaska experienced major transformations in the last 50 years. There also is much we, as citizens, neglected to do.

Those who participated in the statehood crusade in the 1940s and 1950s presented admission to the Union as a panacea which would cure the various social and economic ills of the territory – such as sparse population, inadequate social services, deficient venture and development capital, and poor transportation and communication networks. They also expected that statehood would diminish federal control.

How have we fared as a state during the last 50 years? Contrary to the expectations of many, statehood did not solve all Alaska's problems. It did not appreciably diminish the federal role in the North, it did not result in instant economic growth, and it cost money most of which Alaskans now had to raise themselves.

But statehood had achieved several goals: Alaskans had gained full self-government accompanied by improved efficiency and responsiveness of local government; an increase of local control over natural resources, and the political means of severing the economic constraints of colonialism.

All Alaskans have to be thankful to William A. Egan, the state's first governor, and his team for taking the state constitution as a blueprint in addition to several consultant reports and creating a viable state government. This new creation now offered the wide range of services expected of state governments everywhere. Financial resources, however, were slim.

Governor William A. Egan had called attention to this fact in 1960 when he presented the first complete state budget. He told the legislature that during the last half of the current fiscal year, the state had assumed full responsibility for the management of fish and game resources, and it had fully assumed judicial and other purely state and local functions. He asked how the state would fare beyond June 30, 1961, and answered that most immediately it faced a progressive reduction of the transitional grants available under the Alaska Omnibus Act, a federal aid program. Those grants were to end June 30, 1964. At that time, Egan warned, the state would have to make up several million dollars if it did not want to curtail services.[1]

Egan then presented a balanced budget to the legislature that included proposed tax increases of 2 cents per gallon on highway motor fuel and 1 cent per gallon on marine motor fuel sales, plus

the expenditure of approximately $15 million of federal transi-
tional grants and withdrawals from the general fund surplus. Such
a combination of monies would normally not be available, and the
Alaska State Planning Commission more fully explained just how
far beyond its means the state would be living. At current rates of
income and expenditures, the committee predicted, Alaska would
be about $30 million in debt at the end of the 1966 fiscal year and
$70 million if the financing of a minimum, and sorely needed, cap-
ital improvement program was included.[2]

Clearly, a financial crisis loomed ahead. Alaska's sectionalism
had reasserted itself in bitter squabbling among numerous local
factions over where highways should be located and how boroughs
should be established. One group, located in Anchorage, which
Robert B. Atwood, the publisher of the *Anchorage Daily Times* led,
wanted to move the state capital from Juneau, to the state's population center, while another, which Joe Vogler, the founder of the
Alaska Independence Party, led wanted Alaska to secede entirely
from the Union. Journalist Ray J. Schrick reported that Alaska's
woes would affect American tax-payers because the federal government might well be called upon to foot "as much as 74% of the
bill for a proposed $322 million state construction program in the
next six years."[3]

With some luck, however, such as an expansion in oil and
gas production, income from competitive oil and gas lease sales,
expansion in the fisheries through diversification, and expansion of the forest-product industries and spending restraints the
state hoped to do a fair job managing its financial affairs. Luck
was with the new state. While defense spending, Alaska's major
industry since the 1940s, steadily dropped during the 1960s, the
value of the major natural resources rose encouragingly. By 1967,
oil production was worth $88,187,000 and gas production was
worth $7,268,000. In 1960 the state treasury had received a modest
$3,372,000 from oil and gas production. By 1967 that figure had
increased to $35,613,000.[4]

The 1960 elections ended the overwhelming Democratic predominance and made Alaska a two-party state. Statewide elections between 1958 and 1972 showed a substantial drift toward Republican voting although Democrats still dominated for most of that time.[5]

On Friday, March 27, 1964, one of the greatest recorded earthquakes in North America, measuring 8.4 to 8.7 on the Richter scale, struck south-central Alaska. In a few minutes it caused damage almost beyond description. The loss of life was fortunately relatively low, but property damage was estimated at $380 to $500 million.[6]

The state and federal governments responded speedily and generously, and Alaska quickly returned to normal. President Lyndon B. Johnson, at the urging of Alaska's senior U.S. Senator E.L. Bartlett, established the Federal Reconstruction and Development Planning Commission for Alaska which Senator Clinton P. Anderson (D., N.M) headed. The commission's careful assessment a month later showed that earthquake damage had amounted to $205,811,771 rather than the expected $400 million. On August 14, 1964, the President signed into law legislation that generously assisted Alaska reconstruction.[7]

A few years later, in August 1967, the Chena River, which bisects the town of Fairbanks, overflowed its banks and put much of the city under eight feet of water. Although confined to that one city, property damage was heavy. But once again the federal government lent a helping hand. For example, the Small Business Administration, as in the earthquake disaster, extended necessary long term loans at favorable interest rates to put Fairbanks back on its feet.

Not all was disaster in Alaska. Early in 1968 the Atlantic-Richfield Company struck the world's twelfth-largest oil field and the largest discovered in North America with recoverable reserves of approximately 10,014 barrels of crude oil and condensate and 26 trillion cubic feet of natural gas. The state conducted it 23rd competitive oil lease sale in 1969 and oil companies bid in excess of $900 million. Euphoria reigned. Since statehood Alaska had held a total of twenty-two lease sales, which had netted less than $100 million, but that money had enabled the state to limp financially from lease sale to lease sale. Then, in one day, the state had sold oil leases on less than .001 percent of its total landmass and raised that much money.[8]

The lease sale and the subsequent debate over what to do with all the money were the highlights of that season. In the meantime, the Trans-Alaska Pipeline System (TAPS), an unincorporated joint venture of Atlantic-Richfield, British Petroleum and Humble Oil, applied to the U.S. Department of the Interior in June, 1969, for a permit to construct a hot-oil pipeline across 800 miles of public domain from Prudhoe Bay on the North Slope to tidewater at Valdez on Prince William Sound. TAPS estimated that it would cost about $900 million to build the pipeline. But soon Native villages along the proposed TAPS right-of-way protested, and on April 1, 1970, Judge George L. Hart, Jr., of the federal district court in Washington, D.C., enjoined the Department of the Interior from issuing a construction permit.[9]

In the meantime various environmental organizations sued the Department of the Interior in the same court asking that the TAPS project be halted because it violated both the 1920 Mineral Leasing Act and the new National Environmental Policy Act (NEPA). On April 13, Judge Hart issued a temporary injunction against the TAPS project.[10]

The oil industry then realized that Alaska presented problems that would not be easily overcome, and after much maneuvering, British Petroleum agreed to help lobby for a Native Claims Settlement Act and agreed to persuade other companies in TAPS to join the effort. Nothing happened immediately because TAPS was in the process of reorganization and in the fall of 1977 had become a well-organized Delaware corporation named Alyeska Pipeline Service Company, Inc. It included the same oil companies that had started TAPS. Now they joined the lobbying effort.

Even before the Prudhoe Bay discovery and the proposed pipeline Alaska's Natives had become increasingly uneasy about threats to their lands. On June 19, 1957 the Atomic Energy Commission established the Plowshare Program for the peaceful uses of atomic energy. By the end of 1957 scientists at the Lawrence Radiation Laboratory at the University of California had designed "Project Chariot," a massive explosion equal to 2.4 million tons of TNA, and eventually decided "to blast an artificial harbor – or at least a hole that could be made to look like a harbor – at Cape Thompson" on Alaska's northwest coast. After some study the AEC requested a 1,600 acre land withdrawal in the Cape Thompson area and scheduled an explosion for 1960.[11]

Supporters and opponents rallied, but Eskimos, most affected by such a blast, and public opposition eventually forced the government to abandon "Project Chariot."

Soon state land selections conflicted with Native hunting, fishing, and trapping activities. The first occurred in the Minto Lakes region of interior Alaska in 1961. The Minto villagers asked the Department of the Interior to protect their rights. In response the Bureau of Indian Affairs began filing protests on behalf of the Natives of Minto, Northway, Tanacross, and Lake Alegnagik over approximately 5,860,000 acres which conflicted with some 1,750,000 acres of state selection.[12]

Between 1962 and 1966 threats to Native-claimed lands multiplied, and the story of Minto was repeated over and over again. Natives filed protests to state land selections, and between 1961 and April 1, 1968, Native protest filings covered some 296 million acres. By the middle of 1968 the filings covered almost 337 million acres.[13] In 1967 numerous representatives of Native groups met in Anchorage and formed the Alaska Federation of Natives (AFN). But before the AFN began to function in that year, Secretary of the Interior Stewart Udall imposed a land freeze which stopped transfer of lands Natives claimed – which ended State land selections, until Congress had settled the land-claims issue.[14]

Now the oil companies, contractors, the state, Native and environmental groups lobbied Congress and their efforts bore fruit. Congress passed a compromise bill, and President Richard M. Nixon signed the measure into law on December 18, 1971. Construction on the Trans-Alaska oil pipeline had begun in the summer of 1974, and on 10:05 a.m. on June 20, 1977 oil flowed into the pipeline and oil finally arrived at the Valdez tanker terminal on July 28, 1977.[15]

The Alaska Native Claims Settlement Act (ANCSA) was a milestone in congressional dealing with American Native groups. It gave title to about 44 million acres of land and monetary compensation amounting to $962.5 million. Some $462.5 million was to come from the federal treasury and the rest from mineral revenue sharing with the state. Twelve regional corporations would administer the settlement. All U.S. citizens with one-fourth Indian, Eskimo, or Aleut blood except members of the Metlakatla community on Annette Island who were living when the settlement became law were entitled to become beneficiaries. All eligible Natives were to become stockholders in the business corporations after registering and proving Native ancestry. A Native would be enrolled in the corporation of the region considered home and become the owner of 100 shares of stock.[16]

Congress amended ANCSA numerous time in subsequent years. It also created a 13th regional corporation, without a land base, for Alaska Natives who had left the state over the years. After years of severe birthing pains, bankruptcies, reorganizations and refinancing, many of the regional corporations have become multi-billion dollar powerhouses in Alaska's economy.

During the legislative battle for passage of the Alaska Native Claims Settlement Act (ANCSA), Congress had included section 17(d)(2) in the measure to gain the support of the conservation forces. It authorized the secretary of the interior to withdraw up to 80 million acres of vacant, unreserved, and unappropriated federal public lands for study as possible additions to the national park, forest, wildlife refuge and wild and scenic river systems. Congress, however, had reserved the right to make final decisions on the lands withdrawn for study. Section 17(d)(2) created an uproar in Alaska, and in Congress as well, pitting conservation groups against development-minded interests.[17]

After a prolonged battle, the Senate, after several days of debate and frantic lobbying, voted on August 19, 1980 on the Alaska Lands Bill. It finally passed the substitute bill by a vote of 78 to 14. The measure put 104 million acres in new conservation units; of these, 57 million acres were designated as wilderness. There existed significant differences between the House and Senate versions that would have required a conference committee for resolution. Senate leaders told the House that if it made important changes in the Senate version, Alaska's two senators would filibuster the measure, thereby killing any chances of enacting an Alaska lands bill in that Congress.

In November, 1980 American voters rejected Jimmy Carter and swept Republican Ronald Reagan into the presidency. The Senate gained a Republican majority, and the House, although still Democratic, was more conservative. Representative Morris Udall, the author of the House bill, and House leaders realized that the Senate bill was better than nothing. If the next Congress decided, the leaders reasoned, they would probably lose all the gains they had made in the four-year congressional battle. Thereupon, the House quickly passed the Senate version on November 21, and President Carter signed the Alaska National Interest Lands Conservation Act (ANILCA) into law on December 2, 1980.[18]

ANILCA was a complex measure. Its last part reflected the wishes of Alaska's congressional delegation to end land withdrawals. It not only established the boundaries for federal, state, Native, and private lands but also created a framework for dealing with future land use conflicts. Although the act resolved many important issues, it hardly touched the basic conflict – namely environmental protection versus economic development. Those issues are still being worked out in 2008.

Territorial Alaska had been economically dependent on natural resources, such as fish, timber, and minerals. It quickly became an oil-dependent state with little economic diversification. That had started as early as 1957 with the Swanson River discovery and subsequent development of that oilfield that contained more than 250 million barrels of oil. Soon oil companies leased Cook

Inlet acreage, and in 1962 Pan American Petroleum discovered the Middle Ground Shoal oil field. By the early 1990s fifteen off-shore platforms operated in Cook Inlet.[19]

An important issue that arose with the Prudhoe Bay discovery concerned state regulation and taxation. Governor William A. Egan proposed that the state build and own the pipeline. Egan accurately predicted that oil company ownership of the pipeline would short-change the state's revenue from the Prudhoe Bay field. The pipeline owners would charge high transportation costs to transport the oil and then deduct these tariffs as transportation expenses before paying taxes and royalties to the state; he also believed the oil companies would inflate the costs of construction and pipeline operation.[20]

The legislature established a committee to examine the issue. Oil company representatives testified and vehemently opposed state ownership. It killed Egan's proposal and the state senate voted it down by a large majority.

Chancy Croft, a Democratic state senator from Anchorage, in 1972 proposed that the state impose right-of-way leasing fees on users of the oil pipeline. Through the leasing fee the state charged, it could regulate pipeline tariffs. The oil industry opposed the idea, but the state legislature supported it.[21]

During the same session the legislature passed Governor Egan's cents-per-barrel tax on oil companies, which guaranteed a minimum payment to the state for each barrel of oil produced. It would serve as a replacement for the state's severance tax in case oil prices dropped significantly.[22]

The two laws annoyed Alaska's oil companies and ten of them, Amerada Hess, Amoco, BP, Humble Oil, Humble Pipeline, Gulf, Phillips, Skelly, Sohio, and Union sued the state in superior court. They claimed that the laws violated the doctrine of federal preemption of interstate commerce regulation. They also argued that litigation over the legislation would delay pipeline construction. While Congress debated the TAPS authorization bill, pressure in Alaska intensified to build the pipeline. In 1973, during the legislative session, the governor authorized negotiations with the oil companies. That led to a compromise on Egan's cents-per-barrel levy and the repeal of Croft's right-of-way leasing law.[23]

Egan called the legislature into a special session in October 1973 to consider the compromise package. The governor, however, had not consulted the legislative leadership during the discussions with the oil companies. Many, particularly Democrats, gained the perception that Egan had sold out the state's interests in order to speed pipeline construction. The following were parts of Egan's proposal: a $.025-per-barrel minimum tax; a 20-mill property tax on pipeline facilities; amendments that crippled Croft's right-of-way leasing law, stripping the just-established Alaska Pipeline Commission of tariff-setting authority; a one-eighth-cent-per barrel conservation tax; changes to the 8 percent severance tax; a common-purchase/common-carrier pipeline bill; a measure enabling the pipeline owner companies to purchase the Valdez terminal site.[24]

Legislators changed few of the proposals. They allowed local governments along the pipeline corridor to share in the 20-mill tax on oil and gas production and pipeline assets and required the pipeline to operate as a common carrier, giving all oil producers equal access to it. They also lowered the ceiling for the assessment of the severance tax without raising the rate. Both houses supported Egan's proposals. The state could probably have won better terms from the oil companies but it lacked the expertise and did not have the means to wage an extended legal battle with the oil industry.

From the Prudhoe Bay discovery in 1968 to the Congressional authorization of TAPS in November 1973 was an important period in Alaska state history. The federal government, multinational oil corporations and the Arab oil embargo narrowed Alaska's options. Pipeline construction, which began in earnest in 1974, brought jobs, money and an influx of new residents. From 1977, when oil began to flow, until Prudhoe Bay started to decline in 1989 the state had become largely dependent on the oil industry for its revenues, a dependency determined by the 1973 special session.

After the 1968 Prudhoe Bay discovery there were no comparable large discoveries but rather several smaller fields which the oil companies brought into production. Technological developments enabled the oil industry to develop deposits once considered marginal. After oil had begun to flow in 1977, Alaska took in more royalty and tax revenues than anyone could have imagined. There was, however, a move to change oil taxation, a result of the "Sunshine Boys" reforms of 1974-1980 when Democratic legislators who had been inspired by the post-Watergate period in American politics controlled the House of Representatives.[25]

In 1976 Senator Chancy Croft persuaded his colleagues to establish a $30 million fund to immediately clean up oil spills. Later it was found to be an unconstitutional infringement on interstate oil transportation. Two years later, in 1978, Croft led the attempt to change the way oil companies were taxed. The state taxed companies based on global profits and losses, which enabled industry to transfer large Alaska profits and avoid heavier local taxes. The new legislation taxed oil based on Alaska operations profits. The companies immediately challenged the "separate accounting" method in court. By 1981, the Supreme Court had not settled the issue, and Governor Jay S. Hammond had learned that two states using separate accounting methods had lost their cases to oil companies and had to repay the disputed funds. He decided to support the repeal of the method in the event Alaska lost its case. Also, in 1981, the "Sunshine Boys" era ended when a legislative coup installed Republican control. Revenue Commissioner Tom Williams, who later managed BP's Alaska tax office, drafted the legislative repeal. It easily passed the oil-friendly legislature.[26] Chancy Croft remarked that the repeal of separate accounting marked the day when Alaska capitulated to the oil industry, when the state became a seller rather than a regulator of oil. Separate accounting not only had given the state more revenue, but it had also supplied the state with important information which indicated the limits of taxation. The state no longer possessed the basis to formulate an intelligent policy toward the oil industry. Alaska lost that.[27] The court upheld the validity of separate accounting in 1985, but the legislature did not restore it.

The Republican legislature also refused to fix the Economic Limit Factor (ELF) which gave tax breaks to marginal oil fields. In 1981, the companies applied the ELF to both Prudhoe Bay and Kuparuk. That lowered their taxes by almost $150 million annually. Only after the negative attitudes toward the oil industry following the 1989 *Exxon Valdez* oil spill was Governor Steve Cowper able to persuade the legislature to remove the ELF and pass tough oil-spill and other environmental regulations. Several smaller fields came online in the meantime, but could not replace Prudhoe Bay which, at its peak of production in 1980, put 2.1 million barrels of oil daily through the pipeline, almost 25 percent of domestically produced American oil.

Independent oil companies, which played an important part in Alaska from the start of the twentieth century, gradually lost out to the multinationals. Mergers and acquisitions were driven in the 1990s by declining oil prices and depressions in the global oil markets. For example, in 1998, Exxon Corporation merged with Mobil which created the world's largest oil company in an $8.1 billion deal. BP-Amoco acquired ARCO. The two companies had dominated oil exploration and production in Alaska. The takeover of ARCO ended a dynamic period in the Alaska oil industry.

In the meantime, the idea of a permanent fund to protect some of Alaska's oil wealth for posterity had slowly formed and gathered support. By 1975 and 1976, both the legislature and Governor Jay S. Hammond planned to create a permanent fund. In the November 1976 elections the voters approved the creation of an Alaska Permanent Fund when they approved a Constitutional amendment by a margin of 2 to 1 which directed that at least 25 percent of all mineral lease rentals, royalties, royalty sale proceeds, federal mineral sharing payments and bonuses the state received were to be placed into a permanent fund. The principal was only to be used for those income producing investments specifically designated by law as eligible for permanent fund investments. All permanent fund income was to be deposited into the General Fund unless the law provided otherwise.[28] This was the most important change in the constitution in the state's history. Alaskans discussed many ideas about the use of the fund. The State Department of Revenue issued a paper which was close to a policy statement. It stated that the fund could save money for the future, control government spending, assist in economic diversification, share revenue with local governments, help communities in capital construction projects, pay for services and aid community businesses.[29] The constitutional and statutory language was silent about the fund's objectives. It was simply a permanent fund whose principal had to remain untouched except to produce income. The legislature had the power to appropriate the income for purposes of its choosing to the state's general fund.

In the following four years the legislature and governor explored several options on how to manage the fund and what to do with its income. In 1980 the legislature created the Alaska Permanent Fund Corporation as a government corporation with six trustees. Four of these were to be public members whom the governor appointed to staggered four year terms; the fifth trustee was to be the sitting commissioner of revenue and the governor selected another cabinet member as the sixth trustee. The legislature did not specify the fund's purposes.[30]

Governor Hammond early on had recommended a cash distribution of Permanent Fund income to state residents. The legislature endorsed and adopted the governor's proposal in 1980. It gave every Alaska resident $50 for each year he/she had lived in Alaska since statehood in 1959. Anchorage attorneys Ron and Patricia Zobel, who had been in Alaska less than a year, challenged the concept in court. They argued that durational residency violated their rights to equal protection under the Alaska and U.S. Constitutions. The Alaska Supreme Court sided with the state. The Zobels appealed to the U.S. Supreme Court which sided with them in an 8-1 vote. While awaiting the court's decision, the governor urged the legislature to provide for a dividend under an equal distribution formula. After some debate, the legislature provided dividends in equal amounts to every six-month resident. It passed the legislature in 1982 and the state distributed $1,000 checks to all eligible residents.[31]

Between 1982 and 2006 the dividend program has paid more than $14 billion to eligible Alaskans. Many studies have been conducted about the economic effects of the program. What is certain is that most Alaskans now consider it their birthright, just as they take it for granted that they have no responsibility to contribute to the multitudinous functions of state government through an individual income tax which the legislature abolished in 1981. During years of low oil prices the state suffered severe budget shortfalls. Any proposals to make up these shortfalls with PF earnings have gotten nowhere, as have proposals to re-impose a state income tax. Alaskans have become almost totally dependent on the oil industry to pay state government expenses. This has severed the citizen's stake in government spending, and indeed made all Alaskans recipients of state welfare which the oil companies mostly finance. Alaskans have also come to depend on its lone Congressman and senior U.S. Senator to funnel billions of federal dollars into the state in the form of earmarks. The PF held about $27 billion in early 2009. The income from this fund plus payment of an income tax would enable Alaskans to pay for the services and infrastructure they have enjoyed without any personal contribution. Legislators also rejected repeated suggestions to revise the state taxes levied on the oil industry. In 2006 Governor Frank Murkowski presented to the legislature a draft agreement for a North Slope natural gas pipeline. The oil companies, which were to build the gas pipeline, insisted that they needed fiscal certainty on oil taxes before committing to the project. The governor had negotiated the contract in secrecy, and there was even a suspicion that the governer's team had signed away the right of Alaska's citizens to bypass the legislature and make laws directly by the initiative process. Under Alaska's Stranded Gas Act the legislature supposedly could sign away the right to raise taxes, and many suspected that Murkowski's contract protected the producers against a tax initiative.[32]

Voters in the August 7, 2006 primary handed the governor his walking papers and chose newcomer Sarah Palin. Many issues led to Murkowski's defeat. Some of these were the appointment of his daughter to fill his vacated U.S. Senate seat, abolishing the longevity bonus; the purchase of a jet over the opposition of the legislature and the public; his failed effort to use Permanent Fund' income to support the state budget; his plan to give up the state's rights to change oil taxes for 30 years in exchange for the construction of a gas pipeline; and above all, his overwhelming arrogance. Just before the primary a telling joke made the rounds in Alaska: "What's the difference between Frank Murkowski and God?" "God doesn't think he is Frank Murkowski."[33]

Murkowski, however, has to be credited with overhauling the state's defective oil and gas production tax laws. The issue became entangled in the gasline debate. The governor knew that he would have a tough time selling the new Petroleum Profits Tax, or PPT against the opposition of the industry and fellow Republicans in the legislature. But the governor persuaded the industry and enough lawmakers to accept the PPT. It was the combination of a profits-type tax that indirectly helped high-cost projects, like heavy oil production. It also had investment tax credits that could be exchanged. This allowed new explorers who had not yet achieved production to sell their credits to others thereby reducing their high exploration costs.[34]

Independent analysts for years had pointed out that the state did not receive a fair share from its North Slope oil fields. Richard A. Fineberg, one of these analysts, estimated that from 1993 through 1997 the North Slope producers and their Alaska pipeline affiliate earned about $13.4 billion after taxes on their Alaska operations. The state's royalty and tax payments share was approximately $10.3 billion, while the federal government received an estimated $7.6 billion. During this five year period, North Slope producers and their pipeline affiliates earned an average of $5,500 per minute in inflation adjusted 1998 dollars.[35]

In a 2005 report, Fineberg wrote that oil industry profits on the North Slope amounted to $5.5 billion in 2004, when prices averaged $38.84 a barrel. That came to about $15 million a day, or $625,000 an hour. Even in 1998, when prices had averaged $12.55 per barrel, the industry had made $825 million on the North Slope. At prices of $50 a barrel, Fineberg estimated the industry's North Slope profits at about $5.7 billion a year.[36]

In December 2006, the state department of revenue forecast an extra $1.5 billion in 2007. Some of that money came from higher oil taxes, but most came from the state's new PPT. Passed in August 2006, it was retroactive to April of that year.[37]

In May 2007 the federal government released indictments which charged that two former lawmakers and one current House member misused their offices and violated the public trust in exchange for private gain. A few days later Bill J. Allen, chief executive officer of Anchorage-based VECO Corporation, an oil field services company, and Rick Smith, a vice-president pleaded guilty to bribing state legislators with cash and the promise of jobs and favors for their backing on bills the company supported. The two pled guilty to extortion, bribery, and conspiracy to impede the Internal Revenue Service. The pleas came after the indictments of one current and two former Republican members of the Alaska House of Representatives on federal bribery and extortion charges related to the 2006 negotiations for a new oil and gas tax and a proposed natural gas pipeline.[38] This put a legal cloud over the PPT the legislature had adopted in 2006. By December 2007, two former House members had been sentenced to five and six year jail terms, respectively, and a third one received a prison sentence of three and a half years in 2008.[39]

In late August 2007 FBI agents searched the Girdwood, Alaska, home of senior U.S. Senator Ted Stevens, focusing on records related to his relationship with VECO's Bill Allen as well as those that might shed light on whether federal funds he steered to the Seward SeaLife Center might have enriched a former aide.[40]

Alaska's U.S. Representative Don Young also was under federal investigation over his ties to VECO and his use of earmarks. One of

Young's aides pleaded guilty in the Jack Abramoff lobbying scandal, and Young had ties to the lobbyist. In any event, Young reported that he had spent several hundred-thousand dollars on unspecified legal fees in 2007.[41]

Governor Sarah Palin thereupon developed and introduced Alaska's Clear and Equitable Share plan (ACES) which was a hybrid valuation scheme which incorporated gross and net features that assured that the state would receive appropriate value during high oil prices, share risks during downturns and credit companies for new private sector investments.[42]

She asked the legislature to approve a sensible rewrite of the PPT. Instead, in a special session the legislature passed a measure boosting revenues almost four times more than she had proposed with her ACES plan. Why did an appropriate oil tax bill finally pass? Obviously, the political climate was far more favorable for a tax increase than the governor, the producers and most politicians had guessed. Most legislators had become convinced that corruption had played a role in shaping the 2006 PPT legislation. The three major producers denied that they had anything to do with it. They were, nevertheless, among the chief beneficiaries of the corruption. Furthermore, as global oil prices rose, jurisdictions around the world were boosting their share of the profits. Also, the oil industry's image in Alaska has suffered with North Slope oil spills and BP's big fine for price fixing and environmental crimes. Then there was Exxon's umpteenth oil spill appeal, and all came as producers posted record profits and Americans paid ever increasing prices for gasoline, diesel, and heating oil.[43]

The first fifty years of statehood, most Alaskan residents would agree, have brought monumental changes to the 49th state, some for the better, others for the worse. Alaska is an urban state. Most of its 680,000 inhabitants live in urban centers which offer most of the conveniences found elsewhere in urban America, from box stores to traffic jams. Then there are the Native Alaskans who, if they have not moved to the urban centers, live in more than 200 villages scattered across the state, the majority not connected to the road system, who lack most of these modern conveniences.

Alaskans like to imagine that their state still offers untrammeled freedoms and limitless horizons. This myth lies behind the resistance to all designations of land designed to protect natural landscapes and wildlife habitat, or to prevent environmental degradation. Such attitudes, however, foreclose the freedoms they supposedly defend. There is no escaping into the past of the 1860s before boundary lines and private property, before "No Trespassing" signs, before cities and urban areas had changed the landscapes through which explorers and prospectors traveled laboriously on foot, horseback, dog team, and boat. We are still attracted to the romance of that past, but that world has disappeared. When local activities threaten national parks, national wildlife refuges and national forests, among others, we each lose. Not only our generation but also those of our children and grand children will suffer that loss.

As citizens of this state we must ask before we allow ourselves to be deluded by those who claim to represent our interests which schemes will have unfortunate, unpredictable, and long-term consequences: who will benefit from these multiplying mining sites, highways and bridges to everywhere? Who loses and what are the losses? It is important to keep Alaska a good place to live, maintaining a sense of spaciousness and our individual ties to wild lands so close to our homes. That is a real part of why we live here. It will require vision, wisdom and experience to manage the inevitable changes the next fifty years will bring. The first fifty years of statehood have been, at times, tumultuous. Hopefully we can steer the inevitable changes the next fifty years will bring into avenues that benefit all Alaskan residents and preserve those lifestyles we cherish.

CHAPTER ONE

William H. Seward's Vision

A fter negotiating for three weeks, Secretary of State William H. Seward and Baron Edouard Stoecki, the Russian Minister to the United States, met at Seward's home in Washington, and during a long night of phrasing and rephrasing the working, they finally completed the Treaty of Cession of Russian America. Early in the morning of March 30, 1867, the two weary men signed the document.[1] Even before the money for Alaska was paid to Russia, the territory was officially taken over by the United States. President Andrew Johnson appointed General Lovell H. Rousseau of Kentucky to act as commissioner for the United States government in the ceremonies, with General Jefferson C. Davis to command a military force of about 500 men, stationed at five posts, to maintain peace and order.[2] In a speech at Sitka on August 12, 1868, Secretary Seward dedicated Alaska to future statehood, when he stated, "...nor do I doubt that the political society to be constituted here, first as a Territory, and ultimately as a state or many States, will prove a worthy constituency of the Republic."[3]

President Johnson, when notifying Congress of the transfer which took place at Sitka on October 18, 1867, commented on the indefinite status of Alaska: "Possession having been formally delivered to a military force, awaiting such civil organization as shall be directed by Congress."[4] Congress did not respond to President Johnson's veiled suggestion that some sort of civil government should be established in the new acquisition. Instead, the Fortieth Congress (1867-1869) merely passed an act which made Alaska a customs district of the United States. Violators were to be prosecuted in the United States district courts of Washington, Oregon, or California. Whatever semblance of civil government existed was exercised without any definite legal authority by the commanding general of the troops stationed at Sitka. And, in 1877, the troops were withdrawn from Alaska to help put down the Nez Perce Indian uprising in the Pacific Northwest.[5]

Control of the territory was then officially handed over to the Treasury Department which already was struggling to enforce the customs, commercial, and navigation laws, and to prevent smuggling and the use or importation of liquor and firearms. For the next two years there was no real federal authority at all in Alaska, except what the customs collector at Sitka could conjure out of thin air. In the summer of 1878, the citizens of Sitka, fearing a Native uprising, petitioned for help from the British who responded by sending the warship *Osprey* under the command of Captain H. Homes A' Court for their protection. Shortly thereafter the American sloop of war *Jamestown* under Commander Lester Anthony Beardslee arrived.

Commander Beardslee had been instructed by Secretary of the Navy R.W. Thompson to restore "harmonious relations" between settler and Native, and in the absence of civil government and law., to use his "own discretion in all emergencies that might arise"[6] much to the discomfiture of commander Beardslee, his arrival inaugurated a five-year period during with the Navy exercised the role of the sole government for Alaska. This role was not terminated until 1884, when the passage of the First Organic Act made Alaska a "civil and judicial district" with a governor, district judge, clerk of court, marshal, four deputy marshals, and four commissioners, who had the functions of justices of the peace. The general laws of the state of Oregon then in force were declared to be the law of the district of Alaska, in so far as they might be applicable and not in conflict with the provisions of the act or with the laws of the United States.[7] One historian has declared, "As finally passed, S. 153 was evolved from a composite of honest intentions, ignorance, stupidity, indifference, and quasi-expediency."[8] In short, the First Organic Act provided for a total of thirteen officials who would be responsible for some 586,000 square miles and a population of 32,000 souls, of which 430 were white.

The settlers, who came to Sitka with the Army in 1867, and those who subsequently made the long journey to Alaska, came largely from the other territories and from the states. Most of them had some knowledge of how frontiers in the United States had developed, and they believed that, in the normal course of events, after a suitable period of territorial government, Alaska would join the Union as a state. Alaska, however, did not follow the usual territory to state pattern. It was not until 1884 that, as a previously mentioned, the First Organic Act granted Alaskans even the basic elements of self-government. Historian Earl S. Pomeroy observes that Alaska "stood in an outer political anetoom without the most rudimentary territorial status, governed (when governed at all) more like the Newfoundland fisheries of the Seventeenth-Century British empire than like a territory."[9] Another scholar of territorial government, Jack E. Eblen, has concluded that the Organic Act "provided a cruelly modified first-stage government and made no provision for eventual representative government." Eblen also maintains that although Congress used the time-honored model of the Mississippi Valley area in organizing its noncontiguous territories, including Alaska, it made minor changes in the system which significantly altered the character of administration. In short, the federal government exercised its full powers to assure a tight, imperial control, and thereby created a truly noncontiguous administrative empire, much like those empires created by various European nations in that era of the "white man's burden."[10]

Despite such imperial control, however, the federal government showed little real interest in Alaska. One of the most obvious reasons for this disinterest was that the acquisition coincided
with the post-Civil War preoccupation with Reconstruction. The
nation's priorities simply did not include. Alaska. That faraway and
largely unknown region had few spokesmen to champion its cause,
although the area was by no means terra incognita. In fact, even
before the Civil War American whalers from New England had
brought back news of the wealth of seal furs, walrus ivory, sperm
oil, and baleen obtainable in Alaskan waters. During the war the
Rebel privateer *Shenandoah* had operated in the Bering Sea and
acquainted some Americans with Alaska's existence.[11] Later Senator Charles Sumner of Massachusetts gave a lengthy speech before
the Senate in defense of the Alaskan purchase. In this widely circulated address he extolled the resources and climate of Alaska.
He spoke of the vast forests of pine and fir waiting for the axe and
the mineral resources which included coal and copper, iron, silver,
lead, and gold. The fisheries, he said, were rich beyond any other
on the globe and promised great wealth to the United States.[12] But
despite such accounts of Alaska's riches, even some editors who
were favorably impressed could not resist a facetious remark or
two. James Gordon Bennett of the *New York Herald* commented
in his newspaper that any impoverished European monarchs who
wanted to sell worthless territory should "apply to W.H. Seward,
State Department, Washington, D.C."[13]

It was only with the flood of Klondike-bound gold seekers,
beginning in 1897, that the question of Alaska's form of government
and its resources and their development seemed suddenly pertinent
to the American public and to Congress. The area might just warrant
some serious attention after all. During the decade from 1890 to
1900, Alaska had an influx of more than 30,000 persons due to the
Gold Rush. The census of 1900 showed a total population of 63, 592.
The population continued to grow slowly, except for a period of
decline between 1910 and 1920. This subsequent growth reflected
the successive development of commercial fishing, trapping,

mineral production, and other extractive industries which were characteristic of a colonial economy.[14]

In 1897, President William McKinley, taking notice of the Gold Rush boom, stated in his first annual message to Congress, "The conditions now existing demand material changes in the laws relating to the Territory." In 1899, McKinley again voiced his concern for Alaskan problems when he asserted, "A necessity for immediate legislative relief exists in the Territory of Alaska." The President asked for a system of local government and at least two federal judges. "I see no reason why a more complete form of territorial organization should not be provided," he added.[15]

Under the McKinley administration the Fifty-fifth Congress (1897-99) passed two major pieces of legislation pertaining to the northern territory. One, enacted before the end of 1898, made various provisions for the construction of railroads, and extended the homestead laws to Alaska. The size of the plots was restricted to eighty acres, and the burden of the survey had to be borne by the applicant. Prospective homesteaders were allowed to use soldiers' script. The act also provided that citizens of Canada were to be accorded the same mining rights as American citizens were granted in that Dominion and goods could be transported duty-free between Alaskan ports and Canadian points if Canadians granted reciprocal privileges.[16]

The other piece of major legislation was a clarifying act which provided for the punishment of crime in Alaska and also gave the territory a Code of Criminal Procedure. This act was very complex and lengthy. It codified the laws of Oregon and modified them for Alaska. Included was a system of taxation, the first levied in the district. License fees for some forty occupations were imposed. These varied from $250 per year for banks to $500 for breweries. Mercantile establishments paid on a sliding scale, with a $500 per year fee for those who did a $100,000 business. The sale of liquor was legalized, but a tax was imposed on the dealer. The railroads were taxed $100 for each mile of their operation and salmon canneries were taxed at four cents per case. The funds derived from these taxes and surplus was to go into the United States Treasury.[17] This system of taxation, with only minor modifications, persisted for over fifty years.

A great many Alaska bills were introduced in the Fifty-sixth Congress (1899-1901), including measures pertaining to Native welfare, reindeer, education, the fisheries, the judiciary, and a recurrent request for an Alaskan delegate to Congress. In 1900 Congress passed a civil code and a Code of Civil Procedure. With this last piece of legislation, Congress began to deal directly with the problem of providing a general governmental system for Alaska. The district of Alaska was divided into three parts, and courts were established at Sitka, Nome and Eagle City on the Yukon, with authority to convene elsewhere when necessary.[18] Within the framework of the Organic Act of 1884, which had established Alaska as a civil and judicial district of the United States, the 1900 act provided for the presidential selection of three district judges. It also made possible the incorporation of municipalities for the first time. Communities with 300 or more permanent inhabitants were allowed to organize local governments. The first step was a petition to the United States district court, which had to approve the proposal. At a subsequent local election, the new local governmental scheme was to be approved or disapproved by the inhabitants. In 1904, amending and codifying legislation was passed, and this together with the act of 1900, was the beginning of statutory local self-government in Alaska.[19] The Klondike Gold Rush had brought about some legislation for Alaska. But most important, Alaska had secured official recognition as a pressing problem.

Bills to provide Alaska with a delegate to Congress, as mentioned, had repeatedly been introduced in Congress. In the Fifty-fifth (1897-99), Fifty-sixth (1899-1901), and Fifty-seventh (1901-03) Congresses, delegate bills made some progress, but not enough for enactment. Not until the Fifty-ninth Congress, in 1906, did both houses of Congress take favorable action. The bill provided for the election of a delegate for the short term, that is, the rest of the Fifty-ninth Congress, and for the subsequent election of one for the full session of the Sixtieth Congress (1907-1999).[20] The territorial delegate acted as a nonvoting member of the House of Representatives. He received the same salary and allowances as his colleagues; he served on committees, spoke on the floor, and introduced bills. Since the federal government and its various departments and bureaus played such an important social and economic role in the life of all Alaskans, this representation was extremely important in deciding Alaska's future.

It was not until 1912 that Congress passed the Second Organic Act, which gave an elected legislature to Alaska. Technically, this body was a creature of the federal government, and its work was subject to the veto of a federally appointed governor and to approval (or disapproval) by Congress. The act prescribed the structure of the territorial legislature, the nature of its membership, the method of electing members, and its general internal organization and procedures. Additionally, specific limitations were placed on its authority.[21] Broad responsibility was given to the appointed governor. As a result, territorial legislators, who usually distrusted the Alaskan chief executive, spent much of their time and energy in thwarting this control. They created various boards and elective positions, which eventually resulted in a patchwork of duplication and overlapping of responsibility, making territorial government cumbersome and unwieldy.

Viewing the Alaska government some three decades after its creation, the National Resources Planning Board concluded in 1941:

In many respects Alaska is a Federal province: The Governor is a Federal appointee, the law-enforcement and judicial system is administered by the United States Department of Justice, part of the local taxes are imposed by Act of Congress and collected by Federal officers, the fisheries and wildlife are under the jurisdiction of Federal and quasi-Federal agencies, about 98% of land is in Federal ownership, the national defense program now changing the economic life of the Territory in a radical way is entirely in Federal control.

Edward Lewis "Bob" Bartlett

Architects of Statehood

Edward Lewis "Bob" Bartlett

"Bob" Bartlett was born in Seattle on April 20, 1904. He grew up in Fairbanks where his father had established a freighting business and later also mined for gold. Bob graduated from high school in Fairbanks in 1922 and started a career in journalism at the local paper in 1924. On August 14, 1930 he married Vide Gaustad in Valdez, Alaska. They had known each other since high school. Territorial Senator and Mrs. Anthony J. Dimond witnessed the ceremony.

When Alaskans elected Dimond their delegate to Congress in 1932, he hired Bartlett as his secretary. The Bartletts returned to Alaska in 1934 where Bob accepted the job as assistant territorial director of the Federal Housing Administration in Juneau. He resigned his job in 1936 and took over the family's gold mine in the Circle District.

On February 2, 1939, President Roosevelt appointed him secretary of Alaska, the equivalent of lieutenant-governor, for a four-year term. When Dimond chose not to run for reelection in 1944, Bartlett became a candidate. He won that election and every subsequent one.

In Congress, as a voteless delegate, he successfully steered many bills through Congress. Most important, he championed Alaska's statehood cause. He drafted and introduced many statehood bills, won many converts over the years, and in 1958 saw his dreams fulfilled when Congress admitted Alaska as the 49th State.

Alaskans elected him U.S. Senator in 1958 and reelected him in 1962. He served as the new state's senior U.S. Senator until his death after bypass surgery in Cleveland, Ohio on December 11, 1968.

This picture is remarkably different from the simple pattern of Federal activities that prevailed during territorial days in the States.

On the other hand, the Territory of Alaska is in many respects treated as a state and is expected to assume responsibilities similar to those carried by the states. It is, for example, expected to maintain its own system of elementary, secondary, and higher education...; to maintain a system of social security which will comply with standers laid down for states; to maintain certain technical services in aid of mining and agriculture.[22]

The whole structure of territorial government could have been made more responsive to the popular will had Congress seen fit to make the position of governor elective and to enlarge the powers of the legislature. This would have necessitated an amendment of the Second Organic Act. Proposals for such amendments were introduced time and again by Alaska delegates to Congress but evoked no response in Washington. Delegate E.L. "Bob" Bartlett, who served in the nation's capital from 1945-1958, expressed his frustration on this point when he declared in 1947:

...we have lived under a very limited form of territorial government for 35 years. Delegate James Wickersham...tried to get reforms for the [sic] organic bill. He failed. Anthony J. Dimond failed and I have failed and I have reached the point where I am convinced that it would be just as simple to get a statehood bill through congress as to get through a new organic act.[23]

But despite all its apparent defects, the Organic Act of 1912 ended Alaska's mysterious legal and constitutional status. It specifically stated, "The constitution...shall have the same force and effect within the Territory of Alaska as elsewhere in the United States." As early as 1868, Alaska had been referred to as both the "District of Alaska" and the "Territory of Alaska." These two terms also were used interchangeably in subsequent debates and committee reports, and the First Organic Act of 1884 added to the confusion by making Alaska "a civil and judicial district."[24] The distinction between a territory and a district was a crucial one, because the former was thought capable of exercising at least a limited measure of home rule through a locally elected legislature, while the latter was considered to be incapable of exercising self-government.[25]

It was the Northwest Ordinance of 1787 which had established the philosophical and structural frame work for the American territorial system. The outstanding characteristic of this scheme was its transitional and progressive character looking toward ultimate statehood.[26] Under the provisions of the ordinance the United States had grown from the original thirteen states to forty-eight states, when the last two contiguous territories, New Mexico and Arizona, were admitted to statehood in 1912. The legal and historical precedents of admitting territories, therefore, had deep roots in American history.

Complications had arisen, however, when the United States acquired the Hawaiian Islands and other noncontiguous, remote, and contained an Indian, Eskimo, and Aleut population of modest size. It was grouped with the new lands. The question soon came up whether or not these new acquisitions, populated largely by alien people, were eligible for eventual statehood. The Supreme Court attempted to give an answer in a number of decisions, known as the "Insular Cases," which distinguished between two types of Territories, "incorporated" and "unincorporated."[27] In one of these cases, *Downes v. Bidwell,* the Court dealt with the question of whether or not the constitutional requirement that duties, imports, and excises should be uniform "throughout the United States" applied to Puerto Rico. Specifically, would it invalidate a provision in that island's Organic Act establishing a schedule of custom duties on its merchandise entering the continental United States? The Court decided that Puerto Rico was not a part of the United States for the purposes of this constitutional provision because it had not been incorporated into the United States. Secretary of War Elihu

Root reportedly said of this rather nebulous distinction established by the Court, "...as near as I can make out the constitution follows the flag—but doesn't quite catch up with it".[28]

Historically, statehood was tied to the territorial classification, and, after the Insular Cases, specifically to the incorporated status. On a number of occasions the Court recognized Alaska's incorporated status,[29] and also decided that once an area had been incorporated it could not revert again to an unincorporated status. Furthermore, once Congress had incorporated a territory, it subjected itself to certain limitations to legislate for that region, although these restrictions did not apply when it exercised authority to make laws for an unincorporated area. Most importantly, the act of incorporation was consistently looked upon as a commitment on the part of Congress ultimately to admit the incorporated territory as a state.[30]

Because of such strong historical and judicial precedents, Alaska's eventual admission to statehood was as certain as anything can be in the American political system. But the admission process had often been influenced by political considerations. An example is the case of Nevada. During the Civil War the Republican hierarchy in the Senate had elevated the territory to statehood to give Abraham Lincoln more electoral votes in 1864 and to help ratify the Thirteenth Amendment, although Nevada had a population of only 20,000.[31]

When Delegate James Wickersham introduced Alaska's first statehood bill 1916, the territory had a citizenry of roughly 58,000. At this point the population had not been sufficiently "politicized," and the first statehood movement died due to apathy. When Warren G. Harding visited the territory in 1923, the first President to do so, it gave only a momentary boost to the Alaska statehood movement. The Second World War, however, revolutionized Alaska. Billions of dollars in defense monies flowed into the territory. The dramatic impact of this influx was reflected in Alaska's population growth. Of a total of about 75,000 inhabitants in 1940, approximately 1,000 were members of the military forces. By 1943, the number of people in Alaska had risen to 233,000, of whom some 152,000 were members of the military. Although the total number of inhabitants declined to approximately 99,000 in 1946, the Cold War years and the associated increase in military expenditures again raised Alaska's population to approximately 138,000 in 1950.[32]

The influx of this new population and money during World War II and the Cold War transformed the territory socially and economically. Together with these momentous changes, a new and vigorous movement to gain statehood arose in the mid-1940. This modern statehood movement consisted of two phases. The first lasted from 1943 to 1953. It was propelled by Alaska's governor, the delegate to Congress, and a cross-section of the territory's established business and professional men and women. It had a fairly narrow base. A referendum on statehood was held in 1946. Alaskans, by a margin of three to two, expressed their desire for statehood. In 1949, the territorial legislature responded by creating an official Alaska Statehood Committee. Several congressional hearings were held, in which most of the testimony was favorable to statehood. By 1950, the year an Alaska statehood bill for the first time passed in either house of Congress, the opposition to statehood had crystallized. It was led by the Alaska Salmon Industry, Inc., a trade organization, and included a number of Alaska's newspapers. In Congress, the main support came from representatives and senators of Western public land states, while the opposition was centered mainly in the South and New England.

The second or "populist" phase of the statehood movement began late in 1953 and lasted until 1958. It involved thousands of ordinary Alaskans not connected with any official group of agency. It culminated in a constitutional convention in 1955-56 and the adoption of a constitution in the spring of 1956 by a substantial majority of Alaska's voters.

Throughout the two phases, national as well as local support for Alaska statehood grew. A combination of these pressures resulted in the passage of an Alaska statehood act in 1958 by both houses of Congress.

CHAPTER TWO

Little Government for the Few

I n the eighteenth century, the European exploration of the North Pacific Coast opened up an entire new frontier to the Russian and British fur traders and trappers. This northern region offered an extension of the trade into Alaska, the basis for an enduring colonial structive exploitation of the fur bearing animals as well as numerous other natural resources.[1]

In the 1740's, the Russians began to harvest the fur seals and sea otters together with a variety of land animals bearing valuable pelts. Men from other nations later joined this quest. By the end of the nineteenth century, the sea otters had been virtually destroyed. By the first decade of the twentieth century, the Pribilof Seals had ceased as the result of an international treaty which outlawed pelagic sealing, and, in addition, the United States government took this seal herd. Whaling was big business from 1849, when the first whalers passed through the Bering Strait, until the 1880's, when, due to the growing scarcity of these huge mammals and the substitution of petroleum products for whale oil, the industry began to decline.

Although the fur trade dwindled after the United States acquisition of Alaska in 1867, salmon fishing, which had merely provided for local needs under the Russians, expanded into a thriving
business. The first American saltery was set up in 1968, and the
first cannery began operation at Klawock on Prince Wales Island
in 1878. By 1898, there were fifty-nine canneries in Alaska. Prospectors created another component of Alaska's colonial economy.
Some men searched for minerals, principally gold, in Southeastern
Alaska as early as the 1960s. Actually it all may be said to have
started in 1848 when gold was discovered in California. Soon restless miners spread out from there and began to search for the pre-
cious metal elsewhere, in Nevada and Colorado, Washington and
Idaho, among other places, and northward into British Columbia
as well. In 1857 prospectors found gold at the juncture of the Fraser
and Thompson Rivers in British Columbia. Miners followed the
Fraser River toward its headwaters and discovered gold deposits
in the Cariboo district in 1860 and the filtered into Southeastern
Alaska via the Stikine River route and added to the prospecting
population in the region. Gold was discovered in the Sitka area in
the 1870s and in 1880 Joseph Juneau and Richard T. Harris made a
big strike at the present site of Juneau. Late in the same year the two
men entered a townsite claim which they named Harrisburg.

While hard rock mining grew slowly in southeastern Alaska, a
few prospectors found their way into the Yukon Valley in the early
1970s by way of Hudson's Bay Company route from the Mackenzie
coastal mountains by ascending the Chilkoot Pass and reaching
the upper part of the Yukon River. The discovery of placer gold
in the Yukon Valley led to the establishment of a number of small
mining settlements along that river and its tributaries.

Although the economic development at this time was modest,
it resulted in a substantial influx of white fortune seekers. The first
official census in 1880 reported 33,426 inhabitants, of whom all but
430 were aboriginal Alaskans. The next census, in 1890, showed an
increase of 3,868 whites and a decline among the Eskimos, Indians,

and Aleuts of 7,642, due to the usual traumatic collision between Caucasian and Native cultures.[2]

By 1884 Congress had passed Alaska's first Organic Act, sponsored principally by Indiana's Senator Benjamin Harrison. This framework of government was so patently inadequate that it caused Alaskans to agitate for a territorial form of government and encouraged them to create their own institutions.[3] As Professor Ted C. Hinckley has observed, Alaska was "no different from other Western territories" in that it was "granted a great deal of administrative freedom" from the very beginning.[4] As in so many other regions of the frontier West, Alaskan miners' meetings and law—the so-called miner's code—helped fill the local governmental void. By the authority of this code the miners not only made their own regulations for their claims, but they also enacted rules and regulations which concerned community affairs. Alfred H. Brooks, at one time head of the United States Geological Survey in Alaska, has stated, somewhat romantically:

...there developed democracies of the purest type, resembling in a manner the government in some of the cantons of Switzerland and the earliest colonial settlement of New England. The miners met and by majority vote enacted a community believed that a wrong had been done him, he called a miner's [sic] meeting and he case was settled by majority vote. Similar action was taken in criminal cases. As imprisonment was impractical, there were only three punishments: hanging, banishment, and fines. In the code established at Circle City in 1893, murder was punished by hanging, assault and stealing by banishment and minor infractions by fine.[5]

The miner's code thus helped to fill the local government needs which existed. In the larger settlements, local law enforcement officers, rudimentary court systems, and elected mayors, councils, and other officials began to appear in time.[6]

Meanwhile, the governor, whose office had been established by the First Organic Act of 1884, was marooned in Sitka, Alaska's capital city located on an island in the Alexander Archipelago. Legally, the chief executive was obligated to perform a long list of duties for which he was endowed with an impressive amount of authority. But as one of the governors ruefully remarked, "...authority to require performance of duty, in the absence of any power to compel it, amounts to nothing..."[7] Since the governor had limited means of transportation, he usually was out of touch with most of Alaska. Although still a problem today, the physical and geographical features of Alaska presented almost insuperable barriers to the early pioneers. Southeastern Alaska, where the majority of the white population lived and worked in the 1800s, had ready access to the "outside" (as anything south of Alaska is still referred to in old-fashioned Alaskan idiom) by water transportation. On the other hand, the Gulf coastal area, or the "Westward," and the land mass north of the Alaska Range, or the "Interior" or "Northward," were practically inaccessible and isolated.

Bearing in mind his isolated situation, the governor's annual reports to the President are studies in Alaska politics and territorial administration. If read critically, they give a good insight into many aspects of the history of Alaska. These reports also served to keep territorial affairs before the executive branch of the federal government. Alaska's frontier politicians, Professor Hinckley comments,

> confronted more ponderous problems than those found in many territories. They frequently became very peevish and censorious because of what they felt was glaring inconsideration from Washington, D.C. Damning congressional apathy was a venerable Western habit.[8]

Alaskan governors were especially critical of the Organic Act of 1884. Alfred P. Swineford, the territory's second chief executive, perhaps was typical. In every one of his annual reports he complained about the shortcomings of the Organic Act and expressed doubt that it could be

construed into anything more in harmony with the funda-
mental principles of free representative government then
could one which explicitly declares a qualified executive abso-
lutism. That act, following, as it appears, the always excep-
tional treatment of Alaska, presents an anomaly of law, by
expressly excluding all legislative or representative power
from the people.[9]

What Alaska lacked was people, the foundation of any boom-
ing frontier. From the lack of population, as Professor Hinckley
has written, "everything else suffered. And because it was basically
a problem that could not be remedied by Alaskans, they blamed
their government... [or all their ills]."[10]

Governor Swineford considered a delegate to Congress a necessity and a right which had been extended to every territory except
Alaska. He dismissed as inconsequential the argument that Alaska's
population was too sparse to entitle it to a delegate. Where the question of right was concerned, he asserted, numbers had no significance.[11] Without a legislature and a delegate to Congress, Governor
Swineford stated, Alaska could not develop its wealth and potential. In this last regard he struck a theme which was to be repeated
throughout the years, and which finally found a focus in the statehood movement in the 1950s. Economist George W. Rogers had
remarked that Alaskans, like other colonial peoples, conceived of
economic development as essentially political in nature. Thus the
modern statehood proponents asserted that without two senators
and one representative in Congress, the territory would be unable
to realize its economic potential. Lack of progress, this same group
maintained, was due to the absentee salmon canning, gold mining,
and Seattle shipping interests.[12] While there is no doubt that absentee
economic interests played a significant role in Alaska, as they do in
any colonial economy, they also served as a symbol of the territory's
ills and helped to rally citizens to the statehood cause.

When Congress did not remedy any of the deficiencies of the
Organic Act which Governor Swineford had criticized so vehemently

and so long, he concluded in utter frustration that "the civil government of Alaska is little, if any, better than a burlesque both in form
and substance."[13] Swineford's successors echoed and amplified his
dissatisfactions, and the politically articulate public in Southeastern
Alaska also criticized the shortcomings of the district's governmental
structure. As a matter of fact, political consciousness in Southeastern Alaska became evident soon after the Organic Act of 1884, and
"from this time onward" there was a "desire for home rule, marked
by fairly definite stages."[14] These stages took the form of political conventions which met in Harrisburg in 1881 and in Juneau in 1890. In
each instance a delegate was elected and dispatched to Washington
to plead for, among other things, representation in Congress. Both
times the memorials fell on deaf ears.[15]

After these unsuccessful ventures, concerned Democrats and
Republicans of Southeastern Alaska decided to work through the
regular party machinery. Alaskan Democrats already had received
recognition by their national party when two of the delegates had
been seated at the Democratic National Convention in 1888. Four
years later, both territorial Democrats and Republicans attempted
to seat their representatives at their respective national conclaves.
The Democrats again placed their two men. The Republicans for
the first time were granted two delegates. Both, territorial organizations were also granted a national committeeman.[16] Partly as
a result of these political activities by Alaskans, occasional measures for a delegate had been considered in Congress. One such bill
even received a favorable committee report in 1896 but died in the
House of Representatives.[17]

In that same year, however, there occurred an event in Canada
which profoundly influenced Alaska's political history. In August
of 1896, news of a gold strike came from an obscure creek on the
upper Yukon River. George Washington Carmack, his Indian wife,
and his two brothers-in-law, Skookum Jim and Tagish Charlie, had
found gold on Rabbit Creek, later renamed Bonanza Creek. This
stream flowed into the Klondike River, a tributary of the mighty
Yukon. News of the strike spread rapidly, and before that fall ended,

most of the ground around the creeks that emptied into the Klondike and Indian Rivers was stated out. At the junction of the Klondike and Yukon Rivers a tent camp on a marshy riverbank developed into the frontier city of Dawson.[18]

The rush to the gold fields of the Klondike was one, and since the two major routes led across Alaskan soil, the territory was brought to the attention of millions of Americans. Reported widely in newspaper columns, in scores of magazine articles, and ultimately in "not few than three hundred bound volumes of personal experiences as well as fuller compendia"[19] the Klondike Gold Rush publicized the northland as nothing before had done.

It has been estimated that between 200,000 and 300,000 people started for the Klondike and that approximately 50,000 actually reached the interior of the Yukon Territory and Alaska. Thousands of "stampeders," who were disappointed with the New Eldorado, spread down the Yukon River and up its tributaries into Alaska panning for gold. Just as the Klondike excitement was abating, gold was discovered on the Seward Peninsula near Cape Nome, and the whole story of the Klondike was repeated, and in some respects magnified, because access to the new find was much easier. In 1896 the Seward Peninsula, which forms the nearest approach to Asia in Alaska, was populated by a few hundred Eskimos and a handful of whites. Ten years later it had a permanent population of roughly 4,000 and the summer inhabitants numbered 10,000. In 1902, a gold strike in the Tanana Valley in the interior of Alaska gave birth to the city of Fairbanks. During all this excitement, a great deal of gold was taken from these areas. Between 1896-1906, the Klondike produced $118,725,000 worth of the yellow metal, and the Seward Peninsula between 1896-1906, shipped out $37,247,000 in gold.[20]

In 1897, Governor John G. Brady described the effects of the Gold Rush on Alaska by stating that thousands of fortune seekers had started to the Klondike at once, thousands were waiting for more news from the gold fields, and in addition *shipload after shipload of goldseekers and their freight has [sic] been rushed to the extreme limit of salt-water navigation, and there they have been literally dumped upon the beach, some above high water and many below, as they learned to their sorrow when the water covered them as they slept.[21]*

In 1898 the Governor pleaded for congressional consideration of Alaska's problems, saying:[22]

Alaska is thirteen times larger than Cuba,... it has been in our possession for thirty-one years, and... its value has been unknown and unappreciated. In the light of the recent discoveries who will be so bold as to assert that any square mile of Alaska is a worthless possession. Above all, we beseech Congress to regard us as American citizens, and not undertake to classify us with Kanakas, Filipinos, and Cubans, and as worthy of a long state of probation before the full measure and blessing of the laws can be extended to us.[23]

Again, in 1899, he declared:

Statehood appears to be the only remedy. Alaska is large enough for many states. It might be admitted with definite provisions that as the population advanced within certain areas new States could be created. A people can attain under our form of government to their greatest degree of political happiness under a State and not as a Territory.[24]

The journalist David S. Jordan, writing for the *Atlantic Monthly* in 1898, observed that "the waste and confusion in Alaska arise from four sources—lack of centralization of power and authority, lack of scientific knowledge, lack of personal and public interest, and the use of offices as apolitical patronage." If the United States could not properly care for its colonies, he continued, it should not hoist the flag over such areas to begin with.[25]

In response to such reasoning and to the spectacular publicity enjoyed by Alaska, the federal government moved but cautiously.

Between 1897 and 1901, Congress supplemented the Organic Act of 1884 with a transportation and homestead act (1898), a criminal code and code of criminal procedure (1899), and a civil code and code of civil procedure (1900).[26] These pieces of legislation provided Alaska with a form of civil government. From then on it was only a matter of time before Congress would grant the territory a delegate to represent it in the nation's capital. As pressures for representation continued to grow, various bills providing for a delegate were introduced in Congress.

In 1903, a sympathetic Senate sent a subcommittee traveling through the territory for a first hand look at conditions there. The senators concluded, if nothing else, that "the universal opinion among all classes in Alaska is that the District should be represented by a delegate in Congress."[27] But Congress did not act, and Alaskan reaction to this apathy was reflected in a number of newspaper articles appearing in the *Valdez News* and the Skagway *Daily Alaskan* in 1905. The newspapers recommended that Alaskans establish a legislature on their own, send a delegate to Congress, and, if he was not seated, begin to govern themselves. To lend emphasis to their feelings, a Valdez mass meeting in the same year dispatched a telegram to President Theodore Roosevelt which read: "On behalf of 60,000 American citizens in Alaska who are denied the right of representation in any form, we demand, in mass meeting assembled, that Alaska be annexed to Canada."[28]

Finally, in 1906, Congress enacted a delegate bill.[29] Ernest Gruening, sometime territorial governor and later United States Senator from Alaska, has remarked caustically that "seven consecutive Congresses—from the Fifty-third to the Fifty-ninth inclusive—had found it necessary to discuss intensively, through fourteen years, the enormous concession of one voteless delegate in the lower house."[30]

Ernest Gruening

Architects of Statehood

Ernest Gruening

Ernest Gruening was born on February 6, 1887 in New York City. His father was a noted physician, specializing in diseases of the eye and ear. Ernest and his siblings spoke German at home and English outside of it. The children also learned French after spending a year in Paris in 1894-95.

Ernest attended private schools and entered Harvard in the fall of 1903 at the age of 16. He graduated with an M.D. from Harvard Medical School in 1912 but never practiced medicine. Instead he became a journalist and served as managing editor of the *Boston Traveler* at age 27 and later in that same capacity at the *Boston Journal*. He helped organize the Bureau of the War Trade Board, his first government job.

After more newspaper work and writing *Mexico and Its Heritage*, published in 1928, he took charge of the Portland Evening News in Maine, and in 1932 became one of four editors of *The Nation*.

In 1934, Secretary Harold L. Ickes, with the approval of President Roosevelt, appointed Gruening director of the Office of Territories and Island Possessions, and in 1935 the President appointed Gruening also administrator of the Puerto Rican Reconstruction Administration. After many clashes with Secretary Ickes, the President decided to appoint Gruening governor of Alaska in 1939. He held that position until 1953 and distinguished himself by persuading the territorial legislature to adopt a modern system of taxation for Alaska and vigorously lobbying for statehood. With his nation-wide journalistic connections he helped keep the statehood issue in the national spotlight.

Elected to one of Alaska's Tennessee Plan U.S. Senate seats, he went to Washington, D.C. and lobbied effectively for statehood. Alaskans elected him to one of the state's two U.S. seats in the Senate in 1958. He served with distinction until 1968 and died on June 26, 1974, at age 87, of cancer of the colon.

CHAPTER THREE

Wickersham and the Second Organic Act

M uch of Alaska's history has been a conflict between the nonresident special interests, principally the mining, shipping, and salmon canning industries, and the aspirations of Alaskans for a greater measure of self-government. From 1884 until 1912, these interests worked in Washington to obtain special privileges from an unconcerned Congress, and successfully thwarted territorial desires for home rule. After 1912 and the appearance of a territorial legislature, the special interests also exerted their influence and authority in Alaska. Territorial residents were not totally helpless in counteracting these pressures. This was especially true after the passage of the 1906 delegate act, when James Wickersham, Alaska's third delegate to Congress and the territory's most dominant political figure for the first three decades of the twentieth century, built a highly successful political career primarily on a platform of fighting the "Alaska Syndicate."[1] Wickersham was greatly aided in his battle against the lobby by the conservation issue, highlighted by the famous Ballinger-Pinchot controversy in 1909-10, which drew the nation's attention to its northern territory.[2]

Four years before the Ballinger-Pinchot affair rocked the administration of President William H. Taft, territorial Democrats and Republicans had held conventions to select their first candidates for the new position of delegate. Despite vigorous campaigns, the major party candidates were defeated by the "independent" nominees of the Seward Peninsula and Tanana region miners. In accordance with the 1906 act, Frank Waskey, a prosperous, young miner was elected to serve for the rest of the current Congressional session, while Thomas Cale, a middle-aged, popular but financially unsuccessful pioneer, was victorious for the first full term to start in 1907. The Waskey-Cale platform had included a demand for a territorial form of government. The Democrats had also supported full territorial government, while the Republicans had proclaimed their faith in the general principle of self-government but did not think the territory was quite ready for it.[3] Governor Wilford B. Hoggatt, who had not backed the delegate bill and who also was against a change in the governmental structure, stated nevertheless: "...it is to be hoped that Alaska will be benefited by a ...representative of its people and that the hopes of those who have been asking for representation in Congress for many years may be fully realized."[4]

Shortly before Congress convened late in 1906, President Theodore Roosevelt asked Waskey and the governor to submit to him statements outlining Alaska's political needs. Delegate Waskey wrote to the President that what the territory most urgently needed was special mining legislation, but that the most important matter politically was territorial government. "We are all Americans," Waskey stated, "and as such believe in the inalienable rights and privileges of self-government." Governor Hoggatt disagreed with Waskey and remarked that the conservative businessmen of the territory were almost unanimously opposed to territorial government. He pointed out Alaska's tremendous size, small population, widely scattered settlements, and the instability of the placer mining camps. Most importantly, the cost of such government would have to be borne by the permanent residents of Alaska. Hoggatt felt that much of the agitation for territorial government came from the "saloon element" in Alaska which wanted to decrease the high license fees then imposed upon that business. In addition, the governor stated, some of the demand for self-government had been generated by demagogic statements which claimed that Alaskans were deprived of some of the essential rights of American citizenship.[5] Hoggatt's views made him unpopular with many of the territory's citizens and also had an effect in making home rule a prominent issue in Alaska.[6] The hostility between the governor and the delegate continued during the term of Waskey's successor, Thomas Cale.

President Roosevelt retained an interest in Alaskan affairs, and after conferring with Cale in November of 1907, he recommended to Congress that it provide some form of simple and inexpensive local self-government to that territory. Delegate Cale followed up the message by introducing two measures to achieve the objective, on of them drafted by James Wickersham.[7]

Wickersham had come to Alaska in 1900 at the age of forty-three as a district court judge commissioned by President William McKinley. Wickersham first took up his duties in Eagle on the Yukon River, then moved to Nome in 1901, to Valdez in 1902, and to Fairbanks in 1903. He had established a reputation for efficiency, fairness, courage, and vigor. He did not endear himself to unsuccessful litigants before his bench, some of whom were politically influential. He soon became estranged from Governor Hoggatt and U.S. Senator Knute Nelson (R., Minnesota) for deciding cases against some of their friends. He further antagonized Nelson by blocking creation of a fourth judicial division in Alaska. The senator, thereupon, successfully prevented his confirmation as judge. Roosevelt kept him in office by five recess appointments, but Wickersham tired of the game and handed in his resignation in 1907, but agreed to stay on until a new judge had been appointed, although no later than March, 1908.[8]

Wickersham was no stranger to politics. In the summer of 1903, the Senate Committee on Territories had toured Alaska to investigate its needs. After its return, committee members reported

James Wickersham

Architects of Statehood

James Wickersham

James Wickersham was born in Patoka, Marion County, Illinois, on August 24, 1857. He attended the common schools, studied law and gained admission to the bar in 1880.

President William McKinley appointed Wickersham district judge for the Third Judicial District, headquartered in Eagle, Alaska, after the 65th Congress had passed the Civil Code for Alaska which established the second and third judicial districts for northern Alaska. Sworn into office in June 1900, Wickersham served with distinction.

In 1903, he moved the court's seat to the new town of Fairbanks. In 1908 he resigned and was elected Alaska's delegate to Congress. He secured the passage of Alaska's second Organic Act in 1912, granting Alaska territorial status. He introduced the Alaska Railroad Bill, and legislation to establish Mt. McKinley National Park. He was responsible for the creation of the Alaska Agricultural College and School of Mines, which became the University of Alaska in 1934.

In 1916, he introduced the first Alaska Statehood Bill as a trial balloon. It did not receive a hearing. Wickersham served as delegate to Congress until 1920, and then again from 1930 to 1932. He wrote many articles about Alaska and compiled the first edition of the *Alaska Reports*, a record of all decisions of the Alaska Courts and assembled the first index of all material published about Alaska, the Wickersham Bibliography.

Wickersham died in Juneau on October 23, 1939.

that northern citizens universally desired to be represented in Congress by a delegate who understood Alaska and could represent the north authoritatively. Citizens only disagreed on the delegate selection method. A majority preferred that he be elected while a minority wanted him appointed by the President with the consent of the Senate.[9]

Following that Senate investigation, the House of Representatives had passed a delegate bill. In the Senate, Orville Platt (R., Connecticut) opposed the measure, urging Congress to design special policies for governing noncontiguous territories. He therefore proposed that no language in the measure was to imply "that the territory embraced in the district of Alaska, or any portion thereof, shall at any time hereafter by admitted as a State." This proposal prompted Judge Wickersham to respond. Earlier in the year he had testified before the House Committee on Territories on behalf of the bill. Now, in a public address at Fairbanks, he asked if northern residents would have to create an independent country. A Republic of Alaska could adopt a constitution based on the federal document. The area could be divided into four states: Sitka, with its capital at Juneau; Alaska with its capital of Valdez; Sumner, with its capital at Nome; and finally Tanana with its capital at Fairbanks. But he also suggested that these great natural subdivisions might by admitted into the Union as states once they had gained the necessary population.[10]

Wickersham's drafting of the Cale measure signaled a change of mind, for the Judge had at first taken a dim view of the movement for a territorial government when he had written to Governor Hoggatt early in 1907:

> I regret very much that Waskey and Cale have started off on the mistaken idea of putting territorial government ahead of all other things of Alaska. It certainly is a great mistake and one which will cost the territory dear. You are right in opposing it and you ought not to hesitate. The population is too sparse and the taxable wealth is too small to sustain local

self-government. The population is unsettled, and probably out of the size thousand or eight thousand meant in this mining camp not a hundred of them will admit that they intend to remain in the territory the rest of their lives; nor would one-tenth of them remain if the placer mines were worked out as they are in Dawson and will be here inside of a few years. It is my judgment that a large majority of the people of this district are opposed to local self-government, although there is no difficulty in scaring up resolutions in Fourth of July language in favor of it. You should pay no attention to such resolutions except to try to explain to Congress and the President that they come from a small number of people with nothing else to do and are simply good-naturedly mistaken about what to do.[11]

Hoggatt made this letter public at a Congressional hearing in 1908 which was considering the two territorial government bills introduced by delegate Cale and one of which, as already stated, had been drafted by Wickersham.

By then, however, the judge had given his support to a limited form of territorial government only. As a man who was heavily involved in the mining business of the Tanana Valley, he apparently shared the fears of the canning and mining interests that a full territorial form of government would induce legislators to tax capriciously and spend public funds unwisely. The territorial government bill Wickersham had drafted reflected some of these fears. The measure provided for an appointed upper house and property holding as a qualification for office in the lower house. Wickersham was acutely embarrassed by the letter because he had since changed his position. He also had political ambitions in 1908, and recognized that not intend to jeopardize his political future by adhering to an unpopular position. In addition, both the territorial Republican and Democratic parties endorsed the theory of home rule.[12]

At the territorial convention in 1908, the Regular Republicans nominated "Seattle John" Corson, and the Democrats, John Tonan. J.P. Clum ran independently in the hope of securing support from the interior; Joseph Chilberg was chosen by the northern miners and ran on a pro-labor platform; and Cale was nominated by the Independent Republicans. Wickersham, who had believed that Cale would not run again and wanted to utilize Cale's organization for his own campaign, entered the race for delegate on June 23, 1908. Telegrams announcing his candidacy were sent to various newspapers in Alaska. Shortly thereafter, since Cale had not withdrawn from the race, Wickersham gave up his candidacy. "With both local newspapers against me," he wrote ruefully in his diary, "no money—-and no organization – with my friends at Skagway, Valdez [sic] and Nome for Cale it is a mistake to continue longer in the scramble...." And again, on July 7, Wickersham reflected, "I am sorry that I made such a damned weak display of myself—I went up a little ways in a little baloon [sic] & forgot to take the parachute along." When Cale withdrew from the race in July, however, the irrepressible judge announced that "at the persistent request of many friends throughout the territory I am a candidate for delegate to Congress."[13]

At that point the Alaska Syndicate became involved in the campaign. Formed in 1906, it was a combination of the J.P. Morgan and Guggenheim fortunes. In Alaska the principal mining venture of this organization was the Kennecott-Bonanza copper mine. In order to tap this deposit it began construction of the Copper River and Northwestern Railroad, ruthlessly suppressing competition wherever possible. In addition, the "Guggies" carried on constant warfare against other railroad companies struggling to survive. Since the Syndicate apparently had inexhaustible capital and reportedly controlled steamship transportation and a major part of the salmon canning industry, many Alaskans feared that the wealthy combine would shortly dominate Alaska's politics. It was also common knowledge in the territory that the Syndicate lobby Washington had successfully postponed the delegate bill and opposed any further extension of home rule.[14] A representative of the Morgan–Guggenheim interests, David H. Jarvis, strongly advised candidate Wickersham against running for Congress. The Judge's anti-Guggenheim sentiments were well-known and the lobby did not want to see such a foe in a potentially influential office.

Wickersham construed the Syndicate advice as a challenge and a threat. He immediately revised an address to the people on his candidacy and included a strong plank against Guggenheim domination in mining and transportation matters in Alaska. Then and there the judge recognized the political potential of the nonresident control of Alaskan affairs by the lobby. He ran on an anti-Syndicate platform; in short, one which was generally designed to appeal to many Alaskans. In addition, Wickersham advocated the same form of limited local self-government as recommended by President Roosevelt, and expressed the hope that this government would be as simple and inexpensive as possible and that the elective territorial legislature would be endowed with carefully restricted powers.[15]

In the ensuing campaign, the control of territorial affairs by the Syndicate and the outspoken personality of the Judge were the main issues. Wickersham won the election. His Republican opponent, "Seattle John" Corson, was defeated because of this Guggenheim backing. John Ronan, the Democratic candidate, ran a poor third because the voters identified him as anti-labor. Wickersham's victory, one eminent Alaskan politician and historian has remarked, put "a lusty and resourceful battler" into the position of delegate to Congress "who was able to make the most of the turbulent political situation that was developing."[16]

In November, 1908, delegate-elect Wickersham further explained his stand on an elective Alaskan legislature in a telegram which he sent to President Roosevelt. He asked the President to include in his annual message a recommendation that Congress give the territory a bicameral legislature with carefully limited powers. Specifically, these limitations would include a prohibition against territorial or municipal bonded indebtedness, no county form of government, a fixed limit on the legislature's powers of taxation, and whatever other restrictions might be necessary to give Alaska sufficient, yet simple self-government.[17]

No action was taken under the Roosevelt administration. Delegate Wickersham met the new President, William H. Taft, for the first time in Washington in April, 1909. The delegate used the occasion to urge the Chief Executive to support a territorial government for Alaska. The President remained unconvinced on the ground that Alaska's population was too sparse and transitory. Instead, Taft favored giving Alaska a commission form of government. Wickersham disagreed wholeheartedly with the President's plan and resolved to fight it. On June 9, 1909, he therefore introduced a bill to establish a legislative assembly in Alaska. He mailed numerous copies to the territory in order to get the reactions of Alaskans to his home rule measure.[18]

In September, 1909, the President came to Seattle to attend the Alaska-Yukon Pacific Exposition and to deliver an address. The inspiration for this fair had initially come from a group of Alaskan Gold Rush pioneers who wanted to establish an Alaska exhibit in Seattle to advertise the territory. The idea grew and eventually resulted in the exposition which was to advertise Seattle's pivotal position in relation to the Pacific Rim countries. Upon his arrival in Seattle, President Taft was greeted by a telegram from Alaska which had been signed by sixteen of the territory's nineteen newspapers, seven mayors, and two chambers of commerce. The telegram asked the President to support territorial government. Alaskans at the exposition were greatly disappointed when the President recommended a commission form of government instead of the hoped for home rule. The district presumably was to be put under the Bureau of Insular Affairs in the War Department. There was to be a commission of five or more members exercising local legislative power. These individuals were to be appointed by the President, and their acts were to be subject to review by the Bureau of Insular Affairs. Taft observed that this was very similar to the government which had been given to the Philippine Islands, "although the commission there had more legislative authority than it would be wise or necessary to give the Alaskan commission."[19]

The reaction in the territory to Taft's proposal was bitter. An editorial in the *Fairbanks Times* stated that the President even intended to legislate the office of delegate out of existence by relegating it to a mere advisory position. It was obvious, the newspaper observed, that President Taft's Philippine experience, in which he administered a commission form of government, had been with people who were not born to self-government. "Withhold self-government from a Malay, and he will not know the difference. Deprive an Anglo-Saxon of the same thing, and he feels enslaved." Wickersham remarked that Taft was surprised at the Alaskan reaction. If the President anticipated trouble from the territory over his proposal, the delegate concluded, it was likely to occur, for "I intend to make some myself." If anything, the President's plan for a commission form of government had a unifying effect in Alaska where many changed from mere interest in a local legislature to active advocacy. This became evident when Wickersham asked his constituents to strengthen his position in Washington by holding mass meetings on October 18, 1909, the anniversary of Alaska Cession Day, and by passing resolutions in favor of home rule. Many citizens in the territory complied with his request, and the delegate returned to Washington fortified with these favorable expressions.[20]

There now existed two proposals for a government for Alaska, namely Wickersham's and the President's. Governor Walter Clark, a former newspaperman and Taft appointee, stated that northern residents supported the plan for a legislature for three reasons, namely that Alaska had a constitutional right to self-government such as had been granted to earlier territories; Alaska lawmakers would understand northern problems better than Congressmen from the state; and finally, many believed that tax collections deposited in the United States treasury exceeded Congressional appropriations for the district. With self-government, this money would remain in Alaska and be used to finance internal improvements. Actually, liquor, occupation, and trade license receipts only were deposited in the Treasury if collected from outside incorporated towns. There these funds, as required by the 1905 Nelson Act, were deposited in a special account known as the Alaska Fund. Five percent of these monies were used for the care and maintenance of the insane, 25 percent for educating white children and children of mixed blood who led a civilized life, and 70 percent for the construction and maintenance of wagon roads, bridges, and trails. And in reality Congress appropriated almost double the amount of money collected from all taxes and licenses in Alaska, excluding customs and internal revenue receipts, and also municipal real estate taxes which municipalities levied and spent themselves.[21]

The Washington Wickersham experienced in early 1910 was turbulent. The famous Ballinger-Pinchot controversy had erupted and put Alaska in the national spotlight. This conservation issue centered on thirty-three coal land claims in Alaska and culminated in a joint Congressional investigation.[22] Even though the committee, voting along party lines, absolved Secretary of the Interior Richard A. Ballinger of wrongdoing, public sentiment sided with Gifford Pinchot, the Chief Forester in the Department of Agriculture.

The trouble with the coal land claims reached back to 1906 when President Roosevelt, on the advice of Pinchot, had withdrawn all coal lands in Alaska from entry. Before this executive order became effective, Clarence Cunningham and a group of associates had filed claims in the Bering River area of Alaska. Ballinger, then Commissioner of the General Land Office, had to judge the legality of the claims in the light of the executive order. The investigation by his agent, Louis Glavis, seemed to show that the Cunningham group intended to turn their claims over to the Guggenheims in violation of the law. Ballinger validated the claims, but Secretary of the Interior, James R. Garfield, overturned his decision. Ballinger left the Land Office in 1908 and returned to Seattle while Glavis pursued the matter of the Cunningham claims. As an attorney in Seattle, Ballinger represented the Cunningham group in Washington. When Ballinger became Secretary of the Interior, he removed Glavis from the investigation on a pretense, whereupon the latter complained to Pinchot. The Chief Forester disliked Ballinger and believed Glavis' account. He arranged a meeting between President

Taft and Glavis. The chief executive examined the evidence, upheld his Secretary of the Interior, and fired Glavis. Pinchot felt that the decision had been unfair, and provided information to the press, and finally brought the matter to a head in Congress. Taft dismissed Pinchot, and Ballinger resigned in 1911. The Cunningham claims were eventually denied.[23]

The controversy helped bring about the election of a Democratic house in 1910 and a rift between Roosevelt and Taft. According to Wickersham, the affair

> ...destroyed the friendship between Theodore Roosevelt and President Taft; split the Republican Party into two great factions; defeated President Taft for re-election in 1912; elected Woodrow Wilson President of the United State; and changed the course of history of our country.[24]

In this charged atmosphere, Senator Albert J. Beveridge of Indiana, Chairman of the Senate Committee on Territories, and Representative E.L. Hamilton of Michigan, Chairman of the House Committee on Territories, introduced complementary proposals for a commission form of government without consulting Wickersham. In 1910, hearings on these two bills were held. It soon became evident that there was strong opposition to the President's plan. After some political maneuvering the administration abandoned its proposal. The defeat of these measures was in no small part due to Wickersham's skillful use of the conservation issue to obtain support for Alaskan home rule. The delegate pointed out that the resources of Alaska should be used for the benefit of the entire country. Yet, so far, the territory had been exploited by a few large, absentee-controlled corporations, such as the monopolies which harvested the fur seals and salmon and mined the copper deposits. Home rule, Wickersham asserted, would allow proper utilization of the territory's wealth.[25]

During the conservation controversy, and as a result of it, home rule for Alaska gained measurably. In 1911, there were manifestations of support from the legislatures of Washington and Oregon and commercial associations of those states. The senators and representatives from these areas were instructed to vote for Alaska home rule. Democratic presidential aspirants, such as Woodrow Wilson, Oscar Underwood, and William J. Bryan, were pledged to support the home rule plank of their party. In this favorable atmosphere, hearings on Wickersham's home rule bill began in the spring of 1911 before the House Committee of Territories under its new chairman, Henry D. Flood of Virginia. By late summer of 1911, the passage of the Wickersham measure seemed reasonably assured.[26]

Some Alaskan papers, such as the *Alaska Daily Times* of Fairbanks, were unhappy with the limitations of the delegate's measure. Several newspapers in the territory, the editor stated, "do not enthuse over the bill to establish a debating society in the territory of Alaska, but that does not justify anybody in asserting that they are hostile to home rule." In the face of such remarks, Wickersham wrote in his diary: "[Such editorials]…show how fully the Guggenheim publicity bureau under Gov. W.E. Clark, Governor of the District of Alaska, is at work to kill my elective legislative bill…"[27]

In a special message to Congress on February 2, 1912, President Taft dealt extensively with Alaska. He urged Congress to enact legislation which would help the territory develop its resources. On April 24, 1912, the House unanimously passed Wickersham's elective legislative assembly bill. "It was a glorious Victory!" a jubilant Wickersham exulted in his diary. On July 24, 1912, the Senate passed the delegate's measure in essentially the same form in which its author had drafted it. At that time Wickersham wrote this candid assessment in his diary: "I have won this victory by a single handed fight against all odds—simply by standing at my station and never ceasing the effort." On August 24, 1912, the President signed the Wickersham measure into law. As the author of the Organic Act of 1912, who had also piloted the measure through Congress, the delegate seemed to be content with the provisions of the act. He confided to his diary that the Senate and House conference "agreed to all those things in dispute which I wanted in our Home Rule Bill!"[28]

The Second Organic Act of 1912 gave Alaska a senate of eight members and a house of sixteen to be chosen equally from the four judicial divisions. Since both senators and representatives represented the same constituency, there had been no really reason why Alaska could not have been granted a unicameral legislature, except for the tradition which divided American legislative bodies into two. In 1909 Congress had expanded the number of judicial divisions from three to four: the First Division (southeastern Alaska) at Juneau; the Second Division (northwestern Alaska) at Nome; the Third Division (southcentral Alaska) at Valdez, and later at Anchorage; and the Fourth Division (the interior) at Fairbanks. As with previous territorial governments, the United States Treasury paid the expenses of the legislature. The governor had the power to veto items in appropriation acts but was required to veto other measures, if at all, as a whole. The legislators could override a gubernatorial veto by a two-thirds vote in each house, and Congress could disallow all territorial legislation. The 1912 act directed that the existing executive and judicial structures provided by the First Organic Act of 1884 (as amended in 1900 and thereafter) were not to be changed by the territorial legislature. Both of these branches were to remain appointive by and responsible to the President. The legislature also was prohibited from passing any laws which would deprive the judges and officers of the district county of Alaska of any authority, jurisdiction, of function exercised by similar judges of officers of jurisdiction, or function exercised by similar judges or officers of district courts of the United States.[29]

In fact, the 1912 act became notable for the many restrictions it imposed on the legislature. Some were customary, while others reflected Wickersham's experiences as attorney, judge, and legislator in Washington State. He was concerned, for example, that the legislature might put the territory into debt, and he expected county government to be too expensive. Congress, as well as miners and businessmen objected to the unlimited power of government to borrow and spend. Historian Jeannette P. Nichols pointed out that for the benefit of the "lobbies of the fish conservationists and the big New York game hunters" the federal government retained the power to regulate the territory's fish, game, and fur resources, a function no organized territory had been denied.[30]

The legislature as well as Alaska's municipal government were not allowed to assume bonded indebtedness without Congressional consent, nor could they incur debts except in anticipation of the tax receipts of any one year. The legislature was not allowed to alter the license taxes imposed by the Penal Code of 1899 and the Civil Code of 1900. Territorial property taxes were restricted to one percent of "actual" value, and municipal property taxes were limited to two percent. To add insult to injury, a wide range of "local or special" laws which had been specified in a territories measure of 1886 were excluded from the jurisdiction of the legislature; none of its acts creating county governments could become effective without congressional action.[31] These and numerous other restrictions on the powers of the legislature would cause Alaskans to make tireless efforts to amend and change the Second Organic Act, and eventually contributed to the drive for statehood.

CHAPTER FOUR

The First
Statehood Campaign

M any Alaskans were not enthusiastic about Wickersham's home rule measure, and the delegate knew it. Addressing a joint session of the first Alaska legislature in 1913, Wickersham emphasized the positive aspects of the Second Organic Act. He told the lawmakers that they could deal effectively with a wide variety of matters, including such diverse and important fields as health, vital statistics, education, and welfare. If the legislature acted in all of these areas, the delegate predicted, it would have a busy and fruitful sixty days ahead of it.[1]

Criticism of the Second Organic Act, however, continued. John Troy, who had come to Alaska from the state of Washington in 1897, became one of the act's most vocal critics. In 1899, Troy became the editor of the Skagway *Daily Alaskan*, a position he occupied until the paper changed ownership in 1907. Troy thereupon returned to his home state, but maintained his interest in northern matters and also worked diligently for the Democratic party. In 1913, he returned north and became editor of the Juneau *Alaska Daily Empire*. John Strong, a journalist, had founded the paper in 1912.

Not long thereafter President Woodrow Wilson appointed Strong territorial governor. At that point Troy and three business partners bought the newspaper. As editor, Troy called for "a full territorial form of government, "the kind, he charged, Wickersham had not obtained in 1912. The delegate defended the Organic Act, one of his proudest achievements in Congress, against Troy's criticism. Both men were concerned about Alaska's government, and both competed for political power, although Troy was not interested in elective office.[2]

In his first address on the State of the Union, President Wilson included a request for a full territorial form of government for Alaska which had originated with Juneau Democrats. Wickersham, generally pleased with the President's address, pointed out that, except for a territorial supreme court, such a government already existed. Indeed, a full territorial form of government consisted of an appointive chief executive, an elected legislature, and a court system with appointive judges. Troy criticized the restricted powers of the legislature, enumerating the powers and functions Congress had denied. Wickersham maintained that much could be accomplished with the powers Congress had bestowed.[3]

On March 1, 1915, the second session of the territorial legislature began in Juneau. Addressing that body, Governor Strong compared its powers unfavorably with those of earlier territorial legislatures and even those of Hawaii and Puerto Rico. Strong urged the lawmakers to lobby Congress to enlarge their jurisdiction. Statehood, however, was a different matter, and he predicted that, because of Alaska's noncontiguity, a prolonged struggle in Congress would precede its admission as a state.[4]

Arthur Shoup, a young Republican Representative from Sitka, had listened closely to the governor. He soon introduced a joint memorial in the House which listed many of the powers Congress had denied to the legislature in the Organic Act and requested that these restraints by removed. The memorial passed the House and went to the Senate where the Wickersham and Troy partisans argued the issue on March 29.[5]

The Senate consisted of eight members, two from each of the four judicial divisions. Three were Democrats, namely Josias Tanner, an elderly merchant and civic leader from Skagway; Charles Sulzer; and the owner of a copper mine in the Panhandle town of Sulzer; and Thomas McGann of Nome who had won a by-election on February 27, 1915. He arrived in Juneau at the end of the fourth week of the session after a rather strenuous journey from his home town. The other five Senators were nominal Republicans, more interested in self-interest and issues than party allegiance. Oliver Hubbard, Dan Sutherland and Ole Gaustad supported Wickersham. Hubbard, a lawyer and railroad promoter from Valdez was the only Senator who had never mined for gold. Sutherland, the Senate president, hailed from the mining community of Ruby in the interior of Alaska and had been Wickersham's campaign manager. Norwegian-born Gaustad came from the interior as well and soon was to become the editor and manager of the *Fairbanks Daily News-Miner.* Benjamin Millard, a mining promoter and political rival of Hubbard in Valdez, was not in the Wickersham camp. Neither was Frank Aldrich from Nome who called himself an Independent Democrat, although he voted with the Wickersham faction in organizing the Senate. As a reward he received the chairmanships of two important committees.[6]

When the Shoup memorial came up for debate in the Senate, Hubbard predictably argued that Alaska already had a full territorial of fish, fur and game resources, he pointed out, would add intolerable expenses. Sulzer did not deal directly with the Shoup memorial, but pointed out that Alaska's population had remained stagnant during the previous decade. He blamed the federal government for this lack of growth, noting that members of Congress knew next to nothing about the north. Only home rule, he argued, would remedy the situation. The Senators finally laid aside the House memorial and substituted for it a joint memorial which Millard had introduced earlier in the session. More general than the House Memorial, it merely requested Congress to amend the

Organic Act granting Alaskans the kind of self-government many earlier territories had enjoyed. [7]

Thereupon Senator Hubbard drafted a concurrent resolution which stated that Alaska was ready to enter the Union as a state. The legislature should create a special committee to write a memorial asking for statehood. In addition, a referendum should be conducted on the fourth of July determining whether or not the voters wanted statehood and where the state capital should be located. Hubbard then introduced a resolution asking that the Millard memorial be returned to committee and be replaced by his own proposal.[8]

Senator Millard was upset with Hubbard and accused him of trying to derail his memorial requesting more extensive legislative powers. In fact, Alaska's chance of joining the union were remote, he asserted. Hubbard, however, believed that Alaska could join the Union within three years, while Sulzer thought statehood would be impossible without first gaining the territorial status. After further debate, Hubbard withdrew his resolution and the Senate passed the Millard memorial. After some debate, the House passed the Millard memorial as well.[9]

In the meantime, delegate Wickersham had arrived in Juneau on his way from Washington, D.C., to his home in Fairbanks. A reporter invited a comment from him, whereupon he stated that he favored "a full Territorial form of government for Alaska." To his friends he subsequently explained that Alaska was "entitled to the very fullest form of home rule" and certainly was ready for it. Only statehood would give Alaskans the opportunity to enjoy local government fully, and he revealed that during the next session of Congress he would submit legislation to admit the territory into the Union. The very next morning the Juneau *Daily Alaska Dispatch* became the first northern newspaper to editorially endorse immediate statehood. Ed Russell, the publisher of the paper, followed Wickersham's political leadership, and the *Dispatch* announced that henceforth it would devote its energies to advance the cause of statehood. John Troy, Wickersham's adversary, drily noted that the day was April Fool's day.[10]

Shortly, thereafter, Hubbard's statehood resolution was reported to the Senate without recommendation, and on April 6, the Senators debated it for a few hours, and then held it over for voting until a later day. In the meantime, Wickersham addressed a large crowd in Juneau on the night of April 7, 1915. In his rousing two-hour speech, the delegate recounted his efforts to secure passage of the Organic Act and contrasted his work with that of John Troy and his "reactionary" Democratic friends who did nothing but "howl" for a full territorial form of government. He also reminded his listeners that the act was not nearly as restrictive as Troy would have them believe. Nevertheless, the time had come to move forward on statehood. He also urged legislators to do all in their power to obtain further full territorial government, but also hoped that they would support eventual statehood.[11]

One day after Wickersham's speech, on April 8, the Senate defeated the Hubbard resolution, but undeterred the Senator introduced a joint resolution on April 13 calling for a referendum during the 1916 delegate election providing citizens with the opportunity to vote for full territorial government or for immediate statehood. The resolution, however, was rejected on a point of order.[12]

Wickersham was no fool, and he quickly recognized that he had to publicly deal with John Troy's incessant demands for a full territorial form of government. When he left Fairbanks in the fall to return to Washington, he stopped in Cordova and there announced that he would try to secure broader powers for the legislature. Wickersham also admitted for the first time that he had originally accepted certain limitations in the Organic Act in order to obtain its passage. Now he would work to have these limitations repealed. When he reached Seattle he mentioned that he would agitate for statehood in order to obtain a full territorial government for Alaska from Congress.[13]

By 1916, Wickersham had developed genuine second thoughts about the efficacy of the Organic Act. He blamed the fishing and mining interests, those "invisible forces which organized the opposition to a more perfect government for the people of Alaska under both administrations," for having stymied efforts to amend the act. These "powerful interest," he believed, "desire to seize, own, and exploit the great undeveloped resources of Alaska, free from governmental control." He had hoped that the Wilson administration would remedy the defects of the Organic Act. Instead, opposition to a full territorial form of government now came from the President and his administration. At the time of its passage Wickersham had expressed entire satisfaction with the Organic Act of 1912. But now, recalling the origins of the measure, he complained:

> *The big interests engaged in exploiting Alaska finally contented themselves with procuring the insertion of Amendments in the bill [the Organic Act] limiting the power of the Alaska legislature over the fisheries, schools, roads, and other important matters of the local concern which had always theretofore been controlled by a territorial legislature.*[14]

Wickersham thought that organic acts for territories always had been, always were, and always would be deficient. Since a plank in the Alaska Democratic platform of 1912 referred to territorial government as but an "a temporary makeshift and a preparatory step to complete statehood," the delegate advised Alaskans that the governmental powers they sought could be obtained "through Statehood more certainly than in any other way." [15]

That Wickersham had already given some thought to statehood was evidenced by an article he had written for *Collier's* in 1910, under the suggestive title "The Forty-Ninth Star." Alaska was destined to become a state, he argued, pointing out that the Supreme Court had declared that "under the treaty with Russia ceding Alaska and the subsequent legislation of Congress, Alaska has been incorporated into the United States and the Constitution is applicable to that Territory." Accordingly, Alaska was no different from all the other territories which had become states, and therefore had "the constitutional right to Statehood." The delegate failed to mention that Alaska's noncontiguous status might be an obstacle. In his article, Wickersham did state his intention to introduce a statehood bill for Alaska late in 1910, but for some reason he failed to do so.[16]

In the midst of all this talk about statehood, a newspaper, *The Forty-Ninth Star*, was established in Senator Oliver P. Hubbard's home town of Valdez late in 1915 for the express purpose of promoting the cause of statehood. Its editor, John Frame, was a former attorney and journalist who had come north from the state of Washington during the Gold Rush. Politically allied to Wickersham, he had become chairman of the Progressive-Democratic party. Between 1915-1917 he established and edited newspapers at the new railroad town of Anchorage in addition to the one at Valdez. Frame admonished his prospective readers: "If you are an Alaskan, then be a Forty-niner. Subscribe for this paper and stand by it until the 49th star is placed upon that banner of Freedom."[17]

Following the founding of the paper, the first statehood club in Alaska was also organized in Valdez. The fledgling group elected officers and adopted a twelve-paragraph constitution in which it committed itself to work for statehood. The organizers recognized the inherent and unavoidable imperfections of the territorial form of government. Long experience had shown, the statehood advocates declared, that the full equality and welfare of the people of Alaska could only be achieved by admission as a state.[18]

Wickersham, who was closely associated with the Valdez club, responded to their battle cries by drafting an enabling act for the proposed state of Alaska. He patterned his bill after the 1906 bill, the delegate reasoned, was recent, contained many new ideas, and was liberal in its grants of money and land to the new state, and, therefore, a similar enabling act should find favor with the Wilson administration.[19]

In the meantime, *The Forty-Ninth Star* continued to promote the statehood cause. Not only was the territory entitled to statehood now, the editor asserted, but within five years Alaska would have a population of 100,000. In view of all of Alaska's potentialities,

"...where is there a pessimist or politician who whines that we are not ready for Statehood?" he asked. But the editor had no illusions about the time it would take to achieve statehood. He thought it probably would be several years, but the important thing was to start the effort. Even under the most favorable conditions, he said, statehood could not be attained "until long after we deserve it."[20]

Delegate Wickersham finished his labors on the enabling act early in March, 1916. He sent advance copies of the bill to various Alaska newspapers and asked that the publication of them coincide with the official introduction of the measure on March 30, 1916. Wickersham had carefully chosen this date, which was the forty-ninth anniversary of the signing of the Treaty of Cession of Russian America, to emphasize Alaska's long apprenticeship as a possession of the United State.[21] Even though he submitted the bill as planned, the delegate was not convinced that Alaska was ready for statehood. His enabling act was intended to be a trial balloon. At a talk in Anchorage he pointed out to his listeners that all the costs of administration, now borne by the federal government, would have to be assumed by Alaska's taxpayers. These costs included law enforcement, the operation of the courts, and the expenses of the territorial legislature and the executive department. But since campaigns for statehood were historically lengthy affairs, he consoled his audience, Alaskans did not have to hear these added costs yet. By the time statehood was finally achieved the territory would have the resources to meet the increased financial demands. [22]

As a more realistic goal, Wickersham also introduced two bills designed to enlarge the powers of the territorial legislature. The delegate then teamed up with Senator Key Pitman of Nevada and together they presented identical measures which would have provided a modified commission form of government for the territory. And to cap his efforts, he submitted a bill designed to provide "full territorial government" for Alaska.[23] This measure was designed to correct the deficiencies, real or imagined, of the Organic Act of 1912. Wickersham, however, did not really think that it needed revamping. For, as he confided in his diary, "Am now preparing a follow bill entitled: A bill to establish a full territorial form of government in Alaska etc." Wickersham remarked that the *Alaska Daily Empire* (Juneau) and its editor, John W. Troy, had been "howling" for such a measure. Every time anything went wrong in Alaska, Wickersham complained, the supposed inadequacy of the 1912 act was blamed. "Now I am going to introduce a bill to cover everything they have urged as part of 'full territorial form of government'!" Wickersham was sure that the Democratic administration would reject his proposal. Then he could maintain that he had tried his best but had been foiled by the powers in Washington. The political benefits would be obvious.[24]

The statehood bill itself, the first in a long line of such measures, was simple and skeletal in nature. It contained a provision, standard in enabling acts, that the proposed new state be admitted on a basis of equality with the other states. Alaskans were to hold a constitutional convention and write a document acceptable both to the state and to Congress. The projected government was to be republican in form. There were the usual safeguards, such as those for religious toleration and for the franchise without regard to sex, creed, or color. Creditors were to be protected in that the state was to assume territorial debts. Elementary and higher education were made a state responsibility. The rights of Alaska's, Indians, Eskimos, and Aleuts to lands claimed by them were protected. And the future state was to disclaim all rights and title to any unappropriated public areas which were claimed by the various indigenous groups until Congress extinguished those rights. The state was prohibited from selling the tidelands or banks or beds of waters within its boundaries, but instead would hold title to these areas in perpetuity for the public benefit.

The land grants to the new state generally followed those made to the public land states. There were land grants for public buildings and for the support of public schools, state universities, and charitable, penal, and reformatory institutions. In addition, the new state was encouraged to develop forests and forest reserves. Various sections dealt with the leasing of mineral and coal lands, including oil and gas, and for the disposition of funds derived from the sale and lease of such assets. As an ex-judge, Wickersham gave special attention to the section dealing with the judicial system. He carefully detailed the functions of the various courts, distinguishing between the jurisdictions of the state and federal governments. Arrangements were also specified for the election of state officials. The delegate was very generous when he proposed four Representatives to Congress for Alaska, one from each of the four judicial districts into which Alaska was divided, and the usual two Senators.[25]

As requested by Wickersham, many Alaska newspapers took notice of the first statehood bill, and some reprinted the text in full. The *Daily Alaska Dispatch* of Juneau remarked optimistically that "most of the western Representatives and Senators in other sections of the United States have pledged their support in behalf of the measure." The editor stated that the bill marked another epoch in the history of Alaska, for it meant an end to makeshift government and a firm desire of Alaskans for statehood. A few days later, the same paper summarized the views of those in opposition. "It will be claimed," it stated, "that statehood will cost too much; that Alaska is not ready…; that there are too many isolated districts…; [and that] the distances are too great." The paper maintained that the "reactionary press' approved of statehood in principle, but thought that Alaska was not ready just yet. The objections to statehood were the ones made by the same interests which had opposed the Organic Act of 1912. The paper identified these groups as the fishing industry, the Northern Commercial Company, an absentee-owned trading corporation, and all the other economic groups which preferred to maintain a cozy relationship with federal officials. The opponents always said that they wanted changes in the Organic Act instead of statehood. "to have the organic act amended in spots and to palce [sic] additional patched so the shabby territorial clothes." But in order to get an entire new organic act, the editor predicted, 'will prove more difficult than to secure statehood." He concluded that "halfhearted support would not do. A person is either for statehood or else against it."[26]

Alaska statehood also received some attention in United States newspapers at this time. The publisher of the *San Francisco Chronicle* advised Alaskans to emulate the example of California, organize as a state, and apply to Congress for admission. Success, he told Alaskans, would be assured by following this procedure. His advice was not taken. The *Portland Telegram* however, summed up the movement best when it stated: "We hear the first gentle rapping of Alaska at the door of statehood."[27] One of the reasons the first Alaska statehood movement failed was because "gentle rapping" was not enough. Historically, territories had to pound at the door of Congress for a period of time in order to gain admission. In 1916, no one in Alaska, least of all Wickersham, was prepared for a sustained effort. Furthermore, the delegate was a realistic politician. He knew full well that neither the territory nor Congress was ready for Alaska statehood. Operating the state government, including the courts, enforcing the penal statues and paying the expenses of the legislature and the executive department would be in excess of $500,000 per annum, an expense Alaska was unable to meet.[28]

Why did Wickersham introduce the statehood bill? He had witnessed the Congressional debates over statehood for New Mexico and Arizona and that might have stimulated his desire to guide Alaska's admission into the Union. The most likely explanation, however, is that he introduced the statehood measure to blunt the demands of the Democratic party for a full territorial form of government.

In any event, the attention of delegate Wickersham and his constituents was quickly diverted from the statehood issue to a fight to retain the measure of self-government the territory had already gained under the Organic Act of 1912. The precipitating issue was a tax which the territorial legislature had imposed on the fisheries in 1915. Even though the assessment was nominal, the industry, joined by a number of the larger mining companies, took the subject to court and attempted to have the levy nullified. The federal court upheld the right of the territory to tax, whereupon these groups turned to Congress and tried to obtain federal legislation which would have effectively taken away from the Alaska legislature what little authority it exercised over the fisheries. Wickersham narrowly prevented this attempt to curtail the powers of the territorial legislature. In exasperation, he warned that full territorial government would never by enacted into law "as long as the bureau [of Commerce] and Alaska Fish Trust can prevent it."[29]

Wickersham ran for reelection in 1916 on a platform which ambiguously stated that he favored the "enactment of laws by Congress extending the powers of our Legislature so as to permit the full development of an American type of territorial government in Alaska…" and he also endorsed statehood as soon as it could be organized "in the interest and to the advantage of the people." Statehood clearly was dead for the time being but the issue would resurface at the appropriate time.

CHAPTER FIVE

Secession and President Harding's Alaska Visit

Wickersham's statehood bill did not even receive a hearing in Congress, and perhaps he had not expected that it would. Together with the debate over home rule, however, a great deal of sectionalism developed in the north. Soon many citizens asked that Alaska be divided into several territories, perhaps as many as four.

William Henry Seward, the architect of the Alaska purchase, had expected that Alaska would be divided into several states. And as early as 1897, miners and prospectors had circulated petitions in the Yukon Valley demanding the creation of the territory of Lincoln. Weare, a small trading center at the mouth of the Tanana River was to be the capital. Lincoln was to include all of Alaska's present land area except the Aleutian Islands, the Panhandle, and the intermediate coasts and islands. The petitioners, however, did not push their demands when the Klondike rush absorbed their energies. Next Senator Knute Velson (R, Minnesota) who had visited the north as a member of a Senate committee in 1903 expressed the opinion that Alaska should be divided into three states. One of

these would include the entire southern Alaska coast, including the
Aleutian Islands and the Panhandle; the second would encompass
the Interior region; and the third, Seward Peninsula. A couple of
years later journalist W.E. Beers, Jr. stated that the areas south of
the Yukon and Tanana rivers should be formed into the territory of
South Alaska, excluding the vast area of harsh climate and tundra
farther north.[1]

In 1911, Representative William Sulzer of New Your, the
brother of Charles Sulzer and the owner of mining properties in
Alaska, proposed that Alaska be divided into the territory of Sumner, consisting of the Panhandle; the territory of Seward, consisting
of the region south of the Yukon, and the territory of Alaska which
would embrace the land north of the river. John Troy, the editor of
the *Alaska-Yukon Magazine,* approved of Sulzer's proposal but cautioned that partition be deferred because boundary lines in other
areas had often been drawn unwisely. Troy advised that additional
railroad lines should be built in the north before partition so that
the major development trends might first be perceived.[2]

Soon much controversy arose in the territorial legislature on
how to determine appropriations. All four judicial divisions were
represented equally in the senate and house, and therefore, had
an equal voice in determing how to spend general tax revenues,
the territorial share of receipts from the national forests, and the
monies from the Alaska Fund. The territory derived the bulk of its
revenues from taxes which the legislature had levied on the catch-
ing and processing of salmon, found off the Panhandle coast and
in Bristol Bay. Since territorial, state, or local governments could
not tax national forests, Congress in 1908 allocated to the coun-
ties in which such reserves were located 25 percent of the proceeds
derived from the sale of its timber and other forest products. The
state or territorial legislature was to appropriate these funds for the
support of the public schools and roads of the county. But since
Alaska had no couriers, the money was spent equally throughout
the territory. No great sums were involved, ranging from a low of
$2,685 in 1908 to a high of $41,931 in 1927, but they were derived

from the national forests in the first and third judicial divisions. This equal division of funds regardless of origins irked many residents of the first judicial division.[3]

Many residents of the Panhandle desired a separation from the rest of Alaska, because after that all the taxes collected there as well as the proceeds from the Tongass National Forest would be spent in the region. In addition, a separate Alaska Fund would be established for the region. At the time the Board of Road Commissioners for Alaska, or the Alaska Road Commission, as it was more commonly known, spent seventy percent of the existing fund. The board, consisting of three army officers appointed by the Secretary of War in 1905, had allocated most of the money to projects in the third and fourth divisions which lacked the Panhandle's extensive network of waterways. Legislative reapportionment on the basis of population might have saved the appropriation problem, but unfortunately, Congress had made no provision for this. It would have benefited Southeastern Alaska since it also had experienced population growth in the decade between 1910 and 1920. In 1920, it had a population of 17,402 compared with 15,216 in 1910. All the other regions had lost population. For example, the Southcentral area had declined from 12,900 in 1910 to 11,173 in 1920, and the interior from 13,064 in 1910 to 7,964 in 1920.[4]

Alaska's regionalism increased over the years, and quarrels over the disposition of revenues continued, but there was no happy solution. Citizens of the four judicial divisions always felt slighted by the appropriation process.

When the United States entered the First World War in 1917, talk of partition and demands for self-government died down. And while the First World War created a boom in the contiguous states, Alaska did not share in it. Instead, the territory's economic and population growth slowed down. Census statistics between 1910 and 1920 showed a drop a 9,320 in the population, and many Alaskans as well as citizens in the states blamed the inept Washington bureaus as well as the conservation laws for this stagnation.[5] The simple fact, however, was that the states offered more economic opportunities than the north.

In the meantime, Wickersham had faced Charles A. Sulzer in the 1916 delegate race. Sulzer, a Democrat and a copper mine operator on Prince of Wales Island, had come to Alaska in 1902. He had been elected to the territorial senate in 1914. Alaskan authorities declared that Sulzer had been elected in 1916, but the House of Representatives declared that Wickersham was the rightful winner and seated him. The same thing happened again in 1918, but before Sulzer could assume his office, he died. The Democratic canvassing board nevertheless issued a certificate of election to the deceased. Shortly thereafter, it was decided that a special election be held to fill the vacancy created by Sulzer's death. The Republicans maintained that Wickersham had won the election and therefore did not field a candidate. The Democrats put forth George Grisby, a colorful attorney, who won the special election. The canvassing board issued a certificate of election to Grigsby, who hurried to Washington where the House of Representatives seated him. Eventually, the House reversed itself and declared Wickersham the rightful winner. After his victory, however, Wickersham decided not to run again, and instead support his friend, Republican Dan Sutherland, a miner and a fisherman, in the 1920 election. Sutherland beat Grigsby to win the delegateship.[6]

Before the new delegate took his seat in Congress, the Democrats met for their national convention in San Francisco in the summer of 1920. During the deliberations, the party, for the first time, endorsed "the fullest measure of territorial self-government with the view of ultimate statehood" for Alaska. The Republican did not mention Alaska at all.[7]

Nationally, Warren G. Harding of Ohio gained the presidency in 1920. The Republican victory meant that the new administration would appoint a member of its party to the Alaska governorship. It selected Scott C. Bone, a former editor of the *Seattle Post-Intelligencer* and director of publicity for the Republican National Committee, for the post. With the assurance of a presidential visit to Alaska, Bone left for the north to assume his new position.[8]

By the time the new governor arrived in Alaska, talk about partition had revived once again. Ketchikan residents grumbled that first division tax revenues went to pay for improvements in other divisions, and that the Panhandle was very different and district from the rest of Alaska. The *Daily Alaska Empire* of Juneau opined that statehood for the territory as a whole was remote, particularly because of the unsettled and underdeveloped interior. The situation in southeast Alaska was very different, because the mining and fishing industries were expanding, and there were bright prospects for the establishment of a pulp and paper industry. These developments were certain to attract new settlers, and before long the area would be ready for admission as a state. John Troy advocated immediate partition, but maintained that the Panhandle should join Southcentral Alaska to form a strong state.[9]

Soon residents of Southcentral and interior Alaska began to resent Panhandle pretentions. The *Anchorage Daily Times*, for example, stated that it would not object if the Southeast broke off from the rest of the territory, a sentiment echoed by the Seward and Cordovan newspapers. The *Fairbanks Daily News-Miner* agreed that the Panhandle had little in common with the other divisions, but then asked what the fourth division had in common with the third. Anchorage had always opposed interior goals as strongly as Juneau. In fact, only northwestern Alaska shared common interests with the interior. And in early 1922 the *Alaska Daily Empire* proposed that the territory be divided into West and East Alaska, the former embracing the areas adjacent to the Alaska Railroad, while the latter would encompass the Panhandle, Copper River country, and the upper Yukon Valley in the vicinity of the Eagle and the Forty mile district. Under this scheme country seats would be located at Ketchikan, Juneau, Cordova, and Eagle.[10] In short, sectionalism was alive and well.

While northern residents luxuriated in their quarrels, President Harding left Washington for Alaska. This was the first time a chief executive had visited the territory during his term of office. The visit was of utmost importance to Alaskans, and they looked upon it as an opportunity to present their views to the President on a variety of matters. Harding was interested, among other things, in finding a solution to the administrative tangle which existed in the territory. Five cabinet officers and twenty-eight bureaus exercised authority over that northern land. Many of these agencies were in bitter conflict over how best to develop and utilize the vast resources of the area. Secretary of the Interior Albert B. Fall, for example, had consistently promoted a plan to concentrate the administration of Alaska into one department (presumably Interior), thus allowing private enterprise to exploit the natural resources as speedily as possible. Secretary of Agriculture Henry C. Wallace, in whose department the conservation-minded Forest Service was located, objected to Fall's plan. Harding was torn between these conflicting opinions and wanted to investigate on the spot before making any decisions. This was also an opportunity to draw attention to America's neglected northern territory, and, in addition, the completion of the federal government's Alaska railroad enabled the President to drive the official golden spike.[11]

The President and his party, traveling on the naval vessel *Henderson,* arrived in Metlakatla, Alaska, on July 8, 1923. There the chief executive was greeted by the town's Indian population and territorial Governor Bone. From that village the party traveled on the *Henderson* along the southeastern Alaska coast, stopping at various towns, including Juneau, the capital, and Skagway of Gold Rush fame. The ship then crossed the Gulf of Alaska to Seward, the terminus of the recently completed Alaska Railroad. From that city the presidential entourage traveled to the new town of Anchorage and then to McKinley Park and Nenana on the railroad, where the President drove the symbolic golden spike. From Nenana the party moved on to Fairbanks where Harding addressed most of that town's 1,500 citizens in the ball park. Then the President and his retinue turned south again and finally sailed for Vancouver and Seattle.[12]

During his fourteen days in the territory, Harding had visited eleven different towns and made sixteen speeches. None of these talks was of any particular importance for Alaskan statehood, however, and the President's favorite expression was, "I did not come here to make you a speech. I have come to Alaska to learn and not to talk." For the most part, he spoke in generalities and reserved his conclusions about Alaska for a speech in Seattle upon his return. A week after he gave this address the President died in San Francisco.[13]

Harding's last major talk was delivered in the University of Washington Stadium on July 27, 1923. He spoke of the future of Alaska and indicated that he opposed radical changes in its administration. He rejected the idea of a sudden exploitation of Alaska's resources such as Secretary Fall had advocated, and, instead, endorsed the conservation policies of his predecessors. The President said that he favored a slow, planned evolution which would protect the territory's natural resource endowments but yet permit their gradual use. Equally as important to Alaskans, Harding declared that the territory was destined for ultimate statehood. "Few similar areas in the world present such natural invitations to make a state of widely varied industries and permanent character," he said. "As a matter of fact," he continued, "In a very few years we can well set off the Panhandle and a large block of the connecting southeastern part as a state." He concluded that he had great faith in Alaska's future.[14]

Alaskan reaction to the President's speech was overwhelmingly favorable. The *Ketchikan Alaska Chronicle* asserted that the President's speech "came as a tonic to every Alaskan who has taken off his coat, rolled up his sleeves, and worked for the betterment of the territory." *The Alaska Daily Empire* (Juneau) agreed that "there is nothing the federal government could do that would transform the territory overnight into a populous and wealthy commonwealth." One of the few sour notes was injected by the *Anchorage Daily Times*, which insisted that "the impediments of bureaucracy" would have to be eliminated before Alaska could develop properly.[15]

Responses from newspapers in the continental United States to Harding's speech ranged from favorable to hostile. The Portland *Oregonian* applauded the idea of planned and gradual development, but insisted that governmental regulations over Alaska's resources needed to be relaxed in order to attract capital. The Philadelphia *Evening Public Ledger* favored statehood, as did the New York *Sun*, which stated: "The American ideal of a nation is not a territorial one; we have always been anxious to grant statehood when it is possible." The *Dearborn Independent* argued that Alaska existed under conditions of "taxation without representation," and that in the past territories with less population than Alaska, among them Colorado, Indiana, and Michigan, had been admitted. Opposition to statehood was voiced by the Philadelphia *Record* on the basis that it would grant two Senate seats to a handful of Alaskans and would be patently unfair to the populous Eastern states.[16] As for the conservation forces, they strongly endorsed Harding's stand on Alaska's natural resources and welcomed him as one of their own. *Sunset Magazine,* a Western conservation voice, declared: "Almost with his last breath Warren Harding bequeathed to the Far West a priceless legacy, his support of the forces that desire to build wisely, soundly for the future."[17]

While Harding's Seattle speech and his subsequent death were still being discussed in the nation's press, the Ketchikan Commercial Club asked the mayor and town council to call a convention of the inhabitants of Southeastern Alaska, the territory's most populous and developed section. To approve the secession of the Panhandle and the creation of a cull territorial government preparatory to statehood. The Ketchikan town council responded and issued an invitation. On November 6 residents of all of the larger towns in Southeastern Alaska, except Sitka where the notification did not arrive in time, trooped to the polls and voted 1,344 to 89 in favor of the proposition. Except for Wrangell voting was light everywhere.[18]

After the favorable vote, the cities of Ketchikan, Petersburg, Wrangell, Douglas, Juneau, Haines and Skagway selected delegates for a divisional convention. Ketchikan was given three and Juneau four delegates, while the other towns received one each. In addition to these eleven delegates, Governor Bone appointed two others to represent the unincorporated parts of the Panhandle. On November 15, the delegates met in Juneau, elected officers and appointed three committees. The first was to draft a memorial to Congress, the second to gather materials in support of it, and the third to prepare an organic act for the new territory.[19]

The delegates first dealt with the boundaries of the new territory and decided to include the communities of Prince William Sound and the Copper River region in the new entity. The were invited to join, and five days after the convention had opened, chairman Ralph Robertson announced that he had received a telegram from Cordova which stated that the businessman of that town favored uniting the Prince William Sound and Copper River region with the Panhandle in forming a new territory. After debating several names for the new entity, the delegates settled on South Alaska.[20]

On November 20, 1923 the delegates approved the memorial to Congress and the President which asked for secession. The document argued that the Panhandle had a sizeable population, could expect economic progress, and had different interests from those of the other divisions. The memorial also complained that, although the second and fourth divisions together contributed only one-fourth as much revenue as the first, they received two and one-half times more money than the latter for roads, schools, and other projects. Shortly thereafter, the convention recessed, and during the next few weeks the various town councils which had sent the delegates reviewed the work accomplished. The Juneau town council voted to send Ralph Robertson to Washington, D.C. to present the convention documents to Congress and the President. Skagway, Haines, and Petersburg also contributed funds to help Robertson's mission, while Wrangell did not because it had wanted Wickersham to undertake the mission.[21]

Delegate Sutherland criticized secession, asserting that it followed the views of the exploitative cannery interests, and that Robertson, an attorney who represented about 100 canning and mining corporations, had been sent to lobby for them. In fairness it must be stated that the canning industry did not overly promote secession, although it probably favored it. Republicans sought higher territorial taxes on fish traps while Democrats opposed this. Secession would reduce the revenues of the territory of South Alaska, but it would shrink governmental expenses even more. No longer would funds be spent on road building in the westward and northward, nor for the support of the Alaska Agricultural College and School of Mines or for the support of public schools outside of the Panhandle.[22]

Robertson testified before the House Committee on the Territories when it held hearings on March 27-29 on a measure introduced by its chairman, Representative James Curry of California, to reapportion the legislature of Alaska. The Department of the Interior had drafted the bill at the suggestion of Governor Bone, and it had the backing of Hubert Work, the new secretary. Shortly after the hearings opened, Curry dampened the hope of secessionists when he declared that Alaska was not to be partitioned nor would it be admitted as a state. If and when Alaska had developed economically and attracted a sizeable resident population, then statehood would be bestowed—but not earlier. In fact, it was ridiculous "to think that the United States is going to bear the expense of two territorial governments…with about 50,000 people there altogether," including Indians, Eskimos, and Caucasians. Annual federal expenses for the north amounted to over $7,000,000 annually while tax collections netted only about $400,000. "We are not going to have a two-territory government in Alaska," Curry stated emphatically.[23]

That ended the matter of secession. As to reapportionment, it quickly became clear that Delegate Sutherland opposed the idea because it would reduce the legislative strength of the division in which he had his greatest political support. Chairman Curry respected Sutherland's wishes for postponement, but stated that "this proposition of trying to kill the matter by postponing it from time to time ought to stop…." Had the committee known Sutherlands' sentiments it could 'have saved all these hearing, and put in our time on more important measures."[24]

Committee members had quickly realized that the principal motive behind secession and reapportionment had been the
unwillingness of Alaskans to share revenues. Residents of the first
division also were afraid that the capital could easily be moved
from Juneau at some future date. Several members of the House of
Representatives who had toured Alaska in 1923 had become aware
of the capital site question. Representative John Rankin of Mississippi, for example, remarked that Juneau residents were "scared
about half to death for fear that the capital is going to be moved to
Anchorage." Representative Charles Abernethy of North Carolina
had gained the same impression. He thought that Fairbanks should
have the capital, while his colleagues James Strong of Kansas and
Curry thought that the capital should be located in Seward, the
only good ice-free port on the Alaska Railroad.[25]

The capital site controversy continued into the 1925 session
of the territorial legislature. Hosea Ross, a Fairbanks Republican,
introduced a joint memorial in the House asking that Congress
authorize the people of Alaska to vote on the permanent location
of the capital. It was defeated on a vote of 9 to 6.[26]

This ended secession talk. On June 15, 1925, George Parks was
inaugurated as Alaska's new governor, while Bone returned to journalism. Parks had long lived and worked in Alaska as an official of
the Department of the Interior. There was hardly any mention of
statehood during the eight years Parks served as governor. One such
mention occurred in March and April 1926, when Frank Aldrich
ran against Dan Sutherland for the Republican nomination for delegate to Congress. Both men had served in the territorial senate in
1915, when Sutherland had supported statehood and opposed the
Millard memorial for full territorial government, and Aldrich had
taken the opposite stance. Now the two had reversed their positions.
Aldrich supported statehood, claiming it would cost $50,000 annu-
ally. This sum represented the salaries of the treasure, attorney general, superintendent of schools, highway engineer, superintendent
of the pioneers' home, governor, and the territorial boards. Aldrich
stated that these expenses were offset by an income of $491,770

from the fur seal harvest and $208,553 which had gone into the Alaska Fund in 1925, monies he misleadingly stated, would accrue to Alaska in case of statehood. In addition, the new state would also acquire control of fisheries and tidelands, additional sources of revenue. The *Anchorage Daily Times* found statehood disturbing and stated that it should be discouraged. Instead, Alaskans should strive to have the Organic Act amended to gain increased legislative voters for the territorial legislature.[27]

Sutherland promised to work for gaining increased legislative powers, including an elective governorship and control of the fisheries. He won the primary and general elections. That was to be Sutherland's last term as delegate, for on November 29, 1929 he announced that he would not run for a sixth term. That same night, James Wickersham, now seventy-four years of age, announced that he would seek election to the delegateship. Wickersham promised to work "for a more perfect form of territorial government: and territorial administration of Alaska's game, fur, and fisheries resources. Wickersham defeated John Rustgard, Alaska's attorney general and his rival for the nomination, and went on to defeat Democrat George Grigsby in the November elections to win the delegateship.[28] At the time, nobody knew that the onset of the Great Depression in late 1929 would sweep most Republicans out of office in 1932. The statehood issue became relatively quiescent, not to revive again with any strength until the early 1940s.

The Federal Role in Alaska

ormer Governor and ex-United States Senator Ernest Gruening has characterized Alaskan history as being one of neglect by the federal government. He labels the period of 1867 to 1884 as "The Era of Total Neglect"; 1884 to 1898 as "The Era of Flagrant Neglect", 1898 to 1912 "The Era of Mild but Unenlightened Interest"; and finally the period from 1912 to 1933 as "The Era of Indifference and Unconcern."[1] Alaskan historian Henry W. Clark also complained in 1930, "...the lack of government in Alaska is a blot upon our pretensions toward enlightened democracy. " It was the Gold Rush which made government in Alaska a pressing problem, Clark continued, but not until the outbreak of the First World War did American colonial policy make a real start toward correcting some of the shortcomings.[2] J.A. Hellenthal, an Alaska author and lawyer, echoed the concerns of Gruening and Clark when he stated in 1936: "The government of Alaska is the worst possible under the American flag. The governments that are worse exist under other flags."[3]

It was Gruening, however, who most eloquently summed up the territory's feeling toward the federal government in his address to the Alaska constitutional convention in November 1955. He defined a colony as "a geographic area held for political, strategic, and economic advantage." Alaska fitted this description precisely, he stated, and went on to say:

> The maintenance and exploitation of those political, strategic and economic advantages by the holding power is colonialism. The United States is that holding power.
>
> Inherent in colonialism is an inferior economic status. The inferior economic status is a consequence of the inferior political status.
>
> The inferior economic status results from discriminatory laws and practices imposed upon the colonials through the superior political strength of the colonial power in the interest of its own noncolonial citizens.
>
> We suffer taxation without representation....
>
> We are subject to military service for the Nation... yet have no voice in the making and ending of the wars into which our young men are drafted.
>
> The development of Alaska, the fulfillment of its great destiny, cannot be achieved under colonialism. The whole Nation will profit by an Alaska that is populous, prosperous, strong, self-reliant—a great northern and western citadel of the American idea.[4]

Unlike other colonial areas, Alaska was not inhabited by a large Native population, militantly conscious of its cultural heritage and capable of developing a movement for freedom from colonialism. As a result, the territory was slowly settled by white emigrants from the contiguous United States who were fully aware of their political freedoms and social privileges. As Alaskans they often felt that they had been relegated to second-class citizenship. This impression was sharpened by frustrating dealings with often indifferent and uniformed federal bureaucrats acting on some local matter. In addition, citizens of the territory could not vote in national elections. Not surprisingly, many resented these conditions and were highly vocal in their criticisms of and attacks on the United States government, the most visible symbol of their real and imagined deprivations. For years, therefore, many territorial citizens were engaged in a two-pronged campaign to achieve relief from these circumstances. On the one hand, many Alaskans prodded Congress, through their delegate, to grant greater self-government to the territory, and, on the other, they goaded the local federal bureaucracy to rationalize and expedite its functions in Alaska.

Alaska's delegate to Congress from 1921 to 1931, Dan A. Sutherland, unsuccessfully attempted to persuade Congress to make the office of territorial governor elective. Sutherland and many of his fellow citizens hoped that such a measure would give them not only an elected chief executive of their own choice, but also one who was a resident of Alaska and who would presumably understand its problems. Thus Sutherland introduced a bill for an elective governor in the first session of every Congress between 1923 and 1931.[5]

It was true, as Gruening pointed out, that the federal government was less than attentive to Alaska prior to 1898. The Gold Rush and its accompanying population influx, however, demanded that Washington take a more active role. By 1900 there were only a handful of federal representatives in Alaska, among them the governor, who was an employee of the Department of the Interior, internal revenue and customs collectors, a surveyor—general and his deputies, the staff of the agricultural experiment stations, and three United States district judges.[6] The number of federal personnel, however, grew steadily, and many Alaskans began to view this phenomenon with alarm. For associated with this increase was a continued withdrawal of public lands and natural resources by various federal agencies.[7] The rules and regulations of these various bureaus and agencies could, and did, invalidate those which had been made by the territorial legislature. Alaskans were soon complaining of too much government.

James Wickersham expressed this concern in 1923. He remarked that "the power of national bureaucracy" had found a home in Alaska. It was here, he stated, "that this autocratic enemy to free government is making its last stand for existence among a free people." It was a sad commentary, he insisted, "that there actually exists today a congressional government in Alaska more offensively bureaucratic in its basic principles and practices than that which existed here during the seventy years of Russian rule under the Czar." Comparing the government of Alaska under the Russians with that of the Americans "by executive proclamations and rules and regulations of more than thirty American bureaucrats," Wickersham concluded one could not but admire "the comparative simplicity and reasonableness of the Russian system."[8] Alaska author and lawyer J.A. Hellenthal blamed "the curse of conservation" for Alaska's stagnation. He angrily explained that "at the present rate of progress, it will not be long before an Alaskan will need a license signed by a cabinet officer to kill a mosquito."[9] These and innumerable other expressions of dissatisfaction abounded.

The federal government tried to respond to such criticisms by meeting the increasing complexities of its Alaskan operations. It endeavored to streamline its administration and develop plans for the territory's settlement and economic growth. President Wilson's Secretary of the Interior, Franklin K. Lane, for one, became highly critical of the Alaskan situation. His interest stemmed from the dominant role his department played in the territory. After examining federal management procedures there, he concluded that Alaska had a number of interlocking, overlapping, cumbersome, and confusing governments. Each of these separate units, the Secretary stated, "is intent upon its own particular business, jealous of its own success and prerogative, and all are more or less unrelated in their operations." To correct this situation, Lane urged the creation of a development board of three members. It was to have complete control of the development and conservation of Alaska's resources, the promotion of industries, the development of transportation, and the settlement of the territory.[10]

A Senate bill for such a board was introduced in 1914. It would have vested all federal authority in the development and management of the territory's natural resources in a resident board whose members were to be appointed by the President, confirmed by the Senate, and responsible to the Secretary of the Interior.[11] Like other similar plans, this one was not enacted. In this particular instance, the federal government was too preoccupied with the deepening conflict in Europe.

After the war, in 1921, Secretary of the Interior Albert B. Fall proposed the centralization of all responsibility for the management and development of Alaska's resources under a single, responsible head,[12] presumably himself. Fall, in essence, echoed previous proposals, and his successor, Secretary Hubert Work, also blamed the federal government for the lack of the territory's development. He had no plan for a development board, but asserted that "without the inspiration of self-government and freedom, the country is now being retarded by unnecessary activity of government bureaus...."[13]

The nine major federal departments which controlled Alaskan affairs finally established an interdepartmental coordinating committee in Washington. It consisted of one member from each of these departments. This group, in turn, delegated much of its authority to a similar body in Alaska, composed of the chief field representatives of the nine federal departments. This administrative streamlining did not function as expected. Sherman Rogers, the industrial correspondent for *Outlook*, visited Alaska in 1923 and reported that the attempt had failed. Instead of coordinating and expediting territorial affairs, he stated, it had added greatly to the confusion, red tape, and petty jealousies within the federal administration. Rogers recommended the elimination of the Washington committee and the transfer of executive powers to an Alaskan-based interdepartmental board. This recommendation was strongly endorsed by Secretary of Commerce Herbert Hoover and other federal officials. So far, Hoover remarked, the government had "made about as bad a job of it [Alaska administration] as could have been done if we had set out to do our worst."[14]

After leaving office, Alaska Governor Scott C. Bone, writing in the *Saturday Evening Post*, reviewed Alaska's problems and concluded that governmental reorganization would do little for territorial growth. The remedy, he asserted, lay in full territorial government "preliminary to statehood at the earliest possible date. Then will Alaska grow as the Dakota, Oklahoma, Colorado—indeed, all the continental Union—grew and thrived."[15]

It was not until 1927 that an act of Congress authorized the secretaries of the departments of the interior, agriculture, and commerce each to appoint an ex-officio commissioner for Alaska to whom they could assign and delegate matters under the jurisdiction of that particular department. These commissioners when chosen consisted of the governor of Alaska, representing the Secretary of the Interior, the head of the Bureau of Fisheries field force in Alaska, and the Department of Agriculture's chief territorial field representative in farming and forestry.[16] Little, however, was heard again of these commissioners. It was not surprising, for the strong departmental loyalties of the three members produced only ineffectiveness. After that, no serious attempts at coordinating, consolidating, and streamlining federal operations in the territory were made for several years.

On October 24, 1929, stock market prices fell disastrously on the New York exchange and reached all-time lows in 1932. Nationwide economic activity slowed down in the wake of the crash, unemployment increased tremendously, and America began to experience its worst depression.

The effects of this economic misfortune were soon felt in Alaska. Governor George A. Parks euphemistically reported in 1930 that "during the early summer a surplus of laborers was reported in a few places...." In 1931 he observed that there was more unemployment than usual, and in 1932 that economic conditions had worsened. By 1933 unemployment in the territory, as in the contiguous

United States, had become the major problem.[17] The census of 1930 revealed that Alaska had gained 4,242 people over the census of 1920 which brought its population up to 59,278.[18] This influx was attributable to the unstable economic picture in the Pacific Coast states which led many to seek work in the north.

With the Depression deepening, prices paid for fish and copper, the territory's two chief commodities, declined. This drop, in turn, the new citizens Alaska had recently gained joined the army of the unemployed. The work force in the fishing industries dropped from 29,283 1929 to 12,695 in 1933, while exports from Alaska for the same period, consisting mainly of fish products, minerals, and furs, shrank from 449,944 tons to 260,138 tons. Government employment in the territory was cut back proportionately.[19]

The economic outlook was bleak in April of 1932 when Alaskans chose their delegates to the national party conventions and elected candidates for the delegate ship. The Republican delegation left the territory pledged to the renomination of President Herbert Hoover, while the Democrats favored the nomination of Governor Franklin D. Roosevelt of New York for president. The Democrats chose Anthony J. Dimond out of a field of three candidates for delegate to Congress, while Republican James Wickersham, who had returned from political retirement in 1930 to regain his old seat, was unopposed for a second term.[20]

Dimond was a topflight Alaskan lawyer from Valdez, a former prospector and miner, who had been repeatedly elected mayor of his city, and a one-time member of the territorial Senate. Although the New York Times described him as a man almost entirely lacking in political instinct, a Democrat of longstanding who had never voluntarily sought office, he was rated as the most formidable candidate the Democrats had put into the field in years. Both Wickersham and Dimond campaigned vigorously, the seventy-five-year-old Wickersham fighting for his political life. Dimond electioneered by bush plane and suffered a mishap. He was struck by the plane's propeller on the shoulder and immediately rushed to the hospital in Fairbanks where he was treated for a deep flesh

Anthony J. Dimond

Architects of Statehood

Anthony J. Dimond

Anthony J. Dimond was a tall, somber man who had moved to Alaska from Palatine Bridge, on the Mohawk River in New York, early in the twentieth century. He had taught high school and read some law.

While on a prospecting trip in 1911 a shooting accident forced him to abandon gold mining. He resumed his law studies, and not long after leaving the hospital in Cordova, he was admitted to the territorial bar and began the practice of law. He served as a U.S. Commissioner of the Chisana recording district in 1913 and 1919, as mayor of Valdez for ten years, and territorial senator for two terms.

After a vigorous campaign for the position of Delegate to Congress in 1932 he won the election by a substantial margin. Dimond began his Washington career in an era of political ferment, the New Deal. It was he who initiated the modern drive for statehood.

In the 1941 progress edition of the *Daily Alaska Empire* (Juneau) Dimond attempted to convince Alaskans about the advantages of statehood. On December 2, 1943 Delegate Dimond introduced his own statehood bill. It was a short measure and provided that the federal government convey to the state practically all public lands.

Dimond retired from Congress in 1944 and accepted a federal judgeship in Anchorage.

wound and a broken collar bone. Despite this interruption in his campaign, Dimond won by a substantial margin and Alaska Democrats gained large majorities in both houses of the territorial legislature.[21] The American public also voted for a national political change, and Dimond began his Washington career in an era of tremendous political ferment.

The tall, quiet, dignified delegate quickly made an excellent impression on his colleagues in the House and his acquaintances in the Senate. He worked ceaselessly to expand the powers of the territorial government. In particular, Dimond introduced measures to give Alaska control of the administration of its fish and game resources. In 1938 his efforts were partially rewarded when Congress made a number of reforms which streamlined the administration of the territory's game laws and included many of his suggestions.[22]

During Dimond's six terms in Congress, he generally followed the example of his predecessors and submitted proposals which would have prevented the appointment of a nonresident as governor, and which also provided for the election of a territorial chief executive. He introduced measures which would have permitted the appointment of Alaska residents only to the positions of district court judges and United States attorneys and marshals.[23] All of these proposals were designed to overcome carpetbag charges which were often made against federal appointees, and also to personnel familiar with the territory and its problems. None of the bills ever passed.

In 1934 Dimond joined forces with Hawaii's delegate and submitted legislation which would have given both territories representation in the Senate comparable to that in the house, but without success. His diligent attempts to persuade Congress to extend the Federal Aid Highway Act of 1916 to Alaska likewise were unsuccessful.[24]

Although Alaska failed to gain more self-government as a result of Dimond's efforts, it participated on a modest scale in some of the economic recovery programs of the New Deal. The National Reforestation Act of 1933 provided for the employment of several hundred men. Late in 1933, the federal government raised the price of gold from its fixed price of $20.67 to $35.00 per ounce. This action soon led to an increase in mining activity. The territory also benefited from projects undertaken by the Public Works Administration and the Work Projects Administration as well as the Civilian Conservation Corps. Many programs of enduring worth were completed. These included waterworks, schools, playgrounds, fire stations, and the construction of roads, airfields, and a steel bridge across Gastineau Channel connecting Juneau on the mainland with Douglas on Douglas Island. In addition, trails and shelter cabins were built in the national forests. By 1936, PWA alone had allocated some $4,463,233 for the territory.[25]

In 1935 the famous Matanuska Valley colonization scheme commenced. President Franklin D. Roosevelt envisioned this undertaking as an opportunity to take Americans from depressed agricultural areas and give them a chance to start life anew and become self-sustaining again. In addition, it was to demonstrate Alaska's agricultural possibilities and to stimulate population growth. Some 15,000 letters of application were received once final plans had been announced. The number of prospective settlers was finally limited to 202, who, together with their dependents, would number approximately 1,000 persons. The colonists were chosen from Michigan, Wisconsin, and Minnesota on the assumption that the climatic similarities of these areas to Alaska would best fit the pioneers for life in the Matanuska Valley. The final selection was haphazard. All unsolicited applications were disregarded and colonists were instead recruited and urged to go. Many mistakes were made and numerous people totally unsuited for such an undertaking were brought to Alaska.

In the spring of 1935, 202 families, amidst much fanfare, arrived in the town of Palmer in the center of the valley. They were sponsored by the Federal Emergency Relief Administration under its Rural Rehabilitation Division. Together with some 400 relief workers form the transient camps of California, they set about to clear land for the projected forty-acre tracts each settler was to receive.

They also built living quarters, a school, trading post, cannery, creamery, and hospital.[26]

In the same year another settlement proposal was made by "The Alaska Colonization Branch of the United Congo Improvement Association" with headquarters in Cleveland, Ohio. The organization's letterhead proclaimed optimistically that "Alaska offers the American Negro full political rights." Dr. Joe Thomas, a medical practitioner and the group's head, represented some 2,000 members on relief. Many were farmers, heads of families and war veterans. Although the U.C.I.A., Inc. maintained that Alaska could eventually well support one million Negroes, initial plans were very modest. It asked President Franklin D. Roosevelt to settle some 400 farmers in Alaska, 200 on the Kenai Peninsula and the rest at Iliamna Bay. With existing racial prejudices and prevailing beliefs that only people from the world's northern lands were suited for life in Alaska, Thomas' plan was foredoomed to failure. The proposal was shuttled from agency to agency in the federal government, until it landed on the desk of Ernest Gruening, head of the Division of Territories and Island Possessions, who turned it down.[27]

Although the New Deal quickened Alaska's economic pace, it brought no basic changes. In 1937 the National Resources Committee examined territorial conditions and found that Alaska's was still very small. There were only seven cities with a population of 1,000 or more, and from the beginning until 1937 less than 2,500 miles of public highways had been built in the whole of Alaska. This was equivalent to the mileage regarded as necessary in the contiguous United States to service an area of approximately thirty-six square miles. The committee reported that some fifty-two federal agencies operated in Alaska and that "often their authority and responsibility appear to be poorly defined. There is overlapping of jurisdiction and divided responsibility, resulting in confusion, delay, and excessive 'red tape.'" The committee suggested maximum discretion for federal field officials and the establishment of a coordinating device outside the usual departmental loyalties. In addition, the committee outlined alternate avenues of development Alaska could follow. On the one hand, the territory could simply serve as a source of raw materials for the contiguous United States. In that case, it soon would be destroyed as a future home for Americans. Another possibility was that Alaska could, with considerable government help, develop a diversified economy which would be conducive to population growth. The committee, however, expressed hope that a middle course would be followed.[28]

As a matter of fact, Alaska was soon to be rediscovered and rapidly developed, a circumstance which was neither foreseen nor planned by the federal government. As early as 1933, delegate Dimond had recognized Japan as a threat to America's security and asked Congress for military airfields and planes, a highway to link the territory with the United States, and army garrisons. In 1934, delegate Dimond had recognized Japan as a threat to America's security and asked Congress for military airfields and planes, a highway to link the territory with the United States, and army garrisons. In 1933 he cautioned that it was futile to fortify Hawaii and leave Alaska totally unguarded, because any attack from across the Pacific, he predicted, was bound to come by way of Alaska. In 1935 he stated:

> Is it not obvious that an enemy moving across the Pacific would not come by way of Honolulu, or within 2,000 miles of it, but would rather strike, invade, and take Alaska at one gulp, for at the present time Alaska is absolutely undefended by any military force or installation of any kink...except...a force that is not sufficiently powerful to be of any use against a foreign attack.[29]

He warned his House colleagues in 1937 that Japanese fishermen, ostensibly fishing off Alaska's coast, were actually disguised military personnel seeking information on the depth, defenses, and landmarks of Alaska's harbors. In the same year delegate Dimond attempted to secure a $2,000,000 appropriation to begin construction of an air base near Fairbanks which had been authorized in

1935. He pleaded eloquently, pointing out that if Hawaii was one key to the Pacific, Alaska was the other. At the very least, he urged, Army Air Corps pilots should be trained in cold weather flying. The money was refused. In time he made converts, most importantly General George C. Marshall, the Chief of Staff, and General Henry H. Arnold, head of the Army Air Force. Yet as late as 1938, Dimond reported that Alaska had only approximately 300 infantry troops, stationed at Chilkoot Barracks near Haines, and about six naval airplanes at Sitka, also in Southeastern Alaska.[30]

Congress finally authorized $29,108,285 in 1940 for the construction of navy and army bases and a fort at locations ranging from Unalaska to Kodiak, and from Anchorage to Sitka. The construction of these facilities, however, was stretched in a leisurely fashion over several years. It was not until the invasion of Denmark and Norway by the Nazis in the spring of 1940, Dimond stated later, that military building slowly commenced in the territory. Many congressmen, Dimond believed, for the first time realized that the Scandinavian Peninsula was just over the top of the earth from Alaska, and that bombers which could fly such a distance existed. This sudden insight, the delegate later commented, brought about a turning point in Alaska's fortunes and history.[31] Yet when the Japanese struck Pearl Harbor, none of the Alaskan bases were ready, although construction had been under way since 1940. Pearl Harbor immensely speeded the building of bases at Kodiak Island, Dutch Harbor, Anchorage, Sitka, and Fairbanks.

One contemporary journalist, Richard L. Neuberger, reported early in 1942 that Alaska had not been so conspicuous and prominent in the American press since its purchase in 1867. He anticipated that the war would speed Alaskan development and progress significantly. A rash of articles appeared extolling the strategic importance of Alaska in the defense of the western shores of the United States. Ernest K. Lindley of *Newsweek* reminded his readers early in 1942 that General "Billy" Mitchell in the mid-1930s had emphatically stated that Alaska was the most important strategic spot on the globe in the age of airpower. Nobody had listened at

that time. For years there had been intermittent talk about a highway to the territory, Lindley related. Engineers had surveyed a
route, but the project had remained at the talking stage. As late
as 1940, Secretary of War Henry L. Stimson had thought that the
defense value of such a road connection was at best negligible. But
by October of 1941 the secretary conceded that such a road would
have a desirable long-range value as a defense measure.[32]

Then, on December 7, 1941, Japanese forces attacked the Pacific
fleet at anchor in Pearl Harbor and practically destroyed it. America was at war. In the summer of 1942 enemy forces invaded and
occupied Attu and Kiska on the Aleutian Chain. America's pride
was hurt, and Secretary of the Interior Harold Ickes, who had been
almost totally indifferent to Alaska thus far, suddenly declared that
there was no question that the United States had to defend this
"cherished" territory. Indeed, all Americans were united in their
desire to drive the Japanese out. This attitude was far different from
that expressed by retired Major General Smedley D. Butler, who,
testifying in 1938 before Congress in connection with a naval construction bill, had recommended that the United States abandon
Alaska in case of war.[33]

Far from abandoning its northern outpost, the United States
quickly sent 10,000 soldiers, divided into seven Army Engineer
regiments and supported by 6,000 civilian workers under the direction of the United States Public Road Administration, to start construction of the ALCAN (Alaska-Canadian Military Highway) in
the spring of 1942. Work began simultaneously at three locations:
Dawson Creek, the terminal of a railroad running northwest from
Edmonton, Alberta; at Whitehorse, Yukon Territory, which was
connected by the White Pass and Yukon Railway with Skagway at
tidewater on the coast of Southeastern Alaska; and at Big Delta in
Alaska. The highway was completed with incredible speed, and in
November of 1942 was formally opened for traffic. The construction of 1,671 miles of road over formidable terrain had been an
engineering feat of the first order. It had been estimated that the
cost of construction amounted to roughly $135,000,000 or $56,160

per mile, including the innumerable bridges which cost approximately $23,166,725 to build.[34]

While the ALCAN highway rapidly took shape, thousands of other American soldiers came to Alaska to participate in its defense and prepare for the recapture of Kiska and Attu. Civilian workers toiled practically around the clock to build bases at various locations in Alaska. At the same time, between June 9 and September 13, 1942, Kiska was bombed by planes stationed on Umnak Island. Since these planes had to make a 1,200-mile round trip, they carried a small bomb load but much fuel. This situation improved in September 1942, when the bombers began conducting their raids from the recently completed base on Adak Island, which cut the two-way trip to 500 miles. Next, an advance base was built on Amchitka Island, which was extensively used after February 1943. Throughout the winter of 1942-43, American and Canadian bombers and fighters continued their missions against the Japanese preparatory for the May 11, 1943, amphibious assault on Attu. At the end of May 1943, the island fell into American hands after fierce fighting. Subsequently, construction of airfields proceeded on Attu and Shemya, and August 15, 1943, an amphibious landing was made on Kiska. The troops, however, discovered that the enemy had left the island at the end of July by surface ships and submarines. Following this action, ground forces in Alaska were reduced. From a height of 150,000 men in November of 1943, military personnel of the Alaskan Department had been reduced to 50,000 by March 1945. Forts were closed, bases dismantled, and airfields turned over to the Civil Aeronautics Administration.[35]

The impact of military activities had irrevocably altered the pace and tenor of Alaskan life, and the residual benefits to the civilian economy and the development of Alaska were tremendous. Between 1941 and 1945, the federal government spent well over one billion dollars in the territory. The modernization of the Alaska Railroad and the expansion of airfields and construction of roads benefited the civilian population. Many of the docks, wharves, and breakwaters built along the coast for the use of the Navy, Coast Guard, and the Army Transport Service were turned over to the territory after the war. Thousands of soldiers and construction workers had come north. Many decided to make Alaska their home at the end of the hostilities, a fact reflected in the population statistics. Between 1940 and 1950, the territory's civilian population increased from roughly 74,000 to 112,000.[36] This influx put a tremendous strain on Alaska's social services, such as schools, hospitals, housing, and local government.

In short, the war was the biggest boom Alaska ever experienced, bigger than any of the Gold Rushes of the past. Alaskans themselves were forced into an awareness of the outside world. The territory's isolation, partially self-imposed by the parochial outlook of many of its citizens, and partially caused by the lack of communication and transportation, had ended. The familiar economic pattern of primary resource extraction together with modest supporting services was disrupted and replaced by government and defense-related activities. Government employment rose from 12.1 percent of the total employed labor force in September 1939, to 53.7 percent in April 1950. Self-employment during the same time span dropped from 33.9 percent to 13.7 percent. The change in the commodity-producing industries, such as agriculture, forestry, fisheries, and mining, was even more pronounced. While 62.3 percent of Alaska's total labor force was employed in these primary pursuits in September 1939, it had shrunk to 26.5 percent in April 1950, and continued to fall.[37]

Meanwhile, delegate Anthony Dimond utilized the attention Alaska enjoyed nationally. Between 1943 and 1945 he continued to press for an appointed governor to be chosen from among the territory's residents, for making the governor elective, and for extending the Federal Aid Highway Act of 1916 to Alaska—all to no avail. His proposal to give Alaska proportional representation by electing one territorial senator and one territorial representative for every 4,000 persons was only partly successful. The Organic Act of 1912 had given the territory a Senate of eight members and a house of sixteen. Two Senators and four Representatives were allotted to each of the jour judicial divisions. These geographic units, however, had gained population unequally. According to the 1940 census, the first judicial division showed a population of 25,241; the second, 11,877; the third, 19,312; and the forth, 16,094. With more than twice as many people in the first than the second division, and the population in all, except the second, increasing, the territorial legislature had become less and less representative. As finally passed by Congress, the reform measure gave proportional representation in the house only. It increased the number of Representatives to twenty-four and doubled that of the Senators to sixteen.[38]

With the increase in population, talk about statehood for Alaska was heard again. As early as 1939, the Fairbanks-based "Alaska Home Rule Association" issued a statement in which it assailed "taxation without representation" and asked for future statehood. A bill defeated by the territorial senate in 1941, would have given Alaskans the opportunity of statehood referendum. A similar measure in the 1943 session met the same fate. The modern statehood movement, however, was opened in April 1943, when Senators William L. Langer and Pat McCarran, at Dimond's request, submitted the first statehood bill since Wickersham's measure in 1916.[39]

Dimond followed up with a discussion of the statehood questions over radio station WWDC in Washington. Statehood for Alaska, he asserted, was a foregone conclusion. The territory was ready economically and socially, and entitled to it, although the military might prefer to put off any change in the governmental structure until after the war. Opposition, he predicted, would come from the absentee-owned fishing and mining industries, "who usually cry out in agony at the through that they may be obliged to pay more taxes." Further economic development and statehood, he concluded, were interdependent.[40]

Reactions to the proposal in Alaska varied. Robert B. Atwood, editor and publisher of the *Anchorage Daily Times*, was utterly surprised when he read the news of the Langer-McCarran bill in an Associated Press dispatch. "I had never given statehood any thought or consideration," he recalled. "I wasn't in politics like

Gruening, maybe he thought of it, but I hadn't" Atwood, however, quickly recognized the desirability of statehood and used his newspaper to disseminate this view. The Wrangell Chamber of Commerce passed a resolution strongly urging passage of the measure, while the Juneau Chamber thought that any action should be suspended until the end of the war. The Ketchikan Bar Association unanimously favored it, as did its Juneau counterpart.[41]

Secretary of the Interior Ickes stated that "statehood might be desirable as the ultimate political status for Alaska," but opposed it because of the territory's seasonal economy and unstable population. The Secretary was emphatic in his opposition to Section Three of the bill which proposed to give the future state all vacant and inappropriate public lands. Such action, Ickes asserted, wood give to one state the tremendous natural resources which belonged to all Americans. The secretary recommended against passage of the bill.[42]

On December 2, 1943, Dimond crowned his years in Congress when he submitted a companion measure to the Langer-McCarran bill. The political advantages of statehood, he asserted, were immense. Alaska no longer would be a beggar at the nation's capital, but instead would become a full-fledged member of the Union of States.[43]

CHAPTER SEVEN

Bartlett and Gruening:
Crusaders for Statehood

L ate in the summer of 1939 war clouds were hanging heavy over Europe. Hitler's armies had invaded Poland, and many Americans kept close to their radios to follow the latest developments. Among the many avid listeners were Ernest and Dorothy Gruening, on a vacation in New England from Washington, D.C. where he headed the Division of Territories and Island Possessions in the Department of the Interior. While driving through Rockport, Massachusetts, they heard on the automobile radio that President Franklin D. Roosevelt had appointed him governor of Alaska. The date was September 3, 1939.

Gruening brought an impressive background to his new job. He had received an M.D. from Harvard University in 1912, but instead of practicing medicine, he had pursued a career in journalism. He moved from reporter with the *Boston American* to the *Boston Evening Herald*. Shortly thereafter his paper and the *Boston Traveler* combined, and Gruening continued on the new *Traveler*. He also submitted freelance editorials to the morning newspaper, the *Boston Herald*. Eventually this evolved this evolved into a fulltime position as assistant editorial page editor. When the city editor of the *Traveler* went on vacation, Gruening filled that position, switching back to the evening paper. He performed so well that in October 1914, he received a promotion to the paper's managing editorship. The paper grew in readership and prospered financially.

In the meantime, Gruening had courted a young woman, Dorothy Elizabeth Smith of Norwood, Massachusetts. They were married on November 19, 1914. After some censorship problems on the *Traveler* he resigned and the *Boston Journal* hired him as its managing editor. The paper was financially unstable, and sold out to the *Boston Herald*. After a short stint at the *New York Morning Sun,* he accepted an offer to help organize the Bureau of Imports of the War Trade Board. This was his first government assignment, so he moved his wife and two sons to Washington, D.C. Offered a commission in the Army's Sanitary Corps because of his medical training, but preferring combat, he applied instead to attend a newly organized Field Artillery Officers' Training Camp located near Louisville, Kentucky.

His plans were interrupted when Garet Garrett, the executive editor of the *New York Tribune,* offered him the managing editorship of the paper. He accepted, and moved his family to New York, but his job was short-lived when he quickly locked horns with the executive director whose anti-Wilson bias could not be confined to the editorial pages but was also evident in the news reporting. Gruening had renewed his application for a commission at Camp Zachary Taylor when the defeated Central Powers signed the armistice.

Shorty after his discharge from the United States Army, Gruening accepted the position of business manager of *La Prensa*, a new Spanish language daily in New York. In 1912 he switched jobs once again and became managing editor of *The Nation*, a weekly magazine in New York. While editor of *The Nation*, Gruening became interested in some of the more notable excesses of American foreign policy in Latin America popularly known as "gunboat diplomacy." He became particularly interested in Mexican affairs. Eventually he traveled widely in that country, learned Spanish, and wrote freelance articles telling the story of the Mexican people and their revolution.

After some time, he decided to write a book on Mexico, but found that he did not have enough material. He continued freelancing but put the finished chapters aside for the time being. In 1924 he participated in the presidential election and became director of national publicity for the Progressive Party's presidential standard bearer, Senator Robert Marion LaFollette of Wisconsin. The Senator lost the race, but the Progressive ticket polled an impressive five million votes.

Gruening continued to freelance and returned to Mexico several times. Often separated from his family, he hoped to make up for that in 1929 on a trip to Europe. His third son had been born in 1923; so early in 1926, Dorothy and her three children left for Paris. Gruening joined his family later.

His book, *Mexico and Its Heritage,* appeared in 1928. Considered then, and still today, a standard work on that country, it is recommended by both the U.S. State Department and the Mexicans as required reading.

In the meantime, Gruening went to Portland, Maine in 1927 to take charge of the newly launched *Portland Evening News.* Gruening soon clashed with Samuel Insull, a Chicago public utility tycoon and the head of a large hydro-electric empire, operated throughout 31 states. Eventually, the battle between Gruening's *News* and Insull attracted the attention of the United States Senate. An investigation by the Federal Trade Commission followed. It revealed irregularities and stock juggling and the Insull Empire collapsed and investors lost heavily. Gruening believed that the corruption of the utilities and public officials should be made widely known to avoid a repetition of these abuses. He, therefore, summarized the millions of words of testimony and exhibits in a brief volume, published in 1932, entitled *The Public Pays.*

Late in 1932, Gruening returned to *The Nation.* His Latin American expertise soon brought him to the attention of the Roosevelt administration, and in the fall of 1933 he received an appointment as advisor to the United States delegation to the Seventh Pan-American Conference held at Montevideo, Uruguay, in that year.

His service as advisor singled him out for special praise and shortly thereafter he received an invitation to become a permanent member of President Franklin D. Roosevelt's New Deal Administration. Until 1934, the office of the chief clerk of the Department of the Interior had conducted federal relations with the territories. In that year the president issued an executive order which established the Division of Territories and Island Possessions, also located in the department. Gruening became the first director of the division.

Roosevelt created the Puerto Rican Reconstruction Administration in 1935 and appointed Gruening its administrator. The appointee was totally surprised to find himself holding two jobs. Ickes, who had been displeased with Gruening's forthrightness as director, was even more unhappy now and sharply questioned Gruening as whether he had lobbied for the position.[1] The answer was no.

Gruening's appointment rankled Ickes—he liked to pick his own people—and relations between the two men deteriorated very quickly. The president, who disliked conflict and did not find it easy to fire people, decided to "kick" Gruening upstairs and make him governor of Alaska.

It was not surprising that Gruening, with his background and ambition, came to Alaska determined to make something out of the territory, to demonstrate to the President his capabilities. All his frustrated ambitions he now poured into Alaska. And with a man of his talent, ability, determination, and ego, it was a foregone conclusion that he would have a great impact on the territory.[2]

A contemporary of Gruening's, although considerably younger in years, and a man who also had a great influence on Alaska, was Edward Lewis "Bob" Bartlett. The son of Klondike pioneers, he was born in Seattle and grew up in Fairbanks. He attended the Universities of Alaska and Washington for a time and then, in 1927, became a reporter for the *Fairbanks Daily News-Miner*

where he remained until 1933. He then became secretary to delegate Anthony J. Dimond, remaining in Washington until 1934.
After his return to Alaska he served briefly as an assistant territorial director of the Federal Housing Administration and operated
a placer gold mine until he was appointed secretary of Alaska, a
position comparable to lieutenant governor, by President Roosevelt
in January 1939. Bartlett resigned in February 1944 to become a
candidate for the delegateship.[3]

Gruening and Bartlett, two very dissimilar personalities, the
former aggressive and determined, the latter quiet and persuasive
nevertheless developed a lasting working relationship. But while
the governor soon polarized Alaskan politics into pro- and anti-
Gruening camps by the sheer force of his personality, Bartlett
continued to widen is acquaintances among all elements of the
territory's population and to build political goodwill. Gruening
antagonized many Alaskans, prominent among them territorial
legislators, when he unsuccessfully recommended to the 1941 and
1943 sessions of the Alaska legislature a complete revision of the
antiquated tax laws. Many territorial senators and representatives
went so far as to oppose automatically anything that had the backing of the governor.[4]

The statehood movement soon developed into a crusade under
the leadership of these two men. They did not invent the movement, to be sure, because it already had been ebbing and flowing
in the territory for a long time. They did, however, give it a vitality
and dynamism which it had not possessed before.

Gruening promoted statehood on a broad front. When he went
on lecture tours in the states, he insisted on advertising the issue.
He utilized his connections with the nation's press to advantage.
He clearly defined the devils, the "Outside" interests, including
Seattle's monopolistic control of Alaskan shipping. The people of
the territory had known all along that their freight rates were high.
Gruening explained that this was due to a provision in the Maritime Act of 1920 (sponsored by Washington's Senator Wesley Jones
and known as the Jones Act in the territory) which foreclosed the

alternatives of shipment through the Canadian ports of Vancouver and Prince Rupert, both far more economical, and made Seattle the port through which Alaska trade had to pass. The salmon fisheries had been declining for a number of years. The governor maintained that the White Act of 1924, a measure which had been hailed as the Magna Carta of fishery conservation by both federal officials and industry spokesmen, worked to the detriment of the small operator in Alaska and protected the large companies and their fish traps.[5] In short, Gruening set up the targets and called upon Alaskans to join the movement. He organized the statehood cause within the territory and barnstormed the United States in the service of it.

Bartlett operated in a far different fashion, but just as effectively. He was not as flamboyant as Gruening, although every inch as tenacious. His greatest service for the statehood movement was performed in the halls of Congress. In his 1944 primary fight for the Democratic nomination to replace delegate Dimond, he faced H. Ziegler and Henry Roden, both well-known, old-time political figures. Against the advice of amateur and professional politicians alike, Bartlett ran on a statehood platform. Despite gloomy predictions, he not only defeated his two opponents but went on to win in the general election by 7,255 to 3,763 votes over his Republican adversary, John E. Manders.[6]

After six terms of Congress, delegate Dimond had decided to retire and return to Alaska. In addition, there was the prospect of appointment to a federal judgeship in the territory. When taking leave of his colleagues in the House of Representatives late in 1944, he introduced his successor and recommended him highly to the House membership. Bartlett, he told them, felt as strongly about statehood for the territory as he did. Not surprisingly, then, Bartlett followed his mentor's footsteps and attempted to have the Organic Act of 1912 amended and revised. To this end, he introduced measures for an elective as well as resident governor and secretary of Alaska in almost every session between 1945 and 1955. By 1955, however, he realized the futility of these actions and discontinued submitting such bills. But Bartlett continued to tell his colleagues about Alaska, its promise and problems. He appeared before every committee of the Senate and House which had anything to do with the territory. In addition, he and his Congressional friends began to bombard Congress with statehood bills in almost every session.[7]

World War II ended, at least in Europe, in May of 1945. As previously mentioned, Alaska had profited enormously from the publicity and development it had received thus far in the war. The territorial legislature took advantage of the prevailing idealistic mood, and early in 1945 the House of Representatives sent a memorial to Congress. This document pleaded dramatically for the extension to Alaska of the "Four Freedoms" proclaimed in the Atlantic Charter, which supported the right of small nations and minorities to choose their own form of government and to have control over their own destinies. The memorial was followed shortly by a request to admit Alaska as the forty-ninth state. In the same session Governor Gruening asked the lawmakers to establish provisions for a referendum on the statehood question. The legislature complied, with the vote to be taken in the 1946 general election. Gruening knew that an educational program had to be undertaken at once to assure a large turnout of voters. Congress could not be expected to act on Alaskan statehood without a loud and positive expression from the territorial citizenry. The governor toyed with the idea of engaging either the Library of Congress or the Brookings Institution to make a study of the pros and cons of statehood, but could not find the necessary funds. He decided that George Sundborg, an old friend then working for the Bonneville Power Administration, might be employed to undertake such an analysis at a more modest fee.[8]

At that point, at the suggestion of Gruening, a group of Anchorage statehood enthusiasts, led by Mrs. Evangeline Atwood, the wife of the editor and publisher of the *Anchorage Daily Times*, organized a nonpartisan, nonprofit, territory-wide Alaska Statehood Association. On November 6, Mrs. Atwood sent invitations to many of the territory's citizens which stated:

Evangeline Atwood

Architects of Statehood

Evangeline Atwood

Evangeline Atwood, the daughter of Alaska banker, E.A. Rasmuson, was born and raised in Alaska. She became a social worker in Springfield, Illinois. There, she met Robert Bruce Atwood. They married on April 2, 1932 and moved to Anchorage in 1935, then a city of 2,200.

Evangeline's father enabled her husband to purchase the *Anchorage Daily Times* which had 650 subscribers in the town. The two arrived in Alaska at a time when the ambitions of a few could radically shape the territory. Bob and Evangeline Atwood were pro-statehood and development. They developed the *Anchorage Daily Times* into a media powerhouse.

Both Atwoods were drawn to territorial Governor Ernest Gruening, a Progressive and statehood advocate. At the end of World War II Gruening had asked the territorial legislature to make provisions for a statehood referendum. The legislature complied and the vote was to be taken in the 1946 general election. Gruening knew that an educational program had to be undertaken. He decided to engage George Sundborg, an old friend then working for the Bonneville Power Administration, to make such a study. But there was no money to pay Sundborg. Gruening discussed the idea with Evangeline Atwood. She organized a group of statehood enthusiasts into a non-partisan, non-profit, territory-wide Alaska Statehood Association. It established chapters in ten Alaska cities. It elected Evangeline Atwood as president and authorized her to hire Sundborg to prepare the study. Widely distributed, the study informed voters about the 1946 statehood referendum, which was approved 9,630 to 6,822.

Evangeline Atwood also was an author. She wrote a biography of James Wickersham and an account of the 1935 Matanuska agricultural settlement, among others. Evangeline Atwood died in November 1987 in Anchorage.

Every Alaskan interested in the progress and welfare of the Territory should want his name on this membership list. In the years to come this...list will be a directory of Alaskans who had the foresight, vision and generosity to pioneer this study of statehood.

A membership fee of five dollars was charged. At first Mrs. Atwood had little success in stimulating the establishment of local chapters of the association. But she persisted, and soon chapters had been created in Anchorage, Fairbanks, Juneau, Ketchikan, Sitka, Wrangell, Palmer, Valdez, Kodiak, and Seward. Mrs. Atwood had long been interested in civic affairs. Born in Sitka, she had studied at the universities of Washington and Chicago. She had earned a B.A. degree in sociology from the former and an M.A. degree in social service administration from the latter. She worked as a social worker when she married Robert B. Atwood. Edward Rasmuson, her father, was Alaska's Republican national committeeman, and her brother, Elmer, headed the Bank of Alaska.[9]

On March 12, 1946, the association's headquarters was established at Juneau. About 350 individuals had joined the local chapters by then. The membership elected Evangeline Atwood president and authorized her to hire George Sundborg to prepare the study. Sundborg had first come to Alaska in 1938 as a reporter and editorial writer for the *Daily Alaska Empire*. Later he worked for the Alaska Office of the National Resources Planning Board, and in 1946 he was working as an industrial analyst for the Bonneville Power Administration. He had also authored the well-received book *Opportunity in Alaska*, published in 1945. Sundborg was a capable individual, and Gruening's backing helped him to get the job.[10]

Sundborg faced a difficult task. Materials on which to base the study were limited, and as a full-time employee of the Bonneville Power Administration he could only devote limited time to the project. There also were difficulties in financing the study through the sale of $5 memberships, and the Anchorage chapter decided to ask the territorial legislature, then meeting in special

session, to make a $5,000 appropriation to speed the preparation
and distribution of the study. Although Senator Grenold Collins
introduced a joint memorial, the whole senate postponed the
memorial indefinitely.[11]

During most of the war period, statehood had not been a subject
of serious consideration. By mid-1945, however, even the federal
departments most concerned with Alaska's administration had to
take an official stand. Secretary of the Interior Ickes had voiced his
opposition in 1943. One of his objections was what he considered
the excessive land grants proposed for the new state. In 1945, Jack
B. Fahy, Acting Director of the Division of Territories and Island
Possessions, took the lead. He drafted a memorandum in which
he enumerated the reasons why Alaska should become a state and
cited the activities of Interior designed to further this end. Fahy
circulated his position paper among the policy-making personnel
of the department where it was approved by most except the Fish
and Wildlife Service. Also, the Geological Survey expressed some
doubts. He next sent it to Ickes, mentioning that it had already
gained wide departmental acceptance. Fahy sought to reassure the
secretary when he pointed out that statehood did not mean that
ownership of all the public lands would be vested in the state. As a
matter of fact, he reminded Ickes, past enabling acts had granted
certain acreages for schools, roads, and other public purposes, but
title to the bulk of the lands had always remained with the federal government. Perhaps this argument was convincing enough
to win over the "Old Curmudgeon;" perhaps it was the influence
of wartime idealism. Whatever the reasons, Acting Secretary of the
Interior Abe Fortas announced on August 11, 1945 that statehood
was now a part of the department's policy for Alaska and had been
approved by Secretary Ickes.[12]

While Interior had been formulating a policy, two Congressional groups had traveled to Alaska to investigate conditions on
the spot and hold informal statehood hearings. The House Subcommittee on Appropriations reported that, although the majority of Alaskans favored statehood, the members seriously doubted

the territory's ability to assume the burdens connected with it. The reasons mentioned were the absence of an adequate tax law as well as inadequate social legislation. Representative John Rooney, a member of this committee, amplified these views in a newspaper interview. Any people, he remarked, who allowed a major industry like fishing to take out some $60,000,000 annually and retained only $1,000,000 in taxes obviously were not ready for the responsibilities of statehood. The House Committee on Territories heard statehood widely discussed but found no agreement as to how soon the territory should seek admission. Opponents of statehood, they reported, generally feared increased taxes, while proponents argued that representation in Congress would offset any disadvantages, such as increased costs. The committee members agreed to consider carefully a suggestion by territorial Attorney General Ralph J. Rivers. He proposed that for a five-year period prior to statehood the federal government return a certain portion of the corporate and individual income taxes collected in the territory every year. These funds then could be used to establish a territorial judicial system, to pay the legislature and executive branches of government, and to construct the physical facilities necessary to operate a state. After five years, federal aid could be withdrawn, Rivers believed, and Alaska made a state.[13]

While the statehood forces gathered momentum, Congress reassembled in 1946. In his State of the Union message in January of that year, Truman gave Alaskan statehood a boost when he recommended that the territory be promptly admitted as soon as the wishes of its citizens had been determined. The President also urged Congress to admit Hawaii whose citizens already had opted for statehood. On February 13, 1946, Secretary Ickes resigned his position after having clashed with the President. Truman appointed Julius Krug the new Secretary of the Interior. A large man, thirty-nine years of age, Krug had built a solid reputation on the basis of his work in public utilities regulation and, in the last year of the war, his service as chairman of the War Production Board.[14]

The new secretary visited Alaska in August 1946 to listen and learn, and to determine, among other things, the extent of the statehood movement. He did listen some, but also talked a great deal. Many residents felt that Krug was interested and sincere. The secretary cautioned his audiences that statehood would not solve all of Alaska's problems but "rather it is a step on the way." After returning to Seattle from his ten day visit, he told newsmen that "...Alaska should comprise at least one state and perhaps two or three." When asked what barriers lay in the way of Alaska statehood, he replied that it was the inclination of Congress to move slowly on major decisions unless it was forced to act. Alaska statehood was not an urgent matter. *U.S. News and World Report,* however, predicted that Alaska would soon become the forty-ninth state. The news magazine expected the territory to be America's most important defense frontier in the age of long-range planes and guided missiles. Pollster George Gallup reported in September that 64 percent of American voters favored the admission of Alaska, 12 percent were opposed, and 24 percent were undecided. Gallup went on to say that Americans favored admission mainly because the territory was vital to the defense of the nation, and, in addition, its citizens deserved equal representation.[15]

A few weeks after Krug had left the north, Alaskans had the chance to read Sundborg's statehood report. The author had revised several drafts, and the end product was printed both as a pamphlet, entitled *Statehood for Alaska: The Issues Involved and the Facts about the Issues,* and as a newspaper supplement. William Baker, the proprietor of the *Ketchikan Alaska Chronicle* printed the latter and offered it free of charge to the territory's newspapers. It received wide distribution.[16]

As might be expected, the report clearly showed the sympathies of its author and the sponsoring group, because out of fifty-six pages, only five were devoted to arguments against statehood. Sundborg wrote that the main arguments against statehood were that "Alaska's economy is not sufficiently diversified, its population sufficiently large or its experience in exercising governmental responsibility sufficiently broad to make statehood desirable at the time." But all of these allegations were debatable, he stated, and others, like the idea that Native health and welfare would become a state responsibility, were obviously false.[17]

The bulk of the report consisted of articles partial to statehood. Sundborg observed that most Alaskans probably agreed on the desirability of statehood, but many doubted that the territory was ready to be admitted then. Noncontiguity of both Alaska and Hawaii would prove a stumbling block, he predicted. Historically, territoriality had been an imperfect and temporary form of government, he argued, and therefore had been tolerated.

The center of the report was a long article dealing with Congressional and executive discriminations against Alaska, chiefly in regard to appropriations. Statehood would end such treatment. Sundborg had listened long enough to his mentor, Gruening, and come to share his viewpoint, namely that Alaska never received a just share of federal dollars. The appropriation of highway funds furnished a good example. Under a succession of Federal Aid Highway acts, Congress had appropriated billions of dollars for the construction of primary and secondary road systems in the contiguous states, the District of Columbia, Hawaii and Puerto Rico. Each state's maximum dollar amount was based one-third on its area, one-third on its mileage of rural delivery and star routes, and one-third on its population. No state received less than one-half of one percent of the total Congressional appropriation. To obtain any of this allotment, however, a state had to match federal funds, usually on a dollar-for-dollar basis. In any state in which more then five percent of the area consisted of unappropriated or unreserved public or nontaxable Indian lands, the federal share increased by the percentage which the lands bore to the total area of the state. These public and Indian lands comprised approximately 73 percent of Alaska's area in 1953. Under the prevailing formula, the state would have had to pay about 14 percent of the cost of constructing each mile of federal-aid primary or secondary highway, while the federal government would have paid the remaining 86 percent of the cost.[18] Sundborg argued that if only one-half of Alaska's land area had been computed in the formula, the territory would have received about $160,000,000 in road building funds since 1930; in reality, the department of the interior had spent a piddling $25,511,773 for both construction and maintenance during this period, and of this amount, $2,198,805 had come from the Alaska Fund.

Sundborg made a good point, but he failed to mention that few states had been able to raise sufficient matching funds to receive their full appropriations. Furthermore, federal funds could only be used for construction, not maintenance. The territorial gasoline tax did not raise sufficient revenues for either new construction or maintenance.

In the national forests the Bureau of Public Roads built highways. Again, Alaska had often not been allotted its formula share, but the territory also had not been required to maintain these roads, a privilege not applicable to the contiguous states.[19]

The U.S. Maritime Act, commonly called the Jones Act after its sponsor, Senator Wesley Jones from Washington State, had long annoyed northern residents. The purpose of the act was to build up the American Merchant Marine, but it also restricted Alaskan commerce. All ships engaged in commerce between American ports had to be carried in American-owned and American-built ships. A clause in the act gave shippers the option of using either American- or Canadian-owned forms of transportation in carrying goods from a point of origin in the United State out to any destination on the Atlantic or Pacific oceans, with the single exception of Alaska. Merchandise entering or leaving the territory had to be transported by American carriers. The Jones Act was clearly discriminatory; but as the Supreme Court noted in *Alaska v. Troy*, a suit initiated by the territory in protest, the Constitution of the United States makes clear "that no preference shall be given any regulation of commerce or revenue to the parts of one state over those of another."[20] Since Alaska was not a state, Congress was free to regulate its commerce as it saw fit. That the provisions of the

George Sundborg, Sr.

Architects of Statehood

George Sundborg, Sr.

George Sundborg, Sr. was born on March 25, 1913 in San Francisco, California.

He began his journalistic career in 1934 as the city editor for the *Grays Harbor Washingtonian* in Hoquiam, Washington. He came to Alaska in 1938 and was a reporter and editorial writer for the *Daily Alaskan Empire* and editor of the *Juneau Independent* and later the *Fairbanks Daily News-Miner*.

Sundborg also worked for several months for the North Pacific Planning Project which conducted postwar planning for the entire region. He was Supervisor of the Alaska Merit System from 1940-1941, and general manager of the Alaska Development Board, 1946-47 and 1951-53.

In 1946 the Alaska Statehood Association hired him to research and write a report on the pros and cons of Alaska statehood for a referendum in the 1946 General Election. The 56-page pamphlet was widely distributed as a newspaper supplement. Alaskans voted 3 to 2 for statehood.

Sundborg was one of 55 delegates elected to Alaska's Constitutional Convention and served as the chair of the Committee on Style and Drafting. He served as Senator Gruening's legislative assistant until 1969 and then as Congressional liaison for the U.S. Department of the Interior from 1969-73. He is the author of *Opportunity in Alaska* (1945) and *Hail Columbia* (1954).

At age 95 he lives in a retirement home in Seattle.

Maritime Act most benefitted Seattle, Senator Jones' home city, was not for the court to decide.

There were other instances of Congressional discrimination, but the executive slighted Alaska as well. For example, it took a long time to get a regional office of the Veterans Administration located in Alaska. Before that, lengthy delays occurred because authorization for hospitalization had to be obtained from the Seattle regional office. Another example concerned the International Halibut Commission which regulated the catch off the coasts of Washington, British Columbia and Alaska. The territory had no representative on that body, although the lion's share of the halibut harvest came from territorial coastal waters.

Sundborg also addressed the shortcomings of the Organic Act of 1912 and the restrictions it had imposed upon territorial government. Economic development depended on Congressional action, but that body had rarely acted in a positive fashion. The United States had taken possession of Alaska seventy-nine years ago; only Montana, the Dakotas, Wyoming, and Oklahoma, had waited for statehood longer than Alaska. Critics often mentioned the territory's small population. Sundborg wrote that Arkansas, Florida, Missouri, Nevada, Oregon, and Wyoming had been admitted with a smaller population than Alaska boasted in 1946. Most newly admitted states had gained in population after admission; and while much of this influx was attributable to the general western migration, some of it also was due to the attention statehood had brought. Alaska had a total of 72,524 residents in 1939. Sundborg estimated that this number would grow to 100,000 by 1955, more than qualifying the territory for statehood.

Sundborg estimated that the statehood process would take a few years. Therefore, he admonished his readers not to ask whether or not the territory was ready for statehood now in the upcoming referendum, but rather "am I in favor of statehood in principle, and if so, might Alaska be ready for statehood within the foreseeable future?" He warned that "anything less than decisive approval" at the coming referendum would probably "bury all hopes of statehood for many years to come." In fact, it would probably create a distinctly unfavorable climate toward Alaska's needs and problems both in Congress and nationwide, for it would signify the territory's unwillingness to should adult responsibilities after so many years of territorial apprenticeship.

Those opposing statehood always pointed to the increased expenses. Sundborg conceded that state government was not cheap as the earlier examples of Arizona and New Mexico had shown. He estimated the annual net cost of statehood at about $1,995,000, including $680,000 for the judiciary; $250,000 for the state police and $300,000 for the care of the insane; some $350,000 for the management of the fish and game resources and only $40,000 for the office of the governor and secretary; a mere $25,000 for the legislature, and another $350,000 for the maintenance and amortization of a state capital and any other buildings which might eventually be required.

Sundborg listed several new income sources which might cover the cost of statehood. For example, state courts would collect revenue since they would assume most of the judicial business of the existing United States district courts. During the preceding decade, the federal system had collected an average of about $337,957 a year in fees and various other receipts. Sundborg also suggested that the federal share of the net proceeds of the Pribilof Islands fur seal harvest, which had averaged more than $500,000 a year during the same decade, could well go to the state. Another source of income would accrue to the state by disposing of a portion of its Congressional land grant. Sundborg thought that the new state would most certainly revamp the tax system and for the first time collect equitable revenues from the non-resident fishing, mining and transportation businesses. In short, looking at the potential financial picture Alaskans had to ask themselves if they could afford not to gain statehood.

With statehood, land would become available for settlement and the extraction of resources, he predicted. Furthermore, Alaskans should ask the federal government to make lands available for settlement and economic development in the Tongass and Chugach national forests. Finally, Alaskan management of its game and fisheries was certain to increase revenues from these important resources.

In conclusion, Sundborg stated that historically the absentee interests had always fought a greater measure of self-government for the territory. Opposition to statehood, however also came from sourdoughs and many businessmen who feared a change in the status quo. He predicted that all of the faults statehood was designed to cure would become progressively worse until Alaska was admitted as an equal to the Union of States. Now was the time to start on the long road to statehood.

Sundborg's work was the only comprehensive analysis on the effects of statehood available to voters, and for years it remained the authoritative reference work for the statehood forces. The report, in addition to debates, speeches, meetings, and radio broadcasts, stimulated broad public interest. In the final weeks before the October 1946 referendum, the Alaska Statehood Association sold buttons to raise additional money in order to pay Sundborg and cover the printing cost.[21]

Those Alaskans who went to the polls in the general election in October 1946 were acutely aware of the statehood issues and the attending national attention focused on the territory. Amidst much campaigning and publicity, they reelected delegate Bartlett by a vote of 11,516 to 4,868 over his Republican opponent Almer Peterson. The statehood referendum was approved by a margin of three to two, or 9,630 to 6,822 votes.[22]

Alaskans, like Americans everywhere, desired equality, representation in Congress, and full participation in their government. The referendum results in each judicial division also told much about the old and the new Alaska, about the transformation the territory was undergoing as a result of the war and the new emphasis on defense. In the first judicial division (Southeastern Alaska) the vote was 66 percent in favor and 34 percent against statehood (3,872 to 1,953). Sentiment in this, the territory's most economically advanced part, ran high on the statehood issue, because whatever else statehood might do, it promised to transfer the control of the fishery resources to Alaska. The strength of this sentiment is indicated by the votes in the various towns in this region as shown in Table 1.[23]

TABLE 1
VOTES IN SOUTHEASTERN ALASKA IN THE
1946 STATEHOOD REFERENDUM

Town	For Statehood	Against Statehood
Ketchikan	765	253
Juneau	783	558
Sitka	213	160
Wrangell	152	61
Petersburg	249	57
Skagway	152	67

The third judicial division approved statehood by 60 percent to 40 percent (3,427 to 2,257). Anchorage, a town of 4,229 inhabitants in 1940 and of 11,254 in 1950, approved 66 percent to 34 percent (1,424 to 707). Anchorage was a new town by Alaskan standards. It got its start in 1915 with the construction of the Alaska Railroad. It was the territory's only planned city, and unlike other communities, had not developed around the exploitation of one of the territory's natural resources, such as fish, minerals, or forest products. Instead, its location had become a defense resource. During the Second World War the two largest military bases in the territory had been installed there. Consequently, Anchorage had become a boom town which attracted many newcomers who sought the high wages and opportunities offered by military construction and other government spending. It also quickly became the busiest community in Alaska and contained more new arrivals than any of the other territorial towns or settlements. Many of these war and postwar emigrants from the lower forty-eight States were determined to make Anchorage a modern community. They soon felt the limitations of the Organic Act of 1912. Victor Fischer, one such new resident, recalled, "it was just a preposterous situation; the municipalities were in effect governed by the United States Congress which couldn't care less about Alaska or municipal problems."[24] Thus the city soon became the center for the modern statehood movement.

In the second judicial division 56 percent voted against statehood and 44 percent voted for it (742 to 933). In Nome, the largest city in this division, the story was similar. Here 49 percent voted for statehood and 51 percent against (1,589 to 1,679). Fairbanks, the largest city in this division, went on record in favor of statehood by 737 to 584 votes. Geographically, these two divisions were remote and climatically harsh. The second division embraced the northern areas of Alaska while the fourth division constituted the interior. Nome depended on gold mining and government employment for its livelihood. This helps explain the fairly even division of the vote, because, for instance, the mining interests opposed statehood out of fear of higher taxes. Fairbanks had some gold mining, but the military was becoming the most important economic factor. It therefore was experiencing, although on a much smaller scale, the same influx of newcomers that Anchorage was undergoing. Both Nome and Fairbanks were supply centers for a vast "bush area" inhabited by Indians, Eskimos, and sourdoughs. The first two groups did not participate to any extent in political life. Delegate Bartlett explained the vote of the sourdoughs when he states that they disliked "all the change and commotion that came about in 1940 when the Army started to arm Alaska...; they would rather go back to ...the good old days." George Sundborg, manager of the Alaska Development Board, explained that the negative vote was due to "the sourpuss branch of the sourdough family."[25]

The total vote in the territory had not had not been large. But taking as a base the 1940 census, which listed a population of 72,524 for Alaska, a turnout of 16,384 voters amounted to a respectable 23 percent of the total population. This compared with a high of 47 percent for New Mexico and a low of 2 percent and 1 percent for Mississippi and South Carolina, respectively.[26]

The statehood referendum had reaffirmed the leadership of Gruening and Bartlett. After the October elections, the movement gathered momentum. The Department of the Interior not only pledged to support the movement but also to work closely with Bartlett; and President Truman continued to back Alaska's aspirations. In March of 1947, the Ketchikan Central Labor Council and the American Federation of Labor Unions and Councils of Alaska sponsored a special Alaska statehood and international development edition prepared by the *Ketchikan Alaska Chronicle*. Statehood and self-government, the sponsors stated, were not debatable. Among the many other benefits to be derived would be lower freight rates, because two senators and one representative could have the objectionable and discriminatory Maritime Act of 1920 amended. British Columbia, which stood to gain from such a change, also approved of Alaska statehood and showed it by contributing heavily to the special edition.[27]

At the same time the other Alaska statehood proponents were also at work. They presented admission to the Union as a panacea which would cure the various social and economic ills of the territory, such as a sparse population, inadequate social services, deficient venture and development capital, and poor transportation and communications. Support from the contiguous United States stressed Alaska's key position in the American defensive system. The Japanese invasion of Kiska and Attu during the Second World War was vividly recalled. The possibility of an Alaskan Pearl Harbor with far more serious consequences was to be avoided at all costs.[28]

Although three statehood bills had been submitted to Congress between 1943 and 1946, the exigencies of war had helped prevent their consideration. By 1947, however, Alaska's role in that conflict and in the Cold War generated some support for statehood among Americans in the contiguous United States and members of Congress. Delegate Bartlett therefore introduced a statehood bill on January 3, 1947. This measure was substantially identical to the one he had introduced in 1945 and to the Dimond bill of 1943. However, Bartlett now enlarged the public land grant to the prospective state. He proposed to withdraw from reserve and give to Alaska the Aleutian Islands west of the 172nd meridian west longitude, the Pribilof Islands and all the lands with adjacent waters, and other property set aside or reserved for the use of benefit of the Indians, Eskimos, and Aleuts.[29]

Public hearings on the Bartlett bill before the House Subcommittee on Territorial and Insular Possessions were held in Washington, D.C. between April 16 and 24, 1947. On the first day of the proceedings, Acting Secretary of the Interior Warner W. Gardner recommended the enactment of the statehood measure. He objected, however, to sections 3, 4; and 5 which, with few exceptions, would have transferred to the new state title to practically all public lands. This, he stated, was contrary to the traditional practice which had been followed throughout the American West. Lands had always been granted for schools and internal improvements, but the bulk had been retained by the federal government. Gardner proposed to grant to Alaska about 21,000,000 acres for schools, about 438,000 acres for the university, and another 500,000 acres for various internal improvements.[30]

Garner also objected that Native rights were not protected in the measure. He proposed that the state and its people forever disclaim both the right and title to all land retained by or ceded to the federal government by the statehood bill and to all land owned or held by Natives or Native "tribes, the right or title to which shall have been acquired through or from the United States or any prior sovereignty...." Until the United States either disposed of or extinguished title to such land, it would remain within the exclusive jurisdiction of the federal government and not be taxable by the state. Not only had the Department of the Interior sought such a guarantee of Native rights, but also James Curry, an abrasive Washington, D.C. lawyer for the National Congress of American Indians and the Alaska Native Brotherhood. In fact, Curry stated that the Natives would oppose the statehood bill unless it properly protected their rights.[31] Statehood proponents did not object to the protection of Native rights, but found that the various federal departments as well as conservation groups in the contiguous United States opposed these proposed land grants.

Numerous Alaskans flew to Washington, D.C. to testify in the hearings, and the majority of them spoke in favor of the statehood bill. There were representatives from chambers of commerce, small businessmen, editors and publishers of newspapers, sourdoughs, and federal and territorial officials. Also, some non-Alaskans who supported the movement appeared before the subcommittee. Bartlett, as a member of the subcommittee, made full use of his privilege of questioning the witnesses. He skillfully used the friendly ones to strengthen the statehood case. Among the less friendly witnesses there were some who approved of statehood in principle but said that Alaska was not yet ready. One of these was Herbert L. Faulkner, an attorney and a long-time resident of Juneau. He praised the Bartlett bill, then introduced a formidable array of statistics and detailed information, all designed to totally demolish the case for statehood. The gist of his argument was that Alaska simply would be financially unable to afford statehood. On being pressed by Bartlett, Faulkner admitted that as a lawyer he represented some of the canneries, the largest mining company, a few lumber concerns, and a bank and a telephone business, but he asserted that on this occasion he was representing only himself.[32]

Representative Arthur Miller, a conservative Republican from Kimball, Nebraska who had visited Alaska in 1945 with the House Committee on the Territories, brought up the subject of partition. He suggested that perhaps only the southern one-third of the territory ought to be admitted to the Union. Although all of Alaska was ready for statehood, its vast size would present almost impossible administrative problems in the rest of the area. Representative Mike

Mansfield, a Montana Democrat, reminded Miller that modern methods of communications had alleviated the problems of size, while territorial Attorney General Ralph Rivers observed that territorial administration already extended throughout Alaska. Robert Atwood, the editor and publisher of the *Anchorage Daily Times* testified that partition had already been widely discussed in Alaska and been rejected in principle. If there had to be partition to gain statehood, he suggested that the Yukon River be the boundary.[33]

When Congressmen asked Governor Gruening his opinion about partition, he indicated that, if necessary, any partition should be made either along the Yukon River of the 64th or 65th parallel. There should be a prior understanding, however, that the territory of Tundra should be allowed to join the State of Alaska. Bartlett shared the governor's attitude. He had previously told Gruening that, although he had formerly resisted partition, he had now concluded that if partition was a prerequisite for statehood "I think I would be ready to go along."[34]

Territorial Senator Edward Coffey, an Anchorage Democrat, asked the subcommittee to wait before reporting the measure. He complained that only a few, privileged individuals, mostly government officials who spent public funds for travel to Washington, represented Alaska at the statehood hearings. Alaska's common people, he charged, were hardly represented at all. In addition, he charged, "these public officials, and their representatives, are for statehood under any circumstances" and therefore had little, if any, regard for the kind of provisions Alaskans desired in an enabling act. Coffey had his wish, for eight days after the hearings ended, subcommittee members voted 8-5 to defer reporting the measure until after they had visited Alaska personally.[35]

Hawaii's statehood bill fared much better. The full house voted on the measure on June 30, 1947 and passed it 195-133. That was the first time statehood for either territory had advanced so far. As a result, there was much optimism among statehood advocates.[36]

The House Subcommittee on Territories and Insular Possessions went to Alaska in the early fall of 1947. Of its twenty

members, however, only Bartlett and four Republicans, Fred
Crawford of Michigan, Jay LeFevre of New York, William Dawson of Utah, and Edward Jenison of Illinois, made the trip.
During August 30 to September 12, the subcommittee heard testimony from ninety-two individuals at various Alaskan towns.
At Anchorage, the members found the sentiment for statehood
overwhelmingly favorable. James Wooten, Alaska Airlines' new
president, talked at length about the federal neglect of the territory. Within the next three days, six different people contacted
him and told him that the canned salmon industry disapproved of
his position. Worse, his aggressiveness in the matter, he was told,
would seriously injure his standing with the industry. Alaska Airlines took in approximately $400,000 of cannery travel business
during the fishing season. Shortly before Wooten was to speak
to Senator Hugh Butler's group, the other Congressional group
visiting Alaska, Winton C. Arnold, managing director of Alaska
Salmon Industry, Inc. (a trade organization) and representative of
the powerful Alaskan fishing interests, informally talked to Wooten. Arnold, an affable and knowledgeable lawyer, had gained the
appellation of "Judge" in the 1920's in Hyder, a small silver boom
town at the southeastern tip of Alaska. In 1933, the redoubtable Judge became the Alaska attorney for the cannery operators
and shortly thereafter moved his offices and residence to Seattle.
Although he still lived in that city, Arnold was reputedly the most
powerful man in Alaska because of his influence on the territorial
legislature. In Juneau, where he scrupulously paid his ten-dollar
lobbying fee, he supposedly exerted so much pressure that he was
credited with killing basic tax reforms from 1939 until 1949, when
the legislature finally enacted a basic property and income tax.
Arnold allegedly also used his influence on legislation which dealt
with fishing methods and controls over the fishing industry.[37]

Arnold told Wooten that his position was unwise, because he
was a relatively uninformed newcomer to the territory, and his air-
line also might want to serve the canned-salmon industry. Wooten
ignored Arnold's advice and testified before the Senators, telling

them that he did not sympathize with the salmon industry which paid only a small part of its substantial income in the form of taxes to the territory. In Seattle, Doug Sherrif of the Alaska Packers' Association and Loren Daley, Jr. of the Bristol Bay Packing Company, confronted Wooten and informed him that "you're sticking your neck out of mile, and if you expect to get any of the canned salmon industry business, you sure in hell had better change your position and keep your mouth shut."[38]

Wooten complained about the incident to Representative Crawford and offered to repeat the story in the form of an affidavit. Crawford informed his fellow subcommittee members about the affair, but they overruled his wish to include the letter in the record. Thereupon Crawford released it to the Alaskan press, which, for the most part, gave it headline treatment.[39]

In Seward, the ocean terminus of the Alaska Railroad, they heard relatively little about statehood as such; instead the witnesses concentrated on denouncing the Seattle shipping monopoly and the outrageous prevailing freight rates. In Fairbanks, Al Anderson, secretary of the Alaska Miner's Association, stated his opposition to statehood in terms of the added costs involved. Norman Stines, a Fairbanks resident, complained that the hearing seemed to be packed with statehood advocates. These people, he continued, always claimed to be objective about the issue. Statehood opponents, he concluded, were always labeled as paid agents of the "absentee" owners by the same disinterested and objective individuals. Mrs. Alaska Linck, pioneer resident of the city as well as a past member of the territorial house, was perhaps typical of the "sourdough opposition" to statehood. She said that Delegate Dimond had submitted his statehood bill in 1943 to create new bureaus and agencies, curb individual freedom, and stifle free enterprise and individual industry. She told subcommittee members how she had watched the movement spread, in part though the efforts of the Alaska Statehood Association, but that she had not participated. To be opposed to the movement, Mrs. Linck stated, was not easy because the "anti-statehood" label had become a derogatory one.

She maintained that newcomers did not understand what Alaska needed, and that veterans had been won over by rosy promises of what statehood would accomplish for them. The "New Dealers," she declared in conclusion, were for statehood because they believed in spending now and burdening future generations with unpaid bills.[40]

It was also at Fairbanks that Winton Arnold, the most formidable witness against statehood, was heard. He appeared briefly at Fairbanks and again in Juneau and Ketchikan. His approach in each instance was disarming; never did he come out publicly against statehood. He contended that it was a logical and laudable ambition for Alaskans to aspire to statehood. But he disagreed with those who advertised it as a panacea for all Alaska's problems. Throughout his testimony he hammered at the territory's inability to pay for the increased burdens of statehood. He pointed out that land grants to the new state would overlap aboriginal claims and come into conflict with the reservation policies inaugurated by the Department of the Interior. Whatever the legal complexities, he advised the subcommittee, the Native land issue should be settled once and for all by the federal government before any steps were taken on statehood.[41]

From Fairbanks the subcommittee members made short trips to Barrow, Nome, Kodiak, and Cordova and then flew on to Juneau. There Delegate Bartlett and Mildred Hermann, a lawyer who had been the director of the Office of Price Administration in the territory during the war, critically examined statehood costs Herbert L. Faulkner and Allen Shattuck had submitted. Economist George Rogers had compiled the estimates which Mrs. Hermann gave the Congressmen. It listed the many shortcomings of the territorial tax system, and pointed out where additional revenues could be gained. It certainly gave the subcommittee members a more balanced view of the costs of statehood and of ways of meeting them.[42]

From Juneau the Congressmen traveled to Petersburg, Wrangell, and Ketchikan. In the latter town Governor Gruening delivered a persuasive address on statehood. He complimented the Congressmen on their diligent efforts to learn about Alaska. Once back in Washington, D.C., however, he warned, they would be overwhelmed by national problems and those concerning their own constituencies. It would be next to impossible to transfer their Alaskan impressions to their numerous colleagues, and Alaska would inevitably take a backseat. After eight years under the American flag, Alaska still was without adequate roads, airfields, tuberculosis hospitals, and dependable shipping at reasonable cost. The aboriginal rights issue had not been settled, nor the acquisition of land by homesteaders facilitated. These things had not been done in the past nor would they be accomplished in the future, because of "the system by which distant and changing personnel in Congress and in the executive agencies tries through the complexities of government, to help us without giving us the essential tools... to help ourselves. Those tools are two United States Senators and a Representative in the house with a vote."[43]

Gruening continued by citing numerous examples of Congressional and executive neglect and administration. The governor's eloquence impressed the subcommittee members. Bill Baker of the *Ketchikan Alaska Chronicle*, who admired Gruening, later wrote that the governor had "the tongue of the spellbinder, the logic of Socrates and much of the charm of the late FDR. He has a way of making things seem important and getting others to see them that way."[44] Subcommittee members who had come to Alaska agreed with the principle of statehood but had doubted that Alaskans could finance it. They left the territory with much new information, including facts about Alaska's economic potential and possibilities for gaining increased revenue once the tax system had been modernized.

Gruening had divided his time between the subcommittee and four members of the Senate Public Lands Committee. Butler, who was to take an inordinate interest in Alaska, was a Republican from Omaha, Nebraska. He had amassed a fortune in the flour-milling and grain business. He opposed statehood for any offshore area. In 1946, a delegation of Puerto Ricans attending a meeting of the

Republican National Committee had called on Butler and told him that they wanted statehood. Butler was not sympathetic, telling reporters that he would "never vote for statehood for any offshore area, at least not until the people of this country have been thoroughly educated to the responsibilities that would involve." After the House passed the Hawaii statehood bill in June 1947, a reporter asked Butler what chance the measure had in the Senate. The Senator doubted that the bill could be considered before early 1948, but he advised that his proposal to make Hawaii a county of California should be considered.[45]

Butler's attitude toward Alaska, a part of the North American landmass, became apparent during his visit to the territory. Butler did not intend to hold formal hearings but merely encourage anyone to visit and talk about Alaska's problems. Once in Alaska, the Senators worked hard and held hearings although no record of them was printed. While in Anchorage, Butler declined to commit himself on statehood until a measure came before his committee. On his way back to the states, the Senator stopped in Prince Rupert and told G. Alex Hunter, the editor of the *Prince Rupert Daily News* that Alaska would probably gain statehood in less than ten years, but first the territorial legislature would have to enact a modern tax system.[46]

The 1947 hearings on the statehood bill were important because they placed the issue squarely before Congress. Most of the arguments on both sides were brought into the open. Perhaps most important, the opposition had been ably represented by Al Anderson and Judge Arnold. But also the pro-statehood cause had gained new strength and dimension. By 1948 the increased vigor and enthusiasm for statehood were apparent. The *Anchorage Daily Times* and the *Ketchikan Alaska Chronicle,* as well as *The Alaska Weekly* of Seattle, were lending their editorial voices in support of the cause. Many private citizens were at work as well. Mildred Hermann, president of the Alaska Women's Club, the first woman lawyer in Alaska and an ardent feminist of the old school, assumed a leadership role in Juneau. Ralph J. Rivers of Fairbanks and William A. Egan, territorial senator from Valdez, spent even more time and

William A. Egan

Architects of Statehood

William A. Egan

William A. Egan was born October 8, 1914 in Valdez, Alaska. He held various jobs, including truck driver, bartender, gold-miner, fisherman, and pilot.

Egan served in the U.S. Army Air Corps from 1943 to 1946. On his return to Valdez he became the proprietor of a general merchandise store. He served in the territorial house between 1941 and 1945 and again from 1947 to 1953. Elected to the territorial senate he served one term.

In 1955 fellow constitutional convention delegates chose Egan to preside over their deliberations. He presided with a combination of firmness, fairness, and humor which helped weld a group of comparative strangers into a body of friends and co-workers, united by their mutual respect and common purpose.

Alaskans elected Egan as one of the two Alaska-Tennessee Plan U.S. Senators, and Alaskans elected him the first governor of the new state. There he faced the stupendous task, together with Hugh J. Wade, his secretary of state, of translating the provisions of the state constitution into working political institutions.

Egan served two terms as governor, and then after an interlude of four years, served a third term.

He died on May 6, 1984 at age 69 from lung cancer.

effort than before. Several prominent Tlingit families in southeastern Alaska and many other respected Alaskans, too numerous to mention, joined the movement.[47]

After the House Subcommittee on Territories and Insular Possessions had closed its voluminous Alaskan hearings, it met in Washington, D.C. in February 1948, to discuss Alaska statehood. It soon became apparent that the subcommittee did not agree with the Departments of the Interior and Agriculture on land grants to the new state in support of its schools. Interior insisted on two sections in each township, while the subcommittee and Delegate Bartlett held out for hour. There had been one change, though, for the Department of the Interior now recommended that the state be allowed to select the land from anywhere within the public domain. This was ideal for Alaska, since the state would not have to accept thousands, or even millions of acres covering glaciers, mountains, and tundra. Eventually, an impasse developed, and the delegate was instructed to meet with Interior and Agriculture officials and work out a compromise, which, together with subcommittee amendments, would be incorporated into a new bill. On March 2, 1948, Bartlett submitted such a statehood bill. Two days later the subcommittee approved the new measure, and in April the House Committee on Public Lands unanimously approved the delegate's bill, reporting it with amendments. The committee report briefly discussed the history of Alaska and the territory's inadequate governmental structure and discounted the arguments that Alaska could not support statehood. Instead, the committee member suggested a number of new revenue sources, expressed the conviction that statehood would attract new settlers, and disposed of the argument of noncontiguity as of little importance in the age of modern transportation.[48]

On April 14, 1948, the new statehood bill was reported to the House but was then bottled up in the Rules Committee. Despite a special message from President Truman and a resolution introduced by California's Senator William F. Knowland and on behalf of Hawaii,[49] Senator Hugh Butler, chairman of the Senate Interior and Insular Affairs Committee, refused to allow either the Alaska or Hawaii statehood bills to come up for discussion and debate.

As a result, Alaska statehood died as far as that particular session of Congress was concerned. But the defeat was not decisive or even a major one. For while the Bartlett bill had been debated in the various committees, it was given wide circulation in Alaska newspapers and through Delegate Bartlett's newsletter to his territorial constituents. Bartlett had traveled widely in Alaska and discussed the details of his efforts. In addition, the national press had given considerable attention to the issue. There were many reasons to be optimistic, among them the fact that hearings on Alaska statehood had been held for the first time and that statehood measure had been approved unanimously by a committee of Congress.

Controlling the
Special Interests

Time and again since the first territorial legislature met in 1913 attempts were made to establish a basic and adequate tax system to meet the needs of Alaska, but always without success. Instead, the territory limped along with the inadequate system of license fees and levies which had been established in 1899. Yet, the modern statehood movement could not expect success until Alaska set its own house in order. It must break the influence of the special interests, which, as primary taxpayers, had worked strenuously against anything which would bring self-determination for Alaska a step closer or increase the tax level.

Spurred on by the financial needs of the New Deal period, Governor John W. Troy asked the territorial planning council to make a tax study in the late 1930's. The research was not completed until Troy was replaced by Governor Ernest Gruening. The authors of the report concluded that annual revenue of $10,000,000 was entirely feasible. They recommended the adoption of a modern tax system, and urged that the revenue obtained by invested in a soundly planned and economically executed program of permanent improvements such as roads, schools, hospitals, and public buildings.[1]

It was this tax reform plan which Governor Gruening presented to the 1941 session of the territorial legislature. The study proposed to abolish all obsolete mercantile and license fees, to establish a very modest income and profits tax, and, in addition, to place a nominal levy on property outside of incorporated towns. The legislature not only soundly defeated the Governor's proposal, but also abolished the territorial planning council which had formulated this plan. The defeat was blamed on the mining and canning lobbyists, led by Winton C. Arnold.[2] The legislature, and indirectly the people, were not yet ready to bite the hand that seemed to feed them. The exploitative resource industries still held the threat of total withdrawal of livelihood over many Alaskans.

In the meantime, the estimated value of the combined physical properties of these industries had grown to more then a half billion dollars by the 1940's. Even a modest tax of one percent on these assets would have produced five million dollars annually. In addition, the federal government spent an estimated three billion dollars in Alaska during the war. A small levy on the profits of the contractors and a modest income tax on the salaries of defense workers would have produced a great deal of revenue. But instead, territorial appropriations barely took care of the most pressing needs. Biennial expenditures between 1933 and 1947 were exceedingly small when compared with the potentially available financial resources:

TABLE 2
BIENNIAL APPROPRIATIONS

1935-1935- $2,133,662.67
1937-1937- $2,563,500.00
1939-1939- $3,074,930.00
1941-1941- $3,511,510.00
1943-1943- $4,496,932.00
1945-1945- $4,335,861.39
1947-1947- $5,631,822.00[3]

In 1947, journalist Richard L. Neuberger described Alaska as a feudal barony where the absentee-owned mining and fishing corporations took out millions in natural resources and left next to nothing behind in the form of social and economic benefits. The following year he referred to the territory as the "looted land." Of the 434 fish traps licensed by the Department of the Interior, Neuberger stated, only 38 belonged to Alaskan residents, while 245 were owned and operated by 8 large canning companies. In 1946, a representative year, the value of the fish pack amounted to $56,571,000, on which the industry paid a territorial tax of $630,000, or approximately 24 cents on each case of salmon (one case contained 48 one pound cans). The same year the fishing industry hired 10,956 Alaskans, to whom it paid $3,729,000 in wages. A work force of 12,484 was brought north from the lower forty-eight states. These workers were paid $7,206,000 in wages, which, however, were not distributed to the laborers in Alaska but rather at the end of the season in a lump sum at the point of hire. Territorial merchants, therefore, did not derive any multiplying benefits from these wage dollars. In addition, two Seattle steamship lines, the Alaska Steamship Company and the Northland Transportation Company, both owned by the Skinner family of that city, monopolized the Alaskan trade. These same interests also operated a salmon brokerage. The fishing industry, preferred customers of the shipping monopoly, paid an average of $14.23 a ton for cannery supplies, while other Alaskan customers were charged $28.12 a ton for the transportation of food, staples, and general merchandise north.[4]

It was to the advantage of these interests to keep territorial government and the tax structure at a minimum. The same applied to many established Alaskan businessmen who turned the status quo to their profit. Among such individuals was Austin E. "Cap" Lathrop, Alaska's lone millionaire, and the Lomen brothers, Ralph and Carl, of Nome. Congressman Preston E. Peden of Oklahoma, a member of Subcommittee on Public Lands, told journalist Frank L. Kluckhohn of the *American Mercury* in 1949 that has he had recently dropped in on Lathrop. Peden stated to "Cap" that he favored statehood, whereupon Lathrop replied that if a statehood bill passed, he would immediately sell out for fifty cents on the dollar. When Kluckhohn related this information to Gruening, the governor declared to Kluckhohn that Lathrop's opposition was determined by his economic stake in territorial status. Lathrop paid no territorial taxes on his movie theaters in Fairbanks, Anchorage, and Cordova, but merely a $100 license fee to the municipalities in which they were located. The same was true of the two banks he owned, for which he paid only $250 each. There were no territorial taxes on his two newspapers, two radio stations, and assorted apartment houses, Gruening stated. Lathrop operated a coal company, and there he paid an assessment of less than one cent per ton, which he passed on to his customers. The same advantages were enjoyed by the Lomen brothers, the governor continued, who had monopoly on the lighterage business and paid no taxes whatsoever. These persons and others, according to Gruening, had all lobbied against the basic tax program and statehood because they feared that their privileged position would be destroyed.[5]

The general aim of this combined special interest lobby was a negative one, designed to defeat all measures which would increase governmental costs and to kill any moves which would allow Alaska more control over its natural resources. All that was needed to achieve this objective was a tie vote in one of the two houses of the territorial legislature. The senate was perfect for this strategy with its sixteen members, four from each one of the four judicial divisions regardless of population. The lobby had to control only eight votes out of a total of forty in both houses. Four of the senators were elected from the sparsely settled second judicial division by fewer than 1,000 voters around Nome who depended for a living upon the United States Smelting and Refining Company.[6] The task of the lobby was not a very difficult one under such conditions.

Governor Gruening, who battled these forces, later stated that the longstanding paralysis of the territorial legislature reached its climax in the 1947 session. In the face of Alaska's mounting needs for schools, hospitals, a new physical plant for the University of

Alaska, expanded health services, more assistance for the aged, and legislation to make airport construction possible, the legislature provided revenues of $6,500,000 as against a budget request of $10,500,000. The 1947 legislature, the Governor declared, was the worst in his experience. As a result, the incensed chief executive made a special report to the people of Alaska on the events which transpired during the 1947 session. At issue, he asserted, was whether the territory should be run for its citizens or continues to be governed for and by the large economic interest whose sole concern was the profit motive. He appealed to his fellow Alaskans to elect a legislature which would move the territory forward, presumably toward statehood.[7]

The territorial electorate responded by sending "the Republicans, who in the halls of the territorial legislature…had shown what they would do, what they could do, and what they did do… back to the sidelines."[8] The Governor was unfair in this assessment, because obstruction was not the monopoly of the Republicans alone. Many Democratic legislators had played the same game. In any event, in the 1948 general election the Democrats won control of both houses, and Bartlett was returned to Congress by the decisive margin of 17,520 to 4,789 votes over his Republican opponent R.H. Stock. For the delegate this was an affirmation of his statehood leadership. There also was a referendum on the ballot to determine whether or not Alaskans favored the continued use of fish traps, the symbol of absentee economic control. The vote was advisory in nature only, because these devices were regulated by the federal government. However, Alaskans answered with a resounding "no" of 19,712 to 2,624 "yes" votes. The highly emotional nature of this issue becomes apparent when the votes are broken down by judicial divisions. In the first judicial division, Southeastern Alaska, where the working force was heavily dependent on fishing, the vote was 7,179 against to 1,113 for. In the second judicial division, along the Arctic and Bering Seas, and in the fourth judicial division, the interior of Alaska—both areas where few people had ever seen traps—the tabulations were 1,151 against and 521 for, and 3,665 against and 438 for, respectively. In the third judicial division, which included Anchorage and Kodiak and which had a large and flourishing fishing industry, the vote was 7,727 against and 552 for.[9]

The 1948 election was a turning point for Alaska, because it indicated to the special interests that they would confront a totally different situation in the 1949 territorial legislative session. It signaled the onset of changes and reform. In effect, the legislature which met in Juneau early in 1949 set the territorial house in order and prepared Alaska for statehood.

This legislature adopted a comprehensive but moderate tax program which reached out to include businesses and individuals deriving their income from Alaska but had not been paying any taxes, or at best negligible ones. A territorial income tax was based on ten percent of the federal tax, which made computation of this levy fairly simple. A property tax of one percent was credited against the municipal and school district assessments, and thus duplication was avoided. At the same time the territorial legislature took over and streamlined the old system of license fees from the federal government. For each separate business an initial application fee of $25 was charged. Beyond the initial fee, a sum equal to one-half percent of gross receipts in excess of $20,000 and one-fourth percent above $100,000 received during the income year were to be remitted to the territory. This levy applied to those concerns which, so far, had paid no monies whatever to the Alaska territorial government. These included steamship companies, air and bus lines, lighterage companies, banks and motion picture theaters, oil and construction companies, garages and service stations, newspapers, radio stations, and logging operations. Professional registration, examination, and insurance levies were to be collected by the various professional boards. The tax on the fishing industry was changed from a case tax to one based on the wholesale value of the pack, amounting to four percent of the value of raw fish processed for salmon canneries to one percent of the value of raw material for herring processing plants. The territorial legislature increased fishermen's licenses from $1 to $5 for residents and from $25 to $50 for nonresidents. Fishing gear, such as traps, gill nets, and seines were also taxed. Excise taxes on liquor were raised, and establishments serving alcohol were regulated by fees which varied from $75 to $5,000, according to the type of business, the size of the town, or the volume of the business. In addition, the usual motor fuel taxes, vehicle and drivers' licenses, and tobacco and various miscellaneous taxes were modernized.[10]

Still another important achievement of the 1949 legislative season, in recognition of the popular demand for statehood, was the creation of the official Alaska Statehood Committee. The measure, Senate Bill 49, the number a symbol of the hope that the territory would become the forty-ninth state, was introduced by Senators Frank Peratrovich, the territory's outstanding Tlingit legislator, owner of a general store in Klawock, and president of the Alaska Native Brotherhood; and Victor C. Rivers of Anchorage, a construction engineer and brother of the territorial attorney general. The language of the bill was more indicative of hope than of existing reality at that time:

> *In recognition of near attainment of Statehood for Alaska and the responsibility that will devolve upon the people of Alaska in framing a fundamentally sound and workable state constitution embodying the best provisions that have evolved in the interest of better government in the several states, and in recognition of the many problems that will attend the transition from Territorial status to Statehood, it is deemed necessary in the public interest to establish a Committee, non-governmental in character, to assemble applicable material, make studies and provide recommendations in a timely manner.[11]*

The Alaska Statehood Committee was to accomplish a variety of tasks. It was to hire a qualified researcher who would also act as the executive of the committee and carry out its wishes. The committee was to prepare detailed information and analyses which would help the constitutional convention in drafting a constitution for Alaska; and it was to obtain studies and analyses which would enable the convention to recommend to the first state legislature those procedures necessary to launch the new state government. The committee also was to prepare information which would aid in the transition from territoriality to statehood, and assist the delegate in obtaining enactment of enabling legislation.[12]

The Alaska Statehood Committee was to consist of eleven Alaskans, nominated by the governor and approved by the legislature. As an indication of its bipartisan character, no more than six of the members could belong to the same party. In addition, Governor Gruening, Delegate Bartlett, and his immediate predecessor, ex-Delegate Anthony J. Dimond, were to be ex-officio members. For operating expenses, the legislature voted an appropriation of $80,000 for the committee.

Governor Gruening had the task of selecting at least two members from each of Alaska's four judicial divisions to satisfy regional pride and desire for recognition. Gruening also was determined to appoint one Indian and one Eskimo as well as one woman. He nominated from the first judicial division William L. Baker, a Democrat and the editor and publisher of the *Ketchikan Alaska Chronicle;* Mildred R. Hermann of Juneau, a Republican, one of Alaska's two women lawyers, a feminist, and former president of the territorial Federation of Women's Clubs; and Frank Peratrovich, a Democrat and Tlingit legislator from Klawock. From the second judicial division, he chose Howard Lyng of Nome, a Democrat, miner, and Democratic National Committeeman; and Percy Ipalook, a Republican and an Eskimo Presbyterian minister from Wales. Both were members of the territorial legislature. Gruening selected from the third judicial division Victor C. Rivers, a Democrat from Anchorage, an engineer and architect, and member of the territorial senate; Robert B. Atwood, a Republican of the same city and the editor and publisher of the *Anchorage Daily Times;* Stanley J. McCutcheon, a Democrat, also from Anchorage, an attorney, president of Alaska Airlines, and speaker of the house in the 1949 session; and Lee C. Bettinger, a Republican, mayor of Kodiak, and a businessman. From the forth judicial division, he named Andrew Nerland, a Republican, a businessman from Fairbanks, and a member of the territorial legislature; and Warren A. Taylor, a Democrat from the same city, an attorney, and a legislator who had served several sessions in the territorial house.[13]

Governor Gruening was also obligated to call a meeting of the Alaska Statehood Committee, but since the prospects for the passage of an enabling act looked so promising early in 1949, the governor postponed doing so. Only when it became apparent late in the summer of 1949 that no Congressional action on a statehood measure would be forthcoming did he summon the members of the committee. One of the first obstacles to this new statehood strategy arose when the territorial board of administration froze the $80,000 appropriation for the committee, along with other funds. This action was made necessary because the 1947 legislature had failed to provide the necessary revenue to meet the expenditures it had approved. Undeterred, the members of the committee advanced their own expenses and met in Juneau late in August of 1949 to organize and plan strategy. [14]

It soon became apparent that the road to statehood was still a tedious one. The main task of the Alaska Statehood Committee, it quickly developed, would consist of publicizing and educating the public on statehood both in Alaska and in the contiguous United States. In addition, the committee would have to mobilize expert witnesses for Congressional statehood hearings. One committee member, William L. Baker of Ketchikan, expressed the opinion that Alaska's strategic importance to the defense of the United States would have to be stressed to advance the cause of statehood. In order to generate widespread public support in the state, Baker continued, national labor and fraternal organizations, as well as prominent Americans, would have to be won over to the cause. He concluded that it might be useful to send Alaskan Natives to Washington to plead the territory's case. Other members of the committee disapproved of sending Indians, Eskimos, or Aleuts to Washington in the belief that such action would only stir up additional opposition among racially

Mildred Robinson Hermann

Architects of Statehood

Mildred Robinson Hermann

Mildred Robinson Hermann was born on February 28, 1891 in Indiana. She attended the Universities of Indiana and Washington and received an LL.B degree from LaSalle University through its correspondence program. Hermann began her law studies in James Wickersham's office. She was admitted to the Alaska bar in 1934. She married Russell Royden Hermann, a pharmacist, in Valdez on May 21, 1920. The couple had two children, Barbara Ann and Russell Royden, Jr. Hermann taught school in Yakima, Washington from 1910 to 1919 and in Valdez from 1919 to 1946. She served as president of the Alaska Federation of Women's Clubs from 1941 to 1944. Her husband died in 1944.

Mildred Hermann served for 24 years as the legislative chair of the AFWC. She reported on legislative activities through radio broadcasts and newspaper columns. She also edited the annual special edition of *Alaska Press*, analyzing the legislature. She served as secretary of the Alaska Statehood Committee which the legislature had created in 1949.

At a 1953 House meeting in Washington, D.C. Hermann told Congressmen that Alaska could afford the added annual net cost of statehood, namely $6,799,000.

biased members of Congress and perpetuate the belief that Alaska
was still living in Jack London's era. [15]

At its first meeting, the committee elected as its chairman Robert B. Atwood and named Mildred R. Hermann as secretary. It
also appointed four subcommittees, for education and public relations, legislation, constitution, and state organization. Governor
Gruening recommended the employment of public relations firm
in Washington to do lobbying on behalf of statehood, and suggested the names of a number of available firms. Delegate Bartlett
informed the members that the statehood bill, then buried in the
House Rules Committee, had an excellent chance of passage in the
House in 1950, but cautioned that the four leaders of the House
were adamantly opposed to Alaskan statehood and would have to
be won over. These four were Sam Rayburn of Texas, Joseph W.
Marin and John McCormack of Massachusetts, and Charles Halleck of Indiana. Bartlett urged the committee to organize letter
writing campaigns in the home states of those members of Congress who were opposed to statehood.[16]

After 1949 the Alaska Statehood Committee worked diligently
at its task. Individual members also utilized their association with
national organizations to advertise Alaskan statehood. For instance,
Mrs. Hermann gained the support of Mrs. Leslie B. Wright, legislative chairperson of the General Federation of Women's clubs,
who promised to put her organization squarely behind the Alaskan campaign. The success of these efforts became evident at the
1950 Senate hearings when numerous national groups, fraternal
organizations, labor unions, newspaper editors, and even state
governors testified in favor of the cause. It was Governor Gruening who developed the suggestion of establishing a committee of
distinguished Americans who would support the movement. The
governor capitalized on his experience, first as a newspaper man
and later as a government official in Washington. Through a letter writing campaign, he recruited a "committee of one-hundred"
prominent Americans who supported Alaska's aspirations. This
national committee consisted of citizens from all walks of life. They

included famous personalities such as Eleanor Roosevelt, Rear Admiral Richard E. Byrd, Arctic explorer Vilhjalmur Stefansson, actor James Cagney, novelists Rex Beach and Pearl S. Buck, author John Gunther, General Douglas MacArthur, philosopher Reinhold Niebuhr, and historians Arthur M. Schlesinger, Jr. and Jeannette Paddock Nichols.[17]

1949 was an important year in the Alaska statehood movement. The adoption of tax reform and the establishment of the Alaska Statehood Committee signified that the voting population, and with it the legislature, was at last determined to break the stranglehold of the special interests. From that time on attempts to gain statehood shifted increasingly to the national level and to Washington.

The Fight for Statehood Becomes National

While the territorial legislature was working out long-needed tax reforms in Alaska, Delegate Bartlett and his friends in the House and Senate again submitted some statehood bills in January of 1949. Bartlett's measure differed from his previous bills mainly in its scaled-down land grants. Instead of the 200,000,000 acres asked for in prior measures, he now proposed to transfer sections 2, 16, 32, and 36 in each township for the support of common schools, and section 33 in certain townships in the Tanana Valley for the support of the University of Alaska. In addition, 1,000,000 acres of vacant, inappropriate, and unreserved public lands were to pass to the new state for public buildings, asylums, penitentiaries, reformatories, and other such purposes. In case the particular sections allotted were subject to homestead or aboriginal claims, the state would be given the right of lieu selection, that is, the right to choose land elsewhere. Perfunctory hearings before the Subcommittee on Territorial and Insular Affairs of the House Committee on Public Lands were held in Washington on March 4 and 8, 1949. At that time the Secretaries of the Interior and Agriculture and a representative of the Department of Defense gave favorable testimony. Winton C. Arnold of the Alaska Salmon Industry, Inc., and Al Anderson, executive secretary of the Alaska Miners Association submitted written statements in which their objections, oddly enough, centered on the inadequacy of the land provisions in Bartlett's 1949 statehood bill. They also pointed out that aboriginal claims to Alaskan lands clouded any future title by the state.[1]

Despite these objections, the subcommittee reported the Bartlett measure favorably, and on March 10, the full Public Lands Committee recommended that the statehood bill be passed by the House. The brief report concluded that Alaska was ready for statehood and should be admitted immediately. The bill next went to the House Rules Committee which, however, took no action. Finally, the Public Lands Committee authorized its acting chairman, J. Hardin Peterson of Florida, to take the necessary steps to bypass the Rules Committee. This procedure for circumventing the Rules Committee was possible because on January 3 of that year, in the organization of the House, a reform was approved which barred the Rules Committee from holding for more then twenty-one days a measure which had been approved by one of the other committees. After a specified time period, the chairman of such a committee could move for a bill's consideration on the floor. Peterson took advantage of this reform and filed bypass resolutions for the statehood bills.[2]

On May 16, 1949 President Harry S. Truman and the Democratic House leaders met and selected ten priority bills, among them the Alaska statehood bill—but not the one for Hawaii. Representative Crawford observed that this was a strategic mistake, for the Republicans would never approve of the Alaska bill without the Hawaiian one. A couple of days later the House Rules Committee considered the Alaska measure but did not act on it. Rules Committee Chairman Adolph Sabbath of Illinois and House Speaker Sam Rayburn of Texas well remembered how the Republicans had forced the Hawaiian statehood bill to a House vote in 1947. The

Republicans on the Rules Committee told Sabbath that they would block the Alaska measure unless he agreed to act on the Hawaii bill as well. Sabbath, however, was adamantly opposed to the admission of Hawaii. Southern Congressmen who opposed the admission of both territories were gleeful about the impasse. Since they refused to commit themselves to report the Hawaii measure, the Republicans blocked action on the Alaska bill. Speaker Rayburn, however, did not give up easily, and a couple of months later he prodded the Rules Committee to act on the Alaska bill. The committee, thereupon, held a bitter debate on the statehood issue in July, and finally voted 8-4 to block the measure. Delegate Bartlett thought that the eight negative votes came from Republicans and southern Democrats. Bartlett and Peterson then asked for the Speaker's consent to employ the discharge procedure. Rayburn assented on the condition that the two obtain the agreement of Joseph Martin since the measure could not pass without Republican votes. Martin declined, but stated that he would gladly take up the issue in 1950. [3]

With Congressional action suspended on both statehood bills for 1949, the Hearst newspapers conducted a poll designed to measure support for Alaska and Hawaii statehood in the Senate and House. Asked about immediate statehood for Alaska, 32 Senators were in favor, 21 against, and 43 undecided, and in the House the figures were 171 in favor, 80 opposed and 182 undecided. The comparable figures for Hawaii in the Senate were 33-19-44, and in the House 196-84-153. These figures did not look bad at all, but Congress was eager to adjourn, and statehood proponents were unwilling, under the circumstances, to force a vote on the two measures. That ended the efforts to get the Alaska and Hawaiian bills to a vote.[4]

When Congress reconvened in 1950, both statehood bills were still held by the Rules Committee. Therefore, in early 1950, the House Public Lands Committee once again voted to bypass the Rules Committee and instructed its chairman, J. Hardin Peterson, to take the necessary steps. Speaker Sam Rayburn granted Hardin's request, and the Alaska statehood bill as well as the one for Hawaii came to the floor of the House. The former passed on March 3,

Winton C. Arnold

Architects of Statehood

Winton C. Arnold

Winton C. Arnold was born in 1903 in Walla Walla, Washington. He received a law degree from the University of Idaho in 1924. He moved to Alaska in 1927 and served as U.S Commissioner and Probate Judge in Hyder from 1927 to 1929.

In 1945, Arnold was appointed managing director of Alaska Salmon Industry, Inc. and moved to Seattle. In that job he served as the primary lobbyist for the canned salmon industry in Juneau and Washington, D.C. Because he once had been a commissioner, people generally referred to him as "Judge" Arnold. He was perhaps the most influential lobbyist in Alaska in the 1940s and 1950s.

Arnold became the most effective and articulate opponent of Alaska statehood. Statehood hearings before the U.S. Senate opened on April 24, 1950. Judge Arnold appeared before the committee on the fourth day with an elaborate exhibit of charts and graphs, maps designed to demonstrate the inadequacy of the statehood bill under discussion. His arguments ranged widely. He warned about the confusion that would result from aboriginal land claims. He asserted that less than 1 percent of Alaska's land area had been surveyed. He predicted it would take thousands of years before enough land had been surveyed to transfer title to the state of the acreage granted in the statehood bill.

Arnold's testimony raised questions in the minds of many senators about the adequacy of the traditional western public land state provisions in the case of Alaska. It led the Senate committee to abandon the traditional land grant formula. Instead of awarding Alaska sections 2, 16, 32 and 36 in each township, the proposed new state was granted the right to acquire unappropriated and unreserved lands best suited to its peculiar needs. Congress eventually granted Alaska the right to select 102,550,000 acres.

Arnold died at the Anchorage Pioneer Home in 1989.

1950 by a vote of 186 to 146, and the latter on March 7 by a margin of 262 to 111.[5]

Hawaii's statehood movement went back to 1903 when the territorial legislature had requested Congress to pass an enabling act and make it possible for the islands to adopt a state constitution and be admitted to the Union. It was not until 1935, however, that Congress gave serious consideration to Hawaiian statehood. At that time, the House Committee on Territories held hearings in Washington, and a subcommittee conducted an investigation in Hawaii. The committee, in its report, came to no definite conclusions. Hearings were also held in 1937 and 1946, again in Hawaii. In 1947, the focus shifted to Washington, and after still another inquiry into the matter, the House passed the Hawaiian measure in June of that year by a vote of 195 to 133. From that time until 1958, the Hawaii and Alaska statehood struggles were intertwined. Ernest Gruening asserts that partisanship in relation to statehood for both territories began in 1947 when House Speaker Joseph W. Martin of Massachusetts decided that Hawaii was likely to send a Republican Congressional delegation to Washington upon statehood, whereas Alaska probably would select Democrats. Hawaii's ambitions, therefore, received the Speaker's blessing, but the Alaska measure languished in the House Rules Committee.[6] In subsequent years, arguments based on noncontiguity, racial diversity, disproportionate Senate representation, and the precedent which might be set for other noncontiguous possessions were used against both Alaska and Hawaii.

In 1950, however, there was a great deal of optimism in Alaska because for the first time a statehood measure had passed in one house of Congress. Senate hearings on the Alaska measure were scheduled to begin in April before the Interior and Insular Affairs Committee in Washington. Governor Gruening lost no time in beginning his efforts to sway opinions and change attitudes. Early in April he wrote to Governor Vail Pittman of Nevada and asked him to use his influence with Senator George W. Malone, a Nevada Republican and ardent opponent of statehood. Gruening argued that Malone, as a Westerner, should consider it an honor to help bring not only Alaska into the Union but Hawaii as well. If words alone were not enough, Gruening suggested, Governor Pittman should "build a fire behind him [Malone] and get various organizations in Nevada to communicate with him." Pittman speedily complied with Gruening's request when he pointed out to Malone that the addition of one Representative and two Senators from Alaska would be highly advantageous to the Western block of states.[7] At the same time Governor Gruening and other members of the Alaska Statehood Committee were working to obtain a favorable press for the Alaskan effort. Newspaper support ranged from New York to Texas and from Louisiana to Michigan. The *New York Journal-American* probably summed up the situation best in stating:

> *Alaska wants statehood with the fervor men and women give to a transcendent cause. An overwhelming number of men and women voters in the United States want statehood for Alaska. This Nation needs Alaskan statehood to advance her defense, sustain her security, and discharge her deep moral obligation.*[8]

Opponents of statehood also organized for the upcoming hearings. Delegate Bartlett advised Secretary of the Interior Oscar L. Chapman that the Alaska Salmon Industry, Inc., would be represented at the hearing by Winton C. Arnold, who was "a smooth operator, intelligent and with a pleasing personality." Bartlett cautioned the Secretary that Arnold was the industry's "chief lobbyist," and that he had "fought and is fighting against every liberal and progressive proposal ever made [for Alaska]." Bartlett concluded that a couple of publicity men from McWilkins, Weber and Cole, a Seattle advertising firm handling the salmon industry account, would be in Washington to smooth press relations for Arnold.[9]

When the Senate hearings opened in Washington in April, not only Arnold but also a plane load of Alaskans, mobilized by the Alaska Statehood Committee, appeared as witnesses. The territorial group consisted of mostly older, established residents, including

lawyers, businessmen, ministers, representatives of labor, spokesmen for chambers of commerce, officials from veterans' groups,
and news paper editors.

On April 23, the day after their arrival in the capital, the group
held a strategy session with Bartlett. The delegate probably alerted
them that opponents would certainly propose extensive amendments which might improve the measure, but the real objective
would be to retard its progress. He urged that all efforts be extended
to convince the Senators to approve the House bill with few, if any,
amendments. That same day Gruening and Oscar Chapman, the
new Secretary of the Interior, went to New York to debate statehood on Eleanor Roosevelt's television show with Representative
Leroy Johnson of California and Frederic Coudert of New York.[10]

Alaska statehood hearings before the Senate began on April
24. Since Senator Joseph C. O'Mahoney, the chairman of the Committee on Interior and Insular Affairs, was sick, Senator Clinton
Anderson chaired the hearings. Before his election, Anderson had
been a general insurance agent in Albuquerque, and between 1945
and 1048 he had been President Truman's Secretary of Agriculture.
Secretary Chapman was the first witness to testify. He made a very
strong and impassioned plea for Alaska statehood. He summarized the arguments in favor of admission and disposed of the case
against statehood. The Secretary also cautioned the Senate committee to beware of the economic interests represented by various
witnesses. Glancing around the hearing room, the Secretary noted
the presence of Judge Arnold, whom he descried as "a registered
lobbyist in Alaska for the salmon-packing industry." Governor Earl
Warren of California spoke eloquently for admission, and General
Nathan F. Twining of the air force, then Commander-in-Chief of
the Alaskan Command, testified that statehood for the territory
would strengthen the defenses of America. However, the Reverend
Bernard R. Hubbard of Santa Clara, California, well-known for his
studies of Alaskan glaciers, expressed doubt that the territory could
bear the added costs of statehood.[11]

Several Alaskans appeared before the committee on April 25 in support of the territory's cause. The most effective pro-statehood testimony was given by Mildred R. Hermann. In commenting on the added costs a state government would entail, she stated that $4,242,000 per year above current expenditures would suffice. This amount, she concluded, could be raised from Alaskan sources.[12] On the third day representatives from various national organizations, such as the Veterans of Foreign Wars and the Order of Railway Conductors of America, presented resolutions in favor of statehood. Delegate Bartlett asserted that the salmon industry did not care how much or how little land the state received, but simply opposed statehood. It was inconceivable, he said, that:

> This committee or this Senate is going to allow a single industry, no matter how powerful, to dictate in fields outside its proper boundaries. The plea of that industry in a matter of no direct concern to it at all—namely the amount of land to be conveyed to the new state—is proof that the statehood plan opposition is reduced to a truly desperate expedient in its attempt to block this bill.[13]

Alaskans who testified spoke mainly of the desirability of statehood. Senator Anderson told Judge Dimond that most senators supported statehood, but that they wanted to scrutinize the measure under consideration. Witnesses repeatedly asked the committee not to change the bill in any substantive way lest it be lost in the adjournment rush or defeated on the floor. Senator Anderson listened to this plea several times, and finally told Edward Davis, the attorney representing the Anchorage Chamber of Commerce, that he had no intention of rubber stamping the statehood bill passed by the House.[14]

Judge Arnold appeared before the committee on the fourth day with an elaborate exhibit of charts and graphs, maps and tables, all designed to demonstrate the inadequacy of the statehood bill under discussion. Committee members had been offered a preview of his presentation when Senator Hugh Butler hosted a private luncheon for them in the Vandenberg Room of the Capitol. Butler had introduced Arnold as a man who knew much about the territory and could give them facts about statehood. Arnold addressed the luncheon guests, and at the conclusion handed each one leather-bound booklets containing his visual materials and written testimony on the statehood bill.[15]

In his formal testimony, Arnold's arguments ranged widely from impairment of international treaties and noncontiguity to questions concerned with federal land policies in Alaska and their relationship to the transfer of public lands to the proposed state. Arnold reminded the senators of his earlier warnings about the confusion which would result from the aboriginal land claims. He criticized the Department of the Interior for the erratic policies it had pursued in the territory for years. He asserted that less than one percent of Alaska's land area had been surveyed between 1867 and 1950. At that rate, he continued, it would take thousands of years before enough land had been measured to transfer title of the acreage granted in the statehood bill.[16]

Arnold had offered several Alaskans the opportunity to go to Washington and testify against statehood at the expense of the canned salmon industry. No one had accepted the offer, so on April 28, the second day of his testimony, Arnold introduced the two nonresident witnesses whom he had brought at industry expense to Washington. The first, retired Rear Admiral Ralph Wood, had been the commandant of the Seventeenth Naval District, which included Alaska, during the Second World War. Wood denied that statehood, as claimed by General Twining, would enhance the national security or help substantially in the defense of Alaska. The second witness, Edward W. Allen, was a Seattle attorney and chairman of the International Fisheries Commission. He opposed giving the new state control over its fisheries and other sea resources. Allen insisted that such a transfer would be detrimental to international treaty obligations because of uncertain jurisdiction and dual responsibility which would arise as a result of federal and state participation in the management of this resource. In addition, he pointed to the possibility of imprudent exploitation of these assets under a lax state administration.[17]

On the sixth and final day of the hearings Governor Gruening was given two hours to speak. Gruening found himself in a difficult position. First, there was the time limit, and secondly, the senators often interrupted him with questions. It was obvious that he had to respond to Arnold's presentation. The governor acknowledged that very little land had been surveyed, but, he observed, it was useful and accessible land. Only about 2 million of Alaska's 375 million acres was potential crop land, while another 4 million acres was suitable for nearly year-round grazing of domesticated livestock. Gruening predicted that much of this agricultural land would eventually come under state jurisdiction through lieu land selection and the continuing patenting of land by homesteaders. There was a bright side to federal land ownership, he asserted, because federal match for state highway construction would be higher. Alaska had many land problems, Gruening admitted, but these did not compare to those California faced in 1850. It had received a statehood grant of two sections per township, and not a single acre had been surveyed. In addition, California had confronted aboriginal claims and "Spanish" land grants.[18]

Arnold's testimony, however, had troubled Gruening and he had discussed it with Secretary Chapman. The Secretary had assured him that a 42 million acre land grant was generous and more than the state could use for some time. A larger grant, Chapman pointed out, would put considerable expensive administrative burdens on the new state. The Secretary stated, however, that he would not object if the Senators decided to increase the land grant to eight or even sixteen sections per township. The most important thing was that Alaska gain statehood. To the committee, Gruening suggested that Congress should give Alaska sizable cash grant to speed surveying, and also grant the state a part of the royalties from oil produced on federal reserves. Still, Arnold's statements had troubled Gruening, and he had become vaguely dissatisfied with the measure yet was eager that it be enacted. He suggested that the senators leave intact the proposed land grant of four sections per township. Once both houses of Congress had passed the bill, the House Public Lands and Senate Interior and Insular Affairs committees might meet jointly to determine if more land should be transferred to the state.[19]

The response to Arnold's thorough presentation varied. Delegate Bartlett bitterly observed that the salmon industry was indeed "bleeding with sympathy" for Alaska's well-being. "Do you think," the delegate asked the senators, that "the salmon industry, opposed to statehood in any form, cares at all how much land is granted in the bill?" Answering his own question, Bartlett stated that the industry had merely seized upon the land issue because it believed it would distract Alaskan and Congressional attention. "I have a suspicion," the delegate continued, "that if the statehood bill granted 50 percent of the land or all the land to the state, the salmon industry would be before you protesting the national interest was being violated by such a radical departure from the formula heretofore adopted." Legislation of any kind, he asserted, is always a matter of compromise. He concluded:

> *If I could have my way, the statehood bill would lavish upon the new state grants of various kinds hitherto unheard of in statehood bills. But we statehood advocates are realistic. We know there is a formula of [sic] new western states and that the principal elements of that formula will apply here. If it is desired to tip the scales somewhat on the side of liberality for Alaska, so much the better. But we do not want this bill killed with kindness.*[20]

It seems certain that Arnold's thorough testimony did raise questions in the minds of many senators about the adequacy of the statehood bill under discussion and the applicability of the traditional land grant provisions in the case of Alaska. Senator Ernest McFarland of Arizona expressed this latter concern when he asserted ominously that the committee wanted to write a good bill and would carefully consider all the criticisms.[21, 22, 23]

The Senate hearings ended on April 29, and on June 29 the Senate Interior and Insular Affairs Committee completed its revision of the Alaska statehood bill and reported it favorably. Although the statehood bill died in that particular Congress, the Senate report marked a dramatic turning point in the land grant formula. As Delegate Bartlett related to his listeners in territory-wide broadcasts in July of 1950, the Senate committee had "struck out in a novel and bold and precedent shattering way in determining how land should be transferred to the new state. Instead of awarding to Alaska sections 2, 16, 32, and 36 in each township, regardless of where they happened to be located, the proposed new state was granted the right to take twenty million acres of vacant, unappropriated, and unreserved lands from the public domain best suited to its peculiar needs. This amounted to about two sections in each of Alaska's eventual townships, or about 20,000,000,000 acres, but it could be acquired almost immediately and without waiting for rectangular surveys. Additionally, the measure granted 200,000 acres from the national forests, and again the same acreage adjacent to established or prospective communities, and another million acres for internal improvements. Most recognized that Alaska would not be an agricultural state, and that lands would be far more valuable for their minerals than soils. Starting with the Omnibus Act of 1889, all enabling acts except Utah's had specified that section grants containing minerals had to be retained by the federal government. As compensation, the states concerned had the right to select nonmineral lieu lands of equal size. Congress altered this policy in 1927 as it affected numbered school sections outside of Alaska for which patents had not yet been issued. From that time on such sections could be conveyed to the states regardless of their mineral character. States receiving such lands had the right to sell surface rights to private interests but were required to retain ownership of the minerals. These might be developed but only on lease from the states. All rentals and royalties had to be used for the support of the common schools. This extremely valuable privilege the senators applied to Alaska as well. Title to subsoil mineral rights, except where it conflicted with prior established ownership, was to pass to the new state.

The senators also made a couple of changes in dealing with Native claims. The House had approved a disclaimer clause which applied to federal property generally as well as "to all lands lying within its [Alaska's] boundaries owned or held by any Indians, Aleuts or Eskimos hereinafter called Natives, the right or title to which shall have been acquired through or from the United States or any prior sovereignty…" The senators modified the language "and to any lands or other property (including fishing rights), the right or title to which may be held by any Indians, Eskimos, or Aleuts (hereinafter called Natives) or is held by the United States in trust for such Natives…." When deleting the reference to "any prior sovereignty," the committee members probably based their decision upon a 1947 decision of the Ninth Circuit Court or Appeals which had held, in the case of *Miller v. United States,* that the 1867 Treaty of Cession had transferred unencumbered title to all land in Alaska: the only exception was land which belonged to individual property holders. Whatever claims to lands which they used and occupied, Alaska Natives might have in the future, had to be based on Congressional legislation, particularly the First Organic Act of 1884.

Earlier, Senator Butler had proposed that all orders of the secretary of the Interior which had established Native reservations in Alaska be rescinded and the 1936 authorizing legislation be repealed. Under Butler's concept, the secretary would be allowed to issue patents to Native "tribes and villages or individuals for the lands actually possessed, used, or occupied for town sites, villages, smokehouses, gardens, burial grounds, or missionary stations." Bartlett and Gruening supported the amendment but feared that Native rights advocates in the Department of the Interior would give trouble if such an amendment should be adopted. Finally, Senator O'Mahoney urged a compromise, and the committee complied by providing that no further Native reservations be created until after Alaska had been admitted into the Union as a state. The compromise clause evoked howls of protest from the National Civil

Liberties Clearing House, John Rainier of the National Congress of American Indians, Oliver La Farge, the president of the Association of American Indians, Harold Ickes, and *The Nation*. All maintained that Natives were denied their property rights.[24]

After the Senators finished their deliberations, many pro-statehood Alaskans blamed Arnold for the delays and difficulties the movement had encountered in Congress. To them, he appeared as an obstructionist giant with tremendous forces behind him which were able to thwart the desire of a majority of the territory's citizens. Although this was an oversimplification, Arnold was indeed a very dedicated and skillful advocate for the industry he represented. Dr. George W. Rogers, then an economist on the staff of Governor Gruening, later states:

> *[W.C. Arnold]…spearheaded the anti-statehood forces, and he was very effective, because he was very intelligent, and very energetic, and very ruthless, His testimony before statehood committees was always done very cleverly. He didn't come out and say very bluntly, "I'm against statehood." [Instead, he would say,] "I'm for statehood, but not statehood now." This was his opening remark generally. Then he'd give a devastating case against statehood which ended up to statehood never.*[25]

Ralph J. Rivers, long-time resident of Alaska, erstwhile attorney general of the territory, and later the new state's first elected representative to Congress, recalled that Arnold was loyal to the people he represented and expressed their viewpoint vigorously. "We used to say that we wished we had a W.C. Arnold on our side," Rivers declared. Although the Judge was a good Alaskan, Rivers asserted, he was the "fly in the ointment of the statehood movement." Not until the industry which Arnold represented had practically ruined the salmon runs, Rivers concluded, did the canners begin to relax their opposition to statehood.[26]

Judge Arnold, "the fly in the ointment," later stated that he personally had felt that statehood was inevitable after the first Congressional hearing in 1947, but that he was unable to persuade his employers of this belief. Placed in a difficult position, Arnold asserted, he had fashioned a policy which would serve both the salmon industry and Alaska.[27] This statement might be interpreted to mean that Arnold actually desired immediate statehood and that his actions and testimony were designed to achieve that goal. Mary Lee Council, Delegate Bartlett's administrative assistant for many years, did not see Arnold in the role of a statehood "angle." His testimony, she stated, was designed to defeat the measures. Thus he insidiously and cleverly clouded the real issue as far as the salmon industry was concerned. The industry's opposition, she said, and Arnold's as its spokesman, was based on the knowledge that the new state would take over control of the fisheries and immediately abolish the hated and deadly efficient fish traps. Nevertheless, Ms. Council stated, Arnold inadvertently showed the Senators the way to write a decent statehood bill. Apparently Arnold had been convinced that no such measure could be written because the senators would adhere to the Western public land state model with its small land grants and specific township-section requirements, which were totally inapplicable in Alaska due to its size and peculiar physical characteristics. Much to Arnold's surprise, she maintained, his testimony provided the basis for a unique and generous land selection formula which, even though enlarged in a subsequent years, did not change in concept.[28]

It matters little what motivated Judge Arnold. The fact is that he made a significant contribution to Alaska statehood. He educated his Congressional audience on Alaska's problems and potentials, and his arguments stimulated positive discussion and action.

The Senate hearings ended on April 29, 1950. Early in May, President Truman again gave his support to Alaska and Hawaii statehood and urged the speedy admission of both. Very few of the existing states, the President said, had possessed such great human and natural resources at the time of their admission. Truman asserted that he was disturbed by objections to Alaska and Hawaii statehood because they would be entitled to equal representation in the Senate. This argument was not only entirely without merit, but also belied "a basic tenet of the constitutional system under which this nation had grown and prospered." Without equal representation in the upper house for large and small states alike, the chief executive concluded, "there probably would have been no United States." On June 29, the Senate Interior and Insular Affairs Committee completed its revision of the Alaska statehood bill and reported it favorably, stating that refusal to admit Alaska would break the historic mold in which the United States had grown great. In addition, Alaskans desired and merited statehood, and were willing and able to support it. Statehood, the Senators concluded, would be in the best interest of both the United States and Alaska. The most important achievement of the committee, however, was the changed land selection formula.[29]

The minority report, written by Senator Hugh Butler of Nebraska, asserted that statehood would bring financial chaos and the quick collapse of Alaska. In essence, Senator Butler reiterated Judge Arnold's criticisms, and maintained that Alaska was not yet ready to assume the burdens of statehood. He was willing, Butler stated, to sponsor legislation which would enable Alaskans to elect their own governor and other territorial officials, and thus prepare the territory for eventual statehood. Obviously this was only a sop. Butler failed to explain how an elected governor would be able to overcome the territory's economic handicaps. Despite the improvements in the Alaska measure, the outlook for getting either it or the Hawaii bill before the Senate for a vote appeared rather dim at the end of June, 1950. One June 20, President Truman still insisted that there was time for the Senate to act on the bills. At Bartlett's prompting, the President promised early in July to do all he could to get administration leaders in the Senate to push the statehood measure onto the floor. Editorials in leading national newspapers also urged the Senate to act on both the Alaska and Hawaii bills.[30]

In a brief speech in the Senate on August 8, Senate Democratic leader Scott Lucas of Illinois strongly supported the Alaska measure. He revealed, however, that the Democratic leadership had been told by Senator James Eastland of Mississippi that if either

Harry S. Truman

Architects of Statehood

Harry S. Truman

Harry S. Truman was born May 8, 1884 in Lamar, Missouri. He grew up in Independence and for twelve years was a farmer. He eventually opened a haberdashery in Kansas City.

He became active in the Democratic Party and was elected a U.S. Senator in 1934. During World War II he headed the Senate war investigating committee, checking into waste and corruption and saving perhaps as much as $15 billion.

In 1944 President Franklin D. Roosevelt named him his running mate. During his few weeks as Vice President, Truman scarcely saw the president and received no briefing on the development of the atomic bomb or the unfolding difficulties with the Soviet Union. Suddenly these and many more problems became Truman's to deal with when he became president on April 12, 1945 at the death of President Roosevelt.

In June 1945, Truman witnessed the signing of the United Nations charter. At first he followed his predecessor's policies, but soon developed his own. He presented Congress with a 21-point program, proposing the expansion of Social Security, a full employment scheme, a permanent Fair Employment Practices Act, and public housing and slum clearance – all of which became known as the Fair Deal.

In his January 1946 State of the Union message, Truman gave Alaska statehood a boost when he recommended that the territory be admitted as soon as the wishes of its citizens had been determined. On May 16, 1949, President Truman and the Democratic House leaders met and selected ten priority bills, among them the Alaska statehood measure. Early in May, 1950, the president again gave his support to Alaska and Hawaii and urged the speedy admission of both.

Truman died on December 26, 1972, in Independence, Missouri after a rich life and a highly distinguished career.

statehood bill were brought up, Eastland would try to displace it by promoting the Mundt-Ferguson anti-communist bill. If that happened, Lucas stated, one of the Senators might try to attach a civil rights amendment to the anti-communist measure. Such action, according to the majority leader, held the prospect of a prolonged debate on the Mundt-Ferguson bill and a filibuster on the civil rights amendment which would indefinitely delay the recess of Congress before the elections in the fall. On August 24, Senator Warren G. Magnuson of Washington demanded that the Senate leadership inform the nation of what had happened to the statehood bills. The Senate was stalling, he said, because there were some Senators who did not want to add four members to the upper house and dilute a "voting bloc" namely the southern Democratic-conservative Republican coalition.[31]

Presidential prodding finally prompted the Senate Democratic Policy Committee to put the statehood bills on the list of "essential legislation." This move, however, brought no corresponding promise to push it through the Senate. At that point, a bipartisan group, led by Democratic Senator Richard B. Russell of Georgia, decided to prevent any action on the Alaska and Hawaii bills before the recess of Congress. A few days later, Senate Majority Leader Lucas, anxious to return home to campaign, buckled under and announced that he would have to drop consideration of the measures if the opposition threatened a filibuster which would postpone the pre-election recess.[32] And this is exactly what happened.

In the meantime, however, Andrew Schoeppel, former governor and then the junior Senator from Kansas, addressed his colleagues on September 5, 1950. Schoeppel insisted that he sympathized with the Alaska and Hawaii statehood movements, but then launched into an accusatory speech in which he attacked Chapman's loyalty. He implied that the secretary and one Randolph Feltus, a New York public relations consultant and lobbyist, had served the cause of Russian Communism. Schoeppel revealed that Feltus had advised the Polish Embassy between October 6, 1946 through July 1, 1949, and had also been employed by the Alaska Statehood Committee to promote its cause. The junior Senator from Kansas asked his colleagues to conduct an investigation, a request to which Senator Joseph C. O'Mahoney of Wyoming readily agreed. Chapman believed that Schoeppel's attack had been instigated by opponents of statehood, and he welcomed the five-day hearings which began on September 7, 1950.[33]

Schoeppel, it turned out, only served as a mouthpiece. Personally, he knew little about the charges, but indicated that Frank Bow, his legislative assistant, had gathered the materials on which he had based his speech. Bow had examined Winton Arnold's testimony before the Senate committee, and also contacted the latter for information about the Alaska Statehood Committee's retention of Feltus and the salary paid to him, as well as the political activities of the committee. Arnold could not answer Bow's query, so he turned the matter over to Albert White, an individual with a varied background. Born in San Francisco in 1890, he took over his father's saloon and pool hall in that city. He moved to Valdez, Alaska, in 1908 and stayed until 1917 when he left for Idaho. There he became chairman of the state central committee, worked as deputy collector of internal revenue and special agent of the Department of Justice. In 1934, he became the prohibition administrator for the sates of Idaho, Montana, and Wyoming, and the next year he worked as a Federal Bureau of Investigation agent in San Francisco. In 1926, White returned to Alaska where he served as the U.S. Marshal for the first judicial division until 1934. Admitted to the Alaska bar 1929, he went into private law practice in Juneau in 1934, and served as the chairman of the Republican central committee from 1933-1936. Running unsuccessfully for the position of delegate to Congress in 1938, White became the counsel of the Alaskan Republican Party and its boss, positions he held from 1938 to 1952. In addition, he was a real estate broker and the proprietor of the Bon Marche dry goods store in Juneau. White arranged to have photostats made of the Alaska Statehood Committee warrants sent to Delegate Bartlett as well as the vouchers for them. There was nothing secret about those documents because they were part of the public record. White sent the photostats to Bow.[34]

How had Feltus secured his position with the Alaska Statehood Committee? In 1946, he had contacted Bartlett about a possible job. The delegate merely had asked him to submit a proposal. This Feltus did, and thereafter contacted the delegate about twice a year. He also met Governor Gruening in Washington on numerous occasions. In the summer of 1949, Bartlett, Gruening, Lee Bettinger, a member of the Alaska Statehood Committee, and several Department of the Interior bureaucrats met in the delegate's office to talk to Feltus. Although impressed with the man, he was not hired. His fee—he suggested $3,000 to $6,000 per month for his labor—might have deterred the cost-conscious Alaskans, but also because he indicated that his influence was in the Senate. At that time, the chief struggle was centered on the House. At the request of the governor, Feltus subsequently wrote Gruening and reviewed his substantial professional background and listed many of his references. That ended the Feltus matter for the time being.[35]

In February 1950, Bartlett and Gruening talked again with Feltus. They asked him questions about Senators they knew well and found that his knowledge of their motivations coincided with their own impressions. They were still undecided, however, until Secretary Chapman, one of Feltus' references, recommended him very highly. Chapman's opinion together with Bartlett's fears that if the statehood bill did not pass in 1950, it might cripple Alaskan hopes for quite some time, finally persuaded the delegate to recommend that the Alaska Statehood Committee hire Feltus after the measure passed the House. Bartlett pointed out that Hawaii had spent several hundred thousand dollars on its statehood campaign before 1950 and yet had not advanced farther than Alaska. Still, everything had to be tried to gain admission. So Feltus was hired because of his alleged intimate knowledge of many Senators. Bartlett explained to William Baker, a member of the committee, that Senators like Hugh Butler and Guy Cordon were not about to change their anti-statehood stance just because they read favorable editorials in newspapers or magazines. Rather, these individuals would have "to be persuaded by personal contact from those who knew what makes them tick." Both Bertlett and Gruening had concluded that Feltus had much information about individuals with close ties to opposition Senators "who might be approached and won over to getting their men to act on our behalf." Feltus was to win statehood votes among member of the Senate Interior and Insular Affairs Committee, many of who seemed to be opposed to admission. Feltus later reported to Bartlett that he had discussed the issue with thirty-five Senators and the administrative assistants of another twelve, and also contacted individuals with close personal relationships to various lawmakers. In addition, Feltus had reached many newspapers and radio correspondents, and also attended several strategy meetings with Bartlett as well as the Hawaiian group.[36] In short, Feltus wanted to make certain that Bartlett knew that he was earning his money.

Both the delegate and the governor were impatient for results, and despite the feverish activity of Feltus, they saw no gains. They soon became disillusioned with Feltus. At the end of May 1950, Gruening complained that the lobbyist had worked for two months "on the members of the committee and as far as I can see he hasn't gained a single adherent." Instead, Feltus had proposed complex schemes for converting various Senators, which, however, "depended on a somebody else doing something which have fallen through." Bartlett shared Gruening's disappointment, but cautioned the governor that Feltus had been so ineffective that they could never admit it publicly for fear of being accused of having squandered public funds. Bartlett charged that Feltus "failed to accomplish anything constructive at all...." The lobbyist now thought that he could get Senator Richard B. Russell to work and vote for statehood. Feltus proposed that Russell's brother-in-law talk with the Senator, but thought that he needed about $750 "to sweeten the brother-in-law." The lobbyist wanted to collect some expense money and pay the brother-in-law from those funds. Bartlett was inclined to fire Feltus at this point, but was afraid that this would anger Feltus and he would work against statehood "and then we could be in the unhappy position of discovering he had a bigger following than we no give him credit for." Gruening, however, was ready to call it quits by the beginning of July 1950. He objected mainly to the expense, but the delegate had promised Feltus that he would be retained for a period of five months unless Congress adjourned sooner. During his employment, the lobbyist was to be paid $1,500 per month in salary, and another $500 for necessary expenses. There was to be another $1,500 per month if Congress enacted the Alaska statehood measure during the current session. After Bartlett learned in July that Feltus had once worked for the Polish Embassy to promote Polish-American trade, he at once decided that the agreement had to be terminated. Bartlett was utterly surprised, but should not have been because Feltus had listed the Polish Embassy among his former clients. Bartlett had simply overlooked the possible significance of this connection, for he charged that Feltus had been "delinquent or negligent or evasive in not informing us of this connection." It could hurt statehood. The delegate confronted Feltus with the matter, and the latter immediately offered to disassociate himself from the Alaska Statehood Committee if Bartlett felt its cause might be hurt. Bartlett accepted the resignation, effective July 25, 1950, but though Feltus had only worked for four months, the delegate paid him $7,500 for five months of work but only $500 for his total expenses. Feltus was disappointed because he estimated that he had spent at least $1,600 in expenses. He agreed, however, not to request any more money in case the statehood bill passed that session.[37]

The hearings embarrassed the Alaska Statehood Committee, but did not uncover why Feltus had been hired. Of the principals who testified, no one told the committee all he knew about the matter. Chapman and Feltus were vindicated, but Schoeppel suffered embarrassment. He no longer attended the hearings and told a reporter that perhaps the statements he made on the Senate floor should have been checked more carefully. He also requested that the remaining hearings he held behind closed doors, a wish the committee declined.[38]

It is unclear why Schoeppel and Bow attacked Chapman's loyalty. In the debate following Schoeppel's speech, Senator Lucas suggested that politics might have motivated Schoeppel, but most of the charges against Chapman had already been brought into the open in 1948 before the House Committee on Education and Labor. Schoeppel probably thought that his attack on Chapman might hurt the Truman administration. The Republican Party, however, did not support the Senator, because a couple of days after the incident Senator Robert Taft told reporters that the Senate Republican policy committee "disavows all responsibility for Senator Schoeppel's charges." There is no evidence that the Alaska Salmon Industry was behind Schoeppel, nor that the Senator was desperate to block Alaska's admission. A more plausible explanation is that Bow, who sought election to a Congressional seat from his hometown of Canton, Ohio, was eager to hit the headlines, and apparently determined to emulate Senator Joseph McCarthy of Wisconsin. Bow had talked about Chapman's record throughout his campaign. Like McCarthy, who used the national paranoia of Soviet Communist subversion for his own political ends, Bow also hoped to profit politically. Schoeppel, who had close ties to the private utility companies, had also attacked Michael Strauss, the commissioner of the Bureau of Reclamation, in his Senate speech. The commissioner, a vigorous proponent of the public development of America's hydroelectric resources, had incurred the hostility of private utilities. Schoeppel was in a good position to attack both Chapman and Strauss because the Department of the Interior had no reclamation projects in his home state of Kansas.[39] If nothing else, the Schoeppel affair kept interest in Alaskan statehood alive.

When Congress reconvened late in November of 1950, Senator Lucas, who had been defeated in Illinois by Everett McKinley Dirksen, proposed to bring up the Alaska bill. This action touched off a lengthy debate on the merits of statehood for both territories. Senator Hugh Butler stated that he did not want to "thrust statehood upon the helpless Alaskan." The political immaturity of the territory and its citizens, he declared, was amply demonstrated by

the fact that the Gruening administration "ruthlessly" controlled
the voters of Alaska and perpetuated its own powers. The territory
could not afford statehood because its two major industries, gold
mining and salmon fishing, were declining. This left only the gigan-
tic defense expenditures which one day would have to come to an
end and upon which a stable society could not be built. Senator
John L. McClellan, Democrat of Arkansas, opposed the two statehood bills because of the "communist influence" on Harry Bridges
and his International Longshoremen's and Warehousemen's Union
in Hawaii, and because Bridges now had "his men working in all
the fishery towns in Alaska, trying to put under his thumb every
union in Alaska..." Democratic Senator John Stennis of Mississippi
was shocked to learn that of the 580,000 square miles in Alaska,
the federal government owned 99.7 percent. Privately owned land
amounted to roughly 1,500 square miles, he said, the equivalent of
one large county in Minnesota or two in Mississippi. Yet, such a
small area was to be represented by two senators. The real danger,
Stennis remarked, was that the addition of four senators might
curtail the privilege of unlimited debate. In addition, those four
senators would come from areas not "attached geographically [to
the contiguous United States] and to which in many ways they
are not attached in culture, ideals, and ideas." Once Alaska was
admitted, it would lead to the admission of Hawaii as well. Then,
what would stop the admission of the Virgin Islands, Puerto Rico,
Guam, and Okinawa?[40]

On December 1, Republic Senator Guy Cordon of Oregon
made a speech on the Senate floor in which he dismissed such
arguments as noncontiguity, lack of population, inadequate political maturity, and, in the case of Alaska, meager financial resources.
"If taxation without representation was tyranny in 1776," he stated,
"it is tyranny today." Cordon asserted that the treat of a filibuster
had prevented action on the statehood bills. "I feel," he remarked,
"that my friends in the South have perhaps, as we say in the West,
been too close to the trees for a long time to evaluate the forest."
Nobody could predict what the views of four new senators would

be on civil rights or on any other issue. In addition, Cordon said, public sentiment was overwhelmingly in favor of the admission of both territories. This was a valid point. In 1949, as cited by Cordon, a Gallup poll had revealed that only 68 percent of the American voters favored Alaska's admission, while one year later it had risen to 81 percent. A similar trend was discernible for Hawaii. In 1949, fifty-eight percent of the American people favored Hawaiian statehood, while late in 1950 this percentage had risen to seventy-six.

But the southern Democratic-conservative Republican coalition prevented both the Alaska and the Hawaii bills from coming to the floor of the Senate.[41] This meant, of course, that the whole tedious process of getting a new bill through the House and then through the Senate had to be repeated. But there had been gains. The House had passed an Alaska statehood bill, and the Senate, for the first time, had considered such a measure. In addition, the Senate Interior and Insular Affairs Committee had departed from the traditional Western land grant formula.

With the outbreak of the Korean War in June of 1950, national priorities had shifted rapidly; and as American forces became more deeply involved, Alaska's statehood took a backseat. The years 1951 and 1952 were lean ones for the statehood forces. Even the Alaska Statehood Committee slumped into a moribund condition. Some citizens of the territory, however, were becoming increasingly impatient with Congressional delays and demanded forceful action.

CHAPTER TEN

Alaskans Demand
"Statehood Now"

On January 8, 1951 Senator Joseph C. O'Mahoney, Democrat of Wyoming, submitted an Alaskan statehood measure for himself and eighteen of his colleagues from both parties. With the introduction of three companion bills in the House, the statehood struggle was rolling again.[1]

In the meantime, the Alaska Statehood Committee met in Anchorage in early January 1951. Many statehood proponents had become restless with the inactivity of the committee, and several individuals in the audience urged that "militant and affirmative action be taken," a feeling Delegate Bartlett shared. He suggested that the committee establish an information program for the benefit of Congressmen, national organizations, and Alaskans supporting statehood. Bartlett therefore requested, and the committee approved, funds for printing 5,000 copies of speeches by Senators Mansfield, Anderson, O'Mahoney and others favorable to statehood. At the prompting of Bartlett, the press interviewed Frank Paratrovich on the question of how the Natives viewed the statehood bill Bartlett was about to introduce which omitted the provision prohibiting the creation of Native reservations in Alaska during the period before the official proclamation of admission. Peratrovich stated that the Bartlett bill without the suspension clause would be vigorously supported by the Natives.[2]

The Education and Public Relations Subcommittee was to carry out the information program in cooperation with Bartlett and an $18,000 budget. The subcommittee failed to launch the program, but commissioned the preparation and publication of a report to the legislature on the work of the committee during the last two years. After several drafts, conservative reporter Bob DeArmond described the publication as a "scissors and paste-pot job." It was, however, a success story that told how statehood supporters had overcome all obstacles and only received temporary setbacks. Committee members also discussed the desirability of preparing information and analyses for a constitutional convention, and allotted $12,000 for this task. At the suggestion of Gruening, the committee allocated the remainder of the funds, $25,000, to promoting passage of the statehood bill and related administrative expenses. The Board of Administration released the $55,000 still impounded at the request of the committee, but the territorial legislature failed to provide an additional $50,000. It apparently felt that the committee had not accomplished very much.[3]

The territorial legislature convened on January 22, 1951 for its biennial session. Democrats and Republicans each held eight seats in the senate, while in the house the Democrats occupied fourteen of the twenty-four seats. The house soon formed a Special Committee on statehood. The first item of business the new committee considered was the Republic of Alaska memorial, introduced by Wendell Kay, an Anchorage attorney, on his own behalf and that of his colleagues from the third division. It requested that Alaska be granted statehood. If it could not be done, the memorialists asked that Alaska be given the right to declare its independence of and from the government of the United States and to form a "Republic of Alaska."[4]

Kay's initiative was roundly condemned. An editorial in the *Fairbanks Daily News-Miner* stated that the "memorial would antagonize Congress, make Alaskans look as foolish as their law-makers, tend to weaken the U.S. position in the United Nations, and give Russian propaganda guns new ammunition." The editor suggested that Kay and his fellow memorialists establish a "Repub-lic of the Third Division, and secede from Alaska." The *Anchorage Daily Times* considered the matter a publicity stunt, but asked if the memorialists had thought about the repercussions of either pas-sage or defeat.[5]

In the face of this adverse reaction, Kay withdrew the memo-rial, and February 10, twelve of the fourteen Democrats introduced a joint statehood memorial. No action was taken on it. A house memorial of February 15 which asked the Senate Interior and Insular Affairs Committee to forego further hearings on Alaska statehood and to report Senator O'Mahoney's enabling bill failed of enactment on 12-12 vote. A senate-passed bill appropriating funds for the Alaska Statehood Committee was tabled in the house on a 13-11 vote. Although more Democrats then Republicans sup-ported statehood in the legislature, most representatives did not seem overly enthusiastic about the subject that year.[6]

While the legislature grappled with statehood, the Senate Inte-rior and Insular Affairs Committee began its study of the Alaska measure late in January. Since extensive hearings had been held in the consideration of the Alaska bill was very cursory. On April 3, the committee approved the Hawaii measure 9-4 and the one of the Alaska 7-6. Various amendments had been added to the lat-ter, among them provisions which increased the internal improve-ment grant from 1,000,000 to 2,555,000 acres. Without Senator Guy Cordon's affirmative vote the bill would have failed, but he had changed his negative view of the matter in September of the previous year. The Senator still believed that Alaska did not receive sufficient natural resources in the measure, but had come to believe that this problem could be satisfactorily rectified after admission. The committee rejected a substitute bill, offered by Senator Hugh

Butler, which would have allowed Alaskans to elect their own governor, as an obvious device to defeat statehood.[7]

As already mentioned, the requirement of the Korean War
forced the Senate to devote much of its time for the rest of 1951 to
defense and appropriation bills. The Alaska statehood bill, therefore, was delayed for floor action until 1952. In the meantime,
however, Bartlett, Gruening, Atwood, and Bettinger visited Senators of their respective parties and attempted to win them over to
the cause. Bartlett had learned his lesson from the nearly disastrous
experience with Randolph Feltus. He now hired Emil Hurja and
Hardin Peterson as lobbyists, but requested reports on both from
the House Un-American Activities Committee before signing the
contracts. Hurja was a very interesting individual. He had served as
secretary to Alaska's delegate to Congress, Charles Sulzer, and then
became the executive director of the Democratic National Committee, a post he held from 1932 to 1936. Hurja, however, became
disenchanted with the New Deal and left the Democratic Party,
becoming a journalist, editor, public relations consultant, and a
Republican. Hurja had testified in favor of Alaska statehood in
1947 and again in 1950, and also had harbored the ambition to be
appointed territorial governor. Peterson, a former Congressman,
had spearheaded the attempts in 1949 and 1950 to bring the statehood bills to a vote in the House. He did not run for reelection in
1950 and returned to Florida to practice law. Bartlett hoped that, as
a southerner and former member of Congress he might persuade
his former colleagues to support statehood.[8]

Delegate Bartlett was correct in his assessment that the statehood bills would not be passed without assistance. Senators Robert Taft and Richard Russell supposedly had worked out a strategy
for defeating the bill, planning to return the measure to committee
for hearings. A poll of the lawmakers revealed that such a move
would carry by nine more votes than a Senate majority. While only
43 Senators intended to vote for Alaska, 55 indicated that they
would support Hawaii. When the scheme became known, Senator O'Mahoney, Delegates Bartlett and Farrington, and Governor

Gruening agreed that the Hawaiian measure be scheduled first. The men reasoned that if the Hawaiian measure passed, sufficient numbers of Democrats would overcome their prejudices against Alaska statehood to ensure a continued Democratic majority in the Senate. When the Taft and Russell plan was explained to him, the President approved of the "Hawaii first" strategy, but the Democratic Policy Committee, which decided the order in which bills would be considered for floor action and also directed general party policy and strategy, decided that the Alaska measure should come first. Unfortunately, ten of the sixteen chairmen of the legislative committees of the Senate who composed the Democratic Policy Committee opposed statehood for Alaska. Majority Leader Ernest McFarland was unalterably opposed to the "Hawaii first" scheme since he believed that after admitting the Islands, Republicans would vote against Alaska.[9]

Still, early in 1952 Delegate Bartlett told members of the Alaska Statehood Committee that he had received firm assurances that the Alaska bill would receive favorable consideration in the Senate. The Hearst papers and the Scripps-Howard chain had promised editorial support, Bartlett stated, and all the national organizations which so far had supported the cause had promised to do so again. Bartlett surmised that if the Alaska bill came to a vote in the Senate, it would gain a safe, although small, margin of victory. The delegate accurately predicted that the anti-statehood forces in Congress would try to prevent such a vote so that they would not be forced to go on record against a popular measure. One way they could accomplish this objective, he concluded, referring to the Taft-Russell plan, would be to send the bill back to committee for further study or filibuster it to death.[10]

Both Delegates Bartlett of Alaska and J.R. Farrington of Hawaii wrote to Senator Joseph C. O'Mahoney, chairman of the Senate Interior and Insular Affairs Committee, supporting each other's cause. Bartlett stated that he wanted Hawaii to be admitted in 1952. "I should hope for that result even if by some mischance Alaska's hope were not to be realized. We Alaskans want statehood

Clinton Presba Anderson

Architects of Statehood

Clinton Presba Anderson

Clinton Presba Anderson was born on October 23, 1895 in Centerville, South Dakota. He attended Dakota Wesleyan University from 1913 to 1915 and the University of Michigan in Ann Arbor from 1915 to 1916. He served as U.S. Congressman from New Mexico from 1941 to 1945, U.S. Secretary of Agriculture from 1945 to 1948, and U.S. Senator from New Mexico from 1948 to 1973.

When the U.S. Senate began hearings on Alaska statehood on April 24, 1950, Senator Joseph C. O'Mahoney, the chairman of the Committee on Interior and Insular Affairs was sick. Senator Anderson chaired the hearings and told those testifying that most of his colleagues supported statehood but wanted to scrutinize carefully the measure under consideration. Witnesses repeatedly asked the committee not to change the House-passed bill in any substantive way lest it be lost in the adjournment rush or defeated on the floor. Senator Anderson finally told Edward Davis, the attorney representing the Anchorage Chamber of Commerce, that he had no intention of rubber-stamping the House-passed bill.

After listening to Judge Arnold's testimony, the majority of senators, led by Senator Anderson decided to abandon the traditional formula for granting federal land to the states and allow Alaska to select large blocks of land from the vacant, unappropriated, and unreserved public domain best suited to its needs.

for ourselves," he stated, "but we want it for Hawaii too." Delegate
Farrington echoed these sentiments when he said, "I hope the Senate
will adopt the bill reported by your committee for the admission of
Alaska to the Union as a state without regard to what may be done
with the bill to give statehood to Hawaii."[11]

Debate on the Alaska bill resumed, as scheduled, on February
4, 1952. As early as February 5, however, a poll of Senators showed
that a majority of Republicans and Democrats would vote to send
the Alaska bill back to committee for further study. On February 6,
the Democratic Policy Committee confirmed its earlier decision to
put Alaska first on the agenda. Senator Hugh Butler, as much a foe
of Alaska statehood as ever, confessed that he had great emotional
feeling for Alaska, that he considered it to be a great northern
frontier. But, he said, his desire to help the citizens of the territory
prompted him to reject statehood at that time. He asked his colleagues how they could think of burdening 108,000 Alaskans with
the costs of statehood until it had been ascertained beyond any
doubt that this was what the citizens of the territory really wanted.
Butler asserted that up to that time, Congress had only heard testimony from a small group of Alaskans who had come to Washington "at the taxpayer's expense to present us with their reasons
for desiring statehood." In addition, the Senator introduced voluminous documents, all designed to show that Alaska was totally
unprepared to assume the responsibilities of statehood.[12]

When Senator Stennis asked Senator Magnuson how he
explained the large vote of approximately 6,000 against statehood
in 1946 territorial referendum, Magnuson replied that he could
explain it, although it would not be politically popular for him to
do so.

> Most of the votes in opposition to the granting of statehood to
> Alaska came from my own home town of Seattle, and were
> stirred up by a very small group of people who for a long time
> have been able to go to Alaska, make fortune, help to develop
> Alaska—and I do not blame them—and who would like to

have things remain as they are, in the status quo, without change. That is the source of the opposition. I do not say any-thing is wrong about that; some of those persons have been very good citizens of my state and have also been very helpful in connection with the development of Alaska. But, because it has been so profitable for some of them in connection with mining, fishing, and other commercial activities, they would prefer to preserve the status quo. They live in Seattle, go to Alaska in the summer time, and then return to Seattle. I could discuss the matter of the manipulation of that campaign [the 1946 territorial referendum] in great detail.

A few days later, Senator Magnuson presented editorials from leading newspapers across the nation which urged the Senate to do its duty and pass the Alaska and Hawaii statehood bills.[13]

On February 20, Republican Senator Fred R. Seaton of Nebraska, a newspaper publisher and radio station owner who had been appointed to fill the vacancy created by the death of Senator Kenneth Wherry, delivered his maiden speech in support of Alaska statehood. Seaton had been persuaded to support Alaska' cause by Gruening, who also wrote the speech for him. On the same day, George Smathers of Florida, who had defeated Senator Claude Pepper in 1950, introduced a motion to recommit the Alaska bill to the Committee on Interior and Insular Affairs with instructions to hold hearings on the measure. Smathers, a freshman Senator, was no stranger to Congress for he had served in the House from 1946 to 1950. Smathers led the opposition on the floor, thereby further enhancing his reputation as a reliable member of his bloc. Senator A.S. "Mike" Monroney of Oklahoma requested and received permission from Smathers to included directions which asked the committee also to consider commonwealth status for Alaska and Hawaii. Debate was to begin on February 27, 1952.[14]

Before the scheduled debate was to begin, however, both sides applied strong pressure to wavering and undecided Senators. Republican Senator William Knowland of California informed his colleagues that Monroney's modification of Smather's motion applied to both territories. Republicans, however, wanted to admit Hawaii, Delegate Farrington, together with numerous Alaskans, visited Senators in an effort to overcome indifference and opposition.[15]

Besides Smathers, Senators Hugh Butler, Russell Long, and John Stennis played leading parts in the debate to recommit the Alaska measure. Numerous other Senators opposed the recommittal motion. Democratic Senator Paul Douglas from Illinois spoke eloquently for this group. He maintained that two types of states would lose the most by admitting Alaska. The first were large tax paying states like Illinois, since Alaska would most likely join "the public works block" and receive large amounts of federal funds for economic development. The second were southern states, poles apart on the matter of civil rights with Alaska. After the South had lost voting parity, its Senators had used the filibuster to kill civil rights legislation. It took a two-thirds cloture vote of the total Senate membership to derail a filibuster. The admission of Alaska and Hawaii, he added, would undoubtedly add Senators inclined to vote for cloture, and of this the South was afraid. It really was a matter of national versus regional interests.[16]

When the roll call was taken, eighty-nine Senators answered. Estes Kefauver, who had been campaigning in Iowa, returned to the capital for the occasion, as did Hugh Butler. Senator Thomas Hennings, Jr. of Missouri left his sickbed, and accompanied by his physician, went to vote against recommittal. The vote was tied three times, but finally the Alaska measure was returned to committee by a vote of 45 to 44. As in 1950, a coalition of conservative Republicans and southern Democrats had successfully killed Alaskan statehood for another session of Congress. The House, under these circumstances, saw no need to act at all.[17]

Many Alaskans asked themselves if the Republican vote on Alaska statehood in the Senate could be attributed solely to party politics. Some maintained that it was solely due to party politics, while others thought that Republicans voted negatively because they thought the bill to be inadequate. For example, the land grant was too small, and it did not ensure state control of the fish and wildlife resources. As early as March 1950, the territorial Republican Party adopted a plank in its platform critical of the Alaska statehood bill the House had passed. Members of the Anchorage Republican Club disagreed and supported the measure, charging that the critical platform plank damaged the statehood cause. Walter Hickel belonged to the club. Born in Ellingwood, Kansas in 1919, he ended his formal education at the age of sixteen, and between 1935 and 1940 worked as a carpenter in California. Nearly penniless, the 20 year-old man landed in Alaska in 1940. He worked as a bartender, for the Alaska Railroad, and as a construction worker. Ambitious and energetic, Hickel became a general contractor, building rental units, residential homes, and eventually, hotels. Hickel became a Taft Republican, and soon challenged the Old Guard Republicans, led by Albert White, who long had controlled the party in the territory. Hickel supported the 1950 Alaska statehood bill. In time, however, he and his colleagues modified their support. In 1952, the group drafted a resolution which stated that "we favor and strongly urge statehood for Alaska under a statehood bill providing for Alaskan control of Alaska's resources. They hoped that the national party would incorporate this language into its 1952 platform. Hickel went to Washington to testify against Senator O'Mahoney's Alaska statehood bill in 1952 because of its inadequacies. Alaskans should be able to control the fisheries, he declared, and also receive 100 percent instead of the contemplated 50 percent of the Pribilov fur seal receipts. Most important of all, the land grant was too small. Hickel vigorously lobbied for recommittal, stating that he would rather see a decent measure five years hence than a deficient one today.[18]

In the summer of 1952, the Republican and Democratic Parties held their presidential nominating conventions. Alaska's and Hawaii's delegates to the Republican convention agreed that the 1948 platform plank favoring eventual statehood would no longer suffice. Delegate Farrington demanded immediate statehood for Hawaii, while Fairbanks attorney Maurice Johnson asked for admission under an equitable enabling act. Both were granted their wish, for the term "equitable" was ambiguous, would take much time to exactly determine, allow compromise, and yet enable the Republicans to claim that they were committed to statehood. It also implied that the statehood bills of Democrats Bartlett and O'Mahoney had not been equitable. Better yet, Republicans claimed that they were more attuned to Alaska's needs than the Democrats.[19]

At the convention, two of Alaska's three delegates supported Robert Taft, but the convention chose Dwight D. Eisenhower to be the presidential standard bearer in 1952. With his wide grin, military reputation, and fatherly image, he made an extremely attractive candidate to a nation dominated politically by the Democrats for two decades and tired of the continuing was in Korea. Unlike Taft, Eisenhower was on record as favoring statehood, for on September 17, 1950, while president of Columbia University, he had addressed a crowd at Denver, Colorado. He had told his listeners that he hoped Congress would speedily pass the pending Alaska and Hawaii statehood measures. Such action, he stated, would show the world that America practiced what it preached.[20]

Soon after the Republicans adjourned, the Democrats met for their convention. A plank in the Democratic platform again urged immediate statehood for Alaska and Hawaii, and the party's national convention for the first time gave both territories their alphabetical place in the roll of the states. This lifted them from the bottom of the list as territories, and Alaska became second, right after Alabama. Alaska's delegates cast their votes for Estes Kefauver, but contrary to their expectations, the convention nominated Adlai Stevenson of Illinois, a man who brought considerable intellectual stature and subtle wit into national politics. Statehood seemingly did not suffer a setback, for Stevenson was a member of the National Statehood Committee, a group of ninety-six prominent Americans whom Governor Gruening had persuaded to endorse Alaska's admission. The names of these individuals, in fact, adorned the stationary of Alaska Statehood Committee.[21]

Alaska's Delegate Bartlett did not intend to take any chances on his reelection in view of the strong Republican Presidential candidate. He returned to Alaska late in July to open his campaign. His Republican opponent was Robert Reeve, owner and operator of the Anchorage-based Reeve Aleutian Airlines, who, according to *The New York Times*, belonged to the "statehood in the future" camp. Reeve thought that the territory's population was too small, its financial needs too great to be met locally, and the statehood bills so far considered entirely unsatisfactory. Governor Gruening, in a less charitable frame of mind, referred to Reeve as

> ... a gentleman growling around the territory now rattling the bogey of "creeping or leaping socialism" as part of his Republican campaign. He says we must get away from all government subsidy or assistance. However, this loud-voiced campaigner....has not mentioned that to his success as a private enterpriser the federal government in the last four years has contributed—not loaned, but paid—over half a million dollars in air mail subsidy. That isn't creeping or even leaping socialism.... That would be "flying socialism." Yet I haven't heard that he's refused any of this dough, or offered to turn it back! Why doesn't he practice what he preaches? The fact is, he's just another fellow, who down at heels and out at elbows when he came to Alaska at the end of the Republican era twenty years ago, has been made prosperous by Democratic policies.[22]

Bartlett won a fifth term by beating his opponent 14,219 to 10,893 votes. A referendum on whether or not the federal government should turn over complete control and operation of the fisheries to the territory was overwhelmingly approved by a vote of 20,544 to 3,479. The territorial Republicans, however, brought Democratic dominance to an end and won control of the Alaska legislature. This was the party's first revival since the advent of the New Deal in 1933, and *The New York Times* asked curiously, "As Alaska Goes—?"[23] The November national elections furnished the

Dwight D. Eisenhower

Architects of Statehood

Dwight D. Eisenhower

Dwight D. Eisenhower was born on October 14, 1890 in Denison, Texas, the third of seven sons. He excelled in sports and received an appointment to West Point. In his early Army career he excelled in staff assignments.

Eisenhower served under Generals John J. Pershing, Douglas MacArthur, and Walter Krueger. After Pearl Harbor, General George C. Marshall called him to Washington for a war planning.

Eisenhower commanded the Allied Forces landing in North Africa in November 1942. On D-Day, 1944 he was Supreme Commander of the troops invading France. After the war he became president of Columbia University, then took leave to assume supreme command over the new NATO forces being assembled in 1951.

He was elected President of the United States in 1952 and served two terms from 1953 to 1961. In 1953 he signed a truce that brought an armed peace along South Korea's border. Stalin's death the same year caused shifts in U.S.-Russian relations, and the new Russian leaders consented to a peace treaty neutralizing Austria.

As President, Eisenhower kept most of the New Deal and Fair Deal programs, emphasizing a balanced budget. As desegregation of schools began he sent troops into Little Rock, Arkansas, to assure compliance with federal court orders. He also ordered the complete desegregation of the Armed Forces. He concentrated on maintaining world peace.

He was lukewarm on the issue of Alaska statehood, but his Secretary of the Interior, Fred Seaton, persuaded him to lend his support. President Eisenhower signed the Alaska statehood bill into law on July 7, 1958, and on January 3, 1959 he signed the proclamation officially admitting Alaska as the 49th state into the Union.

Eisenhower died, after a long illness, on March 28, 1969.

answer—" As Alaska Goes, So Goes the Nation"—because nation-ally the Republicans elected their first White House occupant in twenty years, although their control of Congress brought only a tenuous majority of one in the Senate.

Delegate Bartlett expressed his conviction that Alaska's state-hood chances looked dim for the next four years of Republican rule. Senator Hugh Butler of Nebraska, soon to be chairman of the Senate Interior and Insular Affairs Committee, had already told the Delegate that he did not favor the admission of the territory because of its narrow economic base. As a matter of fact, Butler did not think that the issue would even come up. Hawaii, on the other hand, would be dealt with, although the Senator told Bartlett that he was not personally committed to the island territory's cause. Despite these dire predictions, half a dozen Alaskan statehood measures were submitted in the new Congress early in 1953.[24]

In the meantime, the Alaska Statehood Committee met in Juneau on January 28 and 29, 1953. In order to blunt the criticism leveled against the statehood bill by opponents, Governor Gruen-ing suggested that Congress should grant the new state $50 million for the construction of a capital building and a mental institution, and pay for the necessary surveys of the land grant during the first fifteen years after admission. The governor, however, was aware that those opposing statehood would then counter that the territory was not ready for admission if it could not pay for these expenses itself. He considered the proposed 23 million acre grant sufficient, since more acreage would simply put an expensive administrative bur-den on Alaska. The next day committee members met with the leg-islature. Bartlett explained that he would try to have the land grant doubled, but maintained that he and other committee members thought the 23 million acres were adequate. Bartlett also promised that he would include a $50 million cash grant in the measure.[25]

A couple of days before the committee met with the legislature, Howard W. Pollock, a navy veteran, Republican, and freshman rep-resentative from Anchorage, had introduced a bill providing for the abolition of the existing committee and replacing it was a new one consisting of eleven members, three to be appointed by the governor and eight by the lawmakers. Pollock certainly intended to be a member of the committee. The language Pollock had used in the measure implied that neither Bartlett nor the committee members had fulfilled their obligations. The measure stated that the new committee was to prepare an adequate statehood bill conveying control of the territory's natural resources to the state. The draft measure was to receive ample publicity and there were to be ways in which comments, suggestions, and criticism could be incorporated into the bill. After completion, the committee was to petition the governor to conduct a special referendum, and if approved, the measure was to be submitted to the delegate for introduction in Congress. The committee also was to prepare a draft of the future state's fundamental law to be submitted to a constitutional convention after Congress had passed the statehood bill. Although a modified version of Pollock's bill passed the house, the senate rejected it, and the old committee remained intact.[26]

In the nation's capital it soon became evident that statehood had become a strongly partisan issue. The Republican leadership quickly recognized that the admission of Republican-leaning Hawaii would bolster their weak hold on Capitol Hill. If traditionally Democratic Alaska were admitted at the same time, however, Republican gains would be neutralized. President Eisenhower reflected this attitude in his first State of the Union message on February 2, 1953. The President urged that Hawaii be granted statehood "promptly with the first election in 1954," but failed to mention Alaska. The House of Representatives speedily complied with Eisenhower's request and passed a Hawaii bill on March 10, 1953. On the same day, Representative A.L. "Doc" Miller, Republican of Nebraska, the new chairman of the House Interior and Insular Affairs Committee, attempted to placate Alaska statehood advocates in the House when he announced that hearings on an Alaska measure would start on April 14, 1953.[27]

As the date of these hearings approached, Douglas McKay, the new Secretary of the Interior, and an ex-automobile dealer from

Salem, Oregon, expressed his reluctance to appear before the committee. He seemed to reason that since statehood for Alaska was not a part of the administration's plan, the committee hearings would only be a waste of time. Early in April, Chairman Miller warned McKay that failure to appear might be fatal politically. "If you can't do anything but take a neutral stand that should be done," Miller advised. If all else failed, McKay could state that he was "studying the problem." Miller concluded by reminding the secretary that it was "absolutely necessary" to promise hearings on Alaska if the Republicans were to get the Hawaii bill out of the House committee. The political nature of the statehood issue was further emphasized by a political skit performed at the 1953 Washington Gridiron Club Dinner, which the President attended. Miss Hawaii and Miss Alaska Eskimo appeared, with the latter singing to the tune of "Sweet Lielani":

> *Sweet Hawaii, G.O.P. flower*
> *Leaders smile on statehood just for you*
> *They say you'll give them extra power*
> *While I have votes so few*
> *Poor Alaska, we are forsaken*
> *We have no Wai-Ki-Ki like you*
> *No hula girls to charm the senate*
> *You are their dreams come true.*[28]

McKay reflected the President's attitude toward statehood, and supporters of the cause were disappointed. The secretary had to fill a number of positions important to Alaska. For the renamed Office of Territories, McKay chose William C. Strand, a man Senator Butler had recommended as loyal, industrious, and efficient. Strand also knew Alaska well. Born in Chicago, he became a journalist working as a reporter and correspondent in Washington and London. From 1937 to 1948 he wrote for Colonel Robert McCormick's conservative *Chicago Daily Tribune*. In 1948 he became the managing editor of the *Fairbanks Daily News-Miner*. There he became an aggressive partisan critic of the Truman and Gruening Democratic administrations. He also continued the paper's opposition to state-hood as directed by its owner, Alaska's lone capitalist Austin "Cap" Lathrop. After the latter died in a mine accident, Strand finished his contract and left Fairbanks in 1951. In Washington, he became the executive editor of the *Washington Times Herald,* a paper McCor-mick had recently acquired. On May 1, 1953, he assumed the posi-tion Gruening had once held.[29]

McKay faced difficulties in selecting a successor to Ernest Gru-ening. Numerous resident and nonresident politicians competed for the position, including Walter J. Hickel. On February 24, 1953, the secretary announced the appointment of B. Frank Heintzle-man, assistant regional forester of Alaska from 1921 until 1937, and since that time the territory's regional forester. Heintzleman had not applied for the job. Inexperienced politically and with few enemies, he was the ideal compromise candidate. One observer remarked that "any of the partisan groups would prefer Heint-zleman to anyone else except their own candidate." In addition, Heintzleman had a good reputation as an administrator, and the Portland and Seattle business interests trusted him.[30]

Heintzleman was very much the opposite of his predeces-sor. A bachelor, he avoided socializing and possessed no political instincts. He did not campaign, raise issues against the Democrats, nor defend the Republican record. Gruening was an outgoing man, married and a father, who loved to socialize and host as well as attend cocktail parties. He loved politics, was extremely articulate, intellectually preeminent, and very impetuous. Gruening loved to lead, in fact dominated those around him, and often plunged into controversy, often disregarding the views of his superiors. Heint-zleman, by contrast, followed the instructions of his superiors, and was not good at infighting.

Heintzleman was unable to assume his new office because Gruening refused to resign to resign until the end of this term on April 9, 1953. Gruening, however, promised McKay to cooperate in the transition and familiarize Heintzleman with his new duties. When Heintzleman finally assumed office, his ideas on statehood had already been made clear. He had told the Senate Interior and Insular Affairs Committee at the hearing on his nomination that, while looking forward to Alaska's admission as a state, it was still "premature." Instead, Alaskans should concentrate their efforts on developing the region's natural resources. In the meantime, northern residents should be content with an elective governorship.[31]

Back in Washington, the House opened hearings on the Alaska measure, as scheduled, on April 14, 1953. The usual cast of witnesses attended, including the Alaska Statehood Committee and its friends. The military was represented by Undersecretary of the Air Force James H. Douglas. In his testimony, Douglas mirrored the administration's attitude toward the admission of Alaska. He told the committee that while the Department of Defense felt statehood might have long-range military advantages, there would be no immediate benefits. Secretary McKay appeared on April 15, and was predictably noncommittal. The Secretary stated that Alaska should be admitted "when it is ready and under a proper bill so that it can develop, pay its taxes and support itself."[32]

Representatives dealt pleasantly with the witnesses with the exception of John Pillion, a freshman Republican from Lackawanna, suburban Buffalo, New York. Pillion had recently proposed a Constitutional amendment providing that no new state should receive even one senator until its population reached one-half of the average number of people represented by a senator from the other states. In 1950, this amounted to almost 800,000 souls. A new state would receive a second senator only when its population reached one and one-half times the average population represented by a senator, 2,383,938 in 1950. Pillion asked that Alaskan's accept his formula, but delegate Bartlett replied that they would not, and instead insisted on being admitted on the same basis as the existing states. Howard Pollock told Pillion that if his amendment were applied to the existing states, fully thirteen would lose one of their senators, while another thirteen would lose both.[33]

Mildred Hermann had served as the financial expert of the Alaska Statehood Committee on previous occasions. She told the

Congressman that Alaska could afford the added cost of statehood. The territorial legislature had just appropriated its biennial budget. On a yearly basis, this amounted to over $12,000,000, while the tax commissioner had estimated revenues would amount to over $14,000,000 for each of the two years. In addition, the territory had accumulated approximately $4,200,000 in earmarked funds and about another $8,200,000 in its general fund. Doubling the two-cent per gallon gasoline tax would yield an additional $1,250,000 and raising the three-cent per pack cigarette tax to five cents would bring in another $500,000. Other sources of revenue consisted of reimposing the territorial real estate tax which the legislature had just repealed, and levying a severance tax on mining. Taking these figures into account, and assuming that Mrs. Hermann's new estimate of $6,799,000 as the net cost of statehood were not too low, Alaskans would be able to afford it.[34]

Ernest Gruening was the last of the twenty-two witnesses to testify. The former governor reiterated his thesis that the federal government had neglected the territory. Alaskans had conquered nature, but had been frustrated in their battles with bureaucracy, he stated.[35] With that the hearings closed.

Since hearings and investigations into the matter of Alaska statehood had occurred with regularity since 1947, not much new material was added on this occasion. On April 27, 1953, the subcommittee began deliberations on Representative John Saylor's Alaska measure. During the next two and one-half weeks it adopted twenty-three amendments. One of them reduced the $50 million cash grant to $15 million. Subcommittee members felt that the state should construct its own mental, charitable, penal, and reformatory institutions and build many of its roads and harbors without federal assistance. The most important amendment dealt with the land grant. The subcommittee decided to enlarge the basic land grant from 40 million to 100 million acres, to be selected within twenty-five years after statehood. It was to be the state's responsibility to survey, classify and appraise the selected acreage, and also take over fire fighting and other management responsibilities. In addition,

Alaska was to receive another 2,550,000 acres of public lands for internal improvements, as well as 400,000 acres of national forest lands and another 400,000 acres of public land for establishing and expanding community centers and recreational areas. The total land grant of 103,350,000 acres amounted to about 28 percent of Alaska's landmass, or approximately 10 sections out of every township. Significantly, the committee report characterized the amended statehood bill as the "equitable enabling act" called for in the 1952 Republican platform. The subcommittee reported the measure on May 15 by a vote of 12 to 5, and eight days later the bill passed the full committee on a vote of 19 to 4.[36] After this favorable treatment, the Alaska measure promptly disappeared into the House Rules Committee.

In the meantime, the Senate Interior and Insular Affairs Committee considered the House-passed Hawaii measure. It soon became apparent to the Democratic committee members that the Senate's Alaska bill would not even be reported out. To force action, the seven Democrats, lead by Clinton P. Anderson of New Mexico, proposed to add the Alaska measure to the Hawaii bill. The motion passed 8 to 7 on a straight party-line vote, except that Senator George W. Malone, a Republican from Nevada who opposed statehood for either territory, but believed both should get the same chance, voted with the Democrats.[37] The Democrats were simply telling the administration that there would be no admission of Hawaii without reciprocal action for Alaska. Realizing the futility of getting combined bills passed, the Senate Interior and Insular Affairs Committee refused to report the twin measures.

In the spring of the same year, Senator Hugh Butler, now chairman of the Senate Interior and Insular Affairs Committee, had announced his intention of holding hearings in Alaska on a statehood bill. "We are going where we can get the reaction of the little people—not just a few aspiring politicians who want to be Senators and Representatives," Butler stated. In August of 1953, therefore, Butler and five committee members journeyed to the territory. Before the hearings opened he requested that only those who had not yet testified do so now.[38]

Butler's hearings in Alaska were the catalyst which started the "populist" phase of the Alaska statehood movement. His emphasis on wanting to hear the "little people" mobilized a large number of those who had come to Alaska during and shortly after the Second World War. Victor Fischer, then the planning director for the city Anchorage, and Niilo Koponen, a homesteader and surveyor at the time, were typical of this new group of territorial citizens. They had been sympathetic to statehood, but had not been directly involved in it. The indigenous movement so far had been propelled mostly by resolutions from the territorial legislature, formal reports and actions taken by the Alaska Statehood Committee, and editorials in the *Anchorage Daily Times* and other territorial papers. The people who had actively participated were the old-time, established, and yet politically progressive professionals and businessmen who, regardless of party affiliation, had followed the leadership of Gruening and Bartlett generally and on the statehood issue in particular. The "little people" who turned out in great numbers for the Butler hearings included many young lawyers, public officials, small businessmen, housewives, nurses, and homesteaders.[39]

As late as mid-August these statehood forces in Anchorage and Fairbanks had begun to prepare for the upcoming hearings. In Anchorage, the "Little Men for Statehood" movement was formed by two young lawyers, Barrie White and Cliff Groh, and that city's Republican Club and its Chamber of Commerce. In Fairbanks, the local Democrats primarily took the initiative.[40] Victor Fischer, a leader in Anchorage, later recalled the formation of the movement there:

> I remember there were a few phone calls, a few people got together, and we sort of said, what are we going to do. Here the committee is coming, Butler is coming. Somebody said we must have a name for our group. So the natural thing was the LITTLE MEN FOR STATEHOOD. And it happened that one of our little signs that we made up at that point read, "I am a

little man for statehood," and we made up these little signs, we made up big posters, and they were plastered all over Anchorage. And we tried to contact the "little men" we knew in other places, and again, it wasn't done through any formal organization. It was just a bunch of citizens acting together. And we found an empty office somewhere on Fourth Avenue in Anchorage and we painted signs and posters and each of us threw in a couple of dollars. And we got a little printing done. We never had letterhead or a formal organization. We never had a chairman or an executive director.[41]

The Butler committee heard testimony at Ketchikan, Juneau, Fairbanks, and Anchorage. Of the approximately 140 witnesses, fewer than 20 opposed statehood, and most of the latter spoke in Ketchikan and Juneau. Probably typical of those against statehood was Allen Shattuck of Juneau, a successful insurance agency owner and a resident of Alaska since 1897. Shattuck did not favor statehood because he was convinced that the territory could not pay for the added costs of a state government. Carl Heinmiller of Haines belonged to the post-World War II group of Alaskans. He had come to the territory in 1947 as a war veteran to homestead. He wholeheartedly supported statehood, and remarked that he was annoyed with Alaska's old aristocracy who were against statehood because they obviously did not want to pay their share of the added expenses. Nineteen-year-old Jerry Wade of Juneau thought it pathetic that "American citizens had to come here and get down on their knees and plead for the right of complete citizenship." Niilo Koponen told the Senators in Fairbanks that without statehood, Alaska would be unable to provide the stable political environment needed to build solid communities and retain population.[42]

Butler and his fellow Senators arrived in Anchorage on a gray, rainy day in late August. The "Little Men for Statehood" group met them at the railroad depot, uncertain as to how many people would turn out for the occasion. Victor Fischer remembered that he and his friends were concerned because they were so unorganized. They did not know if there would be five or fifty people. As it turned out, there were literally hundreds whole met the train, waving banners and placards proclaiming "Statehood Now."[43]

Of the nearly sixty witnesses in Anchorage, only one opposed a statehood. There were some dramatic moments, when, for example, Mitchell Abood presented the Senators with the signatures of 3,129 individuals who demanded statehood. There was also the testimony of Margaret Rutledge, Republican committeewomen from the third judicial division. She told the Senators of having received an invitation to attend the inaugural ceremonies for the first Republican President in twenty years. But under the McCarran Act, which had become effective late in 1952, persons arriving from Alaska in the contiguous United States were required to pass through immigration to establish their legal citizenship before being granted entry. Mrs. Rutledge described her feelings as she had to stand in line and wait her turn to be cleared before being admitted to the main floor of Sea-Tac air terminal in Seattle-Tacoma. "[As I]…stood in line I was profoundly and unjustly humiliated. I was—and still am—seething with indignation." Mrs. Rutledge concluded that "some degrading influence had robbed me of the thing I value most—my birthright as an American, my freedom in my own country." Thereupon, she broke down in front of the committee and cried. Victor Fischer, also a witness, later stated that the tears of a mature women, a Republican, a pillar of the establishment, impressed the Senators profoundly.[44]

When the hearings concluded on August 27, Senator Butler remarked that the prospects for Alaskan statehood had been improved by the visit. Butler said that he supported a generous land grant for the future state. Then, in his typically ambiguous fashion, he stated that the territory could afford to wait for statehood, but should not be asked to wait too long. Thereupon, the senators left Alaska, except for the tireless Butler, who remained for another three days to investigate the areas where the most economic development was taking place. After his private inquiry, Butler concluded that the federal government should provide the territory with, above all else, an adequate road network, a complete survey of all federal land withdrawals, and to make the acquisition of land title easier, a complete revision of the land laws supplying to Alaska. These measures, Butler remarked, would be far more important than any inadequate statehood bill.[45]

The visit of Butler and his colleagues brought together those Alaskans sympathetic to the statehood cause. Many of those who had before been standing on the sidelines decided, in the words of Victor Fischer, "Hell, this is our fight and not just an official one. We, the people, have to participate." Out of the "Little Men for Statehood" forces there soon evolved another group which dubbed itself "Operation Statehood." In those days the military had made the term "operation" fashionable, and "Operation Statehood" quickly became popular. It had a small executive committee and a series of small committees for special assignments. One committee mounted a campaign to encourage as many newcomers as possible to write to their homestate Congressional delegations and, through their families and friends in the contiguous United States, to exert pressure in Congress for Alaska statehood. A "gimmicks" committee devised unique ways to popularize statehood. A "gimmicks" committee devised unique ways to popularize statehood in Congress. On one occasion, the "gimmick" involved the Forget-me-Not, Alaska's official flower. A group of women made artificial bouquets and mailed them to members of Congress just before an Alaska statehood vote. They included a message which went something like this: "We the people of Alaska, say forget-us-not."[46] In addition, the organization prepared informational packets for wide distribution which included a concise summarization of the reasons why statehood should be granted. Alaskans were urged to send Christmas cards to friends in the contiguous United States which stated:

A merry merry Christmas
With happiness and cheer
And in your Christmas greetings

Give a thought to us up here
Only you can give us statehood
With a short card or a note
To your selected Senator
For we don't have a vote
So for us Alaskans

To make our future bright
Ask your Senator for statehood
And start the New Year right.[47]

Such activities indicated that statehood had become a popular cause, and especially so in the most populous third judicial division. Moreover, many proponents were no longer asking for statehood, but demanding it as a right. Victor Fischer, in 1954 the vice-president of Operation Statehood, later said that most people realized by then that the legal precedents for statehood were inconsequential, and that it was simply a political issue. Fischer likened the fight for statehood to the process of rolling a boulder up the hill and you keep sliding back, and you push it up and it rolls back, and you keep wondering how long you can persevere, pushing that boulder to the top until it stays at the top and rolls down the other.[48]

Popular participation on a large scale had not come a minute too soon. Senator Butler, upon his return to Omaha, Nebraska, stated that he thought he had convinced "the rank and file in Alaska that statehood should not come at this time." Most of "the clamor for statehood," he said, was coming from those "politicians who want to run for office." Democratic Senators Clinton P. Anderson and Earle C. Clements, who had accompanied Butler to Alaska for the hearings, took sharp exception to Butler's statements, accusing him of having completely misread the signs of the times in Alaska. Almost every Alaskan who had testified, the Senators stated, had demanded "statehood…now."[49]

During the Congressional recess after the Butler hearings closed, a major revolution occurred in Republican politics in Alaska.

Victor Fischer

Architects of Statehood

Victor Fischer

Vic Fischer was born on May 5, 1924 in Berlin, Germany, the son of the American writer Louis Fischer and his wife, Bertha. In 1933 life in Nazi Germany had become intolerable and endangered the lives of its Jewish inhabitants. Louis Fischer, an American citizen, and his Lithuanian-born wife and children escaped to Moscow after many adventures.

Vitja, as Victor then was known, grew up in Moscow together with his brother, Juri. His father broke with Stalin after the signing of the Soviet-German Non-Aggression Pact, and the Fischers moved to the United States.

Vic attended the University of Wisconsin, MIT, and Harvard, moving to Alaska in 1950 and working as planning director for the city of Anchorage. In 1953, he helped organize the "Little Men for Statehood" movement in response to U.S. Senator Hugh Butler's (R-Nebraska) visit to Alaska to hear from the "little people." Butler was no friend of statehood.

Vic served as a delegate to the Constitutional Convention where he chaired the committee on the executive branch. Later he served as director of the University of Alaska's Institute of Social, Economic and Government Research, served in the state legislature, and was a professor at the University of Alaska Anchorage. He is retired and lives in Anchorage.

A conservative group led by E. Wells Ervin ran the Anchorage Republican Club. Ervin was an ally of Al White, Alaska's Republican boss, who dominated the party through his control of the central committee. In the middle of December a group of liberals combined to overthrow the leadership of the club by electing Walter Hickel its new president. The ultimate loser in this power struggle was Governor Heintzleman, because Ervin had been supporting the chief executive. The change in leadership meant that the governor had failed to unite the party behind him. Indeed, a few days later the *Anchorage Daily Times* published a letter, signed by eighteen members of the new majority which was critical of the governor, his present administrative program, and the policies of the territorial government in general. Heintzleman apparently lacked interest in statehood, and neglected the Westward in favor of the Panhandle. They suggested that Heintzleman replace his executive assistant, Robert N. DeArmond, with "a progressive man from the Railbelt." The group also faulted the governor for his failure to assert himself against stateside interests allegedly controlling territorial affairs and his inability to secure more federal funds for Alaska.[50] The letter reflected, in part, the anger and frustration so many Republicans felt over the failure of the election victory to bring any immediate rewards or advantages. It also showed that men like Walter Hickel, Elmer Rasmuson, and J.C. Morris, who all had hoped to replace Governor Gruening, were still angry for having been passed over for the position.

Yielding to these and other pressures, Heintzleman asked Secretary McKay that he exert his influence to get the bill of committee and to the floor of the Senate as soon as possible. A majority of Alaskans favored statehood "under equitable enabling legislation" and wanted to know what Congress had to offer.[51] Perhaps Heintzleman also wanted to make sure that the Republican Party be credited for statehood under favorable terms.

In his 1954 State of the Union message, President Eisenhower renewed his request for the immediate admission of Hawaii, but again he did not mention Alaska. *The Washington Post* commented editorially that "a murky cloud of politics" hovered over Eisenhower's request for Hawaiian statehood. A number of legislators were supporting statehood for both territories, while some southern Democrats were anxious to kill any statehood action by adding Alaska to the Hawaii bill. "Much of the politics of statehood," the editor stated the obvious, "lies in the assumption that Hawaii would see Republican Senators to Congress, whereas Alaska would elect Democrats." But with Congress almost evenly divided, the editor observed, "this conjecture assumes disproportionate importance."[52]

It was under this "murky cloud of politics" that a subcommittee of the Senate Committee on Interior and Insular Affairs finally drafted an equitable Alaska statehood bill early in 1954. Senator Guy Cordon of Oregon was the subcommittee chairman. The hearings, which lasted from January 20 to February 24, produced yet another thick volume of information on the territory as well as the statehood bill.[53] This measure proposed to give Alaska 100,000,000 acres of its own choice from the unreserved public lands. In addition, 400,000 acres within the Tongass National Forest in southeastern Alaska and another 400,000 acres from public lands elsewhere were bestowed on the new state to allow room for the expansion of the municipalities in that area and in other localities. A grant of 500,000 acres was made to finance the construction of legislative, executive, and judicial buildings, and 200,000 acres were allocated to aid schools and asylums for the deaf, dumb, and blind. For the partial support of the University of Alaska, the subcommittee granted 500,000 acres. It also provided for a federal grant of $42,000,000 for road construction spread over a six-year period, $30,000,000 for road maintenance over a period of fifteen years, and a $15,000,000 appropriation for land surveys and the improvement and construction of harbors.[54] This was a generous bill and very similar to the House measure of the previous year.

In order to move the Hawaii bill, Senator Butler reversed his previous position and came out for Alaska statehood as early as January 25, 1954. The committee thereupon favorably reported the Hawaii bill two days later.[55] Despite such seemingly encouraging signs, the administration had no intention of seeing Alaska admitted. Reports on the Alaska measure had been requested from the Bureau of the Budget, the agency which determined whether or not a piece of legislation was consistent with the President's program, and from the Departments of the Interior, State, and Commerce as early as January, 1953. No replies had been received by March 11, 1954. Several Alaska statehood proponents in the Senate were afraid that the President would veto a separate Alaska statehood bill. To add to these fears, the House Committee on Interior and Insular Affairs had favorably reported its Alaska bill in June of 1953, and the House Rules Committee had not acted upon it. Senator Clinton P. Anderson spoke for many of this Senate colleagues when he remarked that the only chance the House would have to vote on Alaska statehood would be in the event the Senate passed a combined Hawaii-Alaska measure. On March 11, 1954, the Senate agreed to Senator Anderson' s proposal to join the two statehood bills by a vote of 46 to 43; and on April 1, it passed the twin measures by 57 to 28 votes.[56] This was the first time the Senate had passed the two statehood measures, which was viewed as a good omen by some supporters.

The Senate-passed bill next went to the House, where its fate became fairly certain when House Speaker Joseph W. Martin of Massachusetts announced that he did not see much hope for the combined measure. Martin and the Rules Committee majority were unfriendly to Alaska statehood, as was the President. Hoping that public pressure would help, the Alaska Statehood Committee launched a "write-the-President" campaign. Atwood urged territorial Republican leaders to take the initiative in the drive, for if the bill died, the Republicans would be "washed up in Alaska." Operation Statehood energetically aided the effort.[57]

Operation Statehood played a very important role in the drive for admission. Organized soon after the "Little Men for Statehood" hearings had ended, it adopted a constitution, created several committees, and elected a board of directors to meet weekly until statehood had been achieved. An Anchorage operation, it initially asked Alaskans to urge their friends, relatives, business associates and others in the states to write their own Senators and Representatives on behalf of statehood for the territory.[58]

To finance its work, the organization sold $2 memberships and held a variety of fund-raising events, among them the printing and sale of thousands of Christmas cards showing a Santa Claus carrying a package labeled "Statehood."[59]

After the Senate had passed the combination statehood bill, Operation Statehood urged Alaskans to swamp the White House with telegrams asking for statehood now. With the permission of the Anchorage City Council, the organization used a log cabin set up on the lawn of the city hall where volunteers helped citizens to word their telegrams to the president. Barrie White, a local entrepreneur and the President of Operation Statehood, explained that the objective of the telegrams was to persuade the President not to veto the bill.[60]

While the Senate considered statehood, a number of officials of the Department of the Interior favoring statehood arranged a meeting with the President to determine his position on the subject. So on March 2, 1954, Secretary Douglas McKay, Assistant Secretary Orme Lewis and a few others met with the President and apparently were told to keep the northern and western areas of Alaska out of a future state in order to give the chief executive flexibility in case of a military emergency to move troops about without having to ask permission from the governor. On April 1, Governor Heintzleman and Secretary McKay visited the President and discussed statehood, and a couple of days later the governor, after conferring with Interior officials, wrote a letter to House Speaker Joseph Martin in which he suggested that Alaska be partitioned, with only the populated areas to be incorporated within the boundaries of the new state. The governor's plan would have made a state out of roughly 250,000 square miles which contained the larger population centers and approximately 85 percent of the people. Northern and western Alaska would have remained a territory, to be called "Frontier Alaska" or "Alaska Outpost," until it could be absorbed into the new state. The excluded area was rich in natural resources, such as tin, gold copper, coal, mercury, uranium, undetermined amounts of oil, and various other valuable resources. This suggestion elicited a heated debated amoung Alaskans, and was vigorously opposed by the majority. Delegate Bartlett commented that the governor's suggestion was "a nicely calculated effort to hurt the statehood cause." Leaders of both parties in Anchorage were dismayed at the governor's proposal, but President Eisenhower, while reiterating that he considered Alaska unready for statehood, conceded that he might modify his opposition in view of the partition proposal since it would safeguard the needs of military defense.[61]

There was much speculation about the origins of the partition proposal, for few believed that the governor had acted on his own initiative. Democratic Senator Henry M. Jackson of Washington rendered the most plausible explanation when he stated that "the shock [of Senate passage of the Hawaii-Alaska measure] was so great to the Republican leadership that they had to find some means to knock off statehood for Alaska." Delegate Bartlett recalled that Grant Jackson, the president of the Miners and Merchants Bank of Nome, and Ralph Lomen, Seattle resident and president of the Lomen Commercial Company and who also operated a transfer business at Nome, in 1953 had drawn up a similar proposal and sent the delegate a supply of the pamphlets. In it, the authors suggested that Alaska be divided along the 153 meridian into a state and district, and that the latter be allowed to join the former when it had developed economically and no longer would be a liability to the new state.[62]

It is unclear exactly where President Eisenhower received his notion on partitioning the north. In 1950 Nathan Twining, then the commander-in-chief of the Alaskan Command, had told the Senate Interior and Insular Affairs Committee that statehood would result in economic development and population growth, ease military supply problems, reduce construction costs, and give the Alaskan government stability. Early in 1953, Bartlett was told that Twining, then vice-chief of staff for air, was undercutting the Alaska statehood effort. At the end of February 1953, Lyle O'Rourke, an attorney and Eisenhower supporter, told Bartlett that the President opposed statehood because the military had come out against it. Late in December of that year, Representative A. L. "Doc" Miller, Republican from Nebraska, reinforced O'Rourke's statement when he told Bartlett that the administration opposed statehood because the military did. Bartlett had his doubts, however, because nobody else had reported such a military position.[63]

Furthermore, Atwood had visited Twining early in 1954 who, by then, had become the air force chief-of-staff. Twining told Atwood that he and the air force fully supported statehood, while other military officials told him that the Pentagon did not oppose Alaska's admission. Secretary of Defense Charles Wilson, when asked to comment on the partition proposal prompted by military considerations, stated that the matter had not "gotten far enough that it has been put up to me." Bartlett came to believe that Heintzleman's letter to Speaker Martin had furnished the President with a strategy for deleting Title II, Alaska, from the bill.[64]

By the Spring of 1954, the tandem Alaska-Hawaii statehood bill had become thoroughly ensnarled in partisan politics. In the middle of April 1954, an objection from Sam Rayburn of Texas, the House Democratic leader, blocked the twin measures from going to conference with the Senate. This move further dimmed the chances of a vote in the House on Alaska and Hawaii statehood. As a last ditch effort to try to rescue the tandem measure from the House Rules Committee, members of the Alaska Statehood Committee and Operation Statehood planned to fly to Washington. The suggestion had been made by a Hawaiian statehood group to go to Washington in force and attempt to persuade House Speaker Joseph W. Martin to move the twin bills to the floor of the House. The combined Alaskan group chartered an Alaska Airlines plane. One participant recalled that the majority of Alaskans on the flight consisted of young statehood activists of both political parties from Anchorage and other communities. These were the people who had been brought into the fold by the "Little Men for Statehood"

Henry M. Jackson

Architects of Statehood

Henry Martin "Scoop" Jackson

"Scoop" Jackson was born in Everett, Washington on May 31, 1912. He attended public schools and Stanford University and graduated from the University of Washington law school in 1935 and was admitted to the bar the same year. He practiced law and became prosecuting attorney of Snohomish County 1938-1940.

Jackson was elected to the U.S. House in 1941 and served until 1953. In 1952 he was elected to the U.S. Senate. He was chairman of the Committee on Interior and Insular Affairs from the 89th through the 95th Congresses.

In 1958, the Senate had before it its own Alaska statehood bill and also the House-passed measure. The best chance for the Alaska measure to pass Congress was if the Senate accepted the House version. Delegate Bartlett, therefore, met with Senator Jackson, the floor manager of the Alaska bill. Representative Leo O'Brien, the manager of the House bill, Ernest Gruening, and Bartlett all attempted to persuade Jackson to accept the House bill. To everyone's relief, Senator Jackson did so.

Suddenly, chances for passage of the measure had improved dramatically, and it passed to the Senate on June 30, 1958.

movement. Many had continued in Operation Statehood. On May 10, 1954, they, and members of the Alaska Statehood Committee, in addition to the Hawaiian group, descended upon Congress.[65]

Alaskans were told by A.L. Miller, chairman of the House Interior and Insular Affairs Committee, that statehood chances for the territory would be immeasurably improved if partition of Alaska was accepted. Such a division of Alaska, Miller observed, would permit the establishment of military reservations in case of need. But this plan, he warned, would preclude any chance for future annexation by the state of these areas. Chairman Miller felt confident that such a partition proposal would overcome President Eisenhower's objections to Alaska statehood. If Alaskans rejected this proposal, Miller pointed out to his audience, there would be no statehood for the territory.[66]

The Alaska group also met with President Eisenhower. They found the President perched on his desk when they lined up before him. John Butrovich, a Fairbanks insurance agent and senior Republican in the territorial legislature, told Eisenhower:

> *We feel that you are a great American. But we are shocked to come down here and find that a bill which concerns the rights of American citizens is bottled up in a committee when you have the power to bring it out on the House floor.*[67]

For emphasis, Butrovich reportedly banged his fists on the President's desk as he spoke. Eisenhower is said to have reddened. He replied that he wanted to extend full citizenship to as many Americans as possible, but that Alaska statehood posed many problems which would first have to be resolved. The President obviously referred to the territory's military importance and the safeguarding of these interests through the partition plan. The political ramifications of the issue, Eisenhower told his audience, had only recently come to his attention. He denied, however, that partisanship played any role in the Alaska statehood issue.[68]

After a week of making the rounds in Washington, the weary Alaskans returned home, expressing the belief that their visit, if nothing else, had added to the pressure for statehood. The members of the flight, however, were thoroughly confused by the partition proposal. Ray Plummer, Democratic National Committeeman from Alaska, reflected the feeling of the group:

> No one told us that even if we divide Alaska six ways we would have a better chance of getting statehood than if we stand firm...No one made a firm commitment that 'if you accept partition you will get statehood'.[69]

In any event, another statehood effort had failed for that session of Congress. Between 1953 and 1955, the role of President Eisenhower had been important in delaying statehood for Alaska. With Republican control of Congress, the chief executive might well have exerted the necessary pressure to force a House vote on the issue. Instead, Eisenhower, with an eye on the narrow Republican edge in the Senate, attempted to gain admission for Hawaii alone.

While the President stalled, numerous alternatives to statehood were discussed and debated.

CHAPTER ELEVEN

Elective Governorship and
Commonwealth Status

Not only partition, but also an elective governorship and commonwealth status for Alaska had been mentioned from time to time. Delegate Bartlett had repeatedly introduced elective governorship bill in 1945, 1947, 1948, and again in 1953. Eventually, he rejected the concept because opponents of statehood also sponsored such legislation but considered it to be a substitute for statehood. In any event, under statehood Alaskans could elect their governor. The Department of the Interior shared Bartlett's view, and in the delegate's latest elective governorship bill in 1953, it endorsed the concept only if Congress did not enact statehood. Shortly there-after, the House Subcommittee on Territories and Insular Posses-sions tabled the measure after a brief hearing, for, as Representative John Saylor so well expressed the view of the majority, the elective governor bill would retard statehood by twenty years.[1]

When Senator Butler visited Ketchikan in August 1953, he spoke about his elective governor bill. Under its provisions, the first gubernatorial election was to be held in 1954, but he thought that the measure needed to be amended to allow Governor Heintzleman to serve his full four-year term which ended in 1956. In January of the next year Butler introduced such an amendment, explaining to his colleagues that the filling date of February 1 prescribed by Alaska's election laws was so close that the bill could not possibly take effect that year.[2]

Now the Bureau of the Budget intervened and questioned whether the popular election of a territorial governor would be constitutional since the chief executive would continue to carry out federal as well as territorial functions. The Constitution clearly stated that the President "shall nominate, and, by and with the consent of the Senate, shall appoint ambassadors, other public ministers and consuls, judges of the Supreme Court, and all other officers of the United States, whose appointments are not herein otherwise provided for, and which shall be established by law; but the Congress may by law vest the appointment of such inferior officers, as they think proper, in the President alone, in the courts of law, or in the head of departments." Consequently, as long as the governor administered the interests of the United States his election by the people seemed to be contrary to the Constitution. There also was the question of whether one individual could serve federal and territorial interests without a conflict of interest. Congress had allowed Puerto Ricans to elect their own governor in 1947, but at the same time it also had created the position of a presidentially appointed coordinator of federal agencies. No such position existed in Alaska nor was it mentioned in the elective governor bills. In fact, Congress had passed legislation in 1914 which permitted the legislature to impose nonfederal duties upon the governor and other federal officials in Alaska so long as these were not inconsistent with the performance of their federal responsibilities. In succeeding years the territorial legislature had made the governor a member or ex officio member of numerous boards and agencies and given him the powers of appointment. Often, when disagreeing with the chief executive, there had been suggestions within the territorial legislature to create an elective administrator general who would carry out the purely territorial functions of the governorship.[3]

The authorization to elect the governor would have ended the dual nature of that office. Although widely supported, there also was a good deal of caution. The *Anchorage Daily Times* perhaps best expressed this hesitation when it stated that "Alaska would still be a colony but the interest of the mother country would be lessened." As a territory, the delegate represented Alaskan interests in the capital while being responsible to his constituents. The governor was responsible to the federal government and could expect to be heard at the decision-making level when pleasing the territory's case. An elective governor did not have such access and leverage.[4]

Statehood was not only threatened by an elective governorship, but also by the idea that the territories be transformed into commonwealths. As early as 1952, Senator A.S. "Mike" Monroney, Democrat of Oklahoma, had instructed the Senate Interior and Insular Affairs Committee to consider the commonwealth arrangement for both Alaska and Hawaii. That was the same year Puerto Rico gained commonwealth status, and Monroney might have been inspired by that example. In March of 1954 he revived the proposal in association with George Smathers, William Fulbright, and Price Daniel, three other southern Democrats. Monroney introduced the proposal as an amendment, in the form of a substitute bill for the tandem Alaska-Hawaii measure, which would have granted commonwealth status to both territories. A referendum was to be held in each territory to determine whether its people desired commonwealth status, and if they did, the legislature were to call a convention to draft a commonwealth constitution. The new fundamental laws were to become effective after ratification by the voters of the territories and approval by Congress. Essentially, commonwealth advocates proposed to grant all the rights and responsibilities, except national representation, to Alaska and Hawaii. To sweeten the bait, the two territories were to be granted exemption from federal income taxes, and all the revenues gathered within their borders were to be used locally. Residents of Alaska and Hawaii were to enjoy the complete protection of the Constitution and the Bill of Rights. They would share in the benefits of social security, unemployment compensation, federal housing, and similar legislation. At the same time they would have the full obligations of selective service, but could not participate in

Presidential elections. Commonwealth status, Senator Monroney observed, was the "best way to give justice to the distant areas and at the same time protect the political unity and the present political stature of our 48 contiguous sister states."[5]

The commonwealth proposals for Alaska and Hawaii actually were flimsy and ill-defined. During the 1954 Senate debate, Clinton P. Anderson pointed out that time and again the Supreme Court had designated Alaska and Hawaii as incorporated territories. This implied that both were embryonic states and that all the provisions of the Constitution applied to them. Such was not the case, of course, with unincorporated areas such as Puerto Rico, Guam, and the Virgin Islands. Senator Guy Cordon submitted a report from the Library of Congress which indicated that no incorporated territory had ever been exempted from or been rebated federal taxes. Cordon also submitted a memorandum prepared by two of Hawaii's deputy attorneys general which pointed out that conveying commonwealth status to an incorporated territory was unconstitutional. The same federal taxes paid in a state, the authors argued, also had to be paid in an incorporated territory, and furthermore, that an incorporated territory could not be disincorporated. There was much argument whether or not the Supreme Court would have accepted their arguments. In essence, it was not only a legal but also a political question which would involve, in part, the question of how complete was the power of Congress "to dispose of and make all needful rules and regulations respecting the territory or other property belonging to the United States"? In any event, whatever the court might have decided, the committee defeated Monroney's proposal by a vote of 60 to 24.[6]

Soon, however, commonwealth organizations sprang up in Alaska. Anchorage attorney John Manders, a member of the group called Commonwealth for Alaska, Inc., probably best explained what these Alaskan advocates expected:

Whether you call it commonwealth, territorial status, protectorate or state or home rule the main object of the so-called movement for commonwealth status for Alaska is to take off

the backs of the people the burdensome taxation that is now
plaguing each and every one of them. It makes little differ-
ence what you call it. The main purpose is the elimination
of federal taxation and then whatever you are taxed by your
own legislature is your own fault as to whether or not you are
taxed heavily or lightly.[7]

In the summer of 1954, an Anchorage group organized the Committee for Commonwealth. Alex Bowker of Spenard, the owner of a trailer business, was elected chairman, and Corneil Sherman, a consulting engineer and president of the Alaska Chrome Corporation became co-chairman. Within a short time the committee collected some monetary donations and used these funds to distribute 20,000 copies of a pamphlet explaining commonwealth status. Committee members also solicited the opinion of every member of Congress on the matter.[8]

Another group, Commonwealth for Alaska, filed articles of incorporation in August 1954. John Manders and Harold Sogn, two of the founders of the now defunct organization Statehood for Alaska were among the directors of the new corporation which was "to promote and officially sponsor commonwealth statues for Alaska." While Mander's group immediately became inactive, the Committee for Commonwealth functioned. In the fall of that year Corneil Sherman invited Ingram Stainback, former Hawaiian governor and associate justice of the Hawaiian Supreme court, the address a banquet to Anchorage, attended by about 150 people who paid $25 each. Stainback had once supported statehood for the islands but now favored commonwealth status. The chief attraction, he stated, were the lower taxes. Stainback used the same theme when addressing audiences in Fairbanks and Juneau, the Anchorage Chamber of Commerce, and when he spoke on radio and television. He considered Alaska's chances of obtaining commonwealth status excellent.[9]

Late in 1954, the Committee for Commonwealth finished work on modifying the constitution of the Commonwealth of Puerto Rico to fit Alaskan uses, and prepared a petition which it intended to circulate, asking that Congress authorize commonwealth status for Alaska and include the committee's modified constitution in its bill. Once Congress had passed the measure, Alaskans could skip a constitutional convention and instead conduct a combined ratification referendum and primary election. One month later, in December, the committee filed incorporation papers and shortly thereafter published another pamphlet, entitled *Commonwealth for Alaska: Facts & Comments*. The pamphlet included a copy of the proposed constitution, and explained the proposed statues to mean self government, freedom from federal taxation, and control of a major portion of Alaska's lands and natural resources. It also meant higher taxes since the commonwealth would be expected to assume what, in essence, were state functions such as transportation, a judicial system, health and welfare services, and tax incentives to encourage new industries. Membership dues amounted to five dollars for the first year. The authors of the pamphlet contended that commonwealth would be a stepping stone to statehood.[10]

William Baker, the editor and publisher of the *Ketchikan Alaska Chronicle*, wrote that since there was so much discussion about commonwealth, perhaps Alaskans should have a chance to vote on it as an alternative to statehood. Baker, however, also suspected that the canned salmon industry might be behind the movement, but Delegate Bartlett found the quality of the pamphlet too amateurish and concluded that "the masterminds of the fishing industry" had not been involved in drafting it.[11]

Most Alaskan newspapers supporting statehood generally criticized commonwealth status, while those opposing it, like the *Daily Alaska Empire*, published by Helen Monsen, the daughter of the late Governor John W. Troy, and the *Ketchikan Daily News*, published by Sid Charles, did not promote commonwealth, but did praise some of its advantages. An exception, perhaps, was the *Anchorage Daily News*, whose editor, Norman Brown, had regularly attacked statehood and became an early member of the Committee for Commonwealth.[12]

Obviously, the 1954 elections were on the minds of many Alaskans. One question many asked themselves was whether or not there should be a referendum on commonwealth status. Resident James Walker of Spenard wrote that such a referendum should note a choice between commonwealth or statehood, because almost everyone favored eventual statehood. The ballot should ask: "Are you in favor of obtaining commonwealth status as a stepping stone to eventual statehood? Yes or no." Perhaps in response to this persistent undercurrent, Alice Stuart of Fairbanks, the editor and publisher of the "Alaska Calendar for Engagements," came to Washington in May of 1954 to represent the Alaska Referendum Committee. The committee consisted of herself. She brought with her a petition signed by approximately 1,400 residents asking for a referendum. Miss Stuart met with members of the House Rules Committee, the Senate and House Interior and Insular Affairs committees, Speaker Martin, and even a White House aide. She was unable, however, to meet the President. Her petition asked that there should be a new referendum, worded clearly and in an unbiased manner, such as: "Are you in favor or against immediate statehood for Alaska?" This question, she maintained, should be placed on the 1954 ballot.[13]

When news of Miss Stuart's activities reached Alaska, many of those who had signed her petition were mad. Stuart presented the petition as a request by the signers to delay statehood, yet when soliciting signatures she had said nothing about that purpose. Many of those who signed would not have done so had they known about her intentions. Many had signed, believing that a referendum would show overwhelming approval for immediate admission. Those who had contributed money to finance her trip had thought that she was a member of the Operation Statehood flight to the nation's capital. In short, Miss Stuart had succeeded in deceiving many people and obtaining a free flight to Washington to present her ideas to Congress and the administration.[14]

Two unofficial polls on commonwealth were conducted in 1954. Operation Statehood polled seventy-five candidates for territorial office in the October elections. The questionnaire offered immediate statehood, commonwealth status, and continued territorial status. Fifty-nine candidates responded. Out of this number, fifty-four desired immediate statehood, two preferred commonwealth status, none desired continued territoriality, and the answers of the remaining three did not fit any of the three categories. The Alaska Broadcasting System conducted the second poll at the end of September and the beginning of October 1954. All six of the network's stations in Fairbanks, Anchorage, Seward, Juneau, Sitka, and Ketchikan participated. Listeners were asked to send in signed postcards indicating the kind of government they preferred. The network found that 3,752 desired immediate statehood, 258 statehood later, 784 commonwealth status, and 120 continued territoriality.[15]

The results of the polls were released shortly before the general election. The Republicans suffered overwhelming defeats, winning only three seats to the Democrats' twenty-one in the House and in the Senate, where only half the membership was up for reelection, the new lineup was four Republicans and twelve Democrats.[16]

But while Alaska's media and its citizens generally did not embrace commonwealth status, some national publications rendered favorable interpretations of this new approach. Richard Strout, writing in The New Republic, drew a parallel with the dominion status enjoyed by several members of the British Commonwealth of Nations. Strout maintained that a similar arrangement would be an excellent solution for America's noncontiguous territories. He also asserted that an area with only 129,000 inhabitants was scarcely entitled to two United States Senators, when New York State, with a population of 14,800,000 had only two. Additionally, Strout expressed concern about the precedent the admission of Alaska and Hawaii would set. Could statehood be denied to Guam or the Virgin Islands, he asked? Many of the Senate's most important decisions, he pointed out, were reached by a two-thirds votes. This being the case, Alaska's senators could conceivably neutralize the votes of senators from large populous states.[17] The same argument, of course, could be made with regard to Hawaii's prospective Congressional delegation.

Columnist Walter Lippman also became a convert to the commonwealth cause. He asserted that the admission of outlying territories would constitute a radical change in the structure of the

Union and its external relations. Lippman did not explain how or
why this would happen, nor did he point out that denying statehood to incorporated territories and transforming them into commonwealths would constitute a departure from the American
historical experience. Lippman doubted that the interests of Alaska
and Hawaii were identical to those of Americans in the contiguous
United States and, therefore, questioned whether theses outlying
areas could be successfully assimilated. Like others, he was worried lest Guam, the Carolinas, and even Formosa might someday
take advantage of the precedent set by the admission of Hawaii and
Alaska. Senator Monroney was similarly bothered by the precedent which would be established, and asked, "Must we forever continue... the proposition that all States...[can] come in, no matter
where they...[are] located beyond our land mass, with influence in
the upper chamber equal to the contiguous states....?"[18]

Douglas Smith of the *Washington Daily News* ridiculed such
views, and especially Lippman's argument. Alaska and Hawaii, he
asserted, were the only two incorporated territories left, and the
Supreme Court had repeatedly held that such a territory was in
a state of tutelage in preparation for statehood. The admission of
Hawaii and Alaska would mean no more and no less than the addition of two stars to the flag and of four new senators and an appropriate number of representatives. Each time a territory had been
admitted to statehood, Smith observed, "the Republic survived...
despite the warnings of alarmist...." Delegate Bartlett and Robert B.
Atwood of the Alaska Statehood Committee evaluated the Alaska
commonwealth movement in testimony before a Congressional
Committee in 1955. They stated that the subject seemed to come
up in the territory only when statehood was being discussed before
Congress and there was a possibility of success. Once statehood
legislation failed in a particular session, talk of commonwealth status also quickly subsided.[19]

It was, of course, true, as proponents always asserted, that
Puerto Rico had acquired commonwealth status in 1952 and did
not pay federal taxes. The core of the commonwealth plans for
Alaska and Hawaii promised similar privileges. Delegate Bartlett

reported in 1956 that he had made extensive inquires about the possibility of such freedom from federal taxation. The replies he received had all been negative. Typical was that of Representative Wilbur D. Mills, Democrat of Arkansas and chairman of the House Ways and Means Committee:

> ...*it would appear that the uniformity clause of the Constitution requires that all federal tax laws apply uniformly to Alaska, just as to any other part of the United States. It has also been argued that Congress' power to enact legislation governing the territories is derived from article IV, section 3, clause 2 of the Constitution, and that this power is independent of the prohibition contained in the uniformity clause. This question has never been decided by the courts. However, I am inclined to think that if and when it arises, the courts will decide that the mandate of the uniformity clause must prevail.*[20]

Secretary of the Interior Douglas McKay bluntly stated in 1955 that a federal tax moratorium for Alaska might "be a fine thing," but that it had about as much of a chance of passing Congress as a bill "to replace the stars and stripes on the American flag with the hammer and sickle." Without federal tax exemption, the commonwealth scheme lost its main appeal. But despite the obvious inapplicability of commonwealth status to incorporated territories, the idea did not die easily. As late as 1957, Representative Thomas M. Pelly of Washington proposed it as an alternative to Alaska's admission. In April of that year, the Ketchikan Commonwealth Club requested information on the subject from the Department of the Interior, only to be told that the meaning and implications of commonwealth were entirely unclear.[21]

CHAPTER TWELVE

More Congressional
Deliberations and the
Constitutional Convention

The Republican victory in 1952 had wrought many changes in Alaska's political situation. As already stated, Ernest Gruening, the territory's appointed governor for nearly fourteen years, was a casualty of the 1952 Republican sweep. The man who had been a leader and a catalyst of the statehood movement left office in April 1953. And after long years of dominance, defeat had divided the Democratic Party by bringing to the fore matters which formerly had been disregarded in favor of unity. The dispirited Democrats had to find an issue around which they could rally. Alaska's Republicans, in opposition for such a long time and unaccustomed to political responsibility, served Democratic purposes admirably. The Republican majority in the legislature created a controversial McCarthy-like investigative committee. Besides that, little was accomplished in the 1953 session. According to one Democratic observer, "...that session was one of the worst in territorial history..., members were drunk on the floor..., it was a shambles." The house "never did adjourn, it just disbanded."[1]

These conditions strengthened the Democrat's determination to reorganize and rejuvenate their leadership. Early in 1954 they held a special territorial convention in Juneau, and one of their decisions was to invite Adlai Stevenson, the recent presidential candidate. His visit, it was hoped, would help unify the party. Before Stevenson arrived, however, Secretary of the Interior McKay embarked upon an Alaska inspection trip in July of 1954. While in Anchorage, McKay tongue-lashed an audience who had come to ask him to support statehood. The secretary gave six reasons why statehood had not been achieved. He told his audience that personally he favored statehood, but that the President made policy and he just worked for him. In addition, the chief executive opposed statehood for defense reasons; Alaskans had opposed the partition of the territory: the Senate had tied the Hawaii and Alaska bills together; there were members of Congress who were opposed to the admission of noncontiguous territory; Alaskans had been too belligerent in their demands; and the territory was too underdeveloped. The secretary, not noted for his political tact, told his Anchorage listeners that he was "sick and tired of being kicked around by Alaskans," and that it was time for the people of the territory to "start acting like ladies and gentleman." McKay denied as "just a bunch of horsefeathers" reports that his department wanted to maintain control of Alaska and therefore opposed statehood. "I assure you," McKay concluded, "it would take away a lot of headaches if you got statehood tomorrow."[2]

Stevenson arrived in Alaska a few days after McKay's Anchorage speech. He opened his remarks with an underscored "Ladies and Gentlemen" in an obvious rebuff to the secretary. Statehood advocates felt elated after the Stevenson visit. The bungling of the territorial legislature, the unfriendly attitude of the national administration toward statehood, and Stevenson's appearance helped the territorial Democrats to victory in the fall elections of 1954. After this win, the party faithful gathered in an informal pre-legislative planning session in Fairbanks in the fall of 1954. The group decided to hold a constitutional convention, and in effect, make

Alaska a state prior to Congressional action. Thomas Stewart, then an Assistant Attorney General of Alaska, was assigned the task of writing a preliminary constitutional convention bill.[3]

The idea of such a convention was not a new one in the territory. It had been proposed as early as 1948. At that time, Delegate Anthony J. Dimond had pointed out that such an undertaking should have the active financial support of the territorial legislature in order to make it effective. No such support had been forthcoming. The plan was again promoted in 1951, and, in addition, Alaskans were then urged to elect their Congressional delegation without waiting for action from Congress. The Alaska Statehood Committee rejected this idea as inopportune. Early in 1953, Wendell P. Kay, a lawyer and legislator from Anchorage, submitted a bill for a constitutional convention. The lawmakers debated it fruitlessly, and Kay finally withdrew it. He revived the proposal in the fall of the same year, hard on the heels of the statehood hearings which had been held in Alaska. His obvious intention was to keep interest in the issue at a high level. Nothing came of this suggestion either. Early in June of 1954, with the tandem Alaska-Hawaii bill stalled in the House Rules Committee, Representative A.L. Miller, chairman of the House Interior and Insular Affairs Committee, and supposedly opposed to the territory's admission, suddenly suggested that Alaskans hold a constitutional convention. He indicated that such a positive move might persuade the House Rules Committee to release the measures.[3]

Charles Willis "C.W." Snedden, publisher of the *Fairbanks Daily News-Miner,* was a strong advocate of a constitutional convention. Snedden, a former Washington state newspaperman, real estate investor and former linotype machinist as well as salesman, had been employed by Austin "Cap" Lathrop, then the owner of the paper, to manage the mechanical end of the business. After Lathrop died, Snedden purchased the paper. He also became involved in local affairs as one of the first members of the Fairbanks Municipal Utilities District. This experience had opened his eyes to the inequities of "second-class" citizenship. The board sold two revenue bond issues which totaled $7,000,000. Anywhere in the contiguous states, Snedden asserted, these income tax-exempt bonds would have been sold for not more than 3.25 percent interest. The eastern banking houses, however, judged the territory to be politically unstable and charged 4.75 percent interest on $3,000,000 and 4.25 percent on the other $4,00,000. This amounted to almost $1,500,000 extra paid by the citizens of Fairbanks over the 25-year life of the bonds for the privilege of living in Alaska. This experience motivated Snedden to question the editorial policies of Lathrop's capable editor, William C. Strand, who had been bitterly and consistently opposed to statehood. When Strand left the paper in early 1952, Snedden hired John C. Ryan as editor. The editorial policy of the paper continued automatically until Snedden, having familiarized himself with Alaska and its problems by late 1953, told Ryan to study the whole statehood question. After a few weeks of solitude, Ryan emerged after Christmas, 1953, as a statehood advocate. Snedden concurred with his editor's decision.[4] In a major editorial on February 27, 1954, Snedden himself changed the paper's stand on statehood, when he stated:

> We are American citizens,... and we have the right to enjoy all the privileges for which all our forefathers fought and died.... Alaskans should make it clear that we are demanding full Statehood and nothing less....Alaskans should demand STATEHOOD NOW.[5]

On April 9, 1954, Snedden published a collection of his editorials in a special six-page edition which was widely circulated throughout the territory. This switch on statehood cost him the acquisition of *The Daily Alaska Empire* (Juneau), which bitterly opposed statehood. Snedden later recalled that he had made a firm agreement for the owner. After she received a copy of his February 27, 1954, editorial backing statehood, she called him on the phone and asked to be released from the agreement. Snedden agreed to do so.[6] However, the *Fairbanks Daily News-Miner* added a powerful pro-statehood voice to those of other papers in the territory.

And as so often happens, converts to a cause are much more zeal-
ous than those who are born to it, and Snedden was no exception.

By 1954, several groups of Alaskans were independently preparing measures for a constitutional convention. One such gathering
of interested people, primarily from College, the unincorporated
town near the University of Alaska, formed the Constitutional Study
League in that year. The members of this organization searched the
constitutions of the various states and Canadian provinces for provisions most easily adaptable to Alaskan conditions. A finished bill
for a constitutional convention was entrusted to Robert McNealy,
a Fairbanks attorney and member of the territorial legislature, who
agreed to present the measure in the 1955 session.[7]

Thomas Stewart, an Alaska Assistant Attorney General who
had been given the task by the territorial Democrats of preparing
a constitutional convention bill, resigned his official position and
began to travel widely in the contiguous United States in his quest
to find the best models for his assignment. He visited the political
science departments of major universities and sought advice. He
talked with those who had been involved in the 1947 New Jersey
constitutional convention. Stewart obtained a list of books useful as references for delegates. In addition, he contacted the chief
librarian of the Library of Congress and asked him for the names
of organizations which could furnish staff services for such a convention. Stewart returned to Juneau at the end of 1954 and began
drafting a proposal for a convention to be submitted to the territorial legislature early in 1955.[8]

Throughout 1954 the possibility of such a convention was
widely discussed in the territory. Many of those who were active in
the Anchorage-based Operation Statehood questioned the wisdom
of such an undertaking. Victor Fischer, vice president of the group,
had serious misgivings. He later stated that he and his associates
in the organization regarded a constitutional convention strictly
as a "gimmick" designed to impress Congress sufficiently to grant
statehood. He and his group believed that such a convention would
divert energies needed in Washington. Robert B. Atwood, chairman

of the Alaska Statehood Committee, while agreeing with Fischer's views that the convention would be a "gimmick," disagreed with him about the efficacy of such an undertaking. Atwood stated that his committee had always looked for new approaches to statehood, and felt that such a convention would greatly aid the cause.[9]

When the legislature met in Juneau early in 1955, territorial representative Stewart's constitutional convention bill was the first measure submitted in the house. The members of the joint house senate committee charged with writing a bill acceptable to both houses appointed Stewart their chairman. With the background material he had collected, the copies of the New Jersey and Missouri constitutions, and the document Hawaiians had adopted in 1950, plus the bill prepared by the College group, the joint committee step-by-step completed an acceptable proposal. The provisions of the final measure which emerged from Stewart's joint committee differed greatly from the procedures for a constitutional convention included in the tandem Alaska-Hawaii statehood bill of 1955.[10]

Most importantly, the joint committee agreed to establish twenty-two election districts for choosing delegates. This guaranteed representation for every principal community in the convention, and insured broad support among the various regions of the territory. The joint committee called for adequate appropriations from the territorial general fund to finance the necessary preliminary staff work and the convention itself, and to hire qualified consultants to be utilized by the delegates. The joint committee also fixed a seventy-five day limit for the convention and planned a recess during which the delegates would return home and talk with their constituents. The University of Alaska at College, near Fairbanks, was designated at the meeting place of the convention. This removed it from the political atmosphere which invariably exists in a capital.[11]

In March of 1955, the constitutional convention bill passed the territorial legislature, together with an appropriation of $300,000 for the expenses.[12] With that action, the convention was launched. Alaskans were to go to the polls and elect fifty-five delegates for the November opening of the convention. Robert Atwood was to hire the necessary staff to do the background studies. It had been agreed to secure the services of political scientists from various universities. Instead, early in June 1955, Atwood selected the Public Administration Service of Chicago, a nonprofit organization associated with the Council of State Governments. Thomas Stewart, for one, was nonplussed at Atwood's decision, since the agreement to hire university political scientists had not been kept. But since time was running short and there still was much to be done, he went along with the choice.[13]

As it turned out, the Public Administration Service hired seven political scientists from various universities for the convention itself, who were to be coordinated by Emil Sady of the organization. Next, the Public Administration Service sent a number of consultants to Alaska who traveled throughout the territory with Stewart. These consultants spoke at public meetings and to delegate candidates, and they also prepared material about the upcoming convention for local newspapers. These activities helped to stimulate interest and disseminate a great deal of information about the convention.[14]

While preparations for the constitutional convention proceeded apace, President Eisenhower delivered his State of the Union address on January 6, 1955. He stated that "as the complex problems of Alaska are resolved that territory should expect to receive statehood. In the meantime, there is no justification for deferring admission to statehood of Hawaii." Statehood proponents perked up their ears, because this was the first time in his presidency that Eisenhower had mentioned Alaska statehood in his State of the Union address. The President did not enumerate the complex problems, but presumably they related to military considerations.[15]

Representative Clair Engle, Democrat from California and the new chairman of the House Interior and Insular Affairs Committee, and a leader in the move to join the Hawaii and Alaska measures in 1953, now considered this to have been a mistake. A couple of days after the November 1954 elections he remarked that Hawaii's

Robert B. Atwood

Architects of Statehood

Robert B. Atwood

Bob Atwood was born on March 31, 1907 in Chicago, Illinois. A graduate of Clark University in Massachusetts, he took a job as a newspaper reporter in Springfield, Illinois. There he met Evangeline Rasmuson, the daughter of Alaskan banker E.A. Rasmuson. They married in 1932 and moved in 1935 to Anchorage, a town of 2,200 inhabitants.

With his father-in-law's help Atwood bought the *Anchorage Daily Times*, circulation 650. With drive and imagination, buoyed by the influx of residents, Atwood turned his paper into a media powerhouse that he used to express his pro-statehood and pro-development views. For 52 years Atwood lobbied for what he viewed best for his adopted homeland, from statehood to Native claims, from oil development to moving the capital out of Juneau.

In 1990 Atwood sold the *Times*, as it had been renamed, to Bill Allen, the CEO of VECO, an oil services company. By that time the *Anchorage Daily News* had become the state's dominant paper. Atwood died on January 10, 1997.

chances for achieving statehood should not be tied to Alaska. He predicted that his committee would pass new statehood measures so fast that "they" will smoke from the friction." After the House organization, however, Engle and John Saylor introduced tandem bills. Engle explained that, although he had not changed his mind, he had deferred to the wishes of individuals who were interested in the legislation. Title II of the tandem bill, the Alaska measure, contained one new feature. It allowed the state to select coal, phosphate, sodium, oil, oil shale, and gas lands leased from the Bureau of Land Management before approval of the enabling act. Under this arrangement, existing contracts would not be affected. The state simply replaced the federal government as the contracting party.[16]

When the House Interior and Insular Affairs Committee met on January 25, Representative John Pillion tried to have the tandem measures reviewed at length by the Subcommittee on Territories and Insular Possessions. The committee defeated the move 15 to 7, and decided that the full committee would hold hearings, primarily to benefit new members. Engle also asked that the Departments of the Interior, Agriculture, and Defense submit reports on statehood. They were not to wait for approval from the Bureau of the Budget because that organization was too slow.[17]

As soon as the committee began discussing the Alaska measure, Representative Clifton Young of Nevada opposed the land provisions. The patrimony should be sufficient to launch Alaska on a firm economic footing but not be so lavish as to deplete the public domain, he maintained. In defense, Engle told Young that the administration required that the land grant be adequate, while Representative Arthur Miller denied that the land grant was a simply a give-away. It was important to make Alaska economically strong and independent, he asserted. Wayne Aspinall of Colorado explained that land laws created for the contiguous states simply did not fit Alaskan conditions, but Young insisted that the land grant be reduced to 50 million acres. The committee rejected his amendment 16 to 4. But while Young merely objected to the land grant and not to admission, John Pillion continued his opposition to statehood. He had contacted all the governors and legislators of the 48 states and explained to them that they would lose political power should Alaska and Hawaii be permitted to join the Union. To counter this threat, a number of Constitutional amendments had been proposed. Representative Frederic Coudert had proposed that Congress should determine whether a new state would be granted one, two, or no Senators at all. Another proposal was designed to make the admission of new states as difficult as that of amending the Constitution, requiring a two-thirds approval vote of the House and Senate, and the concurrence of three-fourths of the state legislatures. Representative Coudert sponsored this amendment as well, joined by William Comer of Mississippi, Thomas Dodd of Connecticut, and James Davis of Georgia. Pillion proposed an amendment that would grant Senate representation to a new state on a basis proportional to its population. Existing states would be unaffected because of the Constitutional provision "that no State, without its consent, shall be deprived of its equal suffrage in the Senate. "[18]

Pillion proposed that, until his proposal was accepted, Alaska should be granted full self government, the right to select up to 20 million acres from the public domain, and annual cash grants of $7 million for a five year period in compensation for federal functions the territory would assume. Until admitted to statehood, both Alaska and Hawaii were to be represented by delegates rather than representatives. Pillion concluded that both delegates were lucky in being voteless since they were spared the unpleasantness of voting occasionally for measures detrimental to some of their colleagues.[19]

Secretary McKay appeared before the committee and voiced his displeasure over the fact that the two bills had been combined. He maintained that each territory should be judge on its merits, and that he favored Alaska's admission under a suitable bill. The Secretary thought, however, that the barren wilderness areas of northern and western Alaska would be a financial burden to the new state. Questioned, he implied that his department would approve a measure containing a military reservation. Arthur Miller thereupon

drafted an amendment empowering the President to "establish, by
Executive order or proclamation issued prior to admission...one
or more special national defense withdrawals' within the territory.
The United States was to exercise exclusive jurisdiction over each
such withdrawal. Still, all territorial and federal laws in force in
Alaska prior to admission would also be valid in these withdrawals,
allowing school districts, municipalities, and other political subdivisions to operate as usual—unless the President decided otherwise.
The region in which these special national defense withdrawals
might be made included much of southwestern Alaska, the Aleutian Islands, as well as the area north and west of a line running one
mile from the right bank of the Yukon River. It was a confusing
amendment, because the President already had the power to create
military reservations on the public domain, and indeed, he could
take over private land through condemnation proceedings.[20]

The delegate rejected the amendment, pointing out that neither
the Defense Department nor the President had indicated that it
met their objections. The amendment language was very compli-
cated to boot. Why were the Aleutian Islands included, he asked,
since the air force had downgraded the strategic importance of the
area since the Second World War. He echoed Representative Saylor when stating that the President already possessed the power to
take land for military uses. Most importantly, Bartlett had not been
given the opportunity to analyze the amendment. Shown a map
which contained the proposed boundaries, Bartlett was reminded
that it very much resembled "one of the partition maps." Bartlett
believed that the vast majority of Alaskans opposed the partition
of their territory. Several members tried to convince the delegate
that the amendment was necessary to win the President's approval,
but he persisted and the committee defeated the Miller proposal 14
to 5. Believing that the Alaska measure had no chance without it,
Miller and Saylor moved to strike Title II altogether. The committee, however, rejected this motion by a vote of 15 to 3.[21]

On the afternoon of that eventful day, the committee received
a letter from Secretary of Defense Charles Wilson, containing his

agency's report on the statehood measures. While not objecting
to Hawaii's admission, Wilson stated that in view of Alaska's great
size, small population, limited communications network, strategic
location, and existing international situation it seemed wise not to
change "the political status of this federal area." Bartlett only concluded that nothing had been lost in rejecting the Miller amendment. When the territorial house learned of the Wilson letter, it
dispatched an angry telegram to Representative Clair Engle and
Senator James Murray, denouncing Secretary Wilson and his reference to Alaska as a federal area. For good measure they criticized
President Eisenhower and Secretary McKay as well. All house
members signed the communication.[22]

On February 16 committee members voted on amendments.
They accepted one reducing the gross receipts from the national
forests from 37.5 to 25 percent. Bartlett, having studied the Miller
amendment, found it to be relatively innocuous. Knowing that he
had to make concessions, he changed Miller's language slightly to
make it acceptable to his constituents. He changed the language to
exclude Nome, all of Southwestern Alaska and a good part of the
Aleutian Islands from the withdrawal area. Furthermore, the President would be authorized to create special national defense withdrawals not to exceed 40 percent of the withdrawal area and not
after Alaska had become a state. The committee approved Bartlett's
amendment on a 21 to 5 vote, and Engle's tandem bill 19 to 6. Miller
thereupon stated that he would support the measure.[23]

Meanwhile, on the Senate side, James Murray and twenty-five
of his colleagues reintroduced the measure the Senate had passed
in 1954. Senator Henry Jackson, a Democrat from the state of
Washington and the chairman of the Subcommittee on Territories
and Insular Affairs, was in receipt of the same report Secretary
Wilson had sent to the House committee. Jackson acknowledged
it. The report from the Department of State explained, as it had
in 1950, that admitting the territories into the Union would be in
accordance with the United Nations Charter. It would also give
the United States respect in the eyes of Third World Nations and

contrast sharply with the Soviet Union's denial of political liberties. As it turned out, the Department of State had failed to clear its report with the Bureau of the Budget, and this accounted for the different perspective.[24]

Senator Jackson had pressured the Department of Defense to send a representative to testify. Undersecretary of the Air Force James H. Douglas reluctantly appeared, and told the committee that the department had no wish "to try to prove specific serious difficulties that will certainly arise from Alaskan statehood." Douglas also told committee members that General Nathan Twining had changed his support for statehood and now thought it wise, because of the tense post-Korean War situation, not to change Alaska's political status. Senator Jackson quickly backed Douglas into a corner—there simply was no rational explanation why the Department of Defense opposed Alaskan statehood, it simply echoed the administration's position.[25]

Douglas was unable to answer a number of questions put to him. These he covered in a letter to Senator Jackson in March. He explained that the Department of State had informed him that it deferred to the Department of Defense on the statehood question. The crucial problem seemed to involve the special national defense withdrawals. Finally, the Department of the Interior suggested that the committee adopt Secretary McKay's proposal which would allow the President to establish, prior to the admission, one or more special national defense withdrawals covering any acreage in the withdrawal area which would include the Aleutian Islands and the region north of the main channels of the Porcupine, Yukon, and Kuskokwim Rivers, but would be included within the state. Assistant Secretary of Defense for Legislative and Political Affairs Robert Ross thought that this amendment came closer than any other in meeting defense needs. Still, to find out if Eisenhower agreed, Senator Jackson and Representative Miller put the question to the chief executive. Eisenhower replied on March 31, 1955 that "I am in doubt that any form of legislation can wholly remove my apprehensions about granting statehood immediately. However, a proposal seeking to accommodate the many complex considerations entering into the statehood question has been made by Secretary of the Interior McKay, and should legislation of this type be approved by the Congress, I assure your subcommittee that I shall give it earnest consideration."[26] It left unclear the question of whether or not the President would actually sign an Alaska statehood bill.

After the House Interior and Insular Affairs Committee had reported its tandem bill on February 23, the measure was sent to the Rules Committee. Its new chairman, Howard Smith of Virginia, implacably opposed statehood for either territory. His committee, therefore, refused to grant an "open rule," which would have given the House an opportunity to offer amendments and vote for the admission of either territory. Instead, the Rules Committee gave the tandem bill a "closed rule." A.L. Miller, the mercurial ranking minority member of the House Interior and Insular Affairs Committee, stated, "...those who are opposed to both statehood bills in the House Rules Committee reported out a monstrosity of a rule, a Frankenstein type of monster that in their opinion defeats both bills." Miller said that eight of the twelve members of the Rules Committee were against statehood for either territory. But, he warned, statehood legislation was a privileged matter, and as such, could be brought to the floor of the House without a rule. After debate, the House recommitted the tandem bill on May 10, 1955 by a vote of 218 to 170.[27]

The negative House vote discouraged some statehood advocates. The House had passed an Alaska measure in 1950, and statehood proponents had always thought that, if it came to the floor, the House would surely pass a bill again. The Senate was considered to be the real obstacle. In addition, the issue had been before Congress for nearly a decade. But instead of gaining, the last House vote indicated that statehood was losing ground. Actually, the vote was not as bleak as it appeared to be, because Congressman who opposed one but not the other measure tended to vote against both. Democrats split 105 to 107 on the recommitted motion, while Republicans voted 113 to 63. Statehood opposition was strongest in the South; its Congressmen favored recommittal by 101 to 19, while in the West the vote was 15 to 38. Congressmen from the New England states voted for recommittal 13 to 12, in the Middle Atlantic States 36 to 38, and in the North Central states 53 to 63. Republicans in the last three sections voted for recommittal 90 to 42, but Democrats only 12 to 71. Clearly, the Republican House members decided the issue.[28]

Congress as well as statehood advocates had invested much time and energy in the issue. The thousands of pages of reports and testimony were the mute evidence. Many feared that there seemed to be a mounting danger that the compromise of an elected governor might be agreed upon. This surely would have killed statehood for at least a decade, because Congress undoubtedly would have insisted that Alaskans give this new form of self government a fair chance. Bills to grant Alaska an elected governor were submitted in every year between 1955 and 1957.[29] Delegate Bartlett and the Alaska Statehood Committee refused to endorse such half measures, and none of these bills ever cleared the House or Senate Interior and Insular Affairs Committees.

The administration had wanted recommittal, and the House complied. For example, late in April Homer Gruenther had told Eisenhower's administrative assistant, Bryce Harlow, that the administration should push for recommittal—which could be accomplished if the Republicans stuck together. If the tandem measure was recommitted and then reported separately, Hawaii had a chance. Hawaii's delegate Betty Farrington desired recommittal for the same reason. Ernest Gruening remarked that Joseph Martin and Charles Halleck had worked toward that same end—because they thought that it was uncertain that Hawaii would send Republicans to the Senate.[30]

After recommittal, John Saylor introduced separate measures for Alaska and Hawaii. Delegate Bartlett supported the idea that Hawaii should go first, but John McCormack, the only one of the four House leaders of either party who favored Alaska statehood, insisted that Alaska should go first. Holding the Hawaii measure hostage, he insisted, would protect the Democrats from the risk that only Hawaii would be admitted. Bartlett and Gruening, however, believed that the admission of one territory would trigger the admission of the other. They tried to persuade Senators Jackson and Anderson to go along with that strategy—but the two shared McCormack's view. The Senate subcommittee had not reported either tandem of separate statehood bills, waiting to see what the House would do.[31]

After Congress adjoined, Leo O'Brien and seven other members of the House Subcommittee on Territorial and Insular Affairs came to Alaska to conduct lengthy and broad hearings. O'Brien, a former journalist from Albany, New York, had argued with Pillion about statehood and decided that neither knew what they were talking about. He therefore wanted to inform himself on the spot and travel to Alaska. Pillion, however, decided not to come along because he was afraid that he might change his mind.[32]

Committee members traveled from Point Barrow to Annette Island and also went to King Salmon in Southwestern Alaska. By the time they held their last hearing in Ketchikan, they had heard 234 witnesses. Delegate Bartlett acted as chairman for most of the time during the three week tour. Witnesses talked about a variety of matters, including statehood, the administration of mental health, justice, and fishing matters. The information gained on this trip prompted Congress in 1956 to turn over mental health functions to the territory.[33]

The administration of justice, witnesses complained, was breaking down. Long backlogs developed, and since criminal cases were given priority, civil ones went untried for several years. The problem was that the federal government monopolized the administration of justice, yet about 95 percent of the cases were violations of territorial rather than federal laws. Congress could have relieved the congestion at Anchorage by providing a second district court judge and an additional courtroom, but had refused to do so. In Southeastern Alaska, witnesses talked at length about the declining salmon runs. Criticism was leveled at the U.S. Fish and Wildlife Service and how its officials were so easily influenced by the industry they were supposed to police.[34]

The long hours and many witnesses must have tired the Congressman. Alaskans were used to hearings—they seemed to have become an annual ritual. Congressmen O'Brien was satisfied with the results. To a Juneau audience he confessed that a few years ago "I rather resented begin assigned to a committee which had charge largely of western affairs. But that indifference has been dissipated in the last two weeks."[35] O'Brien became a staunch supporter of Alaskan statehood.

It had been a mixed year for statehood advocates. There had been some gains, but more setbacks. The Alaska constitutional convention thus came at a particularly crucial moment in the statehood movement—when in Congress it had reached its nadir.

In Alaska, the campaign for the election of delegates got under way late in the summer of 1955. There were 55 positions and 171 candidates, indicating the high interest Alaskans showed in this election. Fourteen aspirants were members of the territorial legislature. This posed a dilemma when it was discovered that the Organic Act of 1912 prohibited members of the legislature from serving in positions created by the body of which they had been members. Congress passed a special act to allow these persons to run. The election was nonpartisan. The delegates represented most of Alaska's economic interests. They included lawyers, store owners, fishermen, hotel operators, miners, and housewives. In the Fairbanks district, fifty-five candidates had filed for the seven available positions. According to one observer, the storekeepers, lawyers, politicians, and mining company representatives presented a joint slate designed to maintain their control over Alaska's economy and politics by participating in the writing of the future state's fundamental law. Few of the candidates in the interior took a public stand on any of the important questions which would come before the constitutional convention. Most declared that they possessed an open mind on the merits of a one- or two-house legislatures, the contents of a bill of rights, and other vital questions. Often the election merely centered upon the personal characteristics of the candidates.[36]

A week before the convention opened at the University of Alaska, the Statehood Committee met in Fairbanks and worked out a set of rules and procedures. Approximately ten opening motions were adopted, and when the delegates met, there was a minimum of wasted time. A very smooth beginning was made which was important in setting the tone of the subsequent proceedings. Among the newspapers represented was *The New York Times*, which sent its West Coast representative, Lawrence E. Davies, to cover the event. The *Fairbanks Daily News-Miner* set up a teletype circuit in "Constitution Hall," which it connected with its editorial offices in downtown Fairbanks. The Associated Press wires, which served practically all the newspapers and radio stations in the territory, thus received a constant flow of convention news.[37]

While these preparations were underway, a lifelong resident of New Orleans and the owner of a successful floor covering business, arrived in Alaska. He was determined to help the territory become a state, an undertaking which he had come to consider his civic duty. George H. Lehleitner had originally become interested in Hawaiian statehood while commanding the navy troopship *Rotanin* in the Second World War. In the ship's library he found a copy of Clarence Street's book, *Union Now*. The author argued that unless the older democracies combined into a federal union whose strength would deter dictators, greater conflicts would follow. The reasons for a "Union of the Free" impressed Lehleitner profoundly. He visited Hawaii for the first time in 1945 while depositing several hundred Japanese prisoners at Pearl Harbor. He was distressed to see the "wholly un-American system of government" under which Hawaii operated, especially since the military had largely supplanted the civilian governmental functions. Lehleitner was shocked by the irony of the situation. "For here we were, "he stated, "supposedly fighting a war to maintain our own freedom and to restore it to others from whom it had been stripped." Yet, he continued, "...we Americans were depriving almost a half million of our fellow citizens of many prime essentials that were the proper entitlements of free men!" He realized that an America which withheld statehood from a segment of its own people because of ancestry and distance from the nearest state was not ready to accept Street's idea of a union with other people even farther away. The best way to demonstrate the feasibility of such a union, he decided, was to establish a smoothly functioning state of Hawaii. Therefore, statehood for Hawaii was a must, and he determined to promote this idea when he returned to civilian life in 1945. For the next eight years, Lehleitner concentrated his efforts on helping Hawaii through speaking engagements, a campaign of writing letters, and communicating with Congress. In 1951, he read a paper by Dr. Daniel Tuttle, Jr., of the University of Hawaii, on the so-called "Tennessee Plan." Lehleitner thereupon attempted to persuade Hawaiian statehood leaders to adopt this avenue to reach their goal, but it was rejected by them as too aggressive.[38]

This plan was so named because Tennessee had been the first, although not the last, territory to gain admission by means of it. When it was denied statehood, Tennessee elected its Congressional delegation and sent these men to Washington without waiting for an enabling act. There, the Tennessee delegation made a strong plea for admission, and finally, on June 1, 1796, Tennessee became the sixteenth State of the Union. Six territories, Michigan, California, Oregon, Tennessee, Kansas, and Iowa, elected senators and representatives to Congress before these territories were formally admitted to statehood. In Minnesota, a Congressional delegation was elected after the passage of an enabling act and the framing of a constitution, but before Congress allowed it to become a state. In each case, statehood was hastened by as much as a few months to several years.[39]

In the fall of 1955, Lehleitner determined to acquaint Alaskans with the Tennessee Plan. While in the territory, he contacted the delegates and also received the support of the *Fairbanks Daily News-Miner* although the *Anchorage Daily Times* refused to endorse the scheme. Encouraged by his brief trip, Lehleitner returned to New Orleans, drafted a Tennessee Plan proposal, and sent copies to Alaska's friends in Congress. Receiving uniformly encouraging replies, he photostated some of the letters and put them into packets which he distributed to the convention delegates after he had been invited to address them in January of 1956. By unanimous vote, the convention subsequently adopted the Tennessee Plan in the form of an ordinance attached to the constitution, which would be voted on separately by the people at the ratification of the constitution.[40]

If the ordinance was approved, two senators and one representative were to be chosen at the 1956 general election. Nominations to these positions were to be made at regular party conventions, although Independents could file under established procedures. One senator was to serve the full six-year term which would expire on January 3, 1963, and the other a short term which would end on January 3, 1961. If they were seated, however, the United States Senate would actually prescribe the terms. The Representative was to be elected for a regular two-year term. Until Alaska's admission, members of the Tennessee Plan delegation would be permitted to hold or be nominated for other offices of the United States or the territory. The delegates to the constitutional convention apparently included this stipulation to accommodate Delegate Bartlett as well as members of the territorial legislature. In recognition of Lehleitner's efforts, the members of the constitutional convention named him an honorary member, and also designated him ambassador of good will from Alaska to the people of the United States and to Congress.[41]

The fifty-five delegates opened their deliberations in the new Student Union Building on the campus of the University of Alaska on November 8, 1955. The University administration renamed the structure "Constitution Hall" in honor of the occasion. The *Anchorage Daily Time* described the atmosphere as "friendly, folksy, yet serious…." The Student Union was opened on the day the convention began, and the sounds of construction could still be heard. Many delegates thought that these noises were a fitting background for their labors, together with sitting in a new building on a young campus. As the Anchorage paper described the scene:

The delegates sit in a half circle facing the rostrum on one-armed chairs.... Voluminous literature is stuffed underneath each chair and daily mimeographed reports of the committees are added to these piles. Politics appears to be minimized and President William Egan says that not one delegate has asked him for a committee chairmanship.[42]

Although elected on a nonpartisan basis, Democrats significantly outnumbered Republicans among the delegates, and there were also a few Independents. A close observer of the proceedings has written that the convention members generally respected the expertise of their colleagues as well as that of the hired consultants. As a result, J.C. Boswell, vice president of the U.S. Smelting, Refining, and Mining Company, which had been opposed to statehood, chaired the committee on natural resources; and Leslie Nerland, banker from Fairbanks, the committee on finance and taxation. Veteran members of the territorial legislature headed the committees on apportionment, suffrage and elections, powers of the legislature, and the committee on the executive. Victor Fischer, Anchorage city planner, was secretary of the committee on local government. A political scientist and consultant to the convention, John Bebout, later reported that "few deliberative assemblies have been so fortunate in their choice of chairman." William A. Egan, veteran territorial legislator and storekeeper from Valdez, "presided with a combination of firmness, fairness and humor" which helped to weld a group of comparative strangers, "inclined to be suspicious of one another, into a body of friends and co-workers united by their mutual respect and common purpose."[43]

Not all went smoothly at the convention, however, and there were differences of opinion. But William A. Egan later asserted that in spite of controversies that often flared into heated debate, "political considerations stayed buried." Lawrence E. Davies, correspondent for *The New York Times*, shared this evaluation of the convention's conduct. He noted the high level of intelligence, understanding, sincerity, dedication, and lack of political partisanship shown by most of the delegates. Their emphasis, Davies reported, was not on party but on "the good of Alaska," and their resistance to pressure groups was noteworthy.[44]

Throughout the territory, the convention received phenomenal press coverage. Daily broadcasts told Alaskans about the proceedings, and individual delegates reported to their constituents. During the Christmas-New Year's holiday, the delegates returned home for a recess. At that point, most of the preliminary drafts had been written, and the time was right to consult the citizenry. Individual members of the convention held hearings and discussions throughout Alaska. These activities helped to maintain the high level of interest.

Alaska's constitutional convention had produced a brief document of 14,400 words which the National Municipal League termed as "one of the best, if not the best, state constitutions ever written." The document was short and flexible to allow for the changes which the future would bring. It provided for a government that would foster the growth and development of the whole state and the welfare of all its citizens. The constitution was designed to respect and guard the equal rights and dignity of all Alaskans. The basic law called for a legislature consisting of a senate of twenty members elected for four year terms and a house of representatives of forty members serving for two-year terms, an integrated state administration headed by a governor elected for a four-year term and eligible to succeed himself once, and a unified court system in which judges were selected by the governor on nomination by a judicial council composed of representatives of the bar and the lay public.[45]

A preamble and fifteen articles made up the constitution, and attached to it were three propositions in the form of ordinances. The first of these provided for the ratification of the document at a primary election on April 24, 1956. The second asked the voters to approve the Tennessee Plan. And the third ordinance dealt with the abolition of fish traps in Alaskan waters. The constitution provided for the traditional system of checks and balances, and

avoided the inclusion of matters better handled by statutory law
and administrative code. A number of consultants stated that it
came closer to carrying out the classic pattern of "separation of
powers" than had been achieved in any other state.[46] This separation
had been accomplished though the establishment of three strong
branches of government, the executive, the legislative, and judicial.
Only the governor and secretary of state were elective, and they ran
on the same ticket. All department heads were appointed by the
chief executive. After each federal census, the governor, assisted by
a board, was obligated to reapportion the state.

Tradition prevailed in the division of the legislature into an
upper and a lower house. The legislative apportionment and
apportionment schedule (Articles VI and XIV) were designed to
prevent the rural area dominance of most state upper houses. The
lower body was based on population in twenty-four election districts, while the upper house was apportioned on the basis of both
area and population in sixteen senate districts. These districts were
combinations of at least two house election areas. These, in turn,
were merged into four larger election districts which roughly cor-
responded to Alaska's geographical divisions. The legislature was to
meet annually as long as necessary, and members were to be paid
annual salaries as established by statute. The legislature could override vetoed revenue and appropriation bills or items by a three-
fourths vote by immediately calling a joint session upon receipt of
the veto. Other bills could be overridden by a two-thirds majority. A legislative council composed of legislators was to function
throughout the year.

Article IV, which dealt with the judiciary, was borrowed from
the 1947 New Jersey constitution, and established a unified court
system. It consisted of a supreme court, a superior court, and such
courts as established by the legislature. The judiciary was politically independent, and the administrative head of the court system
was to be the chief justice of the Supreme Court. Judges would be
named by a judicial council, composed of three laymen appointed
by the governor, three lawyers nominated by the state bar, and a

seventh and presiding member who was the chief justice of the Supreme Court. As a popular check on the judiciary, the framers determined that three years after appointment the name of each Supreme Court justice and superior court judge would appear on a nonpartisan ballot for approval or rejection by the voters. Thereafter, each superior court judge was to stand for election every six years, and each Supreme Court justice every tenth year.

Local government (Article X) was placed in boroughs, the Alaska version of unified metropolitan government, and cities. Incorporated boroughs would provide their own local government, while the citizens of unincorporated boroughs assumed limited local responsibility and the state provided whatever assistance was needed.[47] Alaska's natural resources (Article VII) would be developed, wherever possible, according to the sustained yield principle. The state government would retain residual ownership to all state lands and their natural wealth for the benefit of all of its citizens. The initiative and referendum (Article XI) enabled Alaskans to enact laws, and, in the case of the latter, reject acts by the legislature. All elected officials, except judicial officers, were made subject to recall. Article V provided for a voting age of nineteen provided the citizen could read or speak English. Article IX prevented the creation of funds dedicated for specific purposes, except when this action was required to enable the state to participate in federal programs. In addition, the governor had to submit an annual executive budget for the next fiscal year detailing income and projected expenditures. Amendments to the constitution, as provided for by Article XIII, could be added if approved by a two-thirds vote in each house of the legislature, and subsequently, in a statewide election. Every ten years the question of whether to call a constitutional convention would be automatically placed on the ballot by the secretary of state.[48]

It was obvious that the framers believed that Alaska should start with the best constitution possible. In addition, many delegates felt that Alaska had the advantage of learning from the experience and mistakes of other states. In summary, the convention produced a

constitution which confined itself to setting basic policy and to establishing a skeletal structure of government. The executive, legislative,
and judicial branches of government were entrusted with the task of
filling out and adapting the system to changing conditions.

After finishing their labors, the delegates had to sign the document. All looked forward to this task, except Ralph Robertson
from Juneau. He had various objections to the new document,
but he knew that he did not have a chance to persuade his fellow
delegates to vote against the document. He therefore mailed his
resignation to William Egan on February 3, 1956. The other fifty-
four delegates, and more than 1,000 onlookers crowded into the
gymnasium on the University of Alaska campus on the afternoon
of Sunday, February 5. Governor Heintzleman spoke and told the
audiences that charges of imperfection might come "from special
interests, regional points of view and the frequent propensity of
people to consider one feature of a proposition with reference to
how it influences o is influenced by other features of the proposition." Therefore, upon returning home, the delegates had a responsibility to interpret the document to their fellow citizens.[49]

The governor resumed his seat, and then the chief clerk called
the names of each delegate, beginning with Egan's. Very nervous,
the convention president signed the last of fourteen sheets of parch-
ment lying on a table. It was silent except for the recorded music
from chimes while the delegates affixed their signatures. After the
last had signed, Egan addressed the convention. At the conclusion,
the Ladd Choral group sang the "Alaska Flag Song, "and tears slid
down the faces of more than half of the delegates. While the public
left the gymnasium, the delegates remained standing for a while
and looked at the document they had framed.[50]

On Monday, February 6, the seventy-fifth day of the convention, the delegates assembled for the last time. They were weary
from the emotions of the previous day and had expected to be able
to part from each other amicably. The clerk, however, became so
choked with tears that she could barely conduct the roll call. Everybody became sentimental once again, and when a large oil portrait

of Egan was brought into the hall and presented to him as a fight of appreciation from the other delegates, the convention president also lost his composure. Ernest B. Collins, the dean of the convention, afterwards remarked that "this has transcended everything. I thought I was tough. But everyone had skins this morning." Burke Riley, another delegate, observed that at the beginning of the convention nobody "knew what to expect or how much to hope for." Now, nobody wanted the convention to end.[51]

But there was still the matter of ratifying the new constitution. Statehood forces immediately launched a vigorous campaign which lasted until the primary election in April of 1956. They distributed pamphlets throughout the territory urging Alaskans to vote "yes" on the three ordinances. These pamphlets emphasized the representative role of the delegates through the use of the slogan "You Were There." One pamphlet stated, "Your ideas, your background, your feelings and thoughts were there," and still another said that "What was written was the best YOU could write—the best for YOUR future." Alaskans also received brochures which contained a resume of the constitution to facilitate an understanding of it.[52]

In the spring of 1956, the Democrats and Republicans nominated their candidates for the Tennessee Plan positions. The former selected Ernest Gruening and William A. Egan for the Senate seats, and Ralph J. Rivers of Fairbanks for the House position. Rivers had held a variety of public offices, was a territorial legislator, and had been a delegate to the convention. The Republicans chose John Butrovich, an insurance man and territorial senator from Fairbanks, and Robert B. Atwood of Anchorage for the Senate seats. Charles Burdick, the retired assistant regional forester and a resident of Juneau, received the nomination for the House seat.[53]

When Alaskans went to the polls in April of 1956, they approved the constitution by a vote of 17,447 to 8,180, endorsed the Alaska Tennessee Plan 15,011 to 9,556, and overwhelmingly favored the abolition of fish traps by 21,285 to 4,004 votes. In the October 9, 1956 general election, the voters elected all there Democratic candidates for the Tennessee Plan positions. Ernest Gruening won by

14,169 to 13,301 votes over his rival John Butrovich; William Egan by 15,639 to 11,588 votes for Robert B. Atwood and Ralph J. Rivers by 15,569 to 11,345 votes for Charles Burdick.[54]

The constitutional convention had been a great success from the standpoint of Alaska's statehood advocates. It dramatized Alaska's plight as a territory and demonstrated the territory's political maturity through the model constitution" the delegates had drafted. In addition, the overwhelming vote to adopt the basic law presented a reaffirmation of the 1946 referendum on the issue, and a vote of confidence in the course Alaska's statehood leaders had been pursuing. Through broad representation in the convention, the territory's citizens had become involved in the statehood struggle. And finally, with the adoption of the constitution and the approval of the Alaska Tennessee Plan, a head-on assault was launched on Congress—the final effort in a long campaign.

CHAPTER THIRTEEN

The Final Push

etween 1947 and 1956, hearings on Alaska statehood were conducted on seven different occasions in Washington and three times in Alaska. The printed record of these investigations amounted to approximately 4,000 pages. Statehood bills were before Congress almost continuously after 1943. Both Democratic and Republican party platforms included promises of statehood for Alaska and Hawaii. The Democrats had mentioned eventual statehood for the two territories since 1940, and since 1947 had urged the immediate admission of both. In 1948, the Republican platform favored eventual statehood for both, and in 1952, it promised immediate statehood for Hawaii, and eventual statehood for Alaska under an equitable enabling act. In 1956, the statehood plank in the Republican platform reiterated the pledge to Hawaii, and held out admission to Alaska if adequate provisions for defense requirements could be made. In late 1955, a Gallup poll showed that 82 percent of Americans supported the admission of Alaska, while 78 percent favored Hawaii's cause. In addition, some 32 national organizations, such as the American Legion, the American Federation of Labor, and the General Federation of Women Clubs, as well as approximately 95 percent of the nation's newspapers, endorsed statehood for both territories. [1]

Despite President Truman's strong support, an Alaska statehood bill did not come to the House floor for a vote until 1950, at which time it passed. It only reached the floor then because of the previously mentioned twenty-one day rule which had been adopted in 1949. Two years later, this reform of the Rules Committee was repealed.[2] Not until 1955 did a combined Alaska-Hawaii statehood bill come to a vote again in the House. That time it reached the floor because the Rules Committee was fairly certain that under the "closed rule" it had granted, statehood would be defeated. And, as expected, the tandem measure was recommitted.

Between 1953 and 1955, the Eisenhower administration, eager to admit Republican-leaning Hawaii but cool to Democratic Alaska, and a hostile conservative Republican-southern Democratic coalition blocked statehood for both territories. The arguments against Alaska's admission focused on several basic themes. The territory's sparse population did not justify representation in Congress and could not support a state government. Alaska's noncontiguity not only isolated the territory from the main currents of American life, but its admission would set an undesirable precedent, opening the door to statehood for such lands as the Philippines, Guam, and Okinawa. The current defense construction boom in Alaska would end some day, it was said, depriving the territory of its major source of revenue. The territory's resources were still too underdeveloped to attract enough private industry to take the place of federal expenditures. And, finally, statehood would cause sharp increases in various governmental costs which would lead to higher taxes and discourage economic development.

Racism and civil rights also played a vital role in the opposition of some members of Congress, Ernest Gruening reported in 1953 that a common inquiry in private conversations about Hawaiian statehood was a whispered, "How would you like to have a United States Senator called Moto?" Representative John C. Davis of

Georgia perhaps best summed up the Southern attitude toward statehood in a speech before the House. He cited the 1950 census figures for Alaska and Hawaii. The former had a population of 128,643, of whom 33,000 were Indians and Eskimos. The latter had a population of 499,799 which was composed of 183,000 Japanese, 33,000 Chinese, 114,000 whites 87,000 Hawaiians, and 88,000 of other racial or ethnic backgrounds. Davis concluded that his figures did not reflect on the nonwhite population of either territory, but he did contend that "...the crosscurrents of racial feeling create political and administrative whirlpools too dangerous to yet be allowed the authoritative voice in the American Government that goes with full statehood."[3]

These anti-statehood arguments were used successfully year after year, but in 1956, several events occurred which set the stage for the final statehood drive, for Alaska in 1958 and for Hawaii in 1959. In his 1959 State of the Union message, President Eisenhower, as on previous occasions, urgently requested Congress to grant statehood to Hawaii, "a community that is a successful laboratory of brotherhood." As for Alaska, the chief executive was less enthusiastic as he stated, "...in harmony with the provisions I last year communicated to the Senate and House Committees on Interior and Insular Affairs, I trust that progress toward statehood for Alaska can be made in this session."[4] Eisenhower apparently referred to letters he had written in 1955 to Senator Henry M. Jackson, chairman of the Senate Interior and Insular Affairs Committee, and Representative A. L. Miller, the ranking Republican on the House Interior and Insular Affairs Committee. In these letters, the President had said that Alaska's strategic importance required full freedom for federal action. Statehood would impair it. Therefore, unless a formula could be devised an approved by Congress which adequately met these defense needs, it would be imprudent to confer statehood on Alaska.[5] The so-called McKay line, referred to by Eisenhower, modified the partition proposal made by Governor Heintzleman in 1953. McKay's plan intended to set aside, within the boundaries of the new state, some 276,000 square miles which would be subject to defense withdrawals by the President. These areas were located in the sparsely settled northern and northwestern parts of Alaska. No acceptable compromise solution had been found in 1955, and the House, as previously stated, had recommitted the combined Alaska-Hawaii measure by a vote of 218 to 170.[6]

As a result, Eisenhower's comment on Alaska statehood in his 1956 message brought an immediate Democratic response. Senator Jackson remarked, "…if the President comes out flatfooted for Alaska we'll report both it and Hawaii out." Representative Clair Engle, chairman of the House Interior and Insular Affairs Committee, expressed willingness "to give the statehood bills another try if I get definite word what the White House wants in an Alaska statehood bill and assurance that the President will sign it." On the other hand, Delegate Bartlett was encouraged because he felt that Eisenhower's prestige could now be used to rally Republican support for Alaska's cause.[7]

An event of considerable importance in the statehood movement was the resignation of Secretary of the Interior McKay on June 8, 1956. He had been pressured to run for the Senate seat in Oregon held by Wayne Morse. The Secretary, although not unfriendly to Alaska's aspirations, had reflected the administration's unfavorable attitude toward statehood for the territory. After careful deliberation, the President nominated Fred Seaton, a publisher and broadcasting executive from Hastings, Nebraska, to replace the Oregonian as Secretary of the Interior. Seaton had served in the Nebraska legislature in 1945 and 1947 and had been chairman of its legislative council from 1947 to 1949. When Senator Kenneth Wherry died in 1951, the governor appointed Seaton in December to fill the vacancy. While a Senator, Seaton urged Eisenhower to run for the Presidency and later became one of his campaign advisers and speech writers. Seaton decided not to run for election in 1952 and instead returned to his business affairs in Nebraska. In the fall of 1953, Eisenhower appointed him Assistant Secretary of Defense for legislative and public affairs, and in 1955 he moved into the White House as presidential assistant. Alaskans who knew only too well how important the Department of the Interior was in territorial affairs, realized that the attitude of the Secretary could either impede or enhance statehood chances.[8]

Delegate Bartlett welcomed Seaton's nomination, because he remembered Seaton's maiden speech in the Senate. The date had been the 1952 debate on recommitting the statehood bill. Disregarding his party's attitude on the topic, the new Senator had told his colleagues that many of the same objections raised against admitting colleagues that many of the same objections raised against admitting Alaska had been used in the debates on bringing Nebraska, Oregon, Wyoming, and Arizona into the Union. Too long had Alaska been denied its rightful place on the American flag. Ernest Gruening had written the speech for Seaton and was pleased when the Senator delivered it unchanged on the floor. George Sunborg also was busy, writing a number of the pro-statehood speeches which were delivered in the Senate at the time.[9]

Seaton lost no time trying to accommodate statehood with defense concerns. An indication that he was succeeding came in the summer of 1956 as the Democrats and Republicans adopted their party platforms. The former pledged themselves to immediate statehood, while the latter reiterated their 1952 pledge on Hawaii. A resolution in favor of Alaska was in danger of being rejected. Seaton, thereupon, went before the Resolution Committee in support of an affirmative plank which noted the President's concerns. The committee accepted it, and the Republican convention pledged itself to "immediate statehood for Hawaii" and "immediate statehood for Alaska, recognizing the fact that adequate provision for defense requirements must be made." At his news conference on September 11, Eisenhower remarked that if the areas "necessary for defense requirements could be retained under Federal control" and the populated portion made into a state, "it would seem to me to be a good solution to the problem."[10]

C. Willis Snedden, publisher of the *Fairbanks Daily News-Miner*, was especially elated about the appointment of Secretary Seaton. The two had known each other since 1936, and with a

friend of statehood as interior secretary, Snedden decided that the
time had come to pursue admission in an orderly and systematic
fashion. Snedden later recalled that until the constitutional convention, Alaska's statehood forces had never really concentrated
their efforts to achieve the goal. Instead, they had too often used
a shotgun approach by making occasional trips to Washington to
testify at Congressional hearings and by rallying support for local
hearings in Alaska. Snedden asserted that the Alaska Statehood
Committee had rendered yeoman work in obtaining the support
of the various national organizations, such as the Elks, the Kiwanis,
the American Legion, and the Chamber of Commerce of America,
in addition to the active help of many newspapers. But nobody,
with the exception of Delegate Bartlett and ex-governor Gruening,
had pursued the matter steadily and singlemindedly. Now Snedden
was determined to launch an intensive effort to attain the goal.[11]

As a first step in this direction, he phoned the new Interior Secretary a day after his appointment and suggested that the time had
come to make methodical and calculated moves toward statehood.
Seaton agreed, and asked Snedden to recommend an informed
Alaskan who could work in Washington for the Department of the
Interior. Snedden informed him that such a man already occupied
the post of acting legislative counsel of the Department of the Interior. Theodore Stevens had resigned his post as United States Attorney in Fairbanks shortly before Seaton's nomination and taken the
Interior post. Upon Snedden's recommendation, Seaton appointed
him legislative counsel and about a year later, assistant to the secretary as well. On his next trip to the nation's capital, Snedden found
a hand-lettered, cardboard sign on Stevens' office door reading
"Alaskan Headquarters." Stevens quickly became known as "Mr.
Alaska" in the department.[12] And, as a Republican of some standing, Stevens maintained communications between Alaska party
members and the Eisenhower administration.

In the meantime, a group of statehood enthusiasts in Washington were making preparations to assist Alaska's Tennessee Plan
delegation, which was to arrive for the opening of the Eighty-fifth

Congress in January 1957. An unofficial committee, consisting of Delegate Bartlett, D. Ernest Bartley, a professor of political science at the University of Florida, who had been a consultant to the Alaska constitutional convention, and George Lehleitner compiled dossiers on every member of Congress. These files included, among much other information, the attitudes of Senators and Representatives toward Alaska statehood. George Lehleitner also had written a pamphlet which described the historical antecedents of the Tennessee Plan. Together with a cover letter, this booklet was sent to every member of Congress, and was also widely distributed to the editors of daily newspapers, to radio and television network news programs, and to all principal news magazines and periodicals. John Adams, who had been a White House correspondent for the Columbia Broadcasting System during the Truman administration, was hired by Lehleitner as the public relations man for the Alaska Tennessee Plan delegation.[13]

In order to create as broad a base as possible for the Congressional lobbying effort, Snedden and Stevens began to compile a card file on every member of Congress for their own use. This file, like the one being prepared for the Alaska Tennessee Plan delegates, contained not only information about the attitudes of senators and representatives but also extensive personal information on individual members of Congress. Snedden took up residence in Washington on a more or less permanent basis in 1956. To deal with those senators and representatives who still remained doubtful or opposed to the territory's cause, he engaged a detective agency, which was assigned to unearth information on uncooperative legislators which might be used as leverage in obtaining affirmative votes for statehood. "In a few cases," Snedden recalled, "we stumbled across situations where we knew beyond a shadow of a doubt that… [if revealed, it] would end… [a man's career] in public service." As remembered by Snedden, the problem was how to put this intelligence to its best use:

And then the delicate part came in, what to do with it, how to handle it? We got excellent cooperation from all the top people in the press in Washington. Some of the nation's top columnists gave us a hand there.

In short, the information was passed to some sympathetic columnists who would call the person involved and "make a trade." The caller would usually say, "Here's something I ran across. I just wondered whether [I should reveal]… it. It concerns so and so back in such and such time."[14] As a result, several pledges for a vote in support of statehood were obtained.

Snedden also capitalized on his friendship with editors of small newspapers throughout the United States. A poll, which he conducted among these papers and some magazines, was published in *The New York Times* and circulated widely on Capitol Hill. It showed unanimous support for Alaska's admission. The Hearst and Scripps-Howard newspaper chains and *Time* and *Life* joined the struggle. Snedden has said that once he was able to get the attention of a particular newspaperman, statehood "was just like motherhood and being against sin when you explained to them what the situation was." The statehood cause was, as Snedden explained it, "200,000 Alaskans, Americans all, who were held in colonial bondage by the United States government." Secretary Seaton used the power and influence of this office to gather pledges for statehood votes from wavering and undecided members of Congress. The secretary used additions to National Park facilities and personnel increases for the Geological Survey or the Bureau of Land Management, among other incentives, in the districts or states of the senators and representatives in question. According to Snedden, "Fred Seaton did a marvelous job of rounding up a very impressive assortment of pawns."[15]

While the friends of statehood were rounding up votes, Senator-elect Egan and Representative-elect Rivers decided to drive their cars to the nation's capital. Senator-elect Gruening had already flown to Washington. Hearing about the proposed car trip,

Snedden suspected that it could easily be turned into free publicity. He suggested that the Alaska Statehood Committee try to persuade Gruening to return to Alaska and join his colleagues for the trip. Gruening, although fit at age sixty-nine, declined the suggestion. On the afternoon of Sunday, December 9, Egan and Rivers together with their wives were honored at a farewell program in the gymnasium at the University of Alaska. The following afternoon they left Fairbanks in their cars which had been painted white for dramatic effect. The two cars had the Alaska flag, eight stars of gold in a field of blue, painted on each door, in addition to the name and office of each man and a sigh proclaiming, "Alaska, the 49th State." The thermometer stood at a bone-chilling -47F. They drove down the Alaska Highway and through the capitals of the states which had used the Tennessee Plan. After a difficult journey they arrived in Nashville where they were joined by Gruening. The three men and their wives were officially received at the capital and honored at a dinner in the governor's mansion. Finally, on December 31, three weeks after leaving Fairbanks, the weary travelers drove up to the New House Office Building. They had driven over 6,000 miles. Delegate Bartlett received and greeted them, and afterwards they spent nearly an hour before television, newsreel, and press cameras and then answered questions from reporters.[16] Even before Congress reconvened, the delegation had attracted national attention. The question now was: how would the administration and Congress receive them and could the publicity be sustained?

On January 14, 1957, during the noon hour, Florida's Senator Spessard L. Holland asked for the floor. The Senate's presiding officer recognized him, and Holland secured unanimous consent to read an unusual memorial from the Alaska constitutional convention. This document, dated December 9, 1956, asked Congress to "seat our duly—elected representatives and… [to] enact legislation enabling the admission of Alaska to the Union of State." Senator Holland then introduced Alaska's Congressional delegation, which was seated in the diplomatic gallery with their families. Gruening, Egan, and Rivers rose and were greeted with a burst of applause which was followed by speeches from the Senate floor, all forcefully endorsing Alaska statehood.[17]

Despite this magnificent introduction, Congress did not officially seat or recognize the Alaska Tennessee Plan delegation. This refusal did not deter them from pursuing their task as lobbyists. A number of factors retarded this effort at first. Egan had the misfortune to rupture his eardrum, so Gruening, who already knew many of the senators, delayed his lobbying visits until his colleague could accompany him. Rivers went ahead with his job of contacting representatives, studying pertinent information in the Bartley files before he made his visits. Gruening and Egan, after having finished their work in the Senate, came to the aid of Rivers and visited those representatives he had not had time to visit. Eventually, they reported to O'Brien that there were 60 pro-statehood votes among the senators and as many as 238 favorable votes in the House.[18]

That count gave hope for optimism, although Bartlett later recalled that it could hardly have been the result of the short visits Rivers made to the congressmen. Indeed, Rivers was unable "to introduce Bill Snedden to a single member of the Rules Committee on the Democratic side; it was office which I had to perform." In fact, Rivers' acquaintance with House members was so limited that he doubted "very much if Ralph could call by name on sight a dozen members." There also was a problem of space. Until the spring the delegation had no office since Gruening refused to rent space before the legislature had appropriated the necessary funds. In the meantime, Rivers worked out of a corner of Bartlett's office. A couple of weeks after the delegation finally had rented space, Egan and Gruening had a falling—out, and the former moved his office to basement of his home. Without Gruening's contacts, Egan thereafter dealt almost exclusively with Senate staff members. Although such contacts could occasionally be useful, Bartlett chided Egan for spending most of his time in the delegate's office. And instead of taking some member of Congress to lunch, Egan "almost invariably would slip away by himself and have lunch alone in one of the joints…we called Ptomaine Row." Being a very thrifty individual,

Egan tried to save funds the territorial legislature had appropriated for the delegation. Gruening was quite different from Egan, the delegate observed. He was "vigorous and continually active and entertained, as all the members of the delegation should have done." Yet many Senators had privately complained to Bartlett that Gruening "was too persistent, demanded too much time," and talked too much about his favorite theme, federal neglect of and discrimination against the territory.[19]

In the meantime, B. Frank Heintzleman resigned as governor effective January 3, 1957, three months before the expiration of his term. The governor had not been happy in his office. A career bureaucrat with the U.S Forest Service, Heintzleman never developed the kinds of political instincts necessary to survive in such a visible position as chief executive of a territory. On the day he cleared his desk he remarked to a reporter that "I won't miss the job a bit." Subjected to much criticism which he failed to counter, he apparently decided to quit when the 1956 elections put the Democrats back into the control of the legislature. The governor well remembered the 1955 legislative session which had been characterized "by a lack of dignity, vitriolic tirades against public officials," and the usual legislative quarrels and disputes. Heintzleman, then 68 years of age, probably also knew that he would not be reappointed. Secretary Seaton accepted the resignation, and having no particular successor in mind, Waino Hendrickson, the secretary of Alaska, remained acting governor. Seaton apparently doubted that Hendrickson could handle the governorship, but over a period of time he proved to the secretary's satisfaction that he could. It took some time to find a successor to Heintzleman, so Hendrickson occupied the governor's chair throughout the 1957 session of the territorial legislature.[20]

In January 1957, Secretary Seaton visited Alaska for ten days. The tour was designed to acquaint the secretary with the territory and also give him the chance to meet the various aspirants for the governorship. Eventually, Mike Stepovich, a native of Fairbanks,

C. W. Snedden

Architects of Statehood

Charles Willis "Bill" Snedden

Bill Snedden was a newspaper editor-publisher who was born in Spokane, Washington on July 20, 1913. He studied at Oregon State College, the University of Oregon, and Washington State College.

Snedden mastered linotype operations by 1927 and found employment with various Puget Sound newspapers. He engaged in the real estate business and served in the U.S. Army in 1942.

In 1950 he bought the *Fairbanks Daily News-Miner* from Alaska millionaire entrepreneur Austin Eugene "Cap" Lathrop. Snedden became an ardent advocate of Alaska statehood and changed his newspaper's anti-statehood editorial stance. He was a member of the Alaska Statehood Committee from 1957 to 1959.

He recommended that Secretary of the Interior Fred Seaton, a friend since 1936, appoint Theodore "Ted" Stevens, then acting legislative counsel, as legislative counsel. Seaton did, and a year later made him his assistant as well. From then on there was somebody familiar with Alaska in the department.

Snedden and Stevens began to compile a card file on every member of Congress containing not only the member's attitudes toward statehood but much personal information as well. Snedden took up residence in Washington, D.C. on a more or less permanent basis in 1956. To deal with those members of Congress who remained doubtful or opposed to statehood, he engaged a detective agency assigned to unearth information on uncooperative legislators which might be used as leverage—and he used it.

was nominated for the position on May 9, 1957, and Hendrickson was reappointed as secretary.[21]

The senor Stepovich had gone to Fairbanks during the Gold Rush. Michael Anthony was born in that city in 1919, but after his parents divorced, his mother moved to Portland, Oregon. He attended Gonzaga, Notre Dame and Santa Clara Universities. He was thirty-eight years of age when nominated, and had a large family of seven children. An economic conservative, he supported statehood in a modest fashion. He had first gone on record as favoring it at the Congressional hearings in 1953, but until his inauguration he had never occupied a leadership position in the movement. In his inaugural address on June 8, 1957 he told his listeners that now Alaskans had to unite on this issue and work toward statehood.[22]

As governor, Stepovich promoted statehood vigorously and criticized Alaska's sectionalism. The media like the new chief executive, his wife and photogenic family, and even *Time* and *Life* ran human interest stories on him.[23]

With statehood prospects improving, the commonwealth idea revived briefly. Practically a dead issue since 1954, a group of Southeastern dissidents led by Emery Tobin formed the Ketchikan Commonwealth Club in May 1957. Its purposes were to oppose statehood and promote commonwealth for the Panhandle. There were a few other attempts to revive the issue, but the *Anchorage Daily Times* probably summarized the issue best when it stated that it was "a phony movement," designed only to divert attention from statehood, confuse Alaskans, and delay and impede, if possible, Congressional action.[24]

Another issue interfering with statehood was a campaign for tax relief. First raised in 1950 by Neil Moore, Alaska's auditor, it used the slogan "No taxation without representation." Delegate Bartlett immediately requested the Legislative Reference Service of the Library of Congress to research the possibility of exempting individuals and corporations in Alaska from the federal income tax. The answer was an inequivocal no. The issue resurfaced from time to time over the years. On May 14, 1955, Paul Robison, governor Heintzleman's counsel during the 1955 legislative session, publicly challenged the governor and delegate to seek federal tax exemption for "new capital invested in the development of Alaska's resources." Nothing came of it, and then one William Prescott Allen, a native of Olympia, Washington, took up the battle cry in 1956. Allen and his sons published the *Laredo Times* in Texas and the *Montrose Daily Press* in Colorado. For a couple of years he had attempted to buy an Alaska newspaper, and in 1955 he succeeded in buying the Empire Printing Company from Helen Monsen. The operation had been losing money for a number of years, but Allen was willing to absorb the losses. In 1956 Allen wrote Secretary Seaton that he intended to bring statehood to Alaska through a twenty year moratorium on excise and federal income taxes. A year later he proposed to separate southeastern Alaska from the rest of the territory and holding another referendum on statehood. Eventually Allen and publisher Bill Snedden became involved in a long debate. Both made mutually unacceptable offers to be the assets of their respective newspapers as to when Congress would grant statehood or a tax moratorium.[25]

Allen basically was a fool, and a careless one with facts. He reported, for example, that Representative Arthur Miller had stated that if Alaskans petitioned Congress for a twenty year federal tax moratorium it would quite likely be granted. Miller corrected the publisher, stating that he had never endorsed such a proposal and "could no more vote for an income-tax moratorium for Alaska than I could for one for my home State of Nebraska."[26]

After all of these events within the territory and the administration, Congress was ready to deal with Alaska statehood once again. On January 16, 1957, President Eisenhower delivered his budget message to Congress. He again recommended the admission of Hawaii, and "subject to area limitations and other safeguards for the conduct of defense activities so vitally necessary to our national security, statehood.... [for] Alaska." With the introduction of half a dozen statehood bills in that month, the struggle for Alaskan statehood resumed. Four of these measures differed

from previous ones in that they were admission bills rather than
enabling acts, thereby recognizing that Alaskans had written and
ratified a constitution.[27]

In a speech at the University of Alaska at the end of January 1957,
Secretary Seaton underscored the fact that the Eisenhower administration was serious about admitting Alaska. However, if the defense
measures deemed necessary by Washington were rejected, he warned
his audience, statehood might be delayed for scores of years. In an
address to a joint session of the territorial legislatures in Juneau on
the following day, Seaton told the lawmakers that the battle for statehood faced a "long and uphill fight" in Congress, The legislators rose
and gave him a standing ovation when he asserted that the statehood
fight was one "the administration does not intent to lose."[28, 29]

In Washington, Chairman Leo O'Brien of the Subcommittee
on Territorial and Insular Affairs decided to conduct hearings on
the Alaska measure first. The 1957 bills consolidated the 2,550,000
acres of internal improvement grants with the 100,000,000 acre
unspecified grant of public lands, and proceeds from the entire
acreage were not dedicated to any particular use. Since Alaskans
had drafted and ratified their constitution, and Congress had the
opportunity to review the document, the statehood bills declared
that the constitution met all federal requirements and was, therefore, "accepted, ratified, and confirmed." The measures thus became
admission rather than enabling bills.[30]

In March both the Senate and House held hearings on the
admission of Alaska into the Union. Chairman O'Brien planned to
hold five days of hearings, but eventually they exceeded two weeks.
On the Senate side, Henry Jackson of Washington presided over the
hearings. Jackson welcomed new information but was unapprecia-
tive of repetitious evidence. As a consequence, hearings opened on
March 25 and ended the next day.[31]

The first order of business consisted of bringing the measures
into conformity with President Eisenhower's wishes on special
national defense withdrawals. This matter was settled at an interdepartmental conference held on March 5 in the office of Major

General Wilton Persons, the deputy assistant to the President. Conferees decided against partitioning Alaska since it would disfranchise the citizens of northern and western Alaska, be awkward to explain in the United Nations, and perhaps most importantly, deprive the state of valuable mineral resources needed for Alaska's economic development. It also would require annual federal expenditures to the tune of $4 million to support a new territorial government, embarrass Republican politicians in the north, and repudiate previous public statements by Douglas McKay, James H. Douglas, and the President himself that special national defense withdrawals would satisfy the administration. Assistant Secretary of the Interior Hatfield Chilson communicated this decision to O'Brien's subcommittee on March 11, 1957. Under the agreement, the President was to be granted the authority to declare special national defense withdrawals anywhere north and west of the McKay line, embracing an area of approximately 276 million acres.[32]

Within the special national defense withdrawal, the federal government was to possess excusive legislative, executive, and judicial jurisdiction; however, all state and local laws pertaining to municipalities, school districts, and other political subdivisions of the state would continue in effect. All other applicable state laws in force at the time of withdrawal and not in conflict with federal law were to be considered as having been adopted as laws of the United States. The Department of the Interior intended that the state be allowed, with presidential approval, to select lands from within the withdrawal. Since administration support for Alaska statehood hinged on acceptance of the withdrawal provision, Bartlett as well as the Alaska Tennessee delegation agreed to it.[33]

Senator Gruening later remarked that this was a wholly unnecessary request since the President, as head of the armed forces, already had the power to make such withdrawals. "What in time amounted to a face-saving formula for the Administration," Gruening asserted, "was provided as an amendment…. It remained in the Statehood Act…and has been meaningless…ever since."[34]

The O'Brien and Jackson Committees also dealt with federal road funds for Alaska. Both the House and Senate versions included Senator Clinton Anderson's 1954 amendment authorizing $48 million in construction grants over a six-year period and another $30 million in maintenance grants over a sixteen-year period. These the Bureau of the Budget wanted deleted, explaining that if Alaska needed any special provisions to participate as a state in highway apportionments, then Congress should consider this in future highway acts. In 1956 Congress included Alaska on a modified basis in the Federal Aid Highway Act. The legislation eliminated much of the uncertainly about future funding, thus facilitating planning. It also called for the absorption of the Alaska Road Commission by the Bureau of Public Roads. Instead of giving the territory credit for all the public domain and nontaxable Native lands, as would ordinarily have been the case, Congress used one-third of the public domain lands on which the matching formula was based. Under this arrangement, Alaska was to receive $13,390,000 in fiscal year 1958.[35]

The major controversy during the March hearings dealt with transferring jurisdiction over the fisheries to the state. Representatives of several sportsmen's groups and two members of the Washington State Congressional delegation pressed the issue. The former had attempted to persuade the constitutional convention to make provisions for administering the state's fish and game resources by two separate, independent commissions. The convention, however, refused. In 1957, the territorial legislature resisted similar pressure and adopted the single commission, fearing that several commissions would dissipate executive power. The sportsmen's groups tried again before O'Brien's committee, only to be told that this was an internal Alaskan and not a Congressional, concerns. [36]

Republican Representatives Jack Westland of Everett and Thomas Pelly of Seattle were also concerned about the matter. The two submitted a statement to O'Brien's subcommittee from George Johansen, the secretary-treasurer of the Alaska Fishermen's Union, a group consisting primarily of nonresidents. Johansen complained that Alaska's legislature discriminated against nonresidents through reduced employment security benefits and higher charges for fishing licenses. Worse, it had just enacted legislation outlawing commercial salmon fishing by fish traps. These were operated and maintained almost exclusively by nonresident company fishermen. As soon as the federal government relinquished jurisdiction, the trap ban would become effective, destroying their employment.[37]

Representative Westland, therefore, asked that Alaska be prohibited from applying any differential, even though his state of Washington charged nonresidents three times as much as residents for using purse seines and five times as much for using other gear. Representative Thomas Pelly's Congressional district included the cannery operators and fishermen of north Seattle. Pelly advocated commonwealth status for Alaska, and maintained that a twenty year federal tax holiday would equalize Alaska's production costs with those to the south. If Congress admitted the territory before that time, it would simply force the new state to overtax domestic enterprise, and neither properly utilize nor conserve its natural resources. Since Pelly suspected that the subcommittee would vote for statehood, he asked that the federal government retain management authority over Alaska's fisheries and wildlife resources for a period of ten years after the territory had been admitted to statehood.[38]

Generally, the two hearings were perfunctory because many members of the House and Senate committees felt that nothing much that had not already been said could be added to the record. The House Interior and Insular Affairs Committee reported its bill on June 25, 1957, and recommended that the territory be admitted. The committee observed that the traditionally accepted requirements for admission of incorporated territories to statehood appeared to be:

That the inhabitants of the proposed new State are imbued with and sympathetic toward the principles of democracy as exemplified in the American form of government. That a majority of the electorate wish statehood. That the proposed new State has sufficient population and resources to support

State government and at the same time carry its share of the
cost of the Federal Government.

Under this historic pattern, territories had become state. By
each of these historic standards, the committee asserted, "Alaska
is ready and qualified for statehood now." The House bill also provided that Congress accept the Alaskan constitution, and granted
to the proposed state some 182,800,000 acres of vacant, unappropriated, and unreserved land to be selected within a period of
twenty-five years after admittance. The aboriginal land claims were
left in status quo, to be dealt with by future legislative or judicial
action. In August, the Senate committee reported its Alaska statehood measure favorably. In one of its major provisions, Alaska was
given the right to select some 103,350,000 million acres from the
public domain within a twenty-five year period after statehood had
been achieved.[39]

In the meantime, in July of 1957, House Speaker Sam Rayburn
of Texas, hitherto a foe of Alaska statehood, changed his mind and
promised to give the territory "its day in court." This decision sent
the hopes of statehood advocates soaring. Representative Leo W.
O'Brien of New York, chairman of the House Subcommittee on
Territorial and Insular Affairs, predicted that the Speaker's support
would add "at least 20 votes" to the bill when it reached the House
floor. Rayburn recommended, however, that the Alaska measure
not be brought to the floor of the House in the last days of the
session when members of Congress were in no mood to consider
major legislation but merely wanted to hurry home. Rayburn's
advice was accepted by the statehood forces in the House, and the
Alaska bill was put off for consideration until 1958.[40]

There are several versions of why Rayburn changed his mind
about the territory's admission. Mary Lee Council stated that
when the Speaker was asked about it he replied, "I can tell you in
two words, 'Bob Bartlett.'" Another version relates that Lyndon B.
Johnson was interested in the Democratic presidential nomination
as early as 1957, but being a southerner, his close friend and mentor

Rayburn felt he would encounter opposition from northern liberal Democrats. To help overcome this resistance, the Speaker decided to promote a few pieces of legislation favored by these liberals, such as Alaska statehood. Still another explanation was given after Bartlett's death by a journalist of the *Anchorage Daily News*. He disclosed that Bartlett "apparently pledged complete support for Johnson in return for an all-out drive to put the statehood bill over the top...."

According to this writer, Bartlett kept notes on the agreement which would be found in his papers.[41] No evidence has been found, however, which might have corroborated the assertion of the journalist. In any event, Rayburn's support proved to be crucial in the House in overcoming the opposition of the House Rules Committee.

CHAPTER FOURTEEN

Statehood Achieved

In 1957, Congress had passed the civil rights bill that Eisenhower so belatedly had decided to introduce. In its final version, it was a weak civil rights act, but it was the first time since Reconstruction that Congress had approved a specific civil rights measure. Passage of this legislation was the first major defeat for the southern Democrat-conservative Republican coalition in Congress since 1938. A new majority coalition of liberal Democrats and moderate Republicans demonstrated its willingness to pass civil rights legislation, including statehood for the territories. The 1957 civil rights votes also indicated that while four Senators from Alaska and Hawaii might increase liberal strength in the Senate, these additional lawmakers would probably not exert a decisive influence on civil rights. The victory margin in 1957 was wide enough to make the impact of four new votes for civil rights relatively unimportant. It certainly was not necessary to admit Alaska and Hawaii in order to pass the civil rights measure. The civil rights battle of 1957 also suggested that the filibuster would be used sparingly or not at all. Most conservatives reluctantly accepted the fact that their influence could best be maintained through compromises and deals rather than the filibuster. This change in strategy was to be demonstrated in 1958 when conservative Senators failed to invoke the filibuster against statehood and accepted a compromise initiated by moderate Democrats. With that, the South abandoned the obstructionist tactics which had served the white supremacists so well since Reconstruction.[1]

While sectional opposition to statehood was breaking down, political obstacles still remained. In 1957, Hawaii's Delegate John Burns and Alaska's Bartlett agreed to introduce and support separate bills only. After Congress adjourned at the end of August 1957, Burns stated that every effort should be made "to get Alaska statehood approved, without regard to whether Hawaii is right behind." He was certain that the islands would be admitted in the next Congress. And although his position was identical to that which Bartlett had taken in 1955 and 1956 after the recommittal of the Hawaii-Alaska statehood bill, he was roundly criticized by his foes and even some of his friends as a "a great Representative of Alaska, but not... of Hawaii." Burns had taken a chance, for while Alaska's statehood leaders had supported a Hawaii-first strategy, Burns represented a constituency which had long believed that Hawaii had a better claim to and chance for statehood than Alaska.[2]

After Congress reconvened in January 1958, President Eisenhower, in his budget message, for the first time fully supported Alaska statehood. The President urged "that the Congress complete action on appropriate legislation admitting Hawaii and Alaska into the Union as State." But shortly after his message, Eisenhower again dimmed the hopes of Alaska statehood proponents when he advocated that the Hawaii bill should be brought up simultaneously with the Alaska measure. The implications of such a move were obvious to many. *The New York Times* declared that if the two statehood measures were tied together again, neither would get through. Supporters of both territories, however, were adamant that the statehood bills were separate issues, "as different as Alaska and Hawaii were geographically and economically." Once again,

Delegate Burns stated that "nothing should interfere with success in the consideration of [the] Alaska… [statehood bill]." The delegate promised to remove the Hawaii bill from the Senate debate if that was necessary to insure the success of Alaska.[3]

Bartlett managed to talk with Speaker Rayburn about the statehood issue in January. Rayburn told him that as a Westerner, he did not object to Alaska's admission since it was part of the North American continent. Alaska's Native population did not offend him, but he had previously objected to admission because he believed that if Alaska became a state, so would Hawaii. He strongly objected to Hawaii because of its noncontiguity. Yet, despite his strong feelings on the subject, he had decided to help Alaska.[4]

Delegates Bartlett and Burns had tried persistently to get Senator Lyndon B. Johnson to make a commitment on scheduling the statehood bills. Finally, late in January 1958, Johnson convened a private conference of influential Democratic senators which Burns attended. The participants at the meeting agreed that only Alaska would be debated before Congress adjourned. Johnson dropped Hawaii from his agenda, but promised to ensure that southern Democrats would not use procedural devises or the filibuster to defeat Alaska in either chamber. It appeared southern Democrats had accepted this compromise before Johnson presented it to the conferees. Once again, as in the 1957 civil rights legislation, Johnson had brought about a compromise which preserved surface unity within his party by placating southern and liberal Democrats. The compromise also averted an embarrassing and divisive public fight over a southern-led filibuster, and kept the cloture issue safely at bay. The Democratic compromise decision soon became public knowledge when it appeared obvious that Democratic leaders in the House and Senate did not intend to vote on Hawaii in 1958. Yet most Democrats and a large number of Republicans knew that Alaska's admission would inevitably bring quick action on Hawaii. Still, southern Democrats believed that Alaska would meet strong resistance from the Republicans. Southerners agreed to Johnson's compromise in part because they probably anticipated that they could combine with Republicans opposed to the priority given Democratic Alaska and thereby ensure the defeat of the separate measure.[5] Senator James Eastland and his southern Senate colleagues miscalculated in 1958, as events were to show, because Republican resistance to "Alaska first" dissolved. Here Secretary Seaton and administration officials as well as Republican members of Congress sympathetic to Alaska statehood made invaluable contributions.

A few days after Rayburn had talked with Bartlett, the Speaker told House Rules Committee chairman Howard Smith that he wanted a rule on the statehood bill. Bartlett was elated, telling Snedden that "the Rayburn word is a magic one," and that once the Rules Committee met, "the votes are ours in the committee as well as on the floor." Bartlett also talked with Lyndon Johnson who assured him that the Alaska measure would be brought to the Senate floor within ten days and be passed shortly thereafter. Johnson also promised Bartlett that southern Senators would not filibuster the Alaska bill, although some might talk at length to protect their record.[6]

Although the Alaska bill seemed to make good progress, it still faced many uncertainties. One of these occurred on February 4 when the President held one of his regular legislative strategy meetings with his party leaders, Senators William F. Knowland and Styles Bridges, and Representatives Joseph W. Martin and Charles Halleck. The group told the President that the Alaska bill was to come up first. Eisenhower was surprised, and the Congressmen complained that O'Brien's subcommittee had bottled up the Hawaii measure. At a press conference the following day, Eisenhower remarked that he would like to see the two statehood bills considered together. On February 6, Senator Knowland disclosed to the press that he had told Senator Johnson that without a promise that the Hawaiian bill would be dealt with immediately after the Alaska measure, a motion would be made to combine the two. The administration found it unwise to consider only one of the statehood bills. Johnson did not give the assurances Knowland wanted, so the Senate drive for Alaska statehood stopped. The next morning, Bartlett again met with Senator Johnson. He found the senator noncommittal. He related to Bartlett that his office had been swamped by anti-statehood mail. Additionally, bitter opponents such as Senator Richard B. Russell, Democrat of Georgia, and William Prescott Allen, a Texan and the erratic publisher of the anti-statehood *Daily Alaska Empire* of Juneau had been besieging Johnson. Under these circumstances, the Senator did not know what he would do, and even might find it necessary to vote against the measure when it came to the Senate floor. Yet ambiguously the majority leader stated that he intended to act as "a midwife" for Alaska statehood, although he definitely did not plan to be the "doctor" who would "deliver" it. Pressed by Bartlett whether or not Alaska would achieve its goal in 1958, the Senator replied with a firm "no." As if this was not disheartening enough, the Alaska measure still faced the opposition of the House Rules Committee, and particularly its chairman, Howard W. Smith, Democrat of Virginia. *Life* magazine remarked editorially that passage of the Alaska statehood bill was being "held up by the willfulness of one Howard Smith, a Virginia gentleman whose impeccable manners include little real respect for either free enterprise or democracy." Smith had vehemently expressed his feelings toward statehood for either Alaska or Hawaii when he had stated:

> I am opposed to statehood for Alaska. I am opposed to statehood for Hawaii, I am opposed to both of them together, I am opposed to them separately. I am opposed to bringing in Puerto Rico, which has been promised statehood by both of the great political parties like these two outlying Territories have. I am opposed to Puerto Rico, I am opposed to the Virgin Islands, I am opposed to all of them. I want to keep the United States of America on the American continent. I hope I have made my position clear.[7]

With statehood thus blocked in the Senate, the action now centered on the House. On February 25, Clair Engle told Chairman

Frederick Andrew Seaton

Architects of Statehood

Frederick Andrew Seaton

Fred Seaton was born on December 11, 1904, in Washington, D.C. where his father worked for Joseph L. Bristow, U.S, Senator for Kansas. When Fred was six years old his father moved the family to Manhattan, Kansas. There he published the *Manhattan Mercury* and later the *Manhattan Chronicle*.

Fred Seaton graduated from Kansas State University in 1931 and joined his father's newspaper business, eventually becoming associate editor of Seaton Publications. While in Kansas, he met Charles Willis Snedden who later bought the *Fairbanks Daily News-Miner*. In 1937 he moved to Hastings, Nebraska where he published one of the Seaton Family's new acquisition, the *Daily Tribune*. He made the ailing paper financially viable.

Always interested in Republican politics, Seaton held numerous positions within the party. When U.S. Senator Kenneth Wherry died, he was appointed to fill out Wherry's term.

On February 20, 1952 Seaton delivered his maiden speech on the floor of the Senate in support of Alaska statehood. Ernest Gruening had persuaded him to support the cause and had written his speech. Seaton served in several positions in the Eisenhower administration, and in 1956 the president appointed him Secretary of the Interior. As Secretary he advocated cooperative long-range planning between federal and local governments and private enterprise for the development of natural resources, encouraged hydrogenating for the Pacific Northwest, and promoted the long-range development of national parks.

It was Seaton who persuaded a reluctant President Dwight D. Eisenhower to back Alaska's admission as the 49th State.

Smith that unless the Alaska measure received a rule by March 15, he would invoke the privileged status of the bill and bypass Smith's committee. Smith agreed that hearings should be held but doubted that they would occur before the March 15 deadline.[8]

While Delegate Bartlett and his colleagues waited for the hearing, there developed the "John Q. Citizen" movement in Fairbanks. Art Sexauer, a business partner in a restaurant in that town started the movement in February 1958. A political independent heretofore uninvolved in politics, Sexauer wanted to help bring about statehood. About thirty people showed up for the organizing meeting, among them George Sundborg, then the editor of the *News-Miner,* and Ed Merdes, a local attorney. The latter phoned Bartlett and Stevens and asked what Alaskans could do for statehood. Both recommended writing and telegraphing Senators Johnson and Knowland and Speaker Rayburn and Representative Martin. A steering committee thereupon decided to assist citizens in sending messages, and also planned a statehood parade to be held on Washington's birthday. Sexauer then flew to Anchorage where a television station interviewed him about the movement. The next day he had breakfast with Operation Statehood officers and Democratic and Republican party leaders as well as other statehood enthusiasts. The group decided to put a booth on the lawn before the city hall from where they planned to encourage Anchorage residents to send postcards and telegrams to Washington. Furthermore, a section of the annual Fur Rendezvous parade was to be devoted to statehood. Anchorage students were encouraged to make statehood placards and march in the parade. Operation Statehood also asked Bartlett to deliver round-trip tickets to Johnson, Knowland, Rayburn, and Martin so they could preside over the parade. The four then were to be flown to Fairbanks to participate in that city's parade. Predictably, the four Congressional leaders declined the invitations because their Washington duties were too heavy. The parades took place under fair skies and warm weather without the politicians, and enabled thousands of ordinary citizens to publicly display their statehood commitment.[9]

In March, some fourteen million American viewed "See It Now," a popular CBS public affairs program hosted by Edward R. Murrow. It was a one hour program, with the first half devoted to Alaska and the second to Hawaii. Among those speaking for statehood were Delegate Bartlett, Governor Stepovich, and publisher Robert Atwood, and against it Winton Arnold, John Manders, and Senator George W. Malone. The Senator's statements caught the attention of the press. He warned that if noncontiguous Alaska was admitted, Hawaii, Puerto Rico, Taiwan and the Philippines would surely follow. Before long there would be between ten to sixteen offshore Senators in Washington, upsetting the power balance; "you just go off the deep end—one-worlders, and one world free immigration, free trade—that's the ultimate objective... I think in the long run it may be a good many years, but some time you may take all of the Western Hemisphere in one contiguous group." This rambling statement prompted the *Washington Post* to editorialize that the Senator probably did not convert many statehood advocates but that "a few listeners may have developed some queasy doubts about Nevada."[10]

Shortly after the "See It Now" program was shown in the states on March 2, Representative John Pillion charged the CBS had failed to balance its presentation. The network agreed, and Pillion was granted fifteen minutes of prime time television to argue against the admission of Alaska and Hawaii. As expected, Pillion charged that statehood would grant Alaskans and Hawaiians disproportionate representation in the Senate. He also claimed that Harry Bridges, the president of the International Longshoremen's and Warehousemen's Union in Hawaii, would send his communist organizers into Alaska. Soon they would take over its politics, completing the line of discipline from Moscow to the American Communist Party "to Bridges, to Honolulu and Juneau... into our Congress."[11]

In the midst of all of this there appeared William Prescott Allen once again, the publisher of the *Daily Alaska Empire*. He requested a meeting with Bartlett and the Alaska Tennessee Plan delegation. Allen told the group, including Snedden who was present, that statehood did not stand a chance in Congress, and that he wanted their help in asking for a tax moratorium. As usual, Allen's presentation, like his written pieces, was muddled. After listening for a few minutes, Egan got up and asked Allen about an editorial he had published as an advertisement in the *Washington Daily News.* The editorial argued that if Alaska and a Hawaii were admitted now, the "leftist extreme element" in both territories "would undoubtedly run a race in case of war to see which area would voluntarily join the communist bloc first," and with Alaska located next to Russia, it would probably win the race. Allen also rose and admitted the authorship of the piece, whereupon Egan told him that Alaskans did not need an overnight resident from Texas telling them what was best for their future. Allen became mad and shouted that he would not talk to the group again, rushed from the room and slammed the door. Eventually, Senator Richard Russell inserted Allen's editorial in the *Congressional Record.*[12]

At the same time, Representative Pelly stated that he would not vote for statehood unless his constituents were allowed to fish Alaskan waters on the same basis as residents. In order to make certain that this would happen, conservationists and sportsmen, as well as the redoubtable Winton Arnold, had drafted an amendment seeking retention of federal jurisdiction over Alaska's fish and game resources until the Secretary of the Interior certified to Congress that the state had provided for their conservation and nonresident access. The *Fairbanks Daily News-Miner* responded to Pelly by printing excerpts from Edna Ferber's latest novel, *Ice Palace,* which had Thor Storm telling his granddaughter about the Seattle and San Francisco cannery operators who unmercifully exploited Alaska's fisheries and used a small part of their profits to hire smart Washington lobbyists. Alaskans were helpless to stop this plunder because citizens of the United States were not interested in the territory, and northerners lacked voting Congressional representation which alone could remedy this situation. Ferber's book quickly became a bestseller and helped advertise Alaska's plight.[13]

In the meantime, Smith had scheduled hearings on the Alaska bill to begin on March 27, 1958. The chairman stated that the territory's civilian, non-Native population was very small, claimed that Alaska's admission might lead to statehood for Puerto Rico, and that the admission of noncontiguous Alaska and Hawaii could upset the power balance in the United States, and further alleged that the measure represented "the greatest give away of natural resources in history...." Representative O'Brien answered each statement, but Smith soon recessed the meeting. A few days later Snedden overheard Smith telling a colleague that the Alaska bill would only get out of his committee "over my dead body." Snedden repeated Smith's statement to Walker Stone, the editor-in-chief of the Scripps-Howard newspaper syndicate. Stone sketched a dummy of the front page of what became the April Fool's Day issue of the *Washington Daily News*. The illustration showed how "This Little Man Stalls a Vote" of his colleagues on the Rules Committee, and thereby defeated the will of the entire House. In fact, Smith was abusing the function of his committee to assure the smooth functioning of Congress.[14]

On April 23, Speaker Rayburn, although less than enthusiastic about statehood, told Smith that he wanted a rule by the next day. None was forthcoming, and on April 29, Rayburn gave his permission to have the bill brought up as privileged matter a week later, but in order to accommodate Representatives Halleck and Miller, debate was rescheduled for May 14.[15]

In the meantime, O'Brien announced that he would support four more amendments to the Alaska bill. One was Representative Pelly's amendment retaining federal jurisdiction over Alaska's fish and game resources; the second provided for a statehood referendum; the third reduced Alaska's basic land grant from 182,800,000 to 102,550,000 acres, while the fourth permitted the Federal Maritime Board to retain control of Alaska's seaborne trade with other states. Bartlett agreed to all the amendments except Pelly's, which he opposed for reasons of "principle and sentiment." He decided not to fight it, however, because he thought that once Alaska had gained statehood, it would be possible to have Congress repeal the amendment. [16]

After some maneuvering, the effort to bypass the Rules Committee was rescheduled for May 21. The chairman earlier on had learned that there would be an effort to bypass his committee. On May 6 of that year, he appealed to his colleagues in the House to oppose the Alaska statehood bill. He had been informed that the measure would be called up in the House as a "privileged bill." Smith asserted that there were many valid and compelling reasons why statehood should not be granted Alaska, and he reiterated that the strongest was that the contemplated measure constituted the greatest give away of natural resources in American history. Smith objected to the land grant of 182,800,000 acres, including all mineral resources, to the new state. But the real "gimmick" of the bill, Smith observed, was the clause which gave the new state the right for a period of twenty-five years to make its own selections of land in blocks of not less than 5,760 acres. During that period of time, the chairman of the Rules Committee complained, Alaska would only have to watch where the most valuable mineral resources discoveries were made and then choose accordingly. "These natural resources," Smith righteously concluded, "belong to all the people of the United States!"[17]

Smith failed to mention as early as June 1957, that Representative Clair Engle, Democrat of California, chairman of the House Interior and Insular Affairs Committee, had requested him to grant the Alaska bill consideration on the floor. As late as February 1958, not even a time for a hearing had been set. Engle, therefore, had been authorized by the members of his committee "to use all parliamentary methods to secure passage of H.R. 7999," the Alaska statehood bill. In a letter to Smith, Engle asserted that the statehood bill before the House enjoyed privileged status. "I would much prefer to follow the regular procedure and take the bill on the floor under a rule," Engle stated. But unless there was some indication that the Alaska measure would get the "green light" by the middle of March, he would have to bypass the Rules Committee. The procedure Engle had in mind was a little-used device. Under it, statehood and a few other types of legislation were deemed as privileged.[18] This maneuver required that the Speaker of the House recognize the chairman of the legislative committee concerned with this legislation and permit each member of the House, if he wished, to speak for one hour on any amendment.

The Alaska statehood bill was brought up on May 21, 1958 as privileged matter by Representative Wayne Aspinall who spoke for Engle's committee. He moved that the House resolve itself into the Committee of the whole House of the State of the Union. Clarence Cannon of Missouri immediately objected on a point of order. Certain matters, such as the appropriation of federal funds to the new state, deprived the measure of its privileged status, he said. Cannon hoped that he might "have the attention of the Speaker who had looked all along as if he had made up his mind and was not going to change it. I trust he will give attention with an open mind." Speaker Rayburn listened patiently to various other complaints voiced by Representatives Howard V. Smith, Noah M. Mason, and John Taber. Finally, Rayburn ruled that the major features of the Alaska statehood bill dealt with the territory's admission as a state. Lesser provisions did not destroy the privileged status, and the point of order and other objections were overruled. The House, by a roll-call vote of 217 to 172, thereupon agreed to consider the Alaska statehood bill.[19]

With this action the debate on Alaska statehood opened. It was frequently interrupted by delaying tactics from statehood opponents, such as twenty-five minute quorum calls and attempts to attach crippling amendments or to kill the bull outright. John R. Pillion of New York, a bitter statehood foe, found the tactics which had been used by Alaskans to further the cause highly objectionable. Inflammatory slogans such as patriotism, the right to vote, colonialism, second-class citizenship, and taxation without representation, if true, would be a reflection upon "the integrity and wisdom of Congress," and particularly the Committee on Interior and Insular Affairs. Pillion doubted that it was proper for a territorial government to use vast public funds to publicize and promote a purely political objective. "The election by Alaska of three Tennessee plan Congressmen," Pillion declared, "was not only presumptuous but…also a brazen attempt to coerce Congress."[20]

The House accepted an amendment by Representative William A. Dawson 91 to 8 which reduced the land grant to the new state from 182,8000,000 to 102,550,000 acres. An attempt by Walter Rogers of Texas to limit further the acreage to 21,000,000 was defeated. A.L. Miller's proposal to require Alaskans to vote on whether or not the territory should immediately by admitted to statehood was accepted, as was an amendment by Representative Jack Westland of Washington to temporarily retain federal authority over Alaska's fish and wildlife resources. A proposal by Craig Hosmer of California to delay statehood until the territory had attained a population of 250,000 was defeated, as was an attempt by Herbert C. Bonner to reduce from 70 percent to 25 percent Alaska's share in the proceeds from the sales of sealskins. On May 28, Representatives Rogers and Pillion tried to recommit the measure, but were defeated on roll-call votes of 199 to 174 and 202 to 172, respectively.[21]

Victor Fischer, who was working in Washington in 1958, has described the House vote:

I remember walking down the long corridor from the House Office Building through the underground corridor to the Capitol Building, and I had Marge Smith [Bartlett's personal secretary] on my arm, and Bartlett and Mary Lee [Council] were walking ahead. And Marge was just broken up, she was shaking, she said: 'I just can't take this anymore. I just can't take it. If we don't make it now, I just can't go through this again." We sat there, our group, in the House gallery…Mary Lee, and Marge, and I don't know who else was there. And Bartlett sat with [New York Representative Leo W.] O'Brien at that point, and it was really a tremendously tense affair. Representatives kept filing in and out… [and it] looked like a turmoil on the floor, and Bartlett and O'Brien sitting there tallying all this time. And then, finally, Bartlett looks up at us, and gives the

*thumbs-up sign. The gals just sort of broke down at that point.
It was such a phenomenally emotional experience.*[22]

The roll-call vote was 210 to 166, and with that the House sent
the amended Alaska statehood bill to the Senate for action.

In an interview in 1981, twenty-three years after the vote, O'Brien
stated that he did not believe that the Alaska statehood bill would
pass in 1958. In 1981 he still could not explain how the final House
support materialized so dramatically, and although he attributed
much of the final support to the friendship so many lawmakers felt
for Bob Bartlett, he still called the final passage "a miracle."[23]

As in 1950, the House had once again passed an Alaska statehood measure, and by nearly the same ratio. Not only the total vote
but also the sectional and partisan line up had been similar to that
of 1950, when the tally had been 186 to 146. Then, southerners had
voted 41 to 62 for statehood. In 1958, however, the vote had been
27 to 81 for statehood. In 1950 Democrats had voted 125 to 66 in
favor of statehood, and Republicans 61 to 80. In 1958, Democrats
had voted 119 to 82 and Republicans 89 to 84 in favor. Actually,
the victory was greater than Bartlett had expected, for he had predicted passage by only 17 votes.[24]

In 1950, after the Alaska measure had passed the House, it had
subsequently died in the Senate. This time, *The New York Times*
observed, the bill was "considered to have a good fighting chance"
in the upper house. That body now had before it the House bill
as well as its own version. If the Senate went ahead and passed
a measure which varied in any particular from the House bill,
Delegate Bartlett worried, the statehood forces would "be catapulted
into a morass." Any change in the House bill, he observed, meant
that the measure would have to go to conference. Such a step
necessitated unanimous consent, a remote possibility which only
provoked "laughter" in this case. Another alternative was to ask the
House Rules Committee to take charge and provide a rule which
would allow the measure to go to conference. In view of chairman
Howard Smith's hostility, Bartlett stated, there was "about as much

likelihood of that as of unanimous consent." Still another chance
lay in sending the bill back to the House Interior and Insular Affairs
Committee and persuade it to accept the Senate amendments, then
take the measure again to the floor under privileged status and
try for passage. In the delegate's view the foregoing alternatives
did not look promising. He therefore arranged a meeting with
Senator Henry "Scoop" Jackson, Democrat of Washington and
floor manager of the Alaska bill. Bartlett, Leo O'Brien, and Ernest
Gruening, among others, tried at the meeting "to persuade Scoop
to ditch the Senate bill and take the House measure. The delegate
anticipated grave difficulties because Senator Jackson and his
subcommittee had made improvements in the Senate version, and
it differed in some respects from the House bill. To everybody's
relief, however, Senator Jackson accepted the House bill.[25]

The Senators debated the Alaska statehood bill in the latter part
of May and throughout June. In that month, the Southern Senators
caucused to consider action on the pending measures, and a proposal was made to defeat Alaska statehood with a filibuster. Senator Russell Long opposed this course of action, indicating that he
would not only argue against his colleagues but also invoke cloture.
Such talk was heresy for a southerner. The result was that a number
of the most intensely opposed Senators made long speeches against
the bill "for the record," that is, for home consumption, but a southern filibuster did not develop.[26]

On June 27, 1958 Senator Monroney submitted an amendment
to substitute commonwealth status for the statehood measure. It
was rejected by a vote of 50 to 29. Senator Eastland's' point of order
to delete, as unconstitutional, the bill's provision that would permit the President to make defense withdrawals was also defeated
by a count of 53 to 28. On June 30, Senator Eastland introduced
his second point of order on the basis that Alaska's constitution,
endorsed in the statehood bill, violated the United States Constitution because it specified that one Senator was to be elected for
a regular term and one for a short term. It also missed approval
by a vote of 62 to 22. Next, Senator John Stennis' motion to refer

the Alaska statehood bill to the Senate Armed Service Committee with instructions to report it back with thirty days also failed by 55 to 31. Senator Strom Thurmond thereupon introduced an amendment to exclude the proposed defense area from the boundaries of the new state. It likewise suffered defeat on a vote of 67 to 16. At that point Senator Eastland gave up. He had intended, Eastland stated, to offer a motion to refer the statehood bill to the Senate Committee on the Judiciary. But in view of the voting trend so far, "such a motion would be useless...." Instead, he merely asked that his speech he printed in the *Congressional Record*.[27]

With Eastland's move the Southern opposition collapsed, and Senator Henry M. Jackson summarized the Senate effort up to that point:

> *Our work to date has not been the product of a single party. It has been the product of a bipartisan majority. This demonstrates again that Americans can close ranks in the truly great issues. This is not a Republican victory; it is not a Democratic victory; it is simply a victory for Alaskans. Mr. President, it is a victory for all Americans and for the Democratic process.*[28]

Several Senators called "vote, vote," and with Senator Richard Neuberger presiding, the roll-call began. Aiken—yes; Allot—yes; Anderson—yes. There were four more ayes, and then the first nays—Bridges, Bush, Butler, Byrd—then back to the ayes and on until there were 64 ayes and 20 nays. William C. Snedden, one of the many Alaskans in the Senate gallery that day, recalled that when the vote was about half over, "people began to talk. They began to see that we had it, and well, we did. There was spontaneous applause from the galleries and also from the floor." The time at which the roll-call vote ended was 8:02 p.m. Eastern Standard Time.[29] Soon after the vote, Delegate Bartlett and many of the Alaskans who had been sitting in the galleries all day long, headed for the Senate chapel to give thanks for the fulfillment of their hopes and aspirations. For Mary Lee Council, June 30, 1958 was a memorable day:

In all ways it turned out to be a perfect Monday, blue of sky but not blue of mood. So many years had gone into the fight, so many heartbreaks and setbacks had occurred. Success was almost unbelievable—a numbing experience for all who had participated. Something like 8,018,160 minutes passed between April 2, 1943, and June 30, 1958. The first date represents the introduction of the Langer bill and the second the day... [when] the bill passed.[30]

Word reached editor George Sundborg in Fairbanks at the moment the last vote was taken. It was a little past two o'clock in the afternoon in Alaska's interior city, but the staff of publisher Snedden's *Fairbanks Daily News-Miner* worked tireless throughout the rest of that day and part of the night in order to make a token air shipment of the special statehood issue to Washington. It was "for delivery to every member of Congress… as a demonstration of the nearness, under modern transportation conditions, of the nation's capital to the heart of Alaska, the 49th state."[31] The special issue was on the desks of members of Congress on July 1, 1958.

Reaction was jubilant in Alaska. In Fairbanks, "for the five full minutes the combined blast of every civil defense siren from College to North Pole [a small community south of Fairbanks] cried out the news that the U.S. Senate had passed the Alaska statehood bill," reported the *Fairbanks Daily News-Miner*. "Anchorage blows its lid," announced the *Anchorage Daily Times,* as "Alaska's largest city rocked and rolled as the air was split by the sound of sirens, horns, bills, firecrackers, guns—and everything else that could be used to make a noise."[32]

Statehood had been achieved—almost. President Eisenhower still had to sign the measure. He did so on July 7, 1958. But instead of signing the admission bill in public, as was customary, the chief executive decided to do so privately. This action was severely criticized by Senator James E. Murray, Democrat of Montana, who complained to Ernest Gruening:

Rather than to have had pictures taken in the presence of yourself and all those other fine Democrats who played such instrumental roles in bringing about the admission of the 49ᵗʰ state into the Union, he chose to handle this momentous matter as though he were merely signing a private bill for the relief of Mr. "X." Lord knows where he's going to find two Republicans who were sufficiently important in bring [sic] about statehood for Alaska to whom to present the two pens he used in the signing.[33]

Murray exaggerated, of course, because statehood had been very much a bipartisan effort.

On August 26, 1958, Alaskans went to the polls in a referendum and overwhelmingly accepted three propositions which had been inserted in the statehood bill: (1) Shall Alaska immediately by admitted into the Union as a state? (2) Shall the boundaries of the new state by approved? (3) Shall all the boundaries of the statehood act, such as those reserving rights and powers to the United Stated, as well as those prescribing the terms and conditions of the land grants and other property, be consented to? The three propositions were approved, receiving 40,542 to 8,010; 40,421 to 7,766 and 40,739 to 7,500 votes, respectively.[34]

On January 3, 1959, President Eisenhower formally admitted Alaska as the forty-ninth state when he signed the official proclamation. The statehood proclamation recited the action of Congress in 1958 to admit Alaska and the vote of the people in the new state to carry out the provisions of the statehood act. It declared that Alaskans had complied with the requirements set forth by Congress in all respects, and that "admission of the State of Alaska into the Union on an equal footing with the other States of the Union is now accomplished." The President then unfurled the new American flag containing a field of seven staggered rows of seven stars each. The chief executive, briefly addressing himself to the historic occasion, remarked that he felt highly privileged and honored to welcome the forty-ninth state into the Union. To the state itself and to its people he extended, "on behalf of all their [sic] sister states, best wishes and hope of prosperity and success."[35]

***

It is one of the ironic twists of history that finds Alaska, once jestingly referred to as a nearly worthless piece of real estate, now in a position of national, indeed international, prominence. In an age when energy resources determine political and economic relations between countries, oil was discovered at Prudhoe Bay on Alaska's North Slope in 1968. In 1984, nobody questions the wisdom of Alaska statehood.

In retrospect, the arguments used against Alaska statehood are of less significance today than during the struggle. Although the size of the population was always an issue in the admission of territories to statehood, the question actually was settled during the Constitutional Convention in the Connecticut Compromise of 1787, which created two houses, one with equal and the other with proportional representation. Many members of Congress used this argument to conceal their real concern. Not the size, but the racial compositions and the supposedly liberal political philosophy of this frontier area worried the southern bloc.

Over the years, especially after the Second World War, with its attendant revolution in transportation and communications, the objection that Alaska was noncontiguous and too remote became irrelevant. The advances in air transportation and the realization that some of the shortest routes to Europe and Asia were over Alaskan soil lent special significance to the territory. Americans were more anxious to have Alaska as their full-fledged front porch than to worry about it as Asia's and Europe's backdoor to the North American continent. Another argument, that Alaska did not have a sufficiently large population to support state government, was true in some respects. It was especially true because the delegates to the convention drafted a "model constitution" in order to demonstrate the territory's maturity to Congress. But this document would have been more suitable for a heavily populated, urban, industrialized

state like New York or Pennsylvania. The overwhelming majority of Alaskans did indeed live in relatively small, yet surprisingly
sophisticated and modern, urban communities, the myth of the
rugged "last frontier" notwithstanding. A government such as the
one embodied in the Alaska constitution, however, with its complete range of governmental services, was expensive for a state with
limited sources of taxation. Alaska could only boast of a couple
of pulp mills. There were a few producing oil and gas wells, possibilities of hydroelectric power development, the likelihood of
diversification in the fishing industry, some mining, and prospects
for a vastly increased tourist trade. The state's business enterprises
were small and catered mostly to local needs. In addition, Alaska's
population was modest and hardly amounted to more than that of
a medium-sized city in the contiguous United States.

Accordingly, revenues were small. Yet, the demands were great.
The state government had to provide all the governmental service and social overhead required by modern American society.
For instance, it would have been relatively simple to build a few
roads, furnish normal police protection, and establish the customary school facilities. But nothing was normal in Alaska; it was and
remains a land of superlatives. Subarctic engineering is relatively
new, but the state would have to face the problem of permafrost
conditions that frequently cause the road top to buckle and heave.
Police protection would have to provided for an area one-fifth the
size of the forty-eight United State but with very few roads available. Flying would become a way of life for law enforcement officials
as well as other Alaskans—an expensive way of life. "Bush schools"
scattered along the Aleutian chain, through the Yukon Valley,
on the Seward Peninsula, on the Arctic slope, and the islands of
southeastern Alaska were expensive to maintain. It was not until
the discovery of oil on a large scale that the picture changed. By
1970, Alaska's small population had become a virtue rather than a
handicap. The potential oil revenues and a modest population will
make it possible for the state, if it so desires, to pioneer in building
a unique model community with the comforts and conveniences

of twentieth-century life in proximity to and in harmony with the natural environment.

Basically, the same arguments against Alaskan statehood appeared in every discussion and at every hearing between 1916 and 1958. How close were these objections to the real issues? Prior to the Second World War, the lack of action was mostly due to Alaska's small population and physical remoteness, as well as to the opposition and lobbying activity of the special interests. The Second World War rushed Alaska headlong into the modern age and drastically changed the composition of its citizenry. With this population influx came a new awareness, and many of the new arrival were not so willing to acquiesce to the status quo, but wanted to pull Alaska into the mainstream of American Life.

Despite the new involvement of Alaskans, the attitude of Congress had not changed enough. The Old Guard in Congress viewed Alaska and Hawaii as potential dangers. For instance, senators and representatives from these two new states, many feared, would threaten the tradition of the filibuster and endanger cloture. Indeed, in combination with Western, Northern, and Eastern liberal support, these new votes could conceivably be sufficient to abolish XXII. There also was the fear that the admission of Alaska and Hawaii would integrate the hallowed Congressional chambers.

In 1957, Congress, after prolonged debate, passed a new civil rights law, the first since 1870. This new act was meant to protect the Negroes' right to vote by removing some of the obstacles created by state and local officials. Although at first far too weak to overcome the numerous devices used to circumvent it, the new act was indicative of the revelation in race relations in American society generally. These changes led many members of Congress to reassess the limitations of their power and influence. Led by such modern political leaders as Senator Lyndon B. Johnson, these politicians grudgingly acceded to the admission of Alaska, and finally, Hawaii as well.

With Alaska statehood in 1958 and Hawaii statehood in 1959, the land domain of the United State had been rounded out. There are no more new frontiers in a geographical sense. Hopefully, the state of Alaska, especially in view of its temporary oil wealth, will be able to pioneer new realms in the fields of economic and social relationships, and possibly demonstrate that technology and nature are not incompatible.

Endnotes

INTRODUCTION

1   "Message of Governor William A. Egan to the Second Session, First Alaska State Legislature, Recommending Appropriations for Fiscal Year 1961," in State of Alaska Budget Document 1960-1961. (Juneau, Alaska: January 27, (1960), 1-4).
2   Ibid., 7, 20; Alaska State Planning Commission State of Alaska Capital Improvement Program 1960-1966, January 29, 1960, G-4-G-7.
3   Ray J. Schrick, "Alaska's Ordeal," Wall Street Journal, March 16, 1960.
4   Ibid.
5   E. Slotnick, "The 1960 Election in Alaska," Western Political Quarterly, March 1961, 30, Thomas A. Morehouse and Gordon A. Harrison, An Electoral Profile of Alaska (Fairbanks, Alaska: Institute of Social, Economic, and Government Research, (1973), 2-3.
6   State of Alaska, Office of the Governor, "Alaska Earthquake Disaster Damage Report," (preliminary), April 4, 1964, in author's files.
7   E.L. Bartlett Press Release, April 3, 1964, in author's files.
8   Hugh G. Gallagher, Etok: A Story of Eskimo Power (New York: G.P. Putnam's Sons, 1974) 182.
9   Mary Clay Berry, The Alaska Pipeline: The Politics of Oil and Native Land Claims (Bloomington & London: Indiana University Press, 1975), 117-118.
10 Ibid., 117-118.
11 Paul Brooks, The Pursuit of Wilderness (Boston: Houghton Mifflin Co., 1971), 64, 66.
12 U.S. Congress, Senate, Alaska Natives Claims Settlement Act of 1971: Report Together with Additional and Supplemental Views to Accompany S. 35, 92nd Cong., 1st Sess. (October 21, 1971), 96.
13 Mary Clay Berry, The Alaska Pipeline: The Politics of Oil and Native Land Claims (Bloomington & London: Indiana University Press, 1975), 44.
14 Ibid., 48-49.
15 Berry, The Alaska Pipeline, 146-147. Fairbanks Daily News-Miner, June 20, 1978.
16 Robert D. Arnold et. al., Alaska Native Land Claims (Anchorage, Alaska: Alaska Native Foundation, 1976), 146-147.
17 Alaska Native Claims Settlement Act, 92nd Congress, 1st Session.
18 P.L. 96-487, 94 Stat, 2371.
19 Petroleum News-Alaska. Katalla to Prudhoe Bay, 24-25.
20 Jack Roderick, Crude Dreams: A Personal History of Oil and Politics in Alaska (Fairbanks, Alaska: Epicenter Press, 1997), 355-336.
21 Ibid., 347-350.
22 Ibid., 355.

23 Ibid., 363-364.

24 Ibid., 369.

25 Gerald A. McBeath and Thomas A. Morehouse, eds., *Alaska State Government and Politics* (Fairbanks, Alaska: University of Alaska Press, 1987), 246.

26 John Strohmeyer, *Extreme Conditions: Big Oil and the Transformation of Alaska* (New York: Simon and Schuster, 1993), 206.

27 Ibid., 207.

28 Sec. 15, Constitution of the State of Alaska.

29 Kason, "*The Creation of the Alaska Permanent Fund*," 16.

30 Rural Research Agency, "Alaska's Permanent Fund: Legislative History, Intent and Operations," in *The Trustee Papers*, Vol. 5 (Juneau, Alaska: Alaska Permanent Fund Corporation, 1997), 47, 55-56.

31 Clifford J. Groh and Gregg Erickson, "The Permanent Fund Dividend Program: Alaska's Noble Experiment," in *The Early History of the Alaska Permanent Fund: The Trustee Papers*, Vol. 5 (Juneau, Alaska; Alaska Permanent Fund Corporation, 1997), 31.

32 *Fairbanks Daily News-Miner,* June 17, April 2, 2006.

33 *Anchorage Daily News,* September 17, 2006.

34 *Anchorage Daily News*, November 26, 2006.

35 Richard A. Fineberg, *How Much Is Enough? Estimated Industry Profits From Alaska North Slope Production and Associated Pipeline Operations, 1993-1998*, A Preliminary Report to Oilwatch Alaska (Ester, Alaska: December 9, 1998), ES-2.

36 Richard A. Fineberg to Prince William Sound Regional Citizens' Advisory Council," The Profitability and Economic Viability of Alaska North Slope," June 2, 2005.

37 *Fairbanks Daily News-Miner,* December 2, 2006.

38 *Fairbanks Daily News-Miner*, May 5, 8, 2007.

39 *Anchorage Daily News,* December 8, 2007, *Fairbanks Daily News-Miner*, June 2, 2008.

40 *Fairbanks Daily News-Miner*, August 31, *Anchorage Daily News*, August 10, 2007.

41 Ibid., August 5, 2007.

42 *Fairbanks Daily News-Miner,* September 13, 2007.

43 *Anchorage Daily News*, December 2, 2007.

CHAPTER ONE

1 United States Army, Alaska, *The Army's Role in the Building of Alaska* (Headquarters, United States Army, Alaska: Public Information Officer, Pamphlet 360-5, April 1969), p.1. See also Frank A. Golder, "The Purchase of Alaska," *The American Historical Review,* XXV (April 1920), 411-25; Victor J. Farrar, "The Background of the Purchase of Alaska," *Washington Historical Quarterly,*" XIII (April 1922), 92-104; R.H. Luthin, "The Sale of Alaska," *Slavonic Review,*

Endnotes

291

XVI (July 1937), 168-82; Thomas A. Bailey, "Why the United States Purchased Alaska," *Pacific Historical Review*, III (March 1934), 39-49.

2 Stuart Ramsy Tompkins, *Alaska, Promyshlennik and Sourdough* (Norman: University of Oklahoma Press, 1945), p. 191.

3 Speech *of William H. Seward at Sitka, August 12, 1868* (Washington: Philip and Solomons, 1869), p. 16.

4 James D. Richardson, ed., *A Compilation of the Messages and Papers of the Presidents* (New York: Bureau of National Literature, 1912), V, 3778.

5 Mel Crain, "When the Navy Ruled Alaska," *United States Naval Institute Proceedings*, LXXXI (February 1955), 199, states that United States troops were withdrawn as an economy measure by President Rugherford B. Hayes in 1877. Jeannette Paddock Nichols, in *Alaska: A History of Its Administrations, Exploitation, and Industrial Development During the First Half Century Under the Rule of the United States* (Cleveland: The Arthur H. Clark Company, 1924), p. 59, states that the troops were withdrawn because they were needed to quell the Nez Perce Indian uprising in the Pacific Northwest. Ernest Gruening, in *The State of Alaska* (2nd.; New York: Random House, 1968), p. 36, echoes Ms. Nichols.

6 Crain, "When the Navy Ruled Alaska," p. 198

7 Gruening, *The State of Alaska*, pp. 33-52.

8 Nichols, *Alaska*, p. 72.

9 Earl S. Pomeroy, *The Territories and the United States 1861-1890: Studies in Colonial Administration* (Philadelphia: University of Pennsylvania Press, 1947), p. 2

10 Jack E. Eblen, *The First and Second United States Empires: Governors and Territorial Government, 1784-1912* (Pittsburg: University of Pittsburgh Press, 1968), p. 151; Ibid., p. 8.

11 Richard E. Welch, Jr., "American Public Opinion and the Purchase of Russian America," in *Alaska and its History*, ed. Morgan B. Sherwood (Seattle and London: University of Washington Press 1967), pp. 274-88.

12 "Speech of Hon. Charles Sumner, of Massachusetts, on the Cession of Russian America to the United States," in U.S., Congress, House, House Executive Document No. 177, 40 Cong., 2 Sess. (Washington: Government Printing Office, 1868), p. 188. For an excellent description of early Alaska, see William H. Dall, *Alaska and its Resources* (Cambridge: University Press, John Wilson and Sons, 1870).

13 Quoted in Welch, "American Public Opinion and the Purchase of Russian America," pp. 276-77.

14 George W. Rogers and Richard A. Cooley, *Alaska's Population and Economy*, vol. I, *Analysis* (College, Alaska: Institute of Business, Economic and Government Research, 1963), pp. 16-19

15 Richardson, *Compilation of Messages* and *Papers of the Presidents*, VIII, 6269; Ibid., IX, 6400; Ibid., IX, 6401

16 Gruening, *The State of Alaska*, p. 105.

17 Ibid., pp. 107-13.

18 Nichols, *Alaska*, pp. 180-83.

19 Thomas A. Morehouse and Victor Fischer, *The State and the Local Government System* (College, Alaska: Institute of Social Economic, and Government Research, March 1970), p. III-8

20 Gruening, *The State of Alaska*, pp. 138-39.

21 U.S. *Stats. at Large* 512 (1912).

22 National Resources Planning Board, "Postwar Economic Development of Alaska," In *Regional Development Plan—Report for 1942* (Washington: Government Printing Office, December 1941)

23 U.S., congress, House, *Alaska*, Hearings before the Subcommittee on Territorial an Insular Possessions of the Committee on Public Lands, Committee Hearing No. 31, 80 Cong., 1 Sess. (Washington: Government Printing Office, 1947) pp. 366-67.

24 37 U.S. Stats. at *Large* 512 (1912); 15 Stats. at *Large* 240 (1868); 23 U.S. Stats. at *Large* 24 (1884).

25 Max Farrand, "Territory and District," *The American Historical Review*, V (July 1900), 676-81.

26 For an elaboration of this view, see Eblen, The *First and Second United States Empire*, pp. 201-36; Pomeroy, The Territories nd the United States, pp. 1-5.

27 *De Lima v. Bidwell*, 182 U.S. (1901); *Downes v. Bidwell*, 182 U.S. 244 (1901)

28 Robert H. Wiebe, *The Search for Order 1877-1920* (New York: Hill and Wang, 1967), p. 228.

29 See *Rasmussen v. United States*, 197 U.S. 516 (1905); *Nagle v. United States,* 191 Fed. 141 (1911); United States v. Farwell, 76 F. Supp. 35 (1948).

30 See *Balzac v. People of Porto Rico*, 258 U.S. 298 (1922); *McAllister v. United States,* 141 U.S. 174, 188 (1897); *O'Donoghue v. United States*, 289 U.S. 516, 537 (1933). George Washington Spicer described and analyzed some thirty-five key court cases in *The Constitutional Status and Government of Alaska* (Baltimore: The Johns Hopkins University Press, 1917). Alaska statehood proponents in the mid-1940's borrowed heavily from Spicer in their efforts to establish a judicial framework for their cause.

31 Ray Allen Billington, *Westward Expansion: A History of the American Frontier* (3rd ed.; New York: The Macmillan Company, 1967), p. 627.

32 George W. Rogers, *The Future of Alaska: Economic Consequences of Statehood* (Baltimore: The Johns Hopkins Press, 1962), p. 95.

CHAPTER TWO

1   For the various phases of the exploitation of Alaska's resources see Gruening, *The State of Alaska;* Tompkins, *Alaska: Promyshlennik and Sourdough;* Henry W. Clark, *History of Alaska* (New York: The Macmillan Company, 1930); Alfred Hulse Brooks, Blazing Alaska's Trails, ed. Burton L. Fryxell, published jointly by the University of Alaska and the Arctic Institute of North America (Caldwell, Idaho: The Caxton Printers, Ltd., 1953); George W. Rogers, *The Future of Alaska.*

2 Rogers and Cooley, *Alaska's Population and Economy*, vol. II *Statistical Handbook*, p. 7.

3 Eblen, *First and Second United States Empires*, p. 151.

4 Ted C. Hinckley, "Reflections and Refractions: Alaska and Gilded Age America," in *Frontier Alaska, a Study in Historical Interpretation and Opportunity*, Proceedings of the Conference on Alaskan History, June8-10, 1967 (Anchorage, Alaska: Alaska Methodist University Press, 1968), p. 97.

5 Brooks, *Blazing Alaska's Trails*, p. 509.

6 Morehouse and Fischer, *The State and the Local Governmental System*, p. III-6.

7 *Report of the Governor of Alaska for the Fiscal Year 1888* (Washington: Government Printing Office, 1889), p. 46. Hereafter cited as *Annual Report of the Governor of Alaska* with appropriate year in parenthesis.

8 Hinckley, "Reflections and Refractions: Alaska and Gilded Age America," p. 101.

9 *Annual Report of the Governor of Alaska* (1885), p. 15.

10 Hinckley, "Reflections and Refractions: Alaska and Gilded Age America," p. 101.

11 *Annual Report of the Governor of Alaska* (1885), p. 17.

12 Rogers, *The Future of Alaska*, p. 170.

13 *Annual Report of the Governor of Alaska* (1888), p. 45.

14 Nichols, *Alaska*, pp. 121-57,458.

15 *Ibid.*, pp. 66-68, 127-29.

16 *Ibid.*, pp. 125, 134.

17 *Cong. Record*, 54 Cong., 1 Sess., p. 4675 (May 1, 1896).

18 Gruening, *The State of Alaska*, p. 103. By far the best book on the Gold Rush is Pierre Berton, *The Klondike Fever: The Life and Death of the Last Great Gold Rush* (New York: Alfred A. Knopf, 1958).

19 Gruening, *The State of Alaska*, p. 104.

20 Clark, *History of Alaska*, pp. 98-115

21 *Annual Report of the Governor of Alaska* (1897), p. 32.

22 *Ibid.*, p. 37.

23 *Ibid.*, p. 47.

24 *Ibid*, p. p. 49.

25 David S. Jordan, "Colonial Lessons of Alaska," *Atlantic Monthly*, November 1898, pp. 582, 591.

26 Nichols, *Alaska*, pp. 145-793

27 U.S., Congress, Senate, Committee on Territories, *Conditions in Alaska*, 58 Cong., 2 Sess., S. Rept. 2828 to accompany S. Res. 16 (Washington: Government Printing Office, 1904), p. 32.

28 Nicols, *Alaska*, p. 246.

29 U.S. *Stats. at Large* 169 (1906).

30 Gruening, *The State of Alaska*, p. 139. The view that a delegate to Congress was a legal, historical, and moral right is elaborated upon in Everett S. Brown, *The Territorial Delegate of Congress and Other Essays* (Ann Arbor, Michigan: The George Wahr Publishing Co., 1950), pp. 3-38.

CHAPTER THREE

1   The role of the special interests is extensively described in Gruening, *The State of Alaska*, and Nichols, *Alaska.*

2   Herman Slotnick, The Ballinger-Pinchot Affair in Alaska," *Journal of the West*, Vol. X, No. 2 (April 1971), pp. 337-347. Slotnick discusses the Alaskan view of the affair.

3   Nichols, *Alaska,* pp. 274-76.

4   *Annual Report of the Governor of Alaska* (1906), p. 6.

5   U.S., Congress, Senate, *Needs of Alaska in Matters of Legislation and Government,* S. Doc. No. 14, 59 Cong., 2 Sess. (Washington: Government Printing Office, 1906), pp. 4, 2.

6   Nichols, *Alaska,* p. 280.

7   Ibid., pp. 276-77, 280, 298, 300; U.S., President, *A Compilation of the Messages and Papers of the Presidents,* ed. James D. Richardson, 22 v. (New York: Bureau of National Literature, 1897-1929), 16:7103; 60 Cong., 1 Sess., H.R. 4820, December 5, 1907, H.R. 17649, February 20, 1908.

8   Nichols, Alaska, pp. 293-94; for a biography of James Wickersham, see Evangeline Atwood, *Frontier Politics: Alaska's James Wickersham* (Portland, Oregon: Binford & Mort, Thomas Binford, Publisher, 1979).

9   U.S. Congress, Senate, Committee on Territories, Conditions in Alaska; Report to Accompany S. Res. 16, 58 Cong., 2 Sess., S. Rept. 282 (Washington: Government Printing Office, 1904), p. 32.

10 Senate, a 162 Cong. Record, 58 Cong., 2 Sess., p. 3092; Nichols, *Alaska,* p. 228; *Annual Report of the Governor of Alaska* (1904), p. 7. In a 1902 speech before the Seattle and Tacoma Chambers of Commerce, Wickersham had stated that the district should be provided with a territorial government. He also maintained that it should eventually be divided into at least four territories, with the same names he had given in a 1904 speech. In 1902 he had suggested that the capital of Tanana be located at Rampart or Eagle. James Wickersham, *Alaska: Its Resources, Present Condition and Needed Legislation, Being a Synopsis of an Address Delivered by Hon. James Wickersham, U.S. District Judge of Alaska, before the Respective Chambers of Commerce of Seattle, on November 5, 1902, and Tacoma, November 11, 1902* (Tacoma: Allen and Lamborn, 1902), pp. 8-9; U.S. Congress, House, *Biographical Directory of the American Congress, 1774-1961,* H. Doc. 442, 85 Cong., 2 Sess. (Washington: Government Printing Office, 1961), p.1811. This source states that Wickersham resigned to run for delegate to Congress from Alaska. Wickersham, in his diary, says that he resigned from the bench because he "was a poor man and just then had a reasonable and proper opportunity to re-enter the law practice with a fair prospect of accumulating a stake before opportunity failed or old age overtook... [me]." In addition, the Senate had never confirmed him and he had served under repeated recess appointments by President Roosevelt. The Judge did not think that those Senators who had always opposed him would relent now. At that time he had

also had a falling out with Alaskan Governor Wilford B. Hoggatt over a court case involving the career of a young lawyer in which he had rendered a decision contrary to the Governor's Wilford B. Hoggatt over a court case involving the career of a young lawyer in which he had rendered a decision contrary to the Governor's views. The latter thereupon refused to give proper support to the court and Judge Wickersham. On top of it all, his wife Debbie had been in ill health for a number of years and he felt that he had been unable to give her needed personal attention. See James Wickersham Diary, September 9, 1907, Microfilm University of Alaska Archives, Fairbanks, Alaska. Hereafter cited as Wickersham Diary.

11 *Alaska Record* (Juneau), May 27, 1908, quoted in Nichols, *Alaska*, fn. 575, pp. 302-04.

12 Nichols, Alaska, pp. 301-04.

13 Ibid., pp. 300, 295, 303, 312-314; Wickersham Diary, June 23, 1908. Wickersham's progress from retired judge to active politician is chronicled in the following excerpts from his : politician is chronicled in the following excerpts from his diary: "...the end of my political career was reached without a pang of regret—with real genuine feeling of relief—I can now begin to organize my home—library and my own private fortune." (September 8, 1907)
"McGinn [a Fairbanks Republican leader] came to see me again and insisted that I ought to run for Delegate to Congress but can't make up my mind to do so." (February 20, 1908)
"McGinn came today—told him that I would not be a candidate for Delegate to Congress—nor to the National Convention—that I am out of political life and intend to remain out." (March 2, 1908)
"I BECAME A CANDIDATE!!" (March 2, 1908)
Ibid., July 1,6, 7, 14, 1908.

14 James Penick, Jr., *Progressive Politics and Conservation: The Ballinger-Pinchot Affair* (Chicago and London: The University of Chicago Press, 1968), pp. 82-83; Nichols, *Alaska*, pp. 306-09. For the story of the Guggenheims, see Harvey O'Connor, *The Guggenheims: the Making of an American Dynasty* (New York: Covici Friede, 1937).

15 Wickersham Diary, July 17, 1908; "James Wickersham Address to the Voters of Alaska," unidentified clipping in Wickersham Diary, July 17, 1908.

16 Nichols, *Alaska*, p. 316; Gruening, *The State of Alaska*, p. 143.

17 Wickersham Diary, November 17, 1908.

18 Ibid., April 1909, May 31, 1909, June 5, 1909; Ibid., June 7, 1909.

19 George A. Frykman, "The Alaska-Yukon-Pacific Expositions, 1909," *Pacific Northwest Quarterly*, LIII (July, 1962), pp. 89-99; Nichols, *Alaska*, p. 329; *Seattle Post-Intelligencer*, October 1, 1909; Cong. Record, 64 Cong., 1 Sess., p. A1518.

20 Editorial, *Fairbanks Times*, October 3, 1909, clipping in Wickersham Diary, October 3, 1909. For a favorable comment on Taft's commission plan, see Brownell Atherton, "Wanted: A Government for Alaska," *Outlook*, February 26, 1910, pp. 431-40. For the opposite view by "An Alaskan" see "President Taft

Does Not Favor Home Rule," *Alaska-Yukon Magazine*, August 1909, pp. 470-71; Wickersham Diary, October 13, 18, 1909.

21 *Annual Report of the Governor of Alaska* (1911), pp. 30-31; 33 Stat. 616-620; *Annual Report of the Governor of Alaska* (1911), p. 31.

22 See U.S., Congress, Senate, *Investigation of the Department of the Interior and of the Bureau of Forestry*, S. Doc. 719 pursuant to H.J. Res. 103, 61 Cong., 3 Sess. (Washington: Government Printing Office, 1910). A modern account of the controversy between Ballinger and Pinchot is rendered in Penick, *Progressive Politics and Conservation*. For Clarence Cunningham's views on the whole matter, see Cunningham's view on the whole matter, see Cunningham to Martin Harrais, United States Commissioner, September 16, 1935, Harrais Papers, University of Alaska Archives, Fairbanks, Alaska. For Alaskan views on the Ballinger-Pinchot controversy and the conservation issue, see "Conservation Gone Crazy," *Alaska-Yukon Magazine*, February, 1910, pp. 171-73; "Conservation That Locks Up," Ibid., April, 1910, pp. 290-93; and the entire issue of Ibid., May 1910. For a protest against the exploitation of Alaska, see Casey Moran, "A Land to Loot," *Collier's*, August 6, 1910, pp. 19-24.

23 Penick, *Progressive Politics and Conservation*, pp. 77-142.

24 James Wickersham, July 21, 1923, Juneau, Alaska, in Introduction, Nichols, *Alaska*, p. 17.

25 Ibid., pp. 349-58.

26 Ibid., pp. 325-84.

27 Editorial, Alaska Daily Time (Fairbanks), September, 1911, clipping in Wickersham Diary, September, 1911; Ibid., September, 1911. The Delegate not only had trouble with some newspapers over his home rule bill, but also with some irate citizens. After a debate with a local politician in Fairbanks, Wickersham wrote in his diary: I intend to try to convince the people that my legislative bill is good and sufficient...." Ibid., October 27, 1911. Another article in the Alaska Daily Times (Fairbanks), October 29, 1911.

28 Gruening, *The State of Alaska*, p. 150; Wickersham Diary, April 24, July 24, August 17, 1912.

29 37 U.S. *Stats. at Large*, 512 (1912).

30 *Alaska Daily Empire* (Juneau), April 8, 1915; Nichols, *Alaska*, pp. 401-02.

31 37 U.S. *Stats. at Large*, 512 (1912).

CHAPTER FOUR

1 *Speech of Hon. James Wickersham, Delegate to Congress* (Juneau, Alaska [no publisher given], March 10, 1913)

2 *Daily Alaska Empire*, January 28, 1934; *Alaska Daily Empire*, January 20, 1914; *Daily Alaska Dispatch*, April 9, 1915.

3 *Alaska Daily Empire*, September 29, 1914; *Daily Alaska Dispatch*, April 9, 1915.

4 Alaska, Legislature, House, *Journal*, 1915, p.11.

5 Ibid., pp. 53-54, 89.

6 *Alaska Daily Empire*, March 27, 4, 1915

7 Ibid., March 30, 1915; Senate, *Journal*, 1915, pp. 45, 95; Alaska, *Session Laws*, 1915, pp. 210-11.

8 *Daily Alaska Dispatch*, April 7, 1915; *Forty-Ninth Star*, December 18, 1915; Senate, *Journal*, pp. 98-100.

9 *Alaska Daily Empire*, March 31, 1915; Senate, *Journal*, 1915, pp. 100, 150. The Senate passed the Millard memorial by a 6-2 vote, only Hubbard and Sutherland cast the negative votes. The House voted 9-7 to accept the Millard memorial.

10 *Alaska Daily Empire*, March 31, 1915; *Daily Alaska Dispatch*, April 1, 1915; *Alaska Daily Empire*, April 1, 1915.

11 *Daily Alaska Dispatch*, April 7, 8, 9, 1915; *Alaska Daily Empire*, April 8, 1915.

12 Ibid., April 9, 13, 1915; Senate, *Journal*, 1915, pp. 137, 192-93.

13 *Daily Alaska Dispatch*, April 9, 1915; *Alaska Daily Empire*, November 20, December 9, 1915.

14 *Cong. Record*, Appendix, 64 Cong., 1 Sess., p. 1518 (July 25, 1916).

15 Ibid., pp. 1519, 1522.

16 James Wickersham, "The Forty-Ninth Star," *Collier's*, August 6, 1910, p.17.

17 *Forty-Ninth Star*, December 4, 1916.

18 Ibid., March 4, 1916.

19 Wickersham Diary, January 23, 1916.

20 Editorial, *Forty-Ninth Star*, January 8, 1916.

21 Wickersham Diary, January 23, 1916.

22 *Alaska Daily Empire*, March 31, 1916.

23 *Cong. Record*, Index, 64 Cong., 1 Sess., H.R. 4648, p. 170; Ibid., H.R. 6056, p. 189. This action on the part of Wickersham is difficult to understand in light of this vigorous campaign against the Taft proposal for such a form of government just a few years earlier. Ibid., H.R. 232, p. 114, and S. 896, p. 14; Ibid., H.R. 6887, p. 471. For a discussion of this bill, see *Cong. Record*, Appendix, 64 Cong., 1 Sess., pp. 1519-23 (July 25, 1916); Wickersham Diary, December 27, 1915.

24 H.R. 13978, 64 Cong., 1 Sess., in bound volume, R.G. 233, National Archives (hereafter cited as NA)

25 Editorial, *Daily Alaska Dispatch*, March 30, April 1, 8, 13, 15, 1916,

26 Editorials, *San Francisco Chronicle*, quoted in *Forty-Ninth Star*, August 20, 1916; *Portland Telegram*, quoted in *Daily Alaska Dispatch*, April 19, 1916. See also editorial, *Tacoma Daily News*, quoted in Ibid., April 22, 1916, and editorial, *Seattle Post-Intelligencer*, quoted in Ibid., April 27, 1916,

27 *Alaska Daily Empire*, March 31, 1916.

28 For an account of this affair, see *Cong. Record*, Appendix, 64 Cong., 1 See., pp. 1520-22 (July 25, 1916). A pamphlet written to further the modern Alaska statehood movement colorfully describes Wickersham's fight to preserve the authority of the territorial legislature. See Evangeline B. Atwood, *Alaska's Struggle for Self-government... 83 Years of Neglect* (Anchorage, Alaska: Anchorage Daily Times, 1950), pp. 12-13.

29 *Daily Alaska Dispatch*, September 1, 1916.

CHAPTER FIVE

1   *Fairbanks Daily News-Miner*, Golden Days edition, July 18, 1957; *Alaska Monthly*, June 1906, p. 80; W. F. Beers, Jr., "The Government of Alaska, *Alaska-Yukon Magazine*, vol. 4, 1908, p. 373.

2   *Alaska-Yukon Magazine*, vol. 3, 1911, pp. 208, 201.

3   Hugh A. Johnson and Harold T. Jorgenson, *The Land Resources of Alaska* (New York: University Publishers, 1963), pp. 202-203; 35 Stat. 260.

4   George W. Rogers and Richard A. Cooley, *Alaska's Population and Economy: Regional Growth, Development and Future Outlook*, vol. II – Statistical Handbook (College, Alaska: Institute of Business, Economic and Government Research, 1963), p. 17.

5   Ibid., vol. I, Analysis, p. 19. For an excellent study of Alaska's economic growth during the war years, see Joseph L. Fisher, Alaska: *The Development of Our Arctic Frontier* (unpublished PH.D dissertation, Harvard University, 1947)

6   Ernest Gruening, *The State of Alaska* (New York: Random House, 1954), pp. 287-288. For a full account of the affair, see Atwood, *Frontier Politics*, pp. 307-331.

7   Kirk H. Porter and Donal Bruce Johnson, eds. *National Party Platforms, 1840-1960* (Urbana: University of Illinois Press, 1961), pp. 222-223, 238.

8   *Alaska Daily Empire*, July 13,1921.

9   *Alaska Daily Empire*, December 8, 1921, January 7, April 29, 1922.

10 *Ketchikan Alaska Chronicle*, December 7, 1922, January 17, 1923; Anchorage Daily Times, June 11, 1919; *Alaska Daily Empire*, April 29, 1922.

11 See *New York Times*, July 17, 1921, Sec. VII, p. 2, for Secretary Albert B. Fall's plan for the development of Alaska. For the position of Secretary of Agriculture Henry C. Wallace, see "Secretary of Agriculture Wallace on President Harding's Views on Alaska," *The Commercial and Financial Chronicle*, September1, 1923, pp. 959-60. See also Burl Noggle, *Teapot Dome: Oil and Politics in the 1920s* (Baton Rouge: Louisiana State University Press, 1962), pp. 15-31. The account of what motivated President Harding to visit Alaska is based on Robert K. Murray, *The Harding Era: Warren G. Harding and His Administration* (Minneapolis: University of Minnesota Press, 1969), pp. 439-40; and Francis Russell, *The Shadow of Blooming Grove: Warren G. Harding in His Times* (New York & Toronto: McGraw-Hill Book Company, 1968), pp. 572-73.

12 The account of Harding's visit is based on Murray, *The Harding Era*, pp. 445-48; and Russell, *The Shadow of Blooming Grove*, pp. 581-89.

13 James W. Murphy, ed., *Speeches and Addresses of Warren G. Harding, President of the United States* (Washington: Government Printing Office, 1923), p. 307.

14 Ibid., pp. 341-61; *New York Times*, July 28, 1923, pp. 1-2; Murray, *The Harding Era*, p. 448.

15 "Alaska's Problem as President Harding Saw It," *The Literary Digest*, August 18, 1923, p. 18. Excerpts from both Alaska and newspapers from the contiguous states are found in this article.

16 Ibid.

17 Walter V. Woehike, "Warren Harding's Bequest: He Leaves to the Far West an Emphatic Endorsement of the Conservation Policy," *Sunset Magazine*, October 1923, p. 105.

18 *Alaska Daily Empire*, November 7, 9, 1923. U. S. Congress, House, Committee on Territories, *Reapportionment of the Alaska Legislature: Hearings on H.R. 8114*, 68 Cong., IS., March 27-29, 1924 (Washington: Government Printing Office, 1924), p. 20 Alaska's Delegate Dan A. Sutherland criticized the measure. A typewritten note attached to the copy located in the University of Alaska-Fairbanks library states: "This plan to rob Northern Alaska of its share in the revenue of the Territory was instigated by Juneau politicians." Because of the regional differences and jealousies, this note was probably written by a disgruntled Alaskan from the interior of the territory.

19 *Hearings on H. R. 8114*, pp. 14-16. *Alaska Daily Empire*, November 15, 16, 1923.

20 Ibid., November 15, 16, 19, 17, 1923.

21 Hearings on H.R. 8114, pp. 17-20, 7; Memorial of the People of the First Judicial Division of Alaska (Juneau, Alaska, n.d. [1923]); Alaska Daily Empire, Deceember 12, June 14, 1923, March 14, 22, 1924.

22 *Hearings on H. R. 8114*, pp. 6-7, 86-88; *Alaska Daily Empire*, March 14, November 4, 1924.

23 *Hearings on H.R. 8114*, pp. 1-3.

24 Ibid., pp. 1, 84, 97-99.

25 Ibid., pp. 89, 54, 81.

26 House, *Journal*, 1925, pp. 164-250.

27 *Alaska Daily Empire* June 22, February 14, June 16, 1925; *Daily Alaska Empire*, April 19, 1933. *Anchorage Daily Times,* May 15, 1956, March 9, April 9, 1926.

28 Ibid., April 12, 1926; *Daily Alaska Empire*, November 6, 1929, January 28, February 17, 1930.

CHAPTER SIX

1 Gruening, *The State of Alaska*, Table of Contents.

2 Clark, *History of Alaska*, pp. 81, 129.

3 J.A. Hellenthal, *The Alaskan Melodrama* (New York: Leverright Publishing Corporation, 1936), p. 284.

4 Ernest Gruening, "Let Us End American Colonialism," Keynote Address, Alaska Constitutional Convention, University of Alaska, College, Alaska, November 9, 1955, in *Cong. Record*, 85 Cong., 1 Sess., pp. 470-71, 474 (January 14, 1957).

5 *Cong. Record*, Index, 68 Cong., 1 Sess., p. 606 (H.R. 6947 proposed to elect the governor and secretary of the territory); Ibid., 69 Cong., 1 Sess., p. 669 (H.R.

7289 proposed to elect the governor and secretary of the territory); Ibid., 70 Cong., 1 Sess., p. 588 (H.R. 329 provided for the election of the governor only); Ibid., 71 Cong., 1 Sess., p. 279 (H.R. 250 provided for the election of the governor only). None of the bills passed.

6   *Annual Report of the Governor of Alaska* (1904), pp. 15-16.

7   National Resources Committee, *Regional Planning—Part VII, Alaska—Its Resources and Development* (Washington: Government Printing Office, 1938), p. 11. The committee reported that most of Alaska's resources were owned by the federal government. Their development was controlled and regulated under a policy of conservation. Coal lands were withdrawn from entry in 1906 under an executive order on November 12 of that year. A leasing law for coal lands was passed in 1913. Oil lands were withdrawn in 1910 and leasing regulations issued in 1920. An executive proclamation of February 16, 1909, created the Tongass National Forest, and the Chugach National Forest was created by a similar order on February 22, 1909. Ibid.

8   James Wickersham, quoted in Nichols, *Alaska*, p. 33.

9   Hellenthal, *Alaskan Melodrama*, pp. vii, 283.

10 "Red Tape Riddance for Alaska," *The Literary Digest*, June 27, 1914, p. 1530; Franklin K. Lane, "Red Tape in Alaska," Outlook, January 20, 1915, pp. 135-40; typewritten manuscript by Herman B. Walker, special inspector in the Office of the Secretary of the Interior, "Red Tape in the Government of Alaska: The Need for Centralized Responsibility and Accountability" (1914), pp. 1-67, in file 9-1-60, part 1, Central Classified files, 1907-1951, Office of Territories, Record Group 126, National Archives. Hereafter cited as RG, NA.

11 *Cong. Record*, 63 Cong., 2 Sess., p. 2722 (February 2, 1914)

12 *The New York Times*, July 17, 1921, Sec VII, p. 2.

13 Hubert Work, "What Future Has Alaska," *National Spectator in Cong. Record*, 69 Cong., 1 Sess., p. 5126 (March 5, 1926).

14 In the 1930s, nine federal departments were involved in Alaskan affairs. These were Interior, State, Justice, Commerce, Agriculture, War, Treasury, Post Office, and Labor. For the various bureaus operating under the departments, see *Annual Report of the Governor of Alaska* (1931), pp. 120-131; National Resources Committee, *Alaska: Its Resources an Development* (1938); Sherman Rogers, "The Problem of Alaska's Government," Outlook, January 23, 1923, pp. 173-74. Assistant Secretary of Commerce C.H. Huston and Alaska Governor Scott C. Bone also endorsed the proposal. See Ibid., p. 174. Governor Bone, in an article entitled "The Land That Uncle Sam Bought and Then Forgot," *Review of Reviews*, April 1922, pp. 402-10, summarized the contributions Presidents and their administrations had made to Alaskan development, starting with President Benjamin Harrison. He also severely indicted federal red tape in the territory. He concluded that Alaska had been ignored at first, then had been granted a limited form of government, and subsequently had become a problem of conservation politics, only to be dealt with academically.

15 Scott C. Bone, "Alaska from the Inside," *Saturday Evening Post*, August 8, 1926, p. 130.

16 Alaska Law Compilation Commission, *Compiled Laws of Alaska, 1949, Containing the General Laws of the Territory of Alaska, Annotated with Decisions of the District Courts of Alaska, the Circuit Court of Appeals, and the Supreme Court of the United States* (San Francisco; Bancroft-Whitney Co., 1948), title 10, chapter 4, sect. 1,5. Ray Lyman Wilbur, "A New Alaska in the Making," *Current History*, XXXV (October 1931)), 84.

17 *Annual Report of the Governor of Alaska* (1930), p. 1; (1931), p.1; (1932), p. 1; (1933), p.2.

18 George W. Rogers and Richard A. Cooley, *Alaska's Population and Economy: Regional Growth, Development and Future Outlook*, vol. I, Analysis (College, Alaska: Institute of Social, Economic and Government Research, 1963), p.16.

19 National Resources Committee, *New York Times*, April 27, 1932, p. 2, April 28, p. 3, and October 16, Sec. II, p.6.

20 *Biographical Directory of the American Congress*, 1774-1961, p. 813.

21 *New York Time*, October 16, 1932, Sec. II, p. 6; Ibid., November 11, 1932, p.8.

22 Mary Lee Council, "Alaska Statehood" (unpublished manuscript, n.d.) in author's files; Richard L. Neuberger, "Anthony J. Dimond of Alaska," *Alaska Life*, September 1943, in *Cong. Record* Appendix, 78 Cong., 1 Sess., pp. 4282-90 (October 14, 1943). *Cong. Record*, Index, 73 Cong., 1 Sess., H.R. 5205, H.R. 5209, p. 401; Ibid., 74 Cong., 1 Sess, H.R. 163m p. 712; Ibid., 75 Cong., 1 Sess. H.R. 1562, H.R. 1563, p.720; Ibid, 76 Cong., 1 Sess., H.R. 2411, p. 283; Ibid., 77 Cong., 1 Sess., H.R. 79, p.772. H.R. 7844, Which became Public Law 728, 75 Cong., 3 Sess., made some ten changes in Alaska's game laws which embraced many of the recommendations Dimond had made. For details see Public Law 728, *Cong. Record*, Appendix, 75 Cong., 3 Sess., p. 3177 (June 16, 1938.)

23 Ibid., 73 Cong., 2 Sess., H.R. 6378, p. 540; H.R. 6617, p. 545; Ibid., 78 Cong,, 1 Sess., S. 1436, p. 670, provided for the election of a governor and was introduced by Senator William L. Langer at Dimond's request; Ibid., H. R. 2462, p. 742; Ibid., 78 Cong., 1 Sess., H.R. 2977, p. 757.

24 Ibid., 73 Cong., 2 Sess., H.R. 6378, p.540; H.R. 6617, p. 545; Ibid., 73 Cong., 2 Sess., H.R. 8679, p. 589; Ibid., 74 Cong., 1 Sess. H.R. 6861, p. 840; Ibid., 75 Cong., 1 Sess., H.R., 1554, p. 719; Ibid., 76 Cong., 1 Sess., H.R. 1955, p. 155.

25 *Annual Report of the Governor of Alaska* (1933), p. 2, (1935), p. 1; Gruening, *The State of Alaska*, p. 300; *Cong. Record*, 74 Cong., 2 Sess., p. 10876 (June 20, 1936).

26 Gruening, *The State of Alaska*, p. 299; *Annual Report of the Governor of Alaska (1935)*, p. 36. For an excellent account and evaluation of this experiment in subsistence farming, see Orlando Wesley Miller, "The Frontier in Alaska and the Matanuska Valley colony" (Unpublished PH.D dissertation, Columbia University, 1965).

27 Dr. Joe Thomas, The Alaskan Colonization Branch of the United Congo Improvement Association, to C. E. Pynchon, General Manager, Federal Subsistence Homesteads Corporation, Departmetn of the Interior, March 20, 1936, file

9-1-60, Alaska, Development of Resources, Office of Territoreis, RG 126, NA; Dr. Joe Thomas to President Franklin D. Roosevelt, February 18, 1935, file 9-1-60, part 1, Alaska, Development of Resources, Office of Territories, RG 126, NA. For an account of this project see Claus-M. Naske, "A Study in Frustration; Blacks Blocked by Bureaucracy," *The Alaska Journal*, Autumn, 1971, pp. 8-10.

28   National Resources Committee, *Alaska—Its Resources and Development* (1938), pp. 11-14.

29   *Cong. Record*, 73 cong., 2 Sess., p. 8257 (May 7, 1934). See also Arthur R. Robinson, "Will Japan Seize Alaska?" *Liberty Magazine*, March 24, 1934, in Cong. Record, 73 Cong., 2 Sess., pp. 8257-59 (May 7, 1934).

30   *Cong. Record*, 74 Cong., 1 Sess., p. 2343 (February 20, 1935); Richard L. Neuberger, "Anthony J. Dimond of Alaska," Alaska Life, September 1943, in *Cong. Record* Appendix, 78 Cong., 1 Sess., pp. 4288-90 (October 14, 2943); *Cong Record*, 75 Cong., 1 Sess., pp. 4014-15, 4056 (April 29, 30, 1937).

31   Ibid., 76 Cong., 3 Sess., p. 4599 (July 25,1940). The appropriations covered the two fiscal years beginning on July 1, 1939, and ending on July 1, 1941. Richard L. Neuberger, "Anthony J. Dimond of Alaska," *Alaska Life*, September, 1943, in *Cong. Record*, Appendix, 78 Cong., 1 Sess., p. 4289 (October 14, 1943).

32   Richard L. Neuberger, "Alaska—Northern Front," *Survey Graphic*, February 1942, pp. 57-62. "U.S. Strengthens Defenses in Alaska and Bering Straits to Meet Twin Threat of Russian and Japanese Action," *The China Weekly Review*, January 11, 1941, pp. 186-87; "Alaska to be Fortified Against Japanese Invasion: New Northern Airplane route Envisaged," Ibid., May 10, 1941, pp. 318-319; Vilhalmur Stefansson, "Alaska American Outpost No. 4," *Harper's*, June 1941, pp. 83-92; "Alaska's Future is the Responsibility of the U.S.," Fortune, March 1942, p. 114; Bella Doherty and Arthur Hepner, "Alaska: Last American Frontier," *Foreign Policy Reports*, December 1, 1942, pp. 328-47. Ernest K. Lindley, "Alaska: Strategic Stepchild of the Continent," *Newsweek*, March 16, 1942, p. 28.

33   Harold L. Ickes, "Bastion and Last Frontier," *New York Time*, July 26, 1942, Sec IV, p. 7. Ibid., April 9, 1938, p. 10.

34   United States Army, Alaska, *The Army's Role in the Building of Alaska*, pp. 81-85. See also Joseph Driscoll, *War Discovers Alaska* (Philadelphia: J.B. Lippincott Company, 1943); Jean Potter, Alaska Under Arms (New York: The Macmillan Company, 1943).

35   United States Army, Alaska, *The Army's Role in the Building of Alaska*, pp. 88-95.

36   Ibid., p. 96. Rogers, *The Future of Alaska*, p. 95.

37   Rogers and Cooley, *Alaska's Population and Economy*, vol. II, *Statistical Handbook*, pp. 120-23.

38   *Cong. Record*, Index, 78 Cong., 1 Sess., H.R. 344, p. 692; Ibid., H.R. 2462, p. 742. For a companion bill in the Senate introduced by William L. Langer, see S. 1436, Ibid., p. 670; Ibid., 78 Cong., 2 Sess., H.R. 4648, p. 524. Ibid., Appendix, 77 Cong., 2 Sess., p. 4445 (December 16, 1942); Gruening, *The State of Alaska*, pp. 461-63.

39 *New York Times*, March 17, 1939, p. 9. "The Statehood Referendum," *Alaska Frontier*, May-June, 1941, p. 3. William R. Carter, "The Sixteenth Alaska Legislature—A Report to the People," in *Cong. Record*, 78 Cong., 1 Sess. P. 8228 (October 12, 1943). Ibid., 78 Cong., 1 Sess., S. 951, p. 2835 (April 2, 1943).

40 "Notes on a Radio Broadcast, Richard Eaton and Anthony J. Dimond," Personal Correspondence, Statehood Committee—X, Y, Z,— General-Folder Statehood for Alaska, speeches and statements, Box 39, Anthony J. Dimond Papers, University of Alaska Archives, College, Alaska.

41 Interview with Robert B. Atwood, August 26, 1969, Anchorage, Alaska. *Cong. Record*, 78 Cong., 1 Sess., p. 8223 (October 12, 1943); Walter B. King, Ketchikan, to Senator Millard Tydings, June 14, 1943, S. 78A-E1, papers accompanying S. B. 951, April 2, 1943, Senate Committee on Interior and Insular Affairs, RG 46, NA; mimeographed manuscript, Ralph E. Robertson, "Statehood for Alaska: Don't measure Political Rights by Money Cost," Juneau, September 10, 1943, pp. 1-10, Folder Statehood for Alaska, speeches and statements, Box 39, Anthony J. Dimond Papers, University of Alaska Archives, College, Alaska.

42 Secretary Harold L. Ickes to Senator Millard Tydings, September 2, 1943, S. 78A-E1, papers accompanying S.B. 951, Senate Committee on Interior and Insular Affairs, RG 46, NA.

43 *Cong. Record*. 78 Cong., 1 Sess., H.R. 3768, p. 10261 (December 2, 1943). For Dimond's explanation on the principal differences between H.R. 3768 and S. 951, see "Statement by Anthony J. Dimond," December 6, 1943, file 9-1-44, part 2, Alaska-Legal-Statehood, Records of the Office of Territories, RG 126, NA. Anthony J. Dimond, "Statehood for Alaska," December 1, 1943, file 9-1-44, part 2, Alaska-Legal Statehood, Records of the Office of Territories, RG 126, NA.

CHAPTER SEVEN

1 The account of Gruening's early life is based on Ernest Gruening, *Many Battles: The Autobiography of Ernest Gruening* (New York: Liveright, 1973), and Sherwood Ross, *Gruening of Alaska: The Dynamic Career of a Remarkable U.S. Senator* (New York: Best Books, Inc., 1968).

2 Interview with Dr. George W. Rogers, January 19, 1970, College, Alaska. Dr. Rogers was a research economist on the staff of Governor Gruening in the late 1940's. Subsequently he became the the chairman of the Federal Field Committee in Alaska, and later was employed by Resources for the Future, Inc., and the Arctic Institute of North America. He now is research professor of economics, emeritus, at the University of Alaska's Institute for Social and Economic Research.

3 *Biographical Directory of the American Congress*, pp. 522-23.

4 *Annual Report of the Governor of Alaska* (1943), pp. 1-5; William R. Carter, "The Sixteenth Alaska Legislature: A Report to the People," in *Cong. Record*, 78 Cong., 1 Sess., pp. 8226-27 (October 12, 1943).

5 Gruening, *The State of Alaska*, pp. 409, 382-85.

6   Interview with Mary Lee Council, July 20, 1969, Washington D.C. She stated that even "Ernest Gruening was bitterly opposed [and] did everything he could to get Bob not to mention statehood." Gruening told Bartlett that the people of Alaska were not ready for statehood, Miss Council recalled. Election returns were found in "Alaska General Election, September 12, 1944," in the Office of the Secretary of State, Juneau, Alaska.

7   Dimond, Hon. Anthony J., Exercises in Honor of, Original Proceedings on, November 30, 1944, rough draft, House Committee on the Territories, H.R. 78AF36. 1, RG 233, NA; Cong. Record, Index, 79 Cong., 1 Sess., p. 889, H.R. 3323 (election of governor) and H.R 3324 (resident for governor); Iid., 80 Cong., 1 Sess., p. 721, H.R 181 (election of governor) and H.R. 179 (resident of governor); Ibid., 80 Cong., 2 Sess., p. 630, H.R. 6851 (election of governor) and a companion bill in the Senate, S. 2839, introduced by Senator Malone, in Ibid., 80 Cong., 2 Sess., p.548; Ibid., 81 Cong., 1 Sess., p.792, H.R. 218 (Resident for governor) and in the Senate, S. 727 (election of governor in Alaska and Hawaii, introduced by Senator Hugh Butler), in Ibid., 81 Cong., 1 Sess., p. 725; Ibid., 83 Cong., 1 Sess., p.781, H.R. 1916 (election of governor and lieutenant governor) and a companion bill in the Senate, S. 224, introduced by Senator Hugh But-ler, in Ibid., 84 Cong., 1 Sess., p. 672; Senate Bill 41, introduced by William L. Langer, January 11, 1945, 79 Cong., 1 Sess., RG 46, NA; H.R. 1807, introduced by Sam Ervin, January 29, 1945, 79 Cong., 1 Sess., RG 233, NA; H.R. 3898 introduced by E.L. Bartlett, July 21, 1945, 79 Cong., 1 Sess., RG 233, NA.

8   See Richard L. Neuberger, "Alaska—Our Spearhead in the Pacific, "New York Times Magazine, April 12, 1942, in Cong. Record, Appendix, 77 Cong., 2 Sess., pp. 1736-37 (May 7, 1942); Richard L. Neuberger, "Gruening of Alaska," Common Sense, May 1942, in Cong. Record, Appendix, 77 Cong., 1 Sess., pp. 1682-84 (May 11, 1942); Richard L. Neuberger, "Yukon Country Described as Beckoning Mecca for Warriors Imbued with Spirit of the Pioneers who Settled the West." Sunday Oregonian, October 15, 1944, in Cong. Record, Appendix, 78 Cong., 2 Sess., pp. 4432-33 (November 14, 1944); Richard L. Neuberger, "Go North, Young Man!" Collier's, December 23, 1944, in Cong. Record, Appendix, 78 Cong., 2 Sess., pp. 4776-79 (December 15, 1944); New York Times, January 27, 1945, p. 12; Cong. Record, 79 Cong., 1 Sess., p. 2519 (March 21, 1945); Governor Ernest Gruening to Edwin G. Arnold, Director, Division of Territories and Island Possessions, September 5, 1945 and September 26, 1945, file 9-1-44, part 2, Alaska-Legal-Statehood, Records of the Office of Territories, RG 126, NA.

9   Robert B. Atwood, "Alaska's Struggle for Statehood," State Government, Autumn, 1958, p. 205; "Invitation to Join the Alaska Statehood Association," in Personal Correspondence, Statehood Committee—X, Y, Z – General, folder Statehood Committee, Box 39, Anthony J. Dimond papers, University of Alaska Archives, Fairbanks, Alaska.

10   George Sundborg to author, September 25, 1981. In author's files.

11   Jessen's Weekly, (Fairbanks), March 22, 1946; Senate, Journal, 1946, pp. 102, 133, 166.

12   Jack B. Fahy, Acting Director, Division of Territories and Island Possessions, to Secretary of the Interior Harold L. Ickes, July 26, 1945, file 9-1-13, part 3, Records of the Secretary of the Interior, RG 48, NA; News Release, Department of the Interior, August 11, 1945, file 9-1-44, Alaska, Self-Government, General, Classified Files, 1907-51, Records of the Department of the Interior, Box 327, RG 48, NA.

13   U.S., Congress, House Subcommittee of the Committee on Appropriations, *Official Trip of Examinations of Federal Activities in Alaska and the Pacific Coast State*, 79 Cong., 1 Sess. (Washington: Government Printing Office, 1945), p. 11. *Washington Post*, August 14, 1945, clipping in file 9-1-13, part 3, Records of the Office of the Secretary of the Interior, RG 48, NA. U.S., Congress, House, Committee on the Territories, *Official trip to Conduct a Study and Investigation of the Various Questions and Problems Relating to the Territory of Alaska*, H. Rept. 1583 pursuant to H. Res. 236, 79 Cong., 2 Sess. 9Washington: Government Printing Office, 1946), pp. 28-30. For a full account of this plan, as well as an enumeration of the restrictions of the Organic Act of 1912, see Ralph J. Rivers, "Alaska—the 49th State?" *Alaska Life*, December 1945, pp.8-11.

14   Excerpt from the message of the President on the States of the Union and Transmitting the Budget, January 21, 1946, file 9-1-44, part 2, Alaska-Legal-Statehood, Records of the Office of Territories, RG 126, NA; *Anchorage Daily Times*. February 13, 1946; *Daily Alaska Empire*, February 26, 1946.

15   Ibid., August 22, 20, 1946; *Ketchikan Alaska Chronicle*, August 21, 1946; memorandum on Secretary Krug's visit to Alaska, August 21, 1946; memorandum on Secretary Krug's visit to Alaska, August 11-22, 1946, file 9-1-34, part 3, Records of the Office of Territories, R.G. 126, NA; "Alaska: Our Next State; Bolstering Arctic Frontier," *U.S. News and World Report*, September 13, 1946, pp. 19-20; U.S., Congress, House, *Statehood for Alaska*, Hearings before the Subcommittee on Territories and Insular Possessions of the Committee on Public Lands, Committee Hearing No. 9, 80 Cong., 1 Sess. (Washington: Government Printing Office, 1947), pp. 349-50. Hereafter cited as *Statehood for Alaska.*

16   Gruening to Sundborg, July 3, 1946, E.L. Bartlett Papers, Statehood File, box 6, folder Correspondence, General, 1946; Sundborg to Dimond, July 16, 1946, Anthony J. Dimond Papers, Personal File, 1904-53, box 39, folder Statehood for Alaska, Correspondence with G. Sunborg, University of Alaska, Fairbanks, Archives; *Ketchikan Alaska Chronicle*, September 14, 3, 1946; *Anchorage Daily Times*, August 3, September 7, 1946; *Jessen's Weekly*, August 9, 1946.

17   George Sundborg, *Statehood for Alaska: The Issues Involved and the Facts About the Issues* (Anchorage, Alaska: Alaska Statehood Association, August 1946). Sundborg worked closely with Governor Gruening, Mrs. Evangeline Atwood, territoreial Attorney General Ralph J. Rivers and Dimond, then a federal district judge in Anchorage, in the preparation of the pamphlet. Judge Dimond received one of the unfinished copies and commented on it in detail, drawing on his long experience as a lawyer and as Alaska's delegate to Congress. See Anthony J. Dimond to George Sundborg, July 4, 1946, folder of correspondence with

George Sundborg, box 39, Anthony J. Dimond Papers, University of Alaska, Fairbanks, Archives.

18   U.S., Congress, Senate, Committee on Interior and Insular Affairs, *Alaska Statehood: Hearings on S. 50*, 83 Cong., 2 Sess. (Washington: Government Printing Office, 1954), p. 251.

19   *Seattle Daily Times*, May 12, 1948.

20   *Alaska v. Troy*, 258 U.S. 101 (February 27, 1922).

21   *Ketchikan Alaska Chronicle*, October 2, 194.

22   "What Alaskans Say About Statehood," *Alaska Life*, September 1946, p. 9; clipping from *Ketchikan Alaska Chronicle*, September 14, 1946, asking Alaskans to buy one dollar statehood buttons. This money was to be used to pay the costs of printing the Sundborg report as a newspaper supplement and in permanent pamphlet form. Any money left over, the advertisement stated, would be used to persuade Congressmen to enact statehood for Alaska. The Office of Territories attached the following comment to the clipping: "??How much is the price for Congressmen??" File 9-1-44, part 2, Alaska-Legal-Statehood, Records of the Office of Territories, RG 126, NA. See also John L. Manders, "Statehood for Alaska," *Alaska Life*, September 1946, pp. 8-9. The election returns are found in "Official Returns—Territorial Canvassing Board, General Election, October 8, 1946," Office of the Secretary of State, Juneau, Alaska.

23   *Statehood for Alaska* (1947), p. 425; Mary Lee Council, "Alaska Statehood" (unpublished manuscript, n.d.), p. 4, copy in author's files; George W. Rogers, *Alaska in Transition: The Southeastern Region*, A Study Sponsored by the Arctic Institute of North America and Resources for the Future, Inc. (Baltimore: The Johns Hopkins Press, 1960), pp. 3-17; Gruening, *The State of Alaska*, pp. 382-407.

24   *Statehood for Alaska* (1947), p. 425. Rogers and Cooley, *Alaska's Population and Economy*, vol. 1, *Analysis*, p. 46. *Statehood for Alaska* (1947), p. 425; Mary Lee Council, "Alaska Statehood" (unpublished manuscript, n.d.), p. 4, copy in author's files. Interview with Victor Fischer, March 22, 1970, College, Alaska.

25   *Statehood for Alaska* (1947), p. 425. Ibid., p. 275.

26   Ibid., p. 273.

27   Secretary of the Interior Julius A. Krug to Wayne Henrickson, February 7, 1947, file 9-1-34, part 3, Alaska, Secretary's trip to Alaska, Records of the Office of Territories, RG 126, NA; President Harry S. Truman to Secretary Krug, February 8, 1947, file 0-1-13, part 4, Alaska, Administrative, General Records of the Office of the Secretary of the Interior, RG 48, NA. Ketchikan Alaska Chronicle *(Alaska Statehood and International Development Edition)*, March 29,1947.

28   Bob Sikes, "A Congressman's View of Alaska," *Alaska Life*, May 1947, p. 5. See Melvin Price, "Statehood for Alaska, Hawaii, and Puerto Rico," *Cong. Record*, Appendix, 80 Cong., 1 Sess., pp. 1654-58 (April 4, 1947); Wilbur Forrest, "Alaska –a Bastion Unfortified, and an Easy Pearl Harbor No. 2…," *New York Herald Tribune*, December 1, 1947, in *Cong. Record*, Appendix, 80, Cong., 1 Sess., p. 4458, (December 2, 1947); Richard L. Neuberger, "Alaska Now Last

Frontier—Call to New Pioneers—Thousands of Soldiers are Looking North-
ward to Land that Offers Great Opportunities Along with its Hardships," *St.
Louis Post-Dispatch*, February 18, 1945, in *Cong. Record,* Appendix, 79 Cong., 1
Sess., pp. 927-29 (March 1, 1945).

29 H.R. 206, introduced by Bartlett, January 3, 1947, RG 233, NA; S. 56 introduced
by Senator William L. Langer, January 6, 1947, RG 46, NA; and H.R. 1808, submitted by Representative Homer Angell, February 10, 1947, RG 233, NA.

30 *Statehood for Alaska* (1947), pp. 5-21.

31 Ibid., p. 428.

32 Ibid., pp. 73-78, 121-74; interview with Herbert L. Faulkner, August 11, 1969,
Juneau, Alaska. Faulkner stated that his attitude toward statehood had in no
way been influenced by his clients. He simply felt that Alaska could not afford it
financially. Salmon fishing was in decline, he recalled, mining had been going
downhill for a number of years, and there were no prospects of any new industries which could take the place of these two. He told the author that he talked
to Senator Ernest Gruening at the Seattle-Tacoma airport in 1968, and Gruening told him that if oil had not been discovered, the state would have gone
bankrupt. Faulkner felt vindicated in his stand, particularly since nobody could
foresee the impact oil would have on Alaska.

33 *Statehood for Alaska* (1947), pp. 70, 66, 95, 62,71,281, 340; *Ketchikan Alaska
Chronicle*, April 5, 1954.

34 *Statehood for Alaska* (1947), p.424. Bartlett to Gruening, February 15, 1947,
Gruening to Bartlett, March 5, 1947, Bartlett to Gruening, March 8, 1947, E. L.
Bartlett Papers, Statehood File, box 7, folder Correspondence, General, 1947,
University of Alaska, Fairbanks Archives.

35 *Daily Alaska Empire*, April 21, May 2, 1947; *Jessen's Weekly*, May 9, 1947.

36 *Cong. Record*, 80 Cong., 1 Sess., p. 7941.

37 *Daily Alaska Empire*, May 5, 1947; *Alaska Weekly*, July 11, 1947; U.S., Congress,
House, Subcommittee on Territories and Insular Possessions of the Committee
on Public Land pursuant to H. Res. 93, Committee Hearing No. 31, 80 Cong.,
1 Sess. (Washington: Government Printing Office, 1948); pp.120, 132, 374-375,
115. Hereafter cited as *Alaska* (1948); Herbert Hidscher, *Alaska Now* (rev. ed.,
Boston: Little, Brown and Company, 1950), pp. 277, 274.

38 *Anchorage Daily Times*, August 30, September 13, 1947; *Ketchikan Alaska
Chronicle*, September 13, 1947.

39 *Anchorage Daily Times, Ketchikan Alaska Chronicle*, September 13, 1947; *Daily
Alaska Empire,* September 15, 1947.

40 *Alaska* (1948), p. 120.

41 Ibid., pp. 156, 162-63. However, before a subcommittee of the Senate Public
Lands Committee in Anchorage in August 1947, Arnold stated: "The Alaska
Salmon Industry is opposed to statehood. We're paying most of the cost of running the Territory now. We don't propose to pick up the check for the additional
cost of statehood." Ernest Gruening, *The Battle for Alaska Statehood* (College,

Alaska: University of Alaska Press in cooperation with the Alaska Purchase
Centennial Commission, 1967), p. 21.

42   *Alaska* (1948), pp. 213-214, 230-238, 29-33.

43   Ibid., pp. 374-377.

44   Ibid., pp. 377-390; *Ketchikan Alaska Chronicle*, September 15, 1949.

45   Ibid., August 1, 1947; *Daily Alaska Empire*, December 10, 1946; *Anchorage Daily Times*, July 1, 1947.

46   *Ketchikan Alaska Chronicle*, August 1, September 3, 1947; *Alaska* (1948), p. 374; *Anchorage Daily Times*, September 5, 1947; *Jessen's Weekly*, September 12, 1947; *Daily Alaska Empire*, September 12, 1947; *Anchorage Daily Times*, September 5, 1947; *Ketchikan Alaska Chronicle*, September 15,1947.

47   Interview with Dr. George W. Rogers, January 19, 1970, College, Alaska.

48   Memorandum on the chronology of the Alaska statehood legislation with reference to public lands, April 28, 1950, file Persons Leaving Alaska, box 795, Records of the Office of the Governor of Alaska, 1884-1958, Federal Records Center, Seattle, Washington; U.S., Congress, House, *Providing for the Admission of Alaska into the Union*, H. Rept. 1731 to accompany H.R. 5666, 80 Cong., 2 Sess. (Washington: Government Printing Office, 1948), pp. 3-6.

49   *Congressional Quarterly Almanac*, 80 Cong., 2 Sess. (Washington: Washington Congressional Quarterly News Features, 1948), p. 290. *Message from the President of the United States to the Congress of the United states Relative to Enactment of Necessary Legislation to Admit Alaska to Statehood at the Earliest Possible Date*, 80 Cong., 2 Sess. (Washington: Government Printing Office, 1948). *Cong. Record*, 80 Cong., 2 Sess. P. 6123 (May 20, 1948). S. 232, the motion to discharge the bill from the Senate Interior and Insular Affairs Committee, mustered only twenty votes.

CHAPTER EIGHT

1   Hilscher, *Alaska Now*, pp. 275-77.

2   Ibid.

3   Ibid., p. 278; Interview with Ernest Gruening, July 16, 1969, Washington, D.C.; *Statehood for Alaska*, (1947), p. 140.

4   Richard L. Neuberger, "Gruening of Alaska," *Survey Graphic*, October 1947, p. 513; Richard L. Neuberger, "The State of Alaska," *Survey Graphic*, October 1947, p. 513.

5   Frank L. Kluckhohn, "Alaska Fights for Statehood," *American Mercury*, May 1949, pp. 55-62. For a brief biography of Austin E. Lathrop, see Driscoll, *War Discovers Alaska*, pp. 214-28.

6   George W. Rogers, *Alaska in Transition: The Southeast Region*, A Study sponsored by the Arctic Institute of North America and Resources for the Future, Inc. (Baltimore: The Johns Hopkins Press, 1960), p. 164.

7   "A Record of Achievement," Address by Governor Ernest Gruening, Jeffer-
son-Jackson Day Dinner, Fairbanks, Alaska, March 4, 1950, file 37-9, No. 3,
Box 442, Records of the Office of the Governor of Alaska, 1884-1958, Federal
Records Center, Seattle, Washington; Neuberger, "Gruening of Alaska," p. 513.

8   "A Record of Achievement," Address by Governor Ernest Gruening, March
4, 1950.

9   "Official Returns, Territorial Canvassing Board, General Election, October 12,
1948," in Office of the Secretary of State, Juneau, Alaska. For a full discussion of
the trap issue, see Rogers, *Alaska in Transition*, pp. 3-15.

10   Alaska Statehood Committee, *Alaska Statehood: Analysis and Refutation of
Minority Views on S. 50* (Juneau, Alaska, January, 1952), pp. 47-55; Gruen-
ing, The State of Alaska, pp., 317-18. This pamphlet was actually written by Dr.
George W. Rogers.

11   Alaska, *Session Laws*, 1949, pp. 270-71.

12   Ibid.

13   Gruening, *The Battle for Alaska Statehood*, p. 11.

14   Ernest Gruening to Victor C. Rivers, July 25, 1949, file 35-45, Box 436, Records
of the Office of Governor of Alaska, 1884-1958, Federal Records Center, Seattle,
Washington; Minutes of Organizational Meeting of Alaska Statehood Commit-
tee, Juneau, Alaska, August 29-31, 1949, file 68, folder Statehood Committee,
Personal Correspondence, Statehood Committee—X, Y, Z—General, Box 39,
Anthony J. Dimond Papers, University of Alaska Archives, Fairbanks, Alaska.
A brief history of the Alaska Statehood Committee is found in Alaska State-
hood Committee, *Statehood for Alaska: A Report on Four Years of Achievement*
(Juneau, Alaska: Alaska Statehood Committee, 1953)

15   Position Paper by William L. Baker, July 20, 1949, folder Statehood for Alaska,
Personal Correspondence, Statehood Committee—X, Y, Z—General, Corre-
spondence with Gruening, Box 39, Anthony J. Dimond papers, University of
Alaska Archives, Fairbanks, Alaska; Telegram, Lee C. Bettinger to Governor
Gruening, August 28, 1949, file 35-45, Box 436, Records of the Office of The
Governor of Alaska, 1884-1958, Federal Records Center, Seattle, Washington.

16   Minutes of Organizational Meeting of Alaska Statehood Committee, Juneau,
Alaska, August 29-31, 1949, file 68, folder Statehood Committee, Personal
Correspondence, Statehood Committee—X,Y, Z—General, Box 39, Anthony J.
Dimond Papers, University of Alaska Archives, Fairbanks, Alaska.

17   Mildred R. Hermann to all members of the Alaska Statehood Committee,
October 26, 1949, Personal Correspondence, Statehood Committee—X, Y, Z
– General, Box 29, Anthony J. Dimond Papers University of Alaska Archives,
Fairbanks, Alaska; See U.S., Congress, Senate, *Alaska Statehood*, Hearings
before the Committee on Interior and Insular Affairs on H.R. 331 and S. 2036,
81 Cong., 2 Sess. (Washington: Government Printing Office, 1950); Alaska
Statehood Committee, letterhead, in the file of the author. The national committee was completed by February 1950, and the names of its members were
announced by Robert B. Atwood in a formal news release which was sent to

various news services around the country. A direct mailing was made from
Juneau to 718 papers. A copy was addressed to all the newspapers in the hometown of every member of Congress. Along with the release went a separate
brief story for each state, pointing out the people who were on the committee
from that area. Biographies of the ninety-six members were prepared, printed
by the *Ketchikan Alaska Chronicle*, and mailed to every member of the House
of Representatives. George Sundborg designed the letterhead which included
the names of the "committee of one-hundred" for the official use of the Alaska
Statehood Committee. See George Sundborg to Mildred R. Hermann, February
4, 1950, Personal Correspondence, Statehood Committee—X, y, Z—General,
folder Statehood Committee, Box 39, Anthony J. Dimond Papers, University of
Alaska Archives, Fairbanks, Alaska.

CHAPTER NINE

1   *Cong. Record*, Index, 81 Cong., 1 Sess., pp. 787, 844, 759 (H.R. 331, introduced
by Delegate Bartlett; H.R. 25, submitted by Representative Homer Angell; H.R.
2300, introduced by Representative Mike Mansfield; and S. 2036, submitted by
Senator Estes Kefauver); U.S., congress, House, *Statehood for Alaska*, Hearings
before the Subcommittee on Territories and Insular Possessions of the Committee on Public Lands on H.R. 331 and related bills, committee Hearing Serial
No. 3, 81 Cong., 1 Sess. (Washington: Government Printing Office, 1949), pp.
2-3, 14-25, 7-8.

2   U.S. Congress, House, *Providing for the Admission of Alaska Into the Union*, H.
Rept. 255 to accompany H.R. 331, 81 Cong., 1 Sess. (Washington: Government
Printing Office, 1949), pp. 36-52; "Report by Delegate E.L. Bartlett...", July 22,
1949, Records of the Office of the Governor of Alaska, 1884-1958, General
Correspondence, 1934-1953, box 520, folder 58-11-Statehood, Alaska, Federal
Records Center, Seattle, Washington; George B. Galloway, *The Legislative Pro-
cess in Congress* (New York: Thomas Y. Crowell Company, 1955), pp. 343-345.

3   *Anchorage Daily Times*, May 17, 1949; *Ketchikan Alaska Chronicle*, May 18, 17,
June 29, 1949; *Daily Alaska Empire*, May 27, June 29, 1949; Bartlett to Dimond,
July 20, 1949, E.L. Bartlett Papers, Statehood File, box 7, folder Correspon-
dence, General, 1949, University of Alaska Archives, Fairbanks, Alaska; *Ketchi-
kan Alaska Chronicle*, July 22, 23, 1949, Anthony J. Dimond Papers, Personal
File, 1904-53, box 34, folder Bartlett-Statehood Correspondence, University of
Alaska Archives, Fairbanks, Alaska.

4   *Cong. Record*, 81 Cong., 1 Sess., pp. A5107-A5108; *Cong. Record*, 81 Cong., 2
Sess., p. 773; *Ketchikan Alaska Chronicle*, August 9, 1949.

5   Cong, Record, 81 Cong., Sess., pp. 2780-2781 (March 3, 1950). In this instance,
125 Democrats and 61 Republicans against passage of the Alaska statehood bill.
The Rules Committee bypass reform was repealed in 1951.

6   "The Question of Granting Statehood to Hawaii: Pro & Con," *Congressional Digest*, January 1959, p. 9; Gruening, *The State of Alaska*, p. 471.

7   Gruening to Governor Vail Pittman, April 4, 1950, and Pittman to Senator George W. Malone, April 14, 1950, file Persons Leaving Alaska, Box 795, Records of the Office of the Governor of Alaska, 1884-1958, Federal Records Center, Seattle, Washington.

8   Editorial, *New York Journal-American*, March 1950, in *Cong. Record*, Appendix, 81 Cong., 2 Sess., p. 1840 (March 13, 1950). For a sampling of some 300 editorials in favor of Alaska statehood, see Ibid., pp. 2506-2507 (March 29, 1950).

9   Bartlett to Secretary of the Interior Oscar L. Chapman, April 14, 1950, file Alaska Statehood, Records of the Office of the Secretary of the Interior, Office Files of the Secretary of the Interior, Oscar Chapman, Box 33, RG 48, NA.

10 *Ketchikan Alaska Chronicle*

11 U.S., Congress, Senate, *Alaska Statehood*, Hearings before the Committee on Interior and Insular Affairs on H.R. 331 and S. 2036, 81 Cong., 2 Sess. (Washington: Government Printing Office, 1950), pp. 30,, 1-108.

12 Ibid., p. 124.

13 Ibid., pp. 204-205.

14 Ibid., pp. 79, 160-164.

15 *Ketchikan Alaska Chronicle*, April 28, 1950; *Daily Alaska Empire*, April 27, 1950.

16 *Alaska Statehood* (1950), pp. 317-318. The anti-statehood *Daily Alaska Empire* (Juneau) faithfully mirrored the Arnold testimony in its editorial pages. It also had a feature series by Robert N. DeArmond with a decidedly anti-statehood slant which ran from April 24 to May 2, 1950.

17 *Alaska Statehood* (1950), pp. 369-438.

18 Ibid., pp. 481-486, 475, 99-100, 482.

19 Ibid., pp. 481-486, 475, 99-100, 482.

20 Statement of E.L. Bartlett in support of H.R. 331, week of April 24, 1950, E.L. Bartlett Papers, Statehood File, box 164, Legislative History, January-May 1950, University of Alaska, Fairbanks, Archives.

21 *Alaska Statehood* (1950), p. 500.

22 U.S. Congress, Senate, *Providing for the Admission of Alaska Into the Union*, S. Rept. 1929 to accompany H.R. 331, 81 Cong., 2 Sess. (Washington: Government Printing Office, 1950); transcript of E.L. Bartlett radio address, recorded for KINY, Juneau, July 5, 1950, to be used territory-wide, E.L. Bartlett Papers, Statehood File, box 16, folder Legislative History, June-July 1950, University of Alaska, Fairbanks Archives; S. Rept. 1929, p. 11; Bartlett Memorandum, Public Land Provisions in Modern Alaska Statehood Legislation, June 27, 1957, E.L. Bartlett Papers, Statehood File, box 19, Folder Legislative History , June-December, 1957, University of Alaska, Fairbanks archives; U.S. Congress, House, Subcommittee on Territorial and Insular Affairs of the Committee on Interior and Insular Affairs, *Statehood for Alaska: Hearings on H.R. 50, H.R. 628, and H.R. 849, H.R. 340 and H.R. 1242, and H.R. 1243*, 85 Cong., 1 Sess. (Washington: Government Printing Office, 1957), pp. 228-229; Howard W.

Smith to colleague, May 6, 1958, E.L. Bartlett Papers, Statehood File, box 19, folder Legislative History, May 1958, University of Alaska, Fairbanks Archives; 44 Stat. 1026-1027.

23 159 F. 2d 1002, 1005.

24 U.S. Congress, Senate, *Rescinding Certain Orders of the Secretary of the Interior Establishing Indian Reservations in the Territory of Alaska: Report to Accompany S.J. Res. 162*, S. Rept. 1366, 80 cong., 2 Sess. (Washington: Government Printing Office, 1948); *Alaska Statehood* (1950), p. 346; *Daily Alaska Empire,* April 25, 27, 1950; Bartlett to Victor C. Rivers, December 6, 1950, Bartlett to Gruening, August 3, 1950, E.L. Bartlett Papers, Statehood File, box 16, folder Legislative History, August-December 1950, box 8, folder Correspondence, General, July 1950, University of Alaska, Fairbanks Archives; *Cong. Record,* 81 Cong., 2 Sess., pp. 11869-11871; "The Shape of Things to Come," *Nation,* vol. 171. 1950, p. 138.

25 Interview with Dr. George W. Rogers, January 27, 1970, College, Alaska.

26 Interview with Ralph J. Rivers, December 31, 1969, Fairbanks, Alaska.

27 Interview with Winton C. Arnold, August 25, 1969, Anchorage, Alaska.

28 Interview with Mary Lee Council, July 20, 1969, Washington, D.C.

29 President Harry S. Truman to Senator Joseph C. O'Mahoney, chairman, Committee on Interior and Insular Affairs, May 15, 1950, in U.S., Congress, Senate, *Providing for the Admission of Alaska Into the Union,* S. Rept. 1929 to accompany H.R. 331, 81 Cong., 2 Sess. (Washington: government Printing Office, 1950), p. 9; Ibid., pp. 11-12; Ibid., p. 11.

30 Ibid., pp. 31-42; *The New York Times,* July 7, 1950, p. 7; July 8, 1950, p. 4. See editorials, *The New York Times,* June 30, 1950, in *Cong. Record,* Appendix, 81 Cong., 2 Sess., pp. 4890-4891 (July 3, 1950); *St. Louis Post-Dispatch,* July 5, 1950, in Ibid., p. 4958 (July 7, 1950); *Washington Post,* July 19,1950, in Ibid., pp. 5232-5233 (July 19, 1950)

31 Editorial, *Washington Daily News,* August 10, 1950, in *Cong. Record,* Appendix, 81 Cong., 2 Sess., p. 5802 (August 11, 1950); Ibid., p. 13512 (August 24, 1950)

32 *The New York Times,* September 8, 1950, p. 21; September 13, 1950.

33 U.S. Congress, Senate, Committee on Interior and Insular Affairs, *Investigation of Charges by Senator Andrew F, Schoeppel,* 81 Cong., 2 Sess. (Washington: Government Printing Office, 1951). Hereinafter cited as *Investigation of Charges* (1950).

34 Ibid., pp. 296-297, 217-243; Evangeline Atwood and Robert D. Armond, *Who's Who in Alaskan Politics* (Portland, Oregon: Binford & Mort, 1977), for the Alaska Historical Commission), p.105.

35 "Memorandum to Members of Statehood Committee from Delegate E.L. Bartlett," February 27, 1950, Bartlett to Gruening, July 19, 1949, Anthony J. Dimond Papers, Personal File, 1904-53, box 34, folder Bartlett—Statehood Correspondence, Feltus to Gruening, July 25, 1949, E.L. Bartlett Papers, Statehood File, box 1, folder Alaska Statehood Committee File, 1949, University of Alaska, Fairbanks Archives.

36 "Memorandum to Members of Statehood Committee from Delegate E. L. Bartlett," February 27, 1950, Anthony J. Dimond papers, Personal File, 1904-53,

folder Bartlett—Statehood Correspondence, Bartlett to Atwood, February 18, 1950, Bartlett to baker, February 27, 1950, Bartlett to Atwood, February 18, 1950, Feltus to Bartlett, September 22, 1950, E.L. Bartlett Papers, Statehood File, box 1, folder Alaska Statehood Committee, January-May, 1950, folder Alaska Statehood Committee, June-December 1950, University of Alaska, Fairbanks Archives.

37 Gruening to Bartlett, May 29, 1950, Bartlett to Bruening. July 13, May 31, 1950, Gruening to Bartlett, July 10, 1950, Bartlett to Gruening, July 13, 1950, Feltus to Gruening, July 25, 1949, E.L. Bartlett Papers, Statehood File, box 8, folder Correspondence, General, July 1950, box 1, folder Alaska Statehood Committee, 1949, University of Alaska, Fairbanks Archives; *Investigation of Charges* (1950, pp. 54-81.

38 *Daily Alaska Empire*, September 8,11, 1950.

39 *Investigation of Charges* (1950), pp. 303. 4, 167-168; *Daily Alaska Empire*, September 9, 1950; *Investigation of Charges* (1950), pp. 186, 211, 294-296, 350; *Ketchikan Alaska Chronicle*, September 11, 1950.

40 Ibid., pp. 16028-16031 (December 1, 1950).

41 For the debate, see Ibid., pp. 15919-16035 (November 28 to December 1, 1950)

Chapter Ten

1 *Congressional Record*, Index, 82 Cong., 1 Sess. P. 658. Ibid., H.R. 1493, introduced b Bartlett, p. 763; H.R. 1510, submitted by Representative Sam Yorty, p. 764; and H.R. 1863, introduced by Representative Homer Angell, p. 773.

2 "Minutes of the Meeting of the Alaska Statehood Committee," January 6-7, 1951, Records of the Office of the Governor of Alaska, 1884-1958, box 668, Federal Records Center, Seattle, Washington; *Anchorage Daily Times*, January 8, 1951.

3 Alaska Statehood Committee, "Meeting of the Alaska Statehood Committee", January 28, 1953, Alaska Historical Library, Juneau, Alaska; "Meeting of the Publicity and Public Relations Committee, January 8, 1951, Records of the Governor of Alaska, 1884-1958, box 668, Federal Records Center, Seattle, Washington; Atwood to Lee Bettinger, March 9, 1951, E.L. Bartlett Papers, Statehood File, box 1, folder Alaska Statehood Committee, *Statehood for Alaska: A Report on Two Years of Achievement* (Alaska Statehood Committee, 1951); *Fairbanks a Daily News-Miner*, June 26, 1951; "Minutes of the Meeting of the Alaska Statehood Committee," January 6-7, 1951, Alaska, Division of Legislative Audit, "Audit Report: Alaska Statehood Committee, Period from April 1, 1949 to June 30, 1956, Records of the Governor of Alaska, 1884-1958, box 668, General Correspondence, 1952-1958, box 2, folder 65-Statehood Committee, Federal Records Center, Seattle, Washington; Alaska Statehood Committee, "Meeting of the Alaska Statehood Committee," January 28, 1953, Alaska Historical Library, Juneau, Alaska; *Anchorage Daily Times*, November 14, 1951; "minutes of the Meeting of the Alaska Statehood Committee," January 6-7, 1951, Records

of the Governor of Alaska, 18814-1958, box 668, Federal Records Center, Seattle, Washington; *Anchorage Daily Times*, January 8, 25, 191.

4   *Daily Alaska Empire*, January 5, 24, 29, 1951; Alaska, Legislature, House *Journal*, 1951, p. 107.

5   *Fairbanks Daily News-Miner*, February 9, 1951; *Anchorage Daily Times*, January 30, 1951.

6   House, *Journal*, 1951, p. 232-233, 294,295, 322-323, 190; *Daily Alaska Empire*, February 19, 1951; Senate, *Journal*, 1951, pp. 1022-1023

7   *The New York Times*, January 24, 1951. U.S., congress, Senate, *Providing for the Admission of Alaska Into the Union*, S. Rept. 315 to accompany S. 50, 82 Cong., 1 Sess. (Washington: Government Printing Office, 1951). In content this report was very similar to the one of 1950. See U.S., Congress, Senate, *Providing for the Admission of Alaska Into the Union*, S. Rept. 1929 (1950). The latest report had a more extensive minority view and a more complete appendix. This time Senator Butler was supported by Republicans George W. Malone of Nevada and Arthur L. Watkins of Utah, and Democrats Russell B. Long of Louisiana and George A. Smathers of Florida. The minority objected to the specific provisions in the statehood bill and criticized inadequacies, such as insufficient land, no curbs on the "whim of bureaucrats," and the "faulty methods" for selecting delegates to the constitutional convention. The Senators opposed the admission of Alaska in principle because it was noncontiguous and failed to meet the "requirements" for statehood. The minority report contained a list of what was called "instances of the extremely poor leadership in territorial affairs." These, and other criticisms made by Senator Butler and his colleagues, were answer by Dr. George W. Rogers in *Alaska Statehood Committee, Alaska Statehood: Analysis and Refutation of Minority Views on S. 50* (Juneau, Alaska, January 1952). Dr. Rogers stated that the citations of alleged "failures of the territorial administration" were based "upon smear literature produced by the malicious fringe campaigns and recognized at the outset by most Alaskans of all political affiliations as a low form of partisan slander, since amply answered and refuted." Dr. Rogers concluded that it was a deplorable practice to be an objective study," Ibid., pp. 15-16; *Cong. Record*, 82 Cong., 2 Sess., pp. 1530, 1537, 81 cong., 2 Sess., p. 16030.

8   *Cong. Record*, 82 Cong., 2 Sess., 1951, p. 13681; Bartlett Memorandum to Alaska Statehood Committee Members, February 8, 1952, Anthony J. Dimond Papers, Personal File, 1904-53,, box 34, folder Bartlett-Statehood Correspondence, University of Alaska, Fairbanks Archives; Hurja to Sherman Adams, January 24, 1953, Papers of Dwight D. Eisenhowe, Official File, box 314, folder 17-M-1, Endorsement, Hurja, Emil, Dwight D. Eisenhower Library, Abilene, Kansa; *Fairbanks Daily News-Miner*, January 21, 1952.

9   *Daily Alaska Empire*, February 1, 4, January 31, 1952; "Bartlett Statehood Memorandum," April 12, 1951, E.L. Bartlett Papers, Statehood File, box 17, folder Legislative History, 1951, University of Alaska, Fairbanks Archives.

10 Bartlett "Memorandum to all Members of the Alaska Statehood Committee," January 16, 1952, Anthony J. Dimond Papers, Personal Correspondence, Statehood Committee—X, Y, Z—General, folder Statehood Committee, box 39, University of Alaska, Fairbanks Archives.
11 Bartlett to Senator Joseph C. O'Mahoney, Chairman, Senate Interior and Insular Affairs Committee, February 4, 1952, and Delegate J.R. Farrington to O'Mahoney, February 2, 1952, in *Cong. Record*, 82 Cong., 2 Sess., p. 1066.
12 *The New York Times*, February 5, 1952. For the full debate, see *Cong. Record*, 82 Cong., 2 Sess., pp. 751-768, 869-870, 953-955, 1066-1067, 1077-1082, 1115-1128, 1131-1139, 1185-1191, 1194-1198, 1237-1239, 1241-1250, 1253-1256, 1324-1329, 1378-1396, 1409-1411, 1498-1537; Ibid., pp. 1501, 1504-1515.
13 Ibid., pp. 768, 1247-1250.
14 Cong., Record, 82 Cong., 2 Sess., pp. 1194-1197; Gruening, *The Battle for Alaska Statehood*, pp. 57-58; Alfred Steinberg, *Sam Johnson's Boy: A Close-Up of the President from Texas* (New York: The MacMillan Company, 1968), pp. 235, 281; Cong. Record, 82 Cong., 2 Sess., pp. 751, 1183-1184, 1186; *Fairbanks Daily News-Miner*, February 6, March 3, 1952.
15 *Ketchikan Alaska Chronicle*, February 19, 1952; "Shelving Statehood," *Newsweek*, March 10, 1952, p. 28; *Cong. Record*, 82 Cong., 2 Sess., p. 1327.
16 Ibid., p. 1525.
17 *Ketchikan Alaska Chronicle*, March 4, 1952; *Cong. Record*, 82 cong., 2 Sess., pp. 1183-1537.
18 *Anchorage Daily Times*, April 11, 1950; Atwood and DeArmond, *Who's Who in Alaskan Politics*, p. 44; *Anchorage Daily News*, March 4, 1952; *Seattle Daily Times*, January 17, 1952; *Ketchikan Alaska Chronicle*, January 23, 1952.
19 *Fairbanks Daily News-Miner*, July 11, 1952; Kirk H. Porter and Donald Bruce Johnson, *National Party Platforms, 1840-1964* (Urbana: University of Illinois Press, 1961), p. 504. Hereafter cited as Porter and Johnson, *National Party Platforms*.
20 *Denver Post*, September 17, 1950.
21 Porter and Johnson, *National Party Platforms*, pp. 486, 452; Gruening, *The Battle for Alaska Statehood*, pp. 13-14.
22 *Daily Alaska Empire*, July 31, 1952; *The New York Times*, September 2, 1952; "The American Way of Life: A Democratic Achievement – Let's Preserve It," address by Governor Ernest Gruening, Jefferson-Jackson Day Dinner, April 24, 1952, Anchorage, Alaska, Records of the Governor of Alaska, 1884-1958, File 37-9, No. 5, Box 442, Federal Records Center, Seattle, Washington.
23 "Official Canvass of Results, Alaska General election, October 14, 1952, in Office of the Secretary of State, Juneau, Alaska; *The New York Times*, October 18, 1952.
24 Bartlett "Memorandum to all Members of the Alaska Statehood Committee," November 25, 1952, Anthony J. Dimond Papers, Personal Correspondence, Statehood Committee—X, Y, Z—General, folder Statehood Committee, box 39, University of Alaska, Fairbanks Archives; *Cong. Record Index*, 83 Cong., 1

Sess., p. 799 (H.R. 2684). In addition, statehood bills were introduced by Representatives Homer Angell (H.R. 207), Russell V. Mack (H.R. 20), Sam Yorty (H.R. 1746), John P. Saylor (H.R. 2982), and Senator James E. Murray for himself and fourteen colleagues (S. 50); Ibid., pp. 737, 777, 668. Delegate Bartlett introduced a measure for an elective governor and lieutenant—governor (H.R. 1916); Ibid., p. 781.

25 Alaska Statehood Committee, "Meeting of the Alaska Statehood Committee," January 28, 1953, Alaska Historical Library, Juneau, Alaska; Alaska, Legislature, House, *Journal*, 1953, pp. 48-49; Alaska Statehood Committee, "Meeting of the Joint Special Committee on Statehood of the Alaska Territorial Legislature, " January 29, 1953, pp. 55, 68, 96, 113-114, Alaska Historical Library, Juneau, Alaska.

26 House, *Journal*, 1953, pp. 45, 268, 44-447; Senate, *Journal*, 1953, pp. 886-887.

27 Ibid., 83 Cong., 1 Sess., p. 751 (February 2, 1953). The vote on H.R. 3575 was 274 to 138. In the tabulation, 177 Republicans voted for the bill and 37 voted against; 97 Democrats voted for and 100 against; 1 Independent voted against. *Congress and the Nation, 1945-1964* (Washington: Congressional Quarterly Service, 1965), p. 64a; *The New York Times*, March 10, 1953, p. 19.

28 A.L. Miller to Douglas McKay, April 11, 1953, file 9-1-13, part 12, Alaska-Administrative-General, Records of the Office of the Secretary of the Interior, RG 48, NA; *The Daily Alaska Empire*, April 13, 1953.

29 Butler to McKay, July 9, 1953, Papers of Douglas McKay, box 35, folder Bu-Bz, University of Oregon Archives, Eugene, Oregon; Atwood and DeArmond, *Who's Who in Alaskan Politics*, p. 96.

30 *Ketchikan Alaska Chronicle*, February 24, 1953; "Memorandum Re Candidates for Appointment as Governor of Alaska," December 31, 1952, Douglas McKay Papers, box 55, folder Alaska, July 1954, University of Oregon Archives, Eugene, OR.

31 Max Rabb to Sherman Adams, March 4, 1953, Papers of Dwight D. Eisenhower, Official File, box 159, folder 147-D, Dwight D. Eisenhower Library, Abilene, Kansas; U.S. Congress, Senate, Committee on Interior and Insular Affairs, *Nomination of B. Frank Heintzleman: Hearing*, 83 Cong., 1 Sess. (Washington: Government Printing Office, 1953), pp. 5-23).

32 See U.S., Congress, House, *Statehood for Alaska*, Hearings before the Subcommittee on Interior and Insular Possessions of the Committee on H.R. 20, H.R. 207, H.R. 1746, H.R. 2684, H.R. 2982, H.R. 1916, 83 Cong., 1 Sess. (Washington: Government Printing Office, 1953). Hereafter cited as *Statehood for Alaska* (1953).

33 83 Cong., 1 Sess., H.J. Res. 199, February 23, 1953; U.S. Congress, *Hawaii-Alaska Statehood*, Hearings on H.R. 2535 and H.R. 2536, and H.R. 49, H.R. 185, H.R. 187, H.R. 248, H.R. 511, H.R. 555, and H.R. 2531, 84 Cong., 1 Sess. (Washington: Government Printing Office, 1955), p.313. Hereafter cited as *Hawaii-Alaska Statehood* (1955); *Statehood for Alaska* (1953), pp. 64, 119-126.

34 Ibid., pp. 185-194.

35 Ibid., pp. 207-208.

36   U.S. Congress, House, Committee on Interior and Insular Affairs, *Providing for the Admission of Alaska into the Union: Report to Accompany H.R. 2982,* 83 Cong., 1 Sess., H. Rept. 675 (Washington: Government Printing Office, 1953), p. 16; *Ketchikan Alaska Chronicle,* May 25, June 2, 1953; House Rept. 675, pp. 1-7, 14-22.

37   *Congressional Quarterly Almanac,* 83 Cong., 1 Sess. (Washington: Congressional Quarterly News Features, 1953), p. 305.

38   *Daily Alaska Empire,* April 3, 1953, editorial, August 5, 1953.

39   Interview with Victor Fischer, March 17, 1970, Fairbanks, Alaska; Interview with Niilo Koponen, March 10, 1970, Fairbanks, Alaska.

40   *Daily Alaska Empire,* August 13, 1953.

41   Interview with Victor Fischer, March 17, 1970.

42   U.S., Congress, Senate, *Alaska Statehood and Elective Governorship,* Hearings before the Committee on Interior and Insular Affairs on S. 50 and S. 224, 83 Cong., 1 Sess. (Washington: Government Printing Office, 1953), pp. 176-185, 94, 245, 327-328. Hereafter cited as *Alaska Statehood and Elective Governorship* (1953).

43   Interview with Victor Fischer, March 17, 1970.

44   *Alaska Statehood and Elective Governorship* (1953), pp. 471-472; Interview with Victor Fischer, March 17, 1970.

45   *Daily Alaska Empire,* August 27, 1953; *Alaska Statehood and Elective Governorship* (1953), pp. 587-594.

46   Interview with Victor Fischer, March 17, 1970.

47   Christmas card, "Merry Christmas," distributed by Operation Statehood, Anchorage Chapter, copy in the author's files, made available from the private papers of Victor Fischer. Operation Statehood also issued a monthly newsletter and much material in the form of pamphlets, and gave dinners to raise money for lobbying purposes.

48   Interview with Victor Fischer, March 17, 1970.

49   *Daily Alaska Empire,* September 8, 14, 1953.

50   *Anchorage Daily Times,* December 16, 23, 1953.

51   *Daily Alaska Empire,* January 19, 1954.

52   *Cong. Record,* 83 cong., 2 Sess., p. 82; editorial, *The Washington Post,* January 10, 1954.

53   U.S., Congress, Senate, *Alaska Statehood,* Hearings before the Committee on Interior and Insular Affairs on S. 50, 83 Cong., 2 Sess. (Washington: Government Printing Office, 1954), pp. 329-339.

54   U.S., Congress, Senate, *Providing for the Admission of Alaska Into the Union,* S. Rept. 1028 to accompany S. 50, 83 Cong., 2 Sess. (Washington: Government Printing Office, 1954), pp. 30-36.

55   *Cong. Record,* 83 Cong., 2 Sess., p. 682; *Congressional Quarterly Almanac,* 83 Cong., 2 Sess., 1954, pp. 395-398.

56   *Cong. Record,* 83 Cong., 2 Sess., pp. 2909, 3091. The vote followed party lines. Only two Democrats voted against the motion and only two Republicans

opposed it. For the debate on Senator Anderson's proposal to in the two bills, see Ibid., pp. 2905-2919, 2980-2986, 2991-3003, 3065-3090, 4343. In the tabulation, 33 Republicans, 23 Democrats, and 1 Independent Had voted for, and 9 Republicans and 19 Democrats opposed passage. All of the 19 Democrats came from the southern and border states.

57   *Daily Alaska Empire*, April 2, 1954; *Fairbanks Daily News-Miner*, April 2, 3, 1954.

58   Minutes, October 14, 28, November 18, 1953, constitution, Operation Statehood Papers, 1953-1958, box 7, folder 94, Operation Statehood—Minutes of Board of Directors, Call to Order, folder 87, Operation Statehood—Constitution and By-Laws, University of Alaska Archives, Fairbanks, Alaska; Constitution, minutes, October 28, 1953, Operation Statehood Papers, box 7, folder 87, Operation Statehood—Constitution and By-Laws, folder 94, Operation Statehood—Minutes of Board of Directors, call to order; *Anchorage Daily Times*, November 25, 1953.

59   *Fairbanks Daily News-Miner*, April 20, 1954; Ibid., Progress ed., November 7, 1956; *Anchorage Daily Times*, November 10, 1953, February 4, 20, 1954.

60   *Fairbanks Daily News-Miner*, April 3, 1954; *Anchorage Daily Times*, April 3, 1954.

61   Bartlett, "confidential Memo for Statehood Files," E.L. Bartlett Papers, Statehood File, box 10, folder, Correspondence, General, March 1954, University of Alaska Archives, Fairbanks, Alaska; *Ketchikan Alaska Chronicle*, April 2, 1954; *Anchorage Daily Times*, April 12, 14, 1954; Daily Alaska Empire, April 21, 1954. For a report on Alaska's resources, see U.S., Congress, House, *Alaska: Reconnaissance Report on the Potential Development of Water Resources in Territory of Alaska*, H. Doc. 197, 82 Cong., 1 Sess. House, Alaska 1955, Hearings before the Subcommittee on Territorial and Insular Affairs pursuant to H. Res. 30, 84 Cong., 1 Sess. (Washington: Government Printing Office, 1956). Delegate Bartlett stated before the subcommittee that there was "practically a unanimous feeling in Alaska against the partition proposal" which had been advanced by Governor Heintzlean. Bartlett recalled that he could not remember another time "when I have had more mail and telegrams and more unanimously on one side than were sent in opposition to the partition proposal...." Ibid., Part 1, p. 252; *Daily Alaska Empire*, April 5, 6, 7, 1954.

62   *Anchorage Daily Times*, April 19, 1954; U.S., Congress, Senate, Committee on Interior and Insular Affairs, *Alaska Statehood and Elective Governorship*, Hearings on S. 50 and S. 224, 83 Cong., 1 Sess. (Washington: Government Printing Office, 1953), pp. 578-582; Bartlett to Jackson, December 11, 1953, E.L. Bartlett Papers, Statehood Files, box 10, folder Correspondence, General, July-December 1953, University of Alaska Archives, Fairbanks, Alaska.

63   *Alaska Statehood* (1950), pp. 60-61; Bartlett to Atwood, March 2, 1953, E.L. Bartlett Papers, Statehood Files, box 10, folder Correspondence, General, January-March 1953, Bartlett to Atwood, December 30, 1953, E.L. Bartlett Papers, Statehood File, box17, folder Legislative History, 1953, University of Alaska Archives, Fairbanks, Alaska.

64 *Fairbanks Daily News-Miner*, May 19, 22, 1954; Bartlett to Hermann, April 12, 1954, Bartlett to White, April 10, 1954, E.L. Bartlett Papers, Statehood File, box 10, folder Correspondence, General, April 1954, University of Alaska Archives, Fairbanks Alaska; *Anchorage Daily Times*, May 12, 1954.

65 *Daily Alaska Empire*, April 12, 1954; Interview with Victor Fischer, March 17, Fairbanks, Alaska.

66 *Daily Alaska Empire*, May 11, 1954.

67 *Anchorage Daily Times*, May 17, 1954.

68 Ibid.

69 Ibid.

CHAPTER ELEVEN

1 *Jessen's Weekly*, February 19, 1953; *Fairbanks Daily News-Miner*, June 23, 1953.

2 *Alaska Statehood and Elective Governorship* (1953), p. 29; Cong. Record, 83 Cong., 2 Sess., p. 58.

3 U.S., Congress, Senate, Committee on Interior and Insular Affairs, *Alaska-Hawaii Statehood, Elective Governor, and Commonwealth Status*, Hearings on S. 49, S. 399, and S. 402, 84 Cong., 1 Sess. (Washington: Government Printing Office, 1955), p. 140; 61 Stat. 772; 38 Stat. 711; *Fairbanks Daily News-Miner*, December 3, 1952.

4 *Anchorage Daily Times*, January 27, 9, 1956, November 4, 1952, January 2, 1954.

5 A.S. "Mike Monroney," "Let's Keep It 48," *Collier's*, March 4, 1955, p. 32-36.

6 *Cong. Record,* 83 Cong., 2 Sess., p. 4069-4071. Francis D. Wormuth, "The Constitution and the Territories," *Current History*, vo. 29, 1955, p. 340; *Cong. Record*, 83 Cong., 2 Sess., p. 3501.

7 *Daily Alaska Empire*, May 3, 1955.

8 *Anchorage Daily Times*, August 17, 20, 1954.

9 *Daily Alaska Empire*, August 14, 1954; *Anchorage Daily Times*, August 17, September 8, 11, 14, 1954; *Fairbanks Daily News-Miner*, September 23, 1954; *Ketchikan Alaska Chronicle*, September 24, 1954.

10 Commonwealth Committee, *Commonwealth for Alaska: Facts & Comments* (Anchorage: Commonwealth Committee, 1955), Records of the Office of the Governor of Alaska, 1884-1958, box 668, Federal Records Center, Seattle Washington; *Anchorage Daily Times,* August 10, 24, 1954; *Commonwealth Committee, Commonwealth for Alaska: Facts & Comments.*

11 *Ketchikan Alaska Chronicle*, August 16, 11, 1954; Bartlett to William A. Egan, August 19, 1954, E.L. Bartlett Papers, Statehood File, box 18, folder Legislative History, August 1954, University of Alaska Archives, Fairbanks, Alaska.

12 *Daily Alaska Empire*, February 29, 1952; *Anchorage Daily Times*, August 17, 1954.

13 *Jessen's Weekly*, August 26, 1954; *Fairbanks Daily News-Miner,* May 21, 1954; J. William Barba to Bernard M. Shanley, May 17, 1954, Mary R. to Stephens, May 17, 1954, Papers of Dwight D. Eisenhower, Official File, box 753, folder

147-D-1, Alaska Statehood, Dwight D. Eisenhower Library, Abilene, Kansas; *Cong. Record,* 83 Cong., 2 Sess., pp pp, 7067, 7077.

14 *Fairbanks Daily News-Miner,* May 25, 21, 1954; White to George W. Malone, June 8, 1954, Dwight D. Eisenhower Papers, General File, box 135, folder 17-M-4 (2), Dwight D. Eisenhower Library, Abilene, Kansas.

15 *Fairbanks Daily News-Miner,* September 27, 1954; *Alaska-Hawaii Statehood, Elective Governor, and Commonwealth Status* (1955), p. 137.

16 *Jessen's Weekly,* October 14, 1954.

17 Richard Strout, "Alaska and Hawaii: Statehood or Commonwealth Status?" *The New Republic,* February 14, 1955, pp. 13-14.

18 Walter Lippman, "The Alaska-Hawaii Dilemma," *Washington Post and Times Herald,* March 16, 1954; *Alaska-Hawaii Statehood, Elective Governor, and Commonwealth* Status (1955), p. 122.

19 Douglas Smith, "The Issue Over Alaska and Hawaii is Basic and Simple," *Washington Daily News,* March 18, 1954; *Alaska, 1955* (1956), p. 2793

20 *Cong. Record,* 84 Cong., 2 Sess., p. 15477.

21 Ibid., p. 15476; *Daily Alaska Empire,* March 29, 1957; Ketchikan Commonwealth Club to Ruth Van Cleve, Legal Assistant to A.M Edwards, Associate Solicitor for the Territories, April 16, 1957, Acc. No. 66-A-140, Box 169, Interior, Office of the Secretary, Central Files, Section Classified Files, 1954-58, folder Territorial Affairs-Alaska-Political Affairs 9, part 1, RG 48, Washington National Records Center, Suitland, Maryland.

CHAPTER TWELVE

1 Interview with Thomas Stewart, August 20, 1969, Juneau, Alaska.

2 Ibid., *Daily Alaska Empire,* July 21, 1954.

3 N.R. Walker to Dimond, May 30, 1948, Anthony J. Dimond Papers, Personal Correspondence, box 39, Statehood Committee—X,Y, Z—General-folder Statehood for Alaska, General Correspondence, University of Alaska Archives, Fairbanks Alaska; "Minutes of the Meeting of the Alaska Statehood Committee," Anchorage, Alaska, January G-7, 1951, box 668, Records of the Office of the Governor of Alaska, 1884-1958, Federal Records Center, Seattle, Washington; House, *Journal,* 1953, pp. 50-51; *Daily Alaska Empire,* November 27, 1953, June 3, 1954. Delegate Bartlett stated that such a move would bring statehood no earlier, and might even delay it. He agreed, however, that a constitutional convention should be held "whether or not Congress approved statehood at this session." Ibid., June 4, 1954.

4 Interview with C. Willis Snedden, March 25, 1970, Fairbanks, Alaska; editorial *Fairbanks Daily News-Miner,* February 27, 1954; U.S., Congress, House, *Statehood for Alaska,* Hearings before the Subcommittee on Territorial and Insular Affairs on H.R. 50, H.R. 628, and H.R. 849, H.R. 340 and H.R. 1242, and H.R. 1243, 85 Cong., 1 Sess. (Washington: Government Printing Office, 1957), p.

154. For the part Alaska's press played in the struggle for statehood, see Carroll
V. Glines, Jr., "Alaska's Press and the Battle for Statehood." (unpublished M.S.
thesis, American University, 1969).

5   *Fairbanks Daily News-Miner*, February 27, 1954.

6   Ibid., April 9, 1854.

7   Niilo E. Koponen, "The History of Education in Alaska: With Special Reference
to the Relationship between the Bureau of Indian Affairs Schools and the State
School System." (unpublished "special paper" presented in partial fulfillment
of the requirements for a Doctoral degree in Education, Harvard University
Graduate School of Education, June 1964), pp. 68-69; and interview with Niilo
Koponen, March 10, 1970, Fairbanks, Alaska.

8   Interview with Thomas Stewart, August 20, 1969.

9   Interview with Victor Fischer, March 17, 1970, Fairbanks, Alaska; Interview
with Robert B. Atwood, August 26, 1969, Anchorage, Alaska.

10 Interview with Thomas Stewart, August 20, 1969; U.S., Congress, House,
Hawaii-Alaska Statehood, Hearings before the Committee on Interior and Insular Affairs on H.R. 2535 and H.R. 2536, and H.R. 49, H.R. 185, H.R. 187, H.R.
248, H.R. 511, H.R. 555, and H.R. 2531, 84 cong., 1 Sess. (Washington: Government Printing Office, 1955), pp. 8-9. The Alaska bill provided for twenty-seven
delegates to a constitutional convention, apportioned among the four judicial
divisions of Alaska as follows: six delegates from first, three from the second,
ten from the third, and five from the fourth; and three delegates to be elected
at-large. The convention was to meet in Alaska's capital city, Juneau, and was
not to exceed seventy-five days in length.

11 See Chapter 46, *Session Laws of Alaska*, 1955; interview with Thomas Stewart,
August 20, 1969.

12 The *Daily Alaska Empire* (Juneau), March 11, 1955, p. 1.

13 Interview with Thomas Stewart, August 20, 1969.

14 The seven were Drs. Ernest R. Bartley, University of Florida; Dayton D, McK-
ean, University of Colorado; Vincent Ostrom, University of Oregon; Weldon
Cooper, University of Virginia; Kimbrough Owen, Louisiana State University;
Sheldon Elliot, Institute of Judicial Administration, New York University; and
John E. Bebout, National Municipal League. Emil Sady, the representative of the
Public Administration Service, remained at College throughout the convention.
John E. Behout, "Charter for Last Frontier," *National Municipal Review*, April
1956, p. 160. For the background studies prepared for the convention delegates,
see Public Administration Service, *Constitutional Studies*, vols. I-III, prepared
on behalf of the Alaska Statehood Committee for the Alaska Constitutional
Convention, November 1955. (Mimeographed.) Interview with Thomas Stewart, August 20, 1969.

15 U.S., President, *Public Papers of the Presidents of the United States* (Washington: Office of the Federal Register, National Archives and Records Service,
1953-1961), Dwight D. Eisenhower, 1955, p. 28; *Anchorage Daily Times*, February 22, 1955.

16 *Fairbanks Daily News-Miner*, November 4, 1954, January 20, 1955, November 20, 1956; 84 Cong., 1 Sess., H.R. 2535, H.R. 2536. Engle also introduced a single Hawaiian statehood bill, 84 Cong., 1 Sess., H.R. 511; Bartlett to Ancil H. Payne, May 21, 1955, E.L. Bartlett Papers, Statehood Files, box 11, folder Correspondence, General, May-June 1955, University of Alaska Archives, Fairbanks, Alaska.

17 *Hawaii-Alaska Statehood* (1955), pp. 88-112.

18 Ibid., pp. 135, 437, 287-294, 215, 301-313; *Fairbanks Daily News-Miner*, January 4, 1954; 83 Cong., 1 Sess., H.J. Res. 17, 1953; 83 Cong., 1 Sess., H.J. Res. 214, 1953; 83 Cong., 2 Sess., H.J. Res. 361, 1954; 83 Cong., 2 Sess., H.J. Res. 364, 1954; 84 Cong., 1 Sess., H.J. Res.233, 1955; *Hawaii-Alaska Statehood* (1955), pp. 313-314; 84 Cong., 1 Sess., H.J. Res. 208, 1955.

19 *Hawaii-Alaska Statehood* (1955), pp. 319-320.

20 *Daily Alaska Empire*, February 3, 1955; *Hawaii-Alaska Statehood* (1955), pp. 211-223, 342, 337-339; E.L. Bartlett, "Memorandum Seeking to Preserve for the Benefit of History Certain of the Events Which Took Place during the Week Starting February 13 as They Related to Alaska Statehood," February 18, 1955, E.L. Bartlett Papers, Statehood File, box 18, folder Legislative History, January-February 1955, University of Alaska Archives, Fairbanks, Alaska; *Hawaii-Alaska Statehood* (1955), pp. 337-347.

21 *Hawaii-Alaska Statehood* (1955), pp. 397, 350-355; E.L. Bartlett "Memorandum Seeking to Preserve...." February 18, 1955, E.L. Bartlett Papers, Statehood File, box 18, folder Legislative History, January-February 1955, University of Alaska Archives, Fairbanks, Alaska.

22 *Anchorage Daily Times*, February 22, 1955; *Hawaii-Alaska Statehood* (1955), pp. 395-396; *Anchorage Daily Times*, February 16, 1955; Alaska, Legislative, House, *Journal*, 1955, pp. 209-210.

23 *Hawaii-Alaska Statehood* (1955), pp. 399-464; U.S., Congress, Senate, Committee on Interior and Insular Affairs, *Alaska-Hawaii Statehood, Elective Governorship, and Commonwealth Status,* Hearings on S. 49, S. 399, and S. 402, 84 Cong., 1 Sess. (Washington: government Printing Office, 1955), p. 26. Hereafter cited as *Alaska-Hawaii Statehood* (1955); E.L. Bartlett, "Memorandum Seeking to Preserve...." February 18, 1955, E.L. Bartlett Papers Statehood File, box 18, folder Legislative History, January-February 1955, University of Alaska Archives, Fairbanks, Alaska.

24 *Alaska-Hawaii Statehood* (1955), pp. 20-21; *Alaska Statehood* (1950), pp. 46-47.

25 *Alaska-Hawaii Statehood* (1955), pp. 28, 67-70

26 Ibid., pp. 87-88, 27, 36-38; Ross to Engle, March 22, 1955, Papers of Dwight D. Eisenhower, Files of Harlow, Bryce N., box 22, folder Statehood—Alaska and Hawaii, Dwight D. Eisenhower Library, Abilene, Kansas; *Alaska-Hawaii Statehood* (1950), pp. 89-90; *Cong. Record*, 84 Cong., 1 Sess., p. 5880.

27 U.S., Congress, House, *Enabling...Hawaii and Alaska...to be Admitted Into the Union,* H. Rept. 88 to accompany H.R. 2535, 84 Cong., 1 Sess. (Washington:

Government Printing Office, 1955). This report included the minority views; *Cong. Record*, 84 Cong., 1 Sess., pp. 5880, 5975-5976.

28 *Cong. Record*, 84 Cong., 1 Sess., pp. 5974-5976, A246.

29 *Cong. Record*, Index, 84 Cong., 1 Sess., S. 399, p. 640 (introduced by Senator George W. Malone); Ibid., 84 Cong., 2 Sess., H.R. 8113, p. 750 (submitted by Representative William Dawson); Ibid., H.R. 8287, p. 754 (introduced by Representative James B. Utt) Ibid., 85 Cong., 1 Sess., S. 35, p. 856 (introduced by Senator George W. Malone). That support for such a compromise bill existed is indicated in the request from the Director of the Office of Territories to the Department of the Interior to submit a favorable report on S. 399. Memorandum from Legislative Counsel, Office of Solicitor, July 14, 1955 on S. 399, Acc. No. 62-A-401, Box 95, Department of the Interior, Office of Territories, file Alaska-Political Affairs—Election—Legislation, 2, part 1, RG 126, Washington Federal Records Center, Suitland, Maryland. Walter J. Hickel, Alaska Republican National Committeeman, endorsed the elective governor bill. He reminded the Department of the Interior that both parties had come out in favor of it. Hickel to Kirkley Coulter, Assistant Director of the Office of Territories, July 8, 1955, Ibid.

30 Memorandum, Gruenther to Harlow, April 28, 1955, Dwight D. Eisenhower Papers, Files of Harlow, Bryce N., box 22, folder Statehood—Alaska and Hawaii, Dwight D. Eisenhower Library, Abilene, Kansas; E.L. Bartlett, "Confidential Memorandum on Statehood," May 4, 1955, Gruening to Oren Long, May 20, 1955, E.L. Bartlett Papers, Statehood File, box 11, folder Correspondence, General, April 1955, folder Correspondence, General, May-June 1955, University of Alaska Archives, Fairbanks, Alaska.

31 84 Cong., 1 Sess., H.R. 6177, H.R. 6178, May 11, 1955; *Fairbanks Daily News-Miner*, May 12, 17, 1955; Bartlett to Mildred R. Hermann and Robert Atwood, May 20, 1955, E.L. Bartlett Papers, Statehood File, box 11, folder Correspondence, General, May-June 1955, University of Alaska Archives, Fairbanks, Alaska.

32 *Daily Alaska Empire*, September 27, 1955; *Ketchikan Alaska Chronicle*, March 28, 1955.

33 U.S., Congress, House. Subcommittee on Territorial and Insular Affairs of the Committee on Interior and Insular Affairs, *Alaska, 1955*, Hearings Pursuant to H. Res. 30, 5 pts., 84 Cong., 1 Sess. (Washington: Government printing Office, 1956); Daily Alaska Sess. (Washington: Government Printing Office, 1956); *Daily Alaska Empire*, September 27, 1955; *Ketchikan Alaska Chronicle*, March 28 1955; *Alaska, 1955* (1956), pt. 5, pp. 275, 39; Claus-M. Naske, *Edward Lewis Bob Bartlett of Alaska…A Life in Politics* (Fairbanks, Alaska: University of Alaska Press, 1979), pp. 99-114.

34 *Alaska, 1955* (1956), pt. 2, pp. 44, 237; *Fairbanks Daily News-Miner*, August 28, 1958; *Anchorage Daily Times,* June 4, 1958, August 10, 1953; *Alaska, 1955* (1956), pt. 5, pp. 208, 149, 134-137.

35 Ibid., pt. 4, p. 4

36   *Anchorage Daily Times*, September 10, 1955; *U.S. Stats. At Large 299* (1955).
     Fairbanks Daily News-Miner, February 6, 1956; Alaska Constitution Section, p.
     1. Koponen, "The History of Education in Alaska," pp. 71-73.

37   Interview with Thomas Stewart, August 20, 1969; *Fairbanks Daily News-Miner*,
     February 6, 1956; Alaska Constitution Section, p. 5.

38   George H. Lehleitner to Representative James C. Wright, Jr., of Texas, Septem-
     ber 12, 1963, Statehood File, University of Alaska Archives, Fairbanks, Alaska.

39   George H. Lehleitner, "Alaska Seeks Statehood the Tennessee Way ,"*Freedom
     and Union, Journal of the World Republic, II* (April 1956), 16; Mary Lee Coun-
     cil, "Alaska Statehood" (unpublished manuscript, n.d.), p. 19, copy in author's
     files; William R. Tansill, "Election of Congressional Delegations Prior to the
     According of Statehood," October 1955, copy in author's files.

40   George H. Lehleitner to Representative James C. Wright, Jr., of Texas, Septem-
     ber 12, 1963, Statehood File, University of Alaska Archives, Fairbanks, Alaska.
     The vote after a five-hour debate was 53 to 1. *Anchorage Daily Times*, January
     30, 1956, pp. 1, 7. The Alaska Tennessee Plan also received recognition in an
     editorial in *Life*, May 14, 1956, p.48.

41   *Anchorage Daily Times*, January 30, 1956.

42   Ibid., November 16, 1955.

43   Koponen, "The History of Education in Alaska," p. 74; John E. Bebout, "Charter
     for Last Frontier," *National Municipal Review*, April 1956, p. 161.

44   William A. Egan, "The Constitution of the New State of Alaska," *State Govern-
     ment*, Fall 1958, p. 210; *The New York Times*, February 5, 1956, p. 76. For further
     details on the constitutional convention, see Alaska Legislative Council, *Alaska
     Constitutional Convention Proceedings*, November 8, 1955 to February 5, 1956.

45   Editorial, *National Municipal Review,* April 1956, p. 156. Pamphlet, *Proposed
     Constitution for the State of Alaska: A Report to the People of Alaska from the
     Alaska Constitutional Convention* (Fairbanks, Alaska: Commercial Printing
     Co., Inc., 1956); hereafter cited as Proposed Constitution for the State of Alaska,
     1956. Victor Fischer made a copy of this publication available to the author.

46   *Fairbanks Daily News-Miner*, February 6, 1956; Alaska Constitution Section, p. 1.

47   For a perceptive critique of the local government article of the Alaska constitu-
     tion, see Morehouse and Fischer, *The state and the Local Governmental System*,
     chaps. I, IV-IX. The implementation of the local government article is treated
     in Ronald C. Cease, "Area—wide Local Government in the State of Alaska: The
     Genesis, Establishment, and Organization of Borough Government" (unpub-
     lished PH.D dissertation, Claremont Graduate School, 1964); and Ronald C.
     Cease and Jerome R. Saroff, eds., *The Metropolitan Experiment in Alaska: A
     Study of Borough Government* (New York: Frederick A. Praeger, 1968).

48   *The Constitution of the State of Alaska.*

49   *Daily Alaska Empire*, February 6, 1956; *Fairbanks Daily Nes-Miner*, February
     6, 1956.

50 Ibid. In 1960 Ralph Robertson thought better of it and also signed the constitution. Patricia Oakes, *Alaska Voter's Guidebook*, 1ˢᵗ ed. (Central, Alaska: Oakeservices, 1962), p. 20.

51 *Fairbanks Daily News-Miner*, February 6, 1956.

52 Pamphlet, You are Looking at Alaska's Future: What Do You See In It? (Fairbanks, Alaska: Commercial Printing Co., Inc., 1956). Victor Fischer made a copy of this publication available to the author. See also, *Proposed Constitution for the State of Alaska*, 1956.

53 Gruening, *The State of Alaska*, p. 500.

54 Election Results, Acc. No. 66A-140, Box 16.9, Interior, Office of the Secretary, Central Files Section, Classified Files, 1954-58, file Territorial Affairs—Alaska—Political Affairs, 9, part 1, RG 48, Washington National Records Center, Suitland, Maryland; "Official Canvass of Results, Alaska General Election, Tuesday, October 9, 1956," in Office of the Secretary of State, Juneau, Alaska.

CHAPTER THIRTEEN

1 Porter and Johnson, *National Party Platforms*, 1840-1956, pp. 388, 403, 435, 386, 537, 453, 504, 553; Cong. Record, 84 Cong., 1 Sess., p. 5883 (May 9, 1955).

2 Galloway, *The Legislative Process in Congress*, p. 344.

3 Ernest Gruening, "Statehood for Alaska," *Harper's Magazine*, May 1953, p. 73; *Cong. Record*, 84 Cong., 1 Sess. P. 5938 (May 10, 1955).

4 Ibid., 84 Cong., 2 Sess., p. 143 (January 5, 1956).

5 Dwight D Eisenhower to Representative A. L. Miller, March 31, 1955, In *Cong. Record*, 84 Cong., 1 Sess., p. 5880 (May 9, 1955). The same letter was sent to Senator Jackson.

6 For the details of the various debates on the defense safeguard amendments, see *Hawaii-Alaska Statehood* (1955), pp. 336, 55, 396-432.

7 *The Daily Alaska Empire* (Juneau), January 6, 1956, p. 1; January 5, 1956, p.1.

8 *Congress and the Nation*, pp. 99a; U.S., Congress, Senate, Committee on Interior and Insular Affairs, *Nomination of Frederick A. Seaton To Be Secretary of the Interior*, 84 Cong., 2 Sess. (Washington: Government Printing Office, 1956), pp. 2-3.

9 *Cong. Record*, 82 Cong., 2 Sess., pp. 1194-1197; Ernest Gruening, *The Battle for Alaska Statehood* (College, Alaska: The University of Alaska Press, 1967), pp. 57-58; Personal communication from George Sundborg, September 12, 1984.

10 Porter and Johnson, *National Party Platforms*, p. 537; *Daily Alaska Empire*, August 22, 1956; Porter and Johnson, *National Party Platforms*, p. 553; U.S., President, *Public Papers of the Presidents of the United States* (Washington: Office of the Federal Register, National Archives and Records Service, 1953-1961), Dwight D. Eisenhower, 1956, p. 763.

11 Interview with C. Willis Snedden, March 25, 1970, Fairbanks, Alaska.

12 Ibid.

13 George H. Lehleitner to James C. Wright, Jr., September 12, 1963, Statehood file, University of Alaska Archives, Fairbanks, Alaska; Pamphlet, George H. Lehleitner, The Tennessee Plan: How the Bold Became States (New Orleans, La., no publisher, 1956). Copy in author's files; Lehleitner to Wright, September 12, 1963, Statehood file, University of Alaska Archives, Fairbanks, Alaska.

14 Interview with C. Willis Snedden, March 25, 1970, Fairbanks, Alaska.

15 *The New York Times*, October 7, 1956; Interview with C. Willis Snedden, March 25, 1970, Fairbanks, Alaska.

16 *Fairbanks Daily News-Miner*, October 18, November 9, December 10, 1956, January 18, 19, 21, 1957; Snedden to Lehleitner, October 27, 1956, Gruening to Snedden, December 1, 1956, E.L. Bartlett Papers, Statehood File, box 33, folder Tennessee Plan, July-October 1956, folder Tennessee Plan, November-December 1956, University of Alaska Archives, Fairbanks, Alaska; Lehleitner to Wright, September 12, 1963, Statehood File, University of Alaska Archives, Fairbanks, Alaska; *Fairbanks Daily News-Miner*, December 31, 1956; Alaska Division of Legislative Audit, "Audit Report: Alaska Statehood Committee, Period from July1, 1956 to March 31, 1957," Records of the Governor of Alaska, 1884-1958, General Correspondence, 1952-1958, box 2, folder 65—Statehood Committee, Federal Records Center, Seattle, Washington.

17 *Cong. Record*, 85 Cong., 1 Sess., pp. 466-469. For editorials from Tennessee newspapers favoring Alaska statehood, see Ibid., p. 475.

18 Interview with Ralph J. Rivers, December 31, 1957, Bartlett to Hermann, February 11, 1957, E.L. Bartlett Papers, Statehood File, box 33, folder Tennessee Plan, January-February 1957, University of Alaska, Fairbanks Archives; *Fairbanks Daily News-Miner*, October 2, September 17, June 19, 1957.

19 Bartlett to Stewart, January 19, 1967, Bartlett to Hermann, February 11, 1957, E.L. Bartlett Papers, Statehood File, box 33, folder Tennessee Plan, 1958-1967, folder Tennessee Plan, January-February 1957; *Fairbanks Daily News-Miner*, May 8, 1957.

20 *Fairbanks Daily News-Miner*, January 3, 1957; *Daily Alaska Empire*, March 25, 1955; *Fairbanks Daily News-Miner*, July 31, 1958.

21 *Daily Alaska Empire*, January 27, 1957; *Fairbanks Daily News-Miner*, May 9, 1957.

22 Atwood and DeArmond, *Who's who in Alaskan Politics*. P. 95; *Alaska Statehood an Elective Governorship* (1953), p. 326; *Cong. Record*, 85 Cong., 1 Sess., p. A 4651.

23 *Anchorage Daily Times*, July 30, 1957; *Fairbanks Daily News-Miner*, August 2, 1957; "Land of Beauty & Swat," *Time*, June 9, 1958, pp. 18-22; "First Homebred Governor Goes to Work in Alaska," *Life*, August 5, 1957, pp. 53-54, 56.

24 *Anchorage Daily Times*, August 26, 1957; *Daily Alaska Empire*, March 26, 27, April 16, 1957; Snedden to Bartlett, April 18, 1957, E.L. Bartlett Papers, Statehood Files, box 12, folder Correspondence, General, April 1957, University of Alaska Archives, Fairbanks, Alaska. O.E. Darling, the president of Brown and Hawkins Commercial Company, became chairman of a group known as the Alaska Citizens for Commonwealth Committee. For an account of its activities,

see: *Daily Alaska Empire*, August 18, September 6, 1957; *Fairbanks Daily News-Miner*, December 12, 1957; *Anchorage Daily Times*, November 27, 157.

25 Opinion, Robert S. Oglebay to Bartlett, June 21, 1950, Private Papers of Vide Bartlett; *Fairbanks Daily News-Miner*, May 14, June 2, 1955, April 23, 1957; *Ketchikan Alaska Chronicle*, June 3, 1955; Thomas H. Kuchel To Sherman Adams, January 14, 1957, Dwight D. Eisenhower Papers, Official File, box 134, folder 17-M-1, Endorsement, Allen, William Prescott, Dwight D. Eisenhower Library, Abilene, Kansas; *Daily Alaska Empire*, June 1, 1955, May 9, March 29, April 23, 1957, June 11, 1956.

26 *Daily Alaska Empire*, April 23, 30, 1957; *Cong. Record*, 85 Cong., 1 Sess., pp. 5302, 8526-8527.

27 *Cong. Record*, 85 Cong., 1 Sess., p. 608, these bills were S. 49, Ibid., Index, p. 856 (introduced by Senator James E. Murray for himself and 23 colleagues); H.R. 50 Ibid., p.943 (introduced by for himself and 23 colleagues); H.R. 50 Ibid., p. 943 (introduced by Delegate Bartlett); H.R. 340, Ibid., p. 951 (introduced by Representative Russell V. Mack); H.R. 628, Ibid., p. 958 (introduced by Representative Clair Engle); H.R. 849, Ibid., p. 964 (submitted by Representative Leo O'Brien) ; H.R. 1242, Ibid., p. 974 (introduced by Representative John P. Saylor); H.R. 7999, Ibid., p. 1130 (submitted by Representative Leo W. O'Brien); H.R. 1243, Ibid., p. 974 (a tandem Alaska-Hawaii measure submitted by Representative John P. Saylor).

28 *Daily Alaska Empire*, January 29, February 1, 1957.

29 *Fairbanks Daily News-Miner*, January 7, 1957; U.S., Congress, House, Subcommittee on the Territorial and Insular Affairs of the Committee on Interior and Insular Affairs, *Statehood for Alaska*, Hearings on H.R. 50, H.R. 628, and H.R. 849, H.R. 340 and H.R. 1242, and H.R. 1243, 85 Cong., 1 Sess. (Washington: government Printing Office, 1957), p. 91. Hereafter cited as *Statehood for Alaska*, (1957).

30 *Daily Alaska Empire*, January 2, 1957.

31 *Statehood for Alaska* (1957), pp. 92-94, U.S. Congress, Senate, Committee on Interior and Insular Affairs, *Alaska Statehood*, Hearings on S. 49 and S. 35, 85 cong., 1 Sess. (Washington: Government Printing Office, 1957). Hereafter cited as *Alaska Statehood* (1957).

32 Legislative Counsel (Stevens) to Persons, march 6, 1957, Dwight D. Eisenhower Papers, Official File, box 753, folder 14-D-1, Alaska Statehood, Dwight D. Eisenhower Library, Abilene, Kansas; *Statehood for Alaska* (1957), pp. 94-95, 105; *Alaska Statehood* (1957), p. 131.

33 *Statehood for Alaska* (1957), pp. 105-106; *Alaska Statehood* (1957), p. 111; *Statehood for Alaska* (1957), pp 105-129, 131, 135.

34 Gruening, *The Battle for Alaska Statehood*, p. 95.

35 *Alaska Statehood* (1957), p. 7; Claus-M. Naske, *Alaska Road Commission Historical Narrative*, Report No. AK-RD-83-37 (State of Alaska: Department of Transportation and Public Facilities, Division of Planning and Programming, Research Section, 1983), pp. II-V.

36 *Anchorage Daily Times*, January 24, 1956; *Fairbanks Daily News-Miner*, April 21, 1956; *Daily Alaska Empire*, March 12, February 27, 1957; Alaska, *Session Laws*, 1957, p. 60; *Statehood for Alaska* (1957), pp. 250-263.

37 *Alaska* (1955), pt. 5, p. 255; *Statehood for Alaska* (1957), pp. 336-337; Alaska, *Session Laws*, 1957, p. 39.

38 *Statehood for Alaska* (1957), pp. 468, 345, 454-459.

39 U.S., Congress, House, *Providing for the Admission of the State of Alaska Into the Union*, H. Rept. 624 to accompany H.R. 7999 with Minority Report on H.R. 7999 and Minority Views on H.R. 7999 expressed by Hon. Craig Hosmer of California, 85 Cong., 1 Sess. (Washington: Government Printing Office, 1957), pp. 10, 18-19; U.S. Congress, Senate, *Providing for the Admission of the State of Alaska Into the Union*, S. Rept. 1163 to accompany S. 49, 85 Cong., 1 Sess. (Washington: Government Printing Office, 1957), p. 2.

40 *Daily Alaska Empire*, July 26, 1957.

41 Interview with Mary Lee Council, July 20, 1969, Washington, D.C.; Alfred Steinberg, *Sam Johnson's Boy: A Close-Up of the President from Texas* (New York and London: The Macmillan Company and Collier-Macmillan Ltd., 1968), p. 485; *Anchorage Daily Times*, December 12, 1968, in *Memorial Services Held in the Senate and House of Representatives for Lewis Edward Bartlett, Late a Delegate from the Territory of Alaska and a Senator from Alaska*, 91 Cong., 1 Sess. (Washington: Government Printing Office, 1969), p. 81.

CHAPTER FOURTEEN

1 Roger Bell, *Last Among Equals: Hawaiian Statehood and American Politics* (Honolulu: University of Hawaiian Press, 1984), pp. 239-243.

2 Ibid., p. 244; *Fairbanks Daily News-Miner*, August 27, 23, September 5, 1957; *Cong. Record*, 86 Cong., 1 Sess., p. 14979; Bartlett to Oren E. Long, March 6, 1956, Barrie White, Jr. to Bartlett, May 15, 1955, E.L. Bartlett Papers, Statehood File, box 12, folder Correspondence, General, January-April 1956, box 11, folder Correspondence.

3 Editorial, *The New York Times*, February 10, 1958; Bell, *Last Among Equals*, p. 244; John A. Burns to Frank Church, February 5, 1958, in *Cong. Record*, 85 Cong., 2 Sess., p. 7988. Senator Church added his remarks at this time, Ibid., pp. 7983-7994.

4 Val Trimble and Scott Hart interview with E.L. Bartlett, Washington, D.C., August 1, 1965, pp. 4-5, E.L. Bartlett Papers, Statehood File, box 20, folder Legislative History, 1959-1968, University of Alaska Archives, Fairbanks, Alaska.

5 Bell, *Last Among Equals*, p. 245.

6 Bartlett to Snedden, January 28, 1958, E.L. Bartlett Papers, Statehood File, box 13, folder Correspondence, General, February 1958, University of Alaska Archives, Fairbanks, Alaska; *Fairbanks Daily News-Miner*, January 28, 1958.

7   Ibid., February 25, 6, 1958; *Anchorage Daily Times,* February 11, March 3, 1958; President, *Public Papers,* 1958, p. 149, Confidential memorandum for Bartlett's own file, February 7, 1958, E. L. Bartlett Papers, Statehood File, Legislative History, January-April 1958, box 19, University of Alaska Archives, Fairbanks, Alaska; editorial, *Life,* May 5, 1958, clipping in H85A-D8, papers accompanying H.R. 7999, 85 Cong., 1 Sess., NA, Cong. Record, 84 Cong., 1 Sess., p. 5881.

8   *Daily Alaska Empire,* April 3, 1958.

9   *Fairbanks Daily News-Miner,* February 15, 17,18,20, 22, 1958; *Anchorage Daily Times,* February 20,21, 1958; *Fairbanks Daily News-Miner,* February 22, 1958.

10 *Fairbanks Daily News-Miner,* March 13, 14, 1958; Bartlett to Mildred Hermann, March 18, 1958, E.L. Bartlett Papers, Statehood File, box 2, folder Alaska Statehood Committee, 1958-1959, University of Alaska Archives, Fairbanks, Alaska; *Cong. Record,* 85 Cong., 2 Sess., p. 5041; *Anchorage Daily Times,* March 18, 1958.

11 *Fairbanks Daily News-Miner,* April 16, 12, 1958; *Cong. Record,* 85 Cong., 2 Sess., pp. 18186-18187.

12 *Fairbanks Daily News-Miner,* March 13, 14, 1958; Bartlett to Mildred Hermann, March 18, 1958, E. L. Bartlett Papers, Statehood File, box 2, folder Alaska Statehood Committee, 1958, 1959, University of Alaska Archives, Fairbanks, Alaska; *Anchorage Daily Times,* March 24, 1958.

13 *Cong., Record,* 85 Cong., 2 Sess., pp. 4369-4370; *Fairbanks Daily News-Miner,* June 26, 30, May 30, 1958; Edna Ferber, *Ice Palace* (Garden City, NY: Doubleday, 1958), pp. 234-239.

14 Snedden to Lehleitner, May 7, 1964, E.L. Bartlett Papers, Statehood File, box 33, folder Tennessee Plan, 1958-1967, University of Alaska Archives, Fairbanks, Alaska; *Anchorage Daily Times,* April 8, 1958.

15 *Fairbanks Daily News-Miner,* April 24, May 1, 1958; Bartlett to Snedden, April 24, 1958, E.L. Bartlett to Snedden, April 24, 1958, E.L. Bartlett "Confidential Office Memorandum," April 24, 1958, "Memo to Bill Egan and Ralph Rivers," February 28, 1958, box 13, folder Correspondence, General, April 1958, folder Correspondence, General, February 1958, box 19, folder Legislative History, January-April 1958, University of Alaska Archives Fairbanks, Alaska; Anchorage Daily Time, April 25, 30, 1958; *Fairbanks Daily News-Miner,* April 24, May 23, 1958.

16 Ibid., May 13, 15, 1958; Bartlett to Gara H. Lyon, May 6, 1957, E.L. Bartlett Papers, Statehood File, box 12, folder Correspondence, General, University of Alaska Archives, Fairbanks, Alaska.

17 Howard W. Smith to colleagues in the House of Representatives, May 6, 1958, H85A-D8, papers accompanying H.R. 7999, 85 Cong., 1 Sess., RG 233, N.A.

18 Clair Engle to Howard Smith, February 25, 1958, in Excerpt from Full Committee Minutes (Executive Session) of January 18, 1957, H85A-D8, papers accompanying H.R. 7999, 85 Cong., 1 Sess., RG 233, N.A.; Ibid. The procedure Engle had in mind was a rarely used device allowed under Rule XI, clause 20, of the rules of the House of Representatives.

19 *Cong. Record,* 85 Cong., 2 Sess., pp. 9212-9217.

20 Ibid., p. 9225.

21 *Congressional Quarterly Almanac*, 85 Cong., 2 Sess., p. 284; *Cong. Record*, 85 Cong., 2 Sess., pp. 9597-9612, 9743-9757.

22 Interview with Victor Fischer, March 17, 1970, Fairbanks, Alaska. For the scene on the House floor, see *Cong. Record*, 85 Cong., 2 Sess., pp. 9756-9757.

23 John Whitehead interview with Leo W. O'Brien, August 17, 1981, in Claus-M. Naske, John S. Whitehead, William Schneider, Alaska Statehood: *The Memory of the Battle and the Evaluation of the Present by Those who Lived it: An Oral History of the Remaining Actors in the Alaska Statehood Movement* (Fairbanks, Alaska: Alaska Statehood Commission, 1982), p. 115.

24 *Fairbanks Daily News-Miner*, June 5, 1958; *Daily Alaska Empire*, May 29, 1958.

25 *The New York Times*, May 29, 1958; Bartlett to Atwood, Confidential, June 5, 1958, E.L. Bartlett Papers, Statehood File, box 20, folder Legislative History, June 1958, University of Alaska Archives, Fairbanks, Alaska.

26 George H. Lehleitner to Representative James C. Wright, Jr., of Texas, September 12, 1963, Statehood File, University of Alaska Archives, Fairbanks, Alaska. For the opposition speeches, see *Cong. Record*, 85 Cong., 2 Sess., pp. 12015-12021 (Senator A. Willis Rovertson, Democrat of Virginia), 12047-12054 (Senator Strom Thurmond, Democrat of South Carolina), 12175-12179 (Senator James O. Eastland, Democrat of Mississippi), 122292-12298 (Senator A.A. "Mike" Monroney, Democrat of Oklahoma), 12338-12346 (Senator Thurmond), 12441-12447 (Senator Olin D. Johnston, Democrat of South Carolina).

27 Ibid., pp. 12449-12453, 12454-12471, 12602-12611, 12617-12632, 12634, 12637-12641.

28 Ibid., p. 12650.

29 Interview with C. Willis Snedden, March 25, 1970, Fairbanks, Alaska.

30 Mary Lee Council, "Alaska Statehood," pp. 1-3, unpublished manuscript, n.d., in author's files.

31 *Fairbanks Daily News-Miner*, June 30, 1958.

32 Ibid., *Anchorage Daily Times*, June 30, 1958.

33 Senator James E. Murray to Ernest Gruening, Alaska Statehood Committee, July 9, 1958, Alaska Statehood File, Alaska Historical Library, Juneau, Alaska.

34 Memorandum on Statehood Election in 1958, Acc. No. 62-A-401, Box 95, file Alaska-Political-Affairs-Election, file 2, part 1, Department of the Interior, Office of Territories, RG 126, Washington Federal Records Center, Suitland, Maryland.

35 "Admission of the State of Alaska into the Union: A Proclamation by the President of the United States of America," White House Press Release, January 3, 1959. In author's files. *Anchorage Daily News*, January 3, 1959.

Index

Reading Recommendations
for readers interested in the history of Alaska

Accidental Adventurer
Memoir of the First Woman to Climb Mt. McKinley, Barbara Washburn & Lew Freedman, paperback, $16.95

Crude Dreams
A Personal History of Oil & Politics in Alaska, Jack Roderick, paperback, $24.95

Flying Cold
The Adventures of Russel Merrill, Pioneer Aviator, Robert Merrill MacLean & Sean Rossiter, paperback, $19.95

George Carmack
Man of Mystery Who Set Off the Klondike Gold Rush, James Albert Johnson, paperback, $14.95

Good Time Girls of the Alaska-Yukon Gold Rush
A Secret History of the Far North, Lael Morgan, paperback, $17.95

Kay Fanning's Alaska Story
Memoir of a Pulitzer-Prize Winning Newspaper Publisher, Kay Fanning, paperback, $17.95

Mercy Pilot
The Joe Crosson Story, Dirk Tordoff, paperback, $17.95

North to the Future
The Alaska Story, 1959-2009, Dermot Cole, paperback, $14.95

North to Wolf Country
My Life among the Creatures of Alaska, James W. Brooks, paperback, $17.95

Reaching for a Star
The Bold Strategy that Won Statehood for Alaska, Gerald E. Bowkett, paperback, $14.95

Saving for the Future
My Life & the Alaska Permanent Fund, Dave Rose & Charles Wohlforth, paperback, $17.95

Selling Alaska
The White-Collar Adventures of an Advertising Pioneer, Kay Guthrie, paperback, $14.95

The Spill
Powerful Stories from the Exxon Valdez Disaster, Sharon Bushell & Stan Jones, paperback, $17.95

Tales of Alaska's Bush Rat Governor
The Extraordinary Autobiography of Jay Hammond, Wilderness Guide, and Reluctant Politician, Jay Hammond, paperback, $17.95

These titles can be found or special-ordered from your local bookstore, or they may be ordered at 800-950-6663 day or night. More Epicenter titles, including many with historical themes, may be found at www.EpicenterPress.com.

Alaska Book Adventures™
Epicenter Press, Inc.
www.EpicenterPress.com

Printed in the United States
144141LV00003B/2/P